Fighting Different Wars

Experience, Memory, and the First World War in Britain

The popular idea of the First World War is a story of disillusionment and pointless loss. This vision, however, dates from well after the Armistice. Here, Janet Watson separates out wartime from retrospective accounts and contrasts war as lived experience – for soldiers, women, and non-combatants – with war as memory, comparing men's and women's responses and tracing the re-creation of the war experience in later writings. Using a wealth of published and unpublished wartime and retrospective texts, Watson contends that participants tended to construct their experience – lived and remembered – as either work or service. In fact, far from having a united front, many active participants were "fighting different wars," and this process only continued in the decades following peace. *Fighting Different Wars* is an original, richly textured, and multilayered book which will be compelling reading for all those interested in the First World War.

JANET WATSON is Assistant Professor of History at the University of Connecticut.

D1224199

Studies in the Social and Cultural History of Modern Warfare

General Editor
Jay Winter *Yale University*

Advisory Editors
Omer Bartov *Brown University*
Carol Gluck *Columbia University*
David M. Kennedy *Stanford University*
Paul Kennedy *Yale University*
Antoine Prost *Université de Paris-Sorbonne*
Emmanuel Sivan *Hebrew University of Jerusalem*
Robert Wohl *University of California, Los Angeles*

In recent years the field of modern history has been enriched by the exploration of two parallel histories. These are the social and cultural history of armed conflict, and the impact of military events on social and cultural history.

Studies in the Social and Cultural History of Modern Warfare presents the fruits of this growing area of research, reflecting both the colonization of military history by cultural historians and the reciprocal interest of military historians in social and cultural history, to the benefit of both. The series offers the latest scholarship in European and non-European events from the 1850s to the present day.

For a list of titles in the series, please see end of book.

Fighting Different Wars

Experience, Memory, and the First World War in Britain

Janet S. K. Watson

University of Connecticut

CAMBRIDGE
UNIVERSITY PRESS

CAMBRIDGE UNIVERSITY PRESS
Cambridge, New York, Melbourne, Madrid, Cape Town, Singapore, São Paulo

Cambridge University Press
The Edinburgh Building, Cambridge CB2 2RU, UK

Published in the United States of America by Cambridge University Press, New York

www.cambridge.org
Information on this title: www.cambridge.org/9780521831536

First published 2004
This digitally printed first paperback version 2006

A catalogue record for this publication is available from the British Library

Library of Congress Cataloguing in Publication data

Watson, Janet S. K.
Fighting different wars : experience, memory, and the First World War in
Britain / Janet S.K. Watson.
   p.   cm. – (Studies in the social and cultural history of modern warfare)
Includes bibliographical references and index.
ISBN 0-521-83153-9
1. World War, 1914-1918–Social aspects–Great Britain.   2. World War,
1914-1918–Women–Great Britain.   I. Title.   II. Series.
D744.7.G7W386   2003
940.3′41–dc22   2003055515

ISBN-13 978-0-521-83153-6 hardback
ISBN-10 0-521-83153-9 hardback

ISBN-13 978-0-521-03549-1 paperback
ISBN-10 0-521-03549-X paperback

For Lane

Contents

Illustrations

On the cover: The Sheppard family

Acknowledgments

Without the support of a large number of people and organizations, this book could not have been completed. Research in Great Britain was funded by the Fulbright Foundation. Generous support from the Mellon Foundation, the University of Connecticut Research Foundation, the University of Connecticut History Department, and the Stanford University History Department allowed me to focus on writing at different stages of the project. Supplemental grants from the Stanford University Center for European Studies and the Stanford University Institute for Research on Women and Gender were also very helpful.

I am fortunate to have studied at Stanford University. My advisor, Peter Stansky, gave this study his support from its earliest phases. He allowed me the room to follow a subject and approach I found compelling while containing my occasional excesses of enthusiasm. His help throughout the development of this project was invaluable, and his eye for detail always impressive. Lou Roberts gave me her time and attention well beyond the call of a second reader. In courses and directed readings, she was fundamental to my growth as a scholar, and particularly as an historian of gender. Her patient and painstaking readings and re-readings were essential. James Sheehan, Paul Robinson, Keith Baker, Karen Sawislak, and Estelle Freedman all provided useful commentary on sections of the study. I am also grateful to Lynn Lees at the University of Pennsylvania for the guidance she gave me when I really discovered the study of history, and for encouraging me to go on to graduate school. Colleagues (past and present) at the University of Connecticut have been more than supportive. I would particularly like to thank Shirley Roe, Sylvia Schafer, Altina Waller, Nina Dayton, Margaret Higonnet, Nancy Shoemaker, Jackie Campbell, Jeffrey Ogbar, Dan Caner, and Jennifer Baszile (without whom I might not have made it through the first years of teaching). Aaron Windel made the indexing process much more pleasant than I could have expected. Sue Benson generously read a complete draft, helping me to strengthen the manuscript as I entered the publication stage.

A number of people were extremely helpful during my research year in England. Anne Summers of the British Library deserves very special thanks for her support from the funding process through presentation of the material. She was a wonderful resource, balancing the intangible and the practical expertly. I would also like to thank Deborah Thom, Hugh Cecil, and Claire Tylee for their time and useful conversations. It was in England that Jay Winter began his support for this project, and I am delighted now to be part of his series at Cambridge University Press. Both my editors there, Helen Barton and Elizabeth Howard, have shepherded me patiently, skillfully, efficiently, and always pleasantly through the various stages of the publication process. I am also indebted to the Press's anonymous readers for making suggestions that have (I hope) greatly strengthened the final version.

As we all know, archivists exercise great control over the success of our research endeavors. I was lucky in the ones I encountered. Penny Goymer, Nigel Steele, Stephen Walton, and the staff of the Department of Documents at the Imperial War Museum in London were extremely helpful through months of research, accommodating a wide variety of requests, including that of a seat near a power point. At the Peter Liddle 1914–1918 Personal Experience Archives at the University of Leeds, Mr. Liddle was very generous with his rich collection. My thanks also to Carol Walder of the collection, who worked to make my visits to Leeds pleasant ones. Allison Kearns of the British Red Cross Society Archives in Barnett Hill introduced me to one of my favorite parts of the research effort, and also provided frequent and much appreciated rides to the train station. Warm thanks are also due to Peter Waters of the Girls' Public Day School Trust Archives in London, whose stories of life in England and questions about America, as well as his generous photocopying policy, lightened the research process. Thanks as well to the staffs of several GPDST schools for their patience and help, especially Margaret Cullen of South Hampstead High School and Kelly Jones of Wimbledon High School. Librarians at the University of Connecticut, Stanford, the Hoover Institute and the Dodd Center were also extremely helpful. I would also like to take this opportunity to thank by name a number of family members of people whose papers I was privileged to consult at the Imperial War Museum: Mrs. Evelyn Cleverly OBE, Dr. David Cross, Mr. Kenneth Cross, Mrs. R. H. Felstead, Mrs. Ann Mitchell, Mrs. Marion C. Proctor, Rev. Brock Saunders, Mrs. Iris Hilda Sheppard, Mrs. J. Venting, Mr. Ben Watson, and Mr. David Wilby; every effort was made to obtain all appropriate permissions. I cannot begin to express my gratitude to the late Joan Edom, née Beale, for the more than generous access she gave me to her family's papers, and for her warm conversation and support. The Beale letters provided me with an incomparable point of access to my study, and gave me much personal pleasure as well. I am very thankful to have met this family. I would also like to thank Mrs. Edom's daughter-in-law, Gillian Edom, for her ongoing help.

Members of the Stanford community gave me (and this project) invaluable help. Several different sections of this study were presented to different groups, and I would like to thank the members of the European History Workshop, the Gender/Women's/Sexuality History Workshop, the History Dissertation Reading Group, and the 1994–1995 Dissertation Fellows at the Institute for Research on Women and Gender for their extremely helpful comments. I also would like to thank the students in my course on British Narratives of the First World War, who introduced me to other perspectives that forced me to articulate my arguments in new and productive ways. My fellow graduate students at Stanford and elsewhere helped in all the ways that colleagues do, both academically and personally. I want to thank especially Cathy Atwell, Stephanie Brown, Andy Harris, Jordanna Bailkin, Renee Romano, Michelle McClellan, and J. B. Shank. Deborah Cohen provided support and inspiration both from across the Bay and in England, as well as from Washington and Providence (including reading all of the penultimate draft). In Connecticut, I would have found the challenges of juggling career and children much more frustrating without the companionship of Cecilia Forgione. Rachel Morris's friendship has proved a constant gift, everywhere.

Above all, I need to thank my family. All (four) of my educator parents have given steady warm support, as have my parents-in-law. Fran Goldscheider told me that I could accomplish all I set out to, and I am proud to follow in David Kobrin's footsteps by studying history. Sarah Kobrin has shared and supported through graduate school and life – I'm so glad we got over that childhood sibling thing. Benjamin, Timothy, and Rosemary Watson make life joyous and complete (even as they make deadlines a bit more challenging). Without Lane Watson's partnership, confidence, and love, it is unlikely that I would have managed to survive, much less finish a book. This is for him.

Introduction
Experience, memory, and the Great War

In 1946, the English soldier-poet Siegfried Sassoon wrote that 1919 "was a year of rootless re-beginnings and steadily developing disillusionments." He claimed, however, that "few people realized this at the time," and that he, in fact, "was not one of them."[1] Sassoon's observation that disillusionment was only "steadily developing" after the Armistice and that he himself was not aware of the process might seem puzzling, as this disenchantment is one of the best-known features of personal narratives about the war, and Sassoon is regularly invoked as one of its key representatives. The popular image of the First World War intimately connects disillusionment with trench experience, focusing exclusively on the slow attrition of trench fighting punctuated by senselessly bloody battles. Samuel Hynes has called this depiction "the myth of the war," where the "innocent young men . . . who survived were shocked, disillusioned, and embittered by their war experiences."[2] This story of disenchantment centered on men who served in the infantry, and specifically on those with combat experience on the Western front. As Paul Fussell wrote in his seminal study, *The Great War and Modern Memory*, "correctly or not, the current idea of 'the Great War' derives primarily from images of the trenches in France and Belgium."[3] A recent newspaper article commemorating Armistice Day showed the lasting power of this view. It described the Western front as "a pointless, static conflict over strips of earth, which achieved nothing other than the slaughter of millions of young men from both sides." For the soldiers, it was an "existence in hell – subjected to constant shelling, floundering in mud in the winter, baking in the summer, rats and

---

[1] Siegfried Sassoon, *Siegfried's Journey* (New York: Viking, 1946), p. 239.
[2] Samuel Hynes, *A War Imagined: The First World War and English Culture* (London: The Bodley Head, 1990), p. x.
[3] Paul Fussell, *The Great War and Modern Memory* (Oxford: Oxford University Press, 1975), p. ix; Fussell therefore focused his study entirely on the trenches of the Western front, assessing the literary heritage that has resulted from their best-known chroniclers and combining that analysis with an attempt to recapture the details of trench life. Given his focus on highly literary sources – particularly the writings of Graves, Sassoon, and Blunden – it is perhaps not surprising that he found it to be a highly literary war.

1

parasites their constant companions, never knowing whether today's sunrise would be their last, without respite, week after week, month after month, year after ghastly year."[4] The war was not just horrific, but pointlessly, endlessly so.

This familiar story was made famous through the publication and popularity of memoirs and novels, like those of Sassoon as well as Robert Graves, Edmund Blunden, and, for Germany, Erich Maria Remarque. Yet Sassoon, though he himself in 1917 made perhaps the most famous protest against the war, tells us that the disillusionment these accounts all articulate was a postwar phenomenon, the product of distance in time and space from wartime experiences. Inseparably connected with the war in the trenches, the disenchantment of the infantry soldier retrospectively became the story of the First World War in England. If women were being viewed positively, they fit into this picture as the idealized volunteer war nurse – often represented by the ubiquitous Vera Brittain – or, as Susan Grayzel and Nicoletta Gullace have shown, as mother. Jay Winter has also demonstrated the power of the image of woman as the postwar mourner, repository of both personal and aggregate grief.[5]

This retrospective view, however, does not reflect the ways people talked about participating in the war while it was being fought. The war itself was overwhelmingly popular, and the nation came together to a remarkable degree despite critical differences that reflected the nature of divisions in English society. A united nation, however, did not preclude an often-overlooked diversity in the kinds of support that were offered. Ideas about war participation changed with contemporary circumstances, and later versions that focused on disillusionment in the wake of economic difficulties and a war that seemed to have improved nothing left little room for the varied ways that war participation had been presented in personal writings during the conflict. The war, in fact, was a far from unitary experience, whether during the 1914–1918 period or in memory. Men and women, workers, professionals, and the socially elite all talked about their war work in different ways. Battles were constantly being fought over

---

[4] Elaine Murray, "Why We Must Forgive the Men Brutalised by War," *The Scotsman*, November 11, 2000, p. 9.

[5] Vera Brittain, *Testament of Youth: An Autobiographical Study of the Years 1900–1925* (New York: Penguin, 1989 [1933]); see also the BBC miniseries adapted from the memoir. In primary source collections of war narratives, Brittain is often the only woman represented. See also Susan R. Grayzel, *Women's Identities at War: Gender, Motherhood, and Politics in Britain and France During the First World War* (Chapel Hill: University of North Carolina Press, 1999); Nicoletta Gullace, *"The Blood of Our Sons": Men, Women, and the Renegotiation of British Citizenship During the Great War* (New York: Palgrave Macmillan, 2002); Jay Winter, *Sites of Memory, Sites of Mourning: The Great War in European Cultural History* (Cambridge: Cambridge University Press, 1995).

how to represent active participation in the war, present or past. Different ideas about the conflict also existed side by side, sometimes without much awareness of their variance. Even when there was seemingly little or no direct conflict between people's different approaches, many active participants were in fact "fighting different wars," and this process only continued in the decades following the Armistice. War stories have always both reflected and illuminated the workings of the society within which they were written, whether during or after the war itself.

These conflicting accounts, though, are more than mere stories. Rather, they acted as sites for cultural debates about the workings of class and gender identity in English society.[6] Even as they presented a picture of unity contradictions and emphases came to the surface, constantly undermining their own stability. The continued insistence that class was not as important to active war participants as it had previously been, for example, served only to underline its continued influence. If it were not such an important category, after all, would it have merited such careful and repeated attention? Similarly, the constant wartime equation of women's efforts with men's given that *they were performed by women* always served to draw clear lines between the sexes, and to reinforce the importance of gender as a defining factor of English society. Temporary though they were, the debates about parity worked in two directions: notions of gender and class both influenced the image of the war effort and vice versa. In memory, even though the sites for these battles over the nature of war experience were greatly restricted, the same interactive process continued.

In order to see both similarities and distinctions across different populations, during the war and retrospectively, this book is essentially comparative, particularly in three key ways. First, I look at both women and men side by side, paying special attention to families where both brothers and sisters were active in the war effort. This joint focus enables me to examine not just the functioning of gender as a cultural category, but also the times and places where it is subordinate to other ways that people identified themselves.[7] Second, I examine two groups who bring different

---

[6] I consider the path-breaking work on the use of gender in the study of history to be Joan Wallach Scott, *Gender and the Politics of History* (New York: Columbia University Press, 1988). Many historians of Britain have paid special attention to the workings of class especially since E. P. Thompson's seminal study, *The Making of the English Working Class* (New York: Vintage, 1966 [1963]). It has not played a large role in studies of the First World War to date.

[7] Here, as elsewhere, I am particularly influenced by the work of Joan Wallach Scott on the constructed and mutually constitutive nature of experience and identity, especially as they relate to gender: Scott, "The Evidence of Experience," *Critical Inquiry*, 17 (Summer 1991).

attitudes to their wartime efforts: those who saw what they were doing as *work* as well as those better-known war participants who used the language and imagery of *service*. How citizens imagined the work they (and others) were doing proved to be a critical line of demarcation between groups.[8] This division often – though certainly not exclusively – broke down along class lines. "Class" as a category of analysis has been out of favor of late in studies of the First World War, partly because most scholars have focused on specific relatively homogeneous populations (with by far the most attention paid to young service-minded officers). Ideas about class, however, played a fundamentally important role in how many English people saw themselves and their part in the war effort, whether past or present. There is little or no comparative analysis that brings together the well-known veterans with other active soldiers and war workers, though more studies of these working populations have recently appeared. Both "work" and "service" gain new meaning in relation to each other.[9]

Third, my concern with the differences between the construction of *experience* and the workings of *memory* structures the entire book. I divide the subject matter chronologically and consider the accounts that date from the war years separately from those that are retrospective. These have been regularly conflated in scholarly as well as popular literature, which in itself reflects the dominance of the postwar account of disillusionment. By examining how the war was represented while it was being fought, and then the ways it was remembered, we see how the conflicts relate to both different populations and different historical moments. These three comparisons – of gender, class (via attitudes toward work and

---

[8] Patrick Joyce, in "The Historical Meanings of Work: An Introduction," in Joyce (ed.), *The Historical Meanings of Work* (Cambridge: Cambridge University Press, 1987), describes work as "a cultural activity, rather than simply an economic one ... [which] cannot be understood unless it is seen as inseparable from the discursive fields of which it is an integral part" (pp. 1, 12). Valuable studies of professionalization, such as Harold Perkin, *The Rise of Professional Society: England Since 1880* (London: Routledge, 1989), and Roy MacLeod (ed.), *Government and Expertise: Specialists, Administrators, and Professionals, 1860–1919* (Cambridge: Cambridge University Press, 1988), have focused on the overall social process rather than on individual construction of identity. To date, the literature on this idea of work has been predominantly restricted to manual labor. Recent efforts in this direction, however, are rewarding; see Anne Summers, "Public Functions, Private Premises: Female Professional Identity and the Domestic-Service Paradigm in Britain, c. 1850–1930," in Billie Melman (ed.), *Borderlines: Genders and Identities in War and Peace, 1870–1930* (New York: Routledge, 1998), and Angela Woollacott, "Maternalism, Professionalism and Industrial Welfare Supervisors in World War I Britain," *Women's History Review*, 3 (March 1994), and especially Woollacott, "From Moral to Professional Authority: Secularism, Social Work and Middle-Class Women's Self-Construction in World War I Britain," *Journal of Women's History*, 10, 2 (Summer 1998).

[9] As Nicoletta Gullace has recently argued, ideas about service had profound effects on conceptions of citizenship, especially as it related to the expansion of the franchise in 1918: *Blood of Our Sons*.

service), and time − of course still cannot provide a comprehensive picture of a nation at war, or of its memories of the conflict. The breadth they permit, however, exposes the constructed (and frequently divisive) nature of war experience, especially as imagined by individual active participants. It also collapses a distinction much too long maintained in both the scholarly and popular literature: that between the home front and the combat zones.[10] This in turn helps illuminate the functioning of English society as a whole, at different specific historical moments, by means of the ways its members talked and wrote about the war − and about themselves and each other.

Experience, memory, and war participation

The received history of the war starts with idealistic volunteers and ends with shattered veterans and names carved in stone on memorials. This story, though, does not reflect popular views from during the war itself. It is also not self-explanatory − how did the story of the disillusioned trench soldier establish itself as the history of the war? The changing nature of memory, in fact, illuminates different moments in the past. How did the different participants in the war imagine their contributions while it was still being fought? How did popular ideas about the war turn away from the cooperative and diverse effort presented during the war years − and toward the view of useless sacrifice on the part of soldiers and junior officers in the trenches? What happened to other accounts as a result of that shift? What can we learn from these stories about the workings of British society both during and after the war? What role does memory play in historical reconstruction? These are the questions at the heart of this book.

To answer them, I focus first on wartime ideas and then on the contest over retrospective views. For the 1914–1918 period, I position attitudes to war work along a spectrum of ideas about work and service. Some members of the population, both male and female, while generally articulating a clear patriotism, saw their efforts on behalf of the war as work. Professional soldiers and trained nurses, for example, both identified an opportunity for career advancement. Other people, like workers in munitions factories or women leaving domestic service, saw a chance for better wages and working conditions. Many working-class volunteers in the army, as well as vast numbers of their conscript fellows, portrayed the war as the job that had to be done at the time, and therefore also

---

[10] Gullace, *Blood of Our Sons*, and Grayzel, *Women's Identities at War*, are important exceptions.

brought with them into the military the languages and actions of industrial unrest. Other people involved in active war work, including both
some volunteer soldiers and volunteer nurses, identified more strongly
with differing conceptions of service – to king, country, or empire. (This,
of course, is the best-known portrayal of the generation of 1914.) Alternately, some participants framed ideas of service as a response to abstrac-
tions of honor and glory, or to expectations about socially appropriate behavior for members of their class and sex. After the war, people who had
seen the war in terms of service were most likely to frame their memories
as a story of disillusionment. Though the young officers are the ones often talked about, the different attitudes of service went well beyond their
ranks, and included significant numbers of their sisters and other women.
Though the distinctions between work and service are certainly not iron-
clad and at times overlap on a continuum, thinking about the ways they
are distinct provides a useful new means of understanding the wide variety of attitudes people brought to their efforts in wartime, and helps
move the history of the war beyond the divide between home front and
combat.

Here, ideas about work are especially important, as they structured
how many people saw their war contributions, yet have been frequently
overlooked. I examine how different kinds of war work were popularly
described, and how such accounts differed when applied to a variety
of populations. What people thought was the right job for the banker's
daughter, after all, might not have been seen as appropriate for her former maid. These ideas, in turn, were constantly reconstructing popular
perceptions about gender and class difference in wartime British society.
After the war, generation would emerge as a primary fault line, but it
was surprisingly muted in 1914–1918 accounts of national cooperation.
How people thought of gender and class, however, profoundly influenced
how they imagined the experience of different kinds of war work. Then,
in turn, perceptions of those "experiences" changed popular ideas about
gender and class. How, then, did members of each group describe their
contribution to the nation? How were those efforts popularly perceived?
How did ideas about gender and class form those representations, and
how were popular perceptions, in turn, then further changed? Where did
ideas of work and service fit in? These questions are central to my analysis
of each group of war workers.

In 1914, the war led to the articulation of gender and class relations
in new ways. These changes were not straightforward and often were
open to interpretations and challenges. Analyzing these contests in turn
reveals underlying ideas about the nature and constitution of British social structures, and the changes that resulted from the evolving ways that

people talked about war work.[11] The idea of parity, for example, was frequently applied to different kinds of activities in 1914–1918. Women doing full-time volunteer work in hospitals were popularly equated with soldiers in the trenches, as, at times, were women munitions workers (but not men), women working on the land, and the members of the female auxiliary military organizations. This very stamp of approval, however, served at the same time to underline essential ideas about difference. Women could only be equal-but-different, and their efforts were always perceived as those of women in particular, not just citizens.[12] Similarly, popular accounts often focused on alleged mixing of different socioeconomic populations: cross-class cooperation was frequently described both in the trenches and the factories, for example. This emphasis, however, also highlighted ideas about class difference, and demonstrated how central they were to early twentieth-century British society. Otherwise, the ubiquitous lists of workers and soldiers from different social backgrounds would not have been necessary.

The contests over how the war was to be understood are vividly illustrated by differing ideas about war work for women. Members of Voluntary Aid Detachments (called VADs), for example, were volunteer untrained nurses generally from financially comfortable homes. They were consistently praised for their efforts and their patriotic contribution. In many cases, their work as women was even symbolically equated with that of men serving in the army. For others, of course, war work was a part-time concern, the current socially acceptable form of the philanthropy that they had been trained was expected of women of their social and economic position. The often-overlooked women doctors and trained nurses, though patriotic, also found in the war an opportunity to demonstrate their professional capacities, and gain public acceptance for the work they were educated and paid to perform. Perhaps because of this very specific training, they were often considered to be quite separate from women who were taking on new kinds of work because of the war, and excluded from discussions of "women war workers."[13] Other

[11] My interpretation of the reciprocal role of discourse owes much to the work of Michel Foucault. See especially *The History of Sexuality: An Introduction, Volume I* (New York: Random House, 1978), ch. 3, "Method," in Part IV, "The Deployment of Sexuality."

[12] "War," as Denise Riley has argued, "throws gender into sharp relief": Riley, "Some Peculiarities of Social Policy Concerning Women in Wartime and Postwar Britain," in Margaret Randolph Higonnet, et al. (eds.), *Behind the Lines: Gender and the Two World Wars* (New Haven: Yale University Press, 1989). See also Grayzel, *Women's Identities at War*, and Gullace, *Blood of Our Sons*.

[13] See, for example, Gilbert Stone (ed.), *Women War Workers: Accounts Contributed by Representative Workers of the Work Done by Women in the More Important Branches of War Employment* (New York: Thomas Y. Crowell, [1917]). This attitude has persisted through the

populations of women war workers, however, frequently garnered less respect from the public. They also often saw their own contributions to the
war effort in a different light. Some women, long accustomed to waged
labor, found in munitions factories (and other newly available venues)
better pay, more interesting work, and, remarkably, shorter hours and
better living conditions than they had in domestic service. Women in
military-style uniforms (whether they were the socially elite volunteers
who joined paramilitary groups in the early stages of the war or the mainly
working-class women who filled the ranks of the official auxiliary military
organizations that were founded closer to the end of the conflict) were
generally criticized.

Perceptions of class position certainly played a crucial role in how different types of war work were viewed. Ideas about gender were also fundamental, and both criticism and support of war efforts were rooted in
deeply held convictions about the preservation of a certain kind of social
order. When women's war efforts did not fit neatly with cultural expectations, both the work and the women themselves could be perceived as
problematic, and even dangerous. Working-class women, then, whether
in industry or auxiliary military organizations, were condemned for not
being sufficiently interested in the propagation of the war effort, and for
caring too much about the money they required for personal and family
support or pleasure. In particular, they were criticized for the ways they
were perceived to be spending their relative affluence, as the financially
and socially independent working-class woman seemed a threat to the
existing social hierarchy. This order, of course, seemed all the more critical to preserve when men were fighting and dying in France explicitly to
maintain a way of life. Similarly, women in military uniforms could not
consistently be considered the female equivalents of soldiers, since their
very existence as "khaki girls" called into questions the gender divisions
in the society that the soldiers were fighting to maintain. Men defended
women, after all, and women did not take independent action themselves.
Nursing, however, especially volunteer nursing, untainted by any shadow
of female professionalism and only "for the duration," suggested none of
these threats. It was nurturing, healing, inherently the work of women.

Most people who chose to become significantly involved in the war
effort exhibited some level of patriotism. Patriotism, however, was not a
monolithic or easily definable entity, but was in fact highly nuanced and
open to interpretation. The breadth of voices I examine clearly demonstrates that the meaning of patriotism was constantly being redefined.

decades. Barbara McLaren's work of popular propaganda, *Women of the War* (London:
Hodder and Stoughton, 1917), is a notable wartime exception.

To say that most participants were motivated by patriotism, then, raises more questions than it answers about the nature of that patriotism and its relation to the work they were doing. How people perceived both themselves and other workers played a major role in how they thought about war work, and those ideas in turn affected the identities of the workers themselves, both male and female. An emphasis on work does not deny patriotism, but instead argues that patriotism was not the only (or even perhaps the primary) force motivating these participants. Patriotism may have been the basis for their actions, but it did not structure how they saw the tangible tasks they were engaged in. Patriotism could be a motivation, but service (unlike work) translated itself directly into an activity. The familiar young men (particularly the young officers) who volunteered in the early months of the war most famously represent the attitude of service. This approach was also exhibited by many women who, as one contemporary supporter of the war asserted, "have shared to the full in the motives which are stimulating the whole of our compatriots, male and female, throughout the Empire to unprecedented endeavour and sacrifice."[14]

How, then, did popular ideas about the war became focused away from the cooperative and diverse effort presented from 1914 to 1918 and primarily toward the view of useless sacrifice on the part of soldiers in the trenches? This change in perspectives was connected with the rise of trench warfare as the primary symbol of the conflict. By the end of the war itself, the trench was already becoming a powerful metaphor. It caught the public imagination for (at least) two primary reasons, especially as eloquently presented by the poets of the trench. It was the most common experience of soldiers, as the majority of men in uniform were either enlisted or young officers in the infantry. It was also, therefore, what most civilians heard about, whether from members of their own families, friends and neighbors, or the press. Additionally, it was horrifically novel, intriguing because it was so entirely different from what war was expected to be, and from the ways it was previously imagined in both military and civilian minds. Certainly it was far from the only new aspect of the war – women driving ambulances, working in hospitals in large numbers, and traveling away from protective homes without chaperones all caught the popular eye – but they were perceived as new ways to think about women and society, not about war itself. The trench was something different. Naval warfare was not significantly changed, and was not seen as having been central to either the conflict or the ultimate victory. In fact, naval divisions served in the trenches as infantry both in France and at Gallipoli.

[14] Mary Frances Billington, *The Roll-Call of Serving Women: A Record of Woman's Work for Combatants and Sufferers in the Great War* (London: The Religious Tract Society, 1915), p. 218.

Airplanes, though capturing the attention of some, seemed still the stuff of fantasy; witnesses almost invariably described the beauty of the machines in flight. Air warfare also involved a comparatively small number of fighting men, and was not militarily important until the final phases of the war, when pilots' casualty rates exceeded those of infantrymen. The trench, with its obvious and ironic image of the grave that saved lives, was so different from war as popularly imagined that it came to embody the war itself. It replaced previous ways of thinking about warfare instead of merely amending them. This focus on the trench, in turn, shifted the retrospective image of the war exclusively to the inherently masculine realm of combat.[15] During the war, the power of the trench could still be diffused, and women were still represented as having a role in that process. In the years after the Armistice, however, women and non-combatants were pushed out of the history of the war, which became exclusively a "soldier's story," incomprehensible to everyone else. Middle-class men controlled the terms of the debate. Everyone agreed that the war itself had been horrific, but they differed sharply over the effect of those horrors on the men in the trenches as well as about the ultimate impact of the war itself. New battles were being fought – battles over how to remember the war – which acted as codes for disputes over the current and future state of Britain, and over appropriate roles for its citizens. Significantly, narratives that are now seen as fundamental to the soldier's story were often, at the time, considered corrections to it. The history of the war was being recast through the power of memory, and critics selectively identified the texts at the center of the debate. This story of disillusionment was created retrospectively.

Digging out from the trenches

To better understand the war both as experience and as memory, I analyze a diversity of texts: diaries and letters, novels and poetry, and a variety of published non-fiction works. I focus on both public and private narratives, examining how (and why) British society perceived the war at the time, and how these ideas evolved in both the short and longer terms. For the purposes of my analysis, I do not make significant distinctions between fiction and non-fiction *per se*, as both are constructions of experience that simultaneously respond to and contribute to social perceptions. This is perhaps particularly the case with the literature of the war, which was intended to capture the "essence" of experience. Historicization, including

---

[15] For a variety of perspectives on the power of the trench, see also Fussell, *Great War*, Hynes, *War Imagined*, and Grayzel, *Women's Identities at War*.

an awareness of the intended audience for any text, remains critical to understanding what a narrative reveals. This is not to say that all texts have equal truth value, or should be read using identical criteria, but that the divisions between "fiction" and "non-fiction," or "public" and "private," are not necessarily the most important variables for understanding the evolution of war experience.[16] I am not, however, conflating the lives of authors with their fictional counterparts, as has been frequently done with some of the best-known narratives of the First World War. We must read the sources for what they say (and, as importantly, do not say), and, especially, how they say it, instead of just accepting their content as either transparent reality or fictionalization. This book is about how experience and memory were created, and what those processes say about British society.

I chose to focus primarily on war work that achieved some form of social approval, in order to better understand both wartime and postwar British culture. The men who receive considerable attention, then, are those in the military, which was seen as the only truly appropriate arena for their efforts. I discuss other populations of men involved in war-related work, from doctors to miners, only as they illuminate my central analysis. Conscientious objectors, the elderly, and other male non-combatants are generally excluded, along with women who were not occupied, at least part-time, in efforts on behalf of the nation. The diversity of female populations discussed is considerably greater, therefore, because ideas about appropriate women's war work were less obvious or coherent than conceptions of men's obligations (other than a generally unquestioned consensus that women could not be soldiers). I am especially interested in families where men and women members both participated in the war effort.

Most active participants on behalf of the war effort were young adults, whether they were soldiers in active combat or their civilian war worker counterparts. I therefore focus on how predominantly young men and women talked about the war as they experienced it during the years of conflict, and then explore how these descriptions differ from the better-known retrospective accounts of the postwar years. Here, too, though Scotland and Wales play some part, due to both conceptions of national identity and the constraints of sources and archives, this is primarily a

16 For a useful discussion of the use of literature and textual exploration in historical analysis, see Joan W. Scott, "Rewriting History," in Higonnet, et al., *Behind the Lines*, p. 29; Alison Light, *Forever England: Femininity, Literature, and Conservatism Between the Wars* (London: Routledge, 1991), p. 2; and Mary Poovey, *Uneven Developments: The Ideological Work of Gender in Mid-Victorian England* (Chicago: University of Chicago Press, 1988), p. 123.

study of England. These ideas of work and service are also closely tied to a domestic national tradition that frequently invoked the concept rather than the reality of empire. The "experiences" of troops from other parts of the world, therefore, need to be situated in a contextualized study of their own, and are therefore regretfully excluded from my analysis.

When I first became interested in British experiences of the First World War, it seemed to me that the available cultural literature, by its very depth, often seemed to preclude a broader view of the society at war. Though rich and fascinating, most studies by both literary critics and historians have focused on either women or (more often) men. Most have also concentrated on populations engaged in a single form of war work. Even beyond the purview of military histories, the majority of modern analyses focus almost exclusively on male descriptions of the combat experience, and especially on junior officers serving in the front lines. Other analyses have focused on women specifically, but still do not consider the experiences of men and women relative to each other. By conflating texts written in different periods, both during and after the war, many studies also neglect the differences in ideas about the experience of the war during the conflict itself from those which followed it by a decade or more. Further, most studies center on a single social class. The well-educated literary elite, who came from traditions which encouraged personal writing and were in a position to have access to the resources of the publishing industry, were the most clearly heard. Scholars have since explicitly aimed to "restore" the voices of working-class women and their war experiences. Some works rely heavily on oral histories, which again provide only a retrospective viewpoint. Others, in their efforts to argue that the war was a liberating experience for many women, limit their perspective. Munitions workers have recently been the subjects of excellent analyses, but my focus is different both in approach and in its comparative nature. I am especially concerned with how the work and workers were talked about (by themselves and others), and in turn how they compared and contrasted their lot with other active participants. Building on a growing literature on monuments, recent scholarship of the war has focused particularly on how European society reconstructed itself around the recollection of the dead. As Jay Winter has demonstrated, memorializing played a fundamental role in the definition of postwar culture.[17] I

---

[17] Winter, *Sites of Memory*. See also Daniel J. Sherman, *The Construction of Memory in Interwar France* (Chicago: University of Chicago Press, 1999); Alex King, *Memorials of the Great War in Britain: The Symbolism and Politics of Remembrance* (Oxford: Berg, 1998); Joy Damousi, *The Labour of Loss: Mourning, Memory, and Wartime Bereavement in Australia* (Cambridge: Cambridge University Press, 1999); David W. Lloyd, *Battlefield Tourism: Pilgrimage and the Commemoration of the Great War in Britain, Australia and Canada,*

consider the process from a different angle, examining the reconstruction of the memory of lived experience, rather than the cultural work being imposed on the dead. I look at how participation in the war is remembered, and how those memories change. My sources are therefore words rather than monuments, and they describe the living (even if they were to die) rather than those already dead. War work and service, whether experienced or remembered, were functions of the changing structure of modern British society.

This book, then, examines the diverse and numerous representations of war experience during the years of conflict, and then analyzes how they were rewritten or silenced. I do this in order to elucidate the variety of attitudes brought to active war work by different sectors of the population at different times. The "experience" of the Great War became one dominated by the disillusioned trench soldier; this was not its only incarnation, however, either during the war or long afterwards, and the process was fraught with disagreement and debate. The creation of disillusionment embodies the relationship of history and memory at work: articulation of "experience" shifted to reflect historically specific moments. The process thus provides a unique access point to the functioning of early twentieth-century British society; analyzing culture reveals how history is made. Why did people talk about the war the way they did? When did they talk that way? What language was useful for which purposes? What can these details tell us about modern Britain, in a time of political and cultural upheaval? These are the kinds of fundamental perceptions that the comparative study of different populations can give us, climbing out of the trenches and opening up our perspective on the war in fundamentally new ways. Whether in 1914 or decades later, the British have indeed been fighting different wars.

1919–1939 (Oxford: Berg, 1998); Thomas Laqueur, "Memory and Naming in the Great War," in John Gillis (ed.), *Commemorations: The Politics of National Identity* (Princeton: Princeton University Press, 1994); Jonathan F. Vance, *Death So Noble: Memory, Meaning, and the First World War* (Vancouver: University of British Columbia Press, 1997); Adrian Gregory, *The Silence of Memory: Armistice Day, 1919–1946* (Oxford: Berg, 1994); Bob Bushaway, "Name Upon Name: The Great War and Remembrance," in Roy Porter (ed.), *Myths of the English* (Cambridge: Polity Press, 1992).

Part I

Experience and the war

1 Soldiers and "khaki girls": men and women in military and paramilitary organizations

In the summer of 1915, a woman observed four members of an unidentified paramilitary organization, dressed in khaki. She then wrote a letter to the editor of *The Morning Post* hoping to invoke "some regulation forbidding that the King's Uniform be worn in such a manner as to bring it into contempt." She was enraged, specifically, because the marchers were female, and therefore their khaki was "a parody of the uniform" that soldiers in the war had "made a symbol of honour and glory by their deeds." These four women, the writer continued, were "making themselves and, what is more important, the King's uniform, ridiculous."[1] This letter sparked a debate that continued for ten days. Some writers argued on behalf of the women's corps, and Lady Isabel Hampden Margesson stated that uniforms were essential in "stimulating true patriotism."[2] Most opinion, however, was aligned with the anti-suffragist and women's war work advocate Violet Markham. She suggested that "the use of khaki and the adoption of military titles" struck "a wrong and jarring note," because women's activities "hardly give women a claim to assume the uniforms and titles of men who have fallen on the blood-stained fields of Flanders or in the trenches of Gallipoli."[3]

Though the military was usually seen as the only acceptable form of war service for a physically able young man, military organizations for women, including those authorized by the War Office, not only failed to evoke similar approval but were usually the subject of considerable debate and condemnation. Ideas about class and class status – whether the goal was to emphasize or diminish their importance – were key to how both military men and women were then portrayed. As we will see,

---

[1] Letter from "A Woman," *Morning Post*, July 16, 1915, p. 6. The debate continued with the heading "The King's Uniform" on July 19, 20, 21, 22, and 26, with seventeen letters in total. See also the discussion in Jenny Gould, "Women's Military Services in First World War Britain," in Margaret Randolph Higonnet, et al. (eds.), *Behind the Lines: Gender and the Two World Wars* (New Haven: Yale University Press, 1989).

[2] Letter from Isabel Hampden Margesson, *Morning Post*, July 19, 1915, p. 9.

[3] Letter from Violet Markham, *Morning Post*, July 22, 1915, p. 5.

talking about ideas of class as they related to the military could also be a way to convey social concerns that really centered on gender roles. These discussions were also linked to popular ideas about patriotic duty as well as to self-representations of war efforts as different kinds of work or service.

Service by men in the army was regularly described as the ultimate example of patriotism. In itself, this does not seem remarkable. After all, the popular image of the soldier of the Great War is that of the idealistic and socially elite young officer who volunteered immediately in August 1914, only to be disillusioned in the trenches of France, unless he was tragically killed first (which was thought more likely). Junior officers in infantry divisions were alleged to have an average longevity of about three weeks before being killed or wounded.[4] Diversity within the armed forces, however, was much greater than this picture suggests. Enlisted men vastly outnumbered officers, and men continued to volunteer throughout 1915 (and were conscripted from 1916 to the end of the war). By the summer of 1918, a majority of the men on active service were not volunteers but conscripts.[5] All of these soldiers, of course, were in addition to the officers and men of the prewar regular army. Prewar officers and men saw the war as the job they were trained for, paid for, and expected to do. For some of them, it provided a distinct career opportunity through rapid field promotion and more frequent elevation from the ranks. In peacetime, it could be prohibitively costly to hold a commission, especially in one of the elite regiments where expenses far exceeded pay. By 1918, however, the lighter wartime financial obligations of commissions contributed to a remarkably more egalitarian officer corps. Many volunteer soldiers, though certainly motivated by the call of their country, still saw soldiering as work to be accomplished; their recruitment rates were affected by the need to settle civilian affairs and to ensure adequate pensions for their wives and families, and in some cases by changing civilian wage rates. Their views, especially later in the war, were often not significantly different from those expressed by conscripts. Many of these men demonstrated a certain resignation to the inevitability of their military work and resolved to "get the job done," as is perhaps illustrated by the

---

[4] That statistic is a myth; the average subaltern served approximately six months in the front lines before leaving for any of a variety of reasons. Obviously, there is much variation within these statistics. See Keith Simpson, "The Officers," in Ian F. W. Beckett and Keith Simpson (eds.), *A Nation in Arms: A Social Study of the British Army in the First World War* (Manchester: Manchester University Press, 1985), pp. 86–87. See also J. M. Winter, *The Great War and the British People* (Cambridge, MA: Harvard University Press, 1986).

[5] Ilana R. Bet-El, "Men and Soldiers: British Conscripts, Concepts of Masculinity, and the Great War," in Billie Melman (ed.), *Borderlines: Gender and Identities in War and Peace, 1870–1930* (New York: Routledge, 1998), p. 74.

language of the workplace and of industrial action. The better-known idealistic young officers were a minority, though a vocal one.

Similarly, women joined military organizations for many reasons. Different opportunities were available to women at specific points in the war, some privately operated and others later officially sanctioned by the War Office. In the early years of the war, the Women's Volunteer Reserve (WVR) and Women's Legion were controversial for their marching and use of khaki uniforms. In 1917, the official Women's Army Auxiliary Corps (WAAC) was founded, to be followed in 1918 by the much smaller Women's Royal Naval Service (WRNS) and the Women's Royal Air Force (WRAF). Many members of these organizations shared the "work" attitude of the men in the ranks. The WAAC, for example, paid better, was less supervised, and offered more interesting opportunities than domestic service usually could. Some other women saw service in the paramilitary and auxiliary military organizations in patriotic terms similar to the language being employed by their brothers who were becoming junior officers. When one young woman heard that a women's army auxiliary was going to be formed, she wrote to her mother that she would like to join it, as she "should love to form an actual part of the Army!"[6] Many of the women in these organizations explicitly considered themselves to be "in" – or at least equivalent to – the army. Observers did not agree, however. Though this idea of parallel service was often popularly utilized for women in other forms of war work (and particularly for volunteer nurses in hospitals), it was much more rarely applied to women in military and paramilitary organizations despite the government's best efforts. Here, parallel status was sexually – and therefore culturally – dangerous. As Nicoletta Gullace has argued, "within the wartime vocabulary of gender definitions, men were those who protected; women those who required protection."[7] When boys were being called on in adventure novels to "train yourselves to defend your homes, your mothers, your sisters, your country, all that you hold dear," then "military women" was an oxymoron.[8]

One of the powerful ways in which anxiety about the blurring of gender differences was expressed was through talk about class. Ideas about class

---

[6] Eleanora Pemberton to her mother, February 21, 1917: Miss E. B. Pemberton, Imperial War Museum Department of Documents (hereafter IWM-DD) 85/33/1.

[7] Nicoletta F. Gullace, *"The Blood of Our Sons": Men, Women, and the Renegotiation of British Citizenship During the Great War* (New York: Palgrave Macmillan, 2002), p. 43; see ch. 2, "The Making of Tommy Atkins: Masculinity, Propaganda, and the Triumph of Family Values."

[8] Escott Lynn, Prefatory Letter, *In Khaki for the King* (1915), quoted in Samuel Hynes, *A War Imagined: The First World War and English Culture* (London: The Bodley Head, 1990), p. 46.

differences (or lack thereof) were used either to authorize or deny gender-appropriate activity in wartime. Patriotic, masculine military service was therefore described as minimizing class differences. Allegedly, soldiers from different socioeconomic backgrounds served together, learned about each other, and were united in their efforts to defeat the enemy. In fact, however, class distinctions inside the military remained clear and important. Women's military organizations, in contrast, were denied that uniform patriotic stamp of approval. They, in turn, frequently suffered from class-based criticism at both ends of the economic spectrum. The more elite members of the WVR were described as merely filling the empty time of the socialite, while the working-class WAACs were repeatedly charged with sexual "immorality."[9] Clearly, wartime conceptions of military service and military work were both deeper and more intricate than the too-familiar ideas of male patriotism, honor, and sacrifice.

Fighting as a job: military work

Many members of military organizations, male and female, described the war in terms of different kinds of work. The idea that war could be a soldier's profession has been often overlooked in the literature of the First World War, due both to an emphasis on the volunteers who were so powerfully articulate and to the condemnation of the horror of trench warfare in the decades after the Armistice. Ideas about war as work jarred with the postwar emphasis on disillusionment; they were too prosaic – or too practical – for the realm of tragedy. For most of the members of the prewar army, however, both officers and men in the ranks, war was the job they were trained to do. As one officer explained it, "we were regular soldiers and our business was war."[10] This perspective was shared by the working-class women who joined the "ranks" of the women's auxiliary military organizations. They described feeling good about doing something for the country (and were resentful when those inspirations were maligned), but were also clearly responding to higher pay and better working conditions than many of them could find in civilian work. To think of the military as work rather than as service was not to deny patriotism. It was, however, to suggest a different perspective on how the

[9] For important investigations into other aspects of the complex relationships between class, sexuality, and gender roles, see especially Gullace, *Blood of Our Sons*, and Susan R. Grayzel, *Women's Identities at War: Gender, Motherhood, and Politics in Britain and France During the First World War* (Chapel Hill: University of North Carolina Press, 1999).

[10] A. B. Beauman, *Then a Soldier* (London: Macmillan, 1960), p. 27. See also W. J. Reader, *At Duty's Call: A Study in Obsolete Patriotism* (Manchester: Manchester University Press, 1988), p. 32.

war experience was constructed. As Doron Lamm has argued, "patriotism, remunerated work, and personal autonomy were inseparable" in the minds of the women who joined the WAAC.[11]

The British regular army, with the divisions and traditions inherent in the regimental system, is not easy for outsiders to understand. Loyalties in the prewar regular army were quite intense, but they were specifically regimental. There was no real overarching structure, and at some points no commander-in-chief. The regiments, with their histories and their unusual names, provided distinct identities: the Coldstream Guards, the Black Watch, the King's Own Yorkshire Light Infantry, the Sherwood Foresters, for example – all had different connotations, which were critically important (at least to their members).[12] The regular army was relatively small, and it served most actively in India and Africa. In the nineteenth century, it was not the military mainstay of the nation. The strength of the empire was based more on the Royal Navy, which, of course, "rule[d] the waves."

By 1914, the army had become a highly trained professional force, but this was a relatively recent development. The regular army evolved significantly in the years preceding the Great War. Its reputation in the Victorian era was quite different from that of the modern fighting organization it became by 1914, described by the military historian Corelli Barnett as "the best equipped, organized and prepared army that Britain had ever sent abroad at the beginning of a war."[13] As recently as the late nineteenth century, in contrast, officers had little respect for the profession of the soldier, and the ranks were drawn from the dregs of society, desperate for any option to support themselves.[14] Parade drill in distinctive regimental uniforms was the main substance of training procedures, and the powerful conviction remained that "when a regiment can march and drill like the Guards Brigade, there is no fear of its conduct in the sternest battle."[15] Soldiers spent much more time marching than practicing with

---

[11] Doron Lamm, "Emily Goes to War: Explaining the Recruitment to the Women's Army Auxiliary Corps in World War I," in Melman, *Borderlines*, p. 392.

[12] See Edward M. Spiers, *The Army and Society 1815–1914* (London: Longman, 1980), p. 2; Maj. R. Money Barnes, *The British Army of 1914: Its History, Uniforms, & Contemporary Continental Armies* (London: Seeley Service & Co., 1968), p. 14. Some of the volunteers, like Robert Graves, also participated wholeheartedly in the politics of the regimental system.

[13] Correlli Barnett, *Britain and Her Army 1509–1970: A Military, Political and Social Survey* (New York: William Morrow, 1970), p. 372.

[14] Figures vary, but even in the Edwardian years more than half (and possibly as many as 90 percent) of all recruits were unemployed; see Reader, *Duty's Call*, p. 6; Spiers, *Army and Society*, pp. 45–47.

[15] An "officer," quoted in Byron Farwell, *Mr. Kipling's Army: All the Queen's Men* (New York: Norton, 1981), p. 103.

firearms (perhaps contributing to the belief of some women that they, too, could be like soldiers). After the Boer War, the army recognized institutionally that parade drill alone was not sufficient, so it was combined with extensive fieldwork and fire training. This shift was part of a new emphasis on professionalism among regular soldiers, combined with official efforts at reforming the military.[16] The new orientation was supported by a small but significant change in the composition of men accepting commissions. There was a marked tendency away from the peerage and baronetage and toward sons of the professional classes; the officer corps was becoming more of a career and less a place to send younger sons.[17] Parade drill and regimental loyalties, though, remained significant parts of the new orientation. The new soldiers who excelled at parade as well as with firearms, however, would bring an attitude of professionalism – indeed of work – to the propagation of war in 1914. Though the wartime volunteers frequently alleged that drill was more ornamental than directly useful in modern warfare, it remained deeply rooted in the regular army creed. Sir Ian Hamilton, a professional soldier with an illustrious career, explained that "men who are smart on parade are more alert, more readily controlled, more obedient, and move more rapidly and with less tendency to confusion or panic than troops which depend entirely on their individual qualities."[18] Even as more directly practical training became universal in the army, ideas about parade and drill were closely connected to perceptions of a competent, professional force.

One thing did not change: both before and after the rise of military professionalization, class distinctions were the lifeblood of the army. Officers were gentlemen, and other ranks were men. Relations between the two could be strained, and in fact they lived quite separate lives with relatively little contact off the parade grounds. Lord Wolseley wrote of the late Victorian era that the soldier was "a daring and self-sacrificing fellow, [but] he must be well led, and as a general rule I believe that leader must be a British gentleman."[19] Life for men in the ranks before the war was roughly consistent across the regiments. The men were fed and clothed in addition to their pay. By the end of the century, term (rather than life) enlistment was well established and wages had increased significantly. By 1914, enlisted men were no longer the economic outcasts they had

---

[16] Edward M. Spiers, "The Regular Army in 1914," in Beckett and Simpson, *Nation in Arms*, pp. 48–49, 57.
[17] Barnett, *Britain and Her Army*, pp. 344–345, 362–363, 367; Spiers, *Army and Society*, p. 9.
[18] Remarks circulated by the Lieutenant-General Commander-in-Chief Southern Command to Volunteer Brigades: quoted in Spiers, "Regular Army," p. 47.
[19] Quoted in Farwell, *Kipling's Army*, pp. 135–136.

been for much of the 1800s.[20] Soldiers joined because they wanted to, not because they had to. Corporal Leigh recalled he had joined the army "to have an easy time as I thought, and also to see a bit of the outside world."[21]

Military life was very different for officers. They paid their own mess bills and had their own uniforms made, so regimental differences were critically important both socially and financially. Personal income, often in significant amounts, was a necessary supplement to pay. This remained true even after the system of purchasing commissions was abolished and the government effectively bought out the army. The memoir of A. B. Beauman, gazetted to the South Staffordshire Regiment in 1908, made clear what the costs could be. Though the Staffordshires were not comparable in status to the Guards, for example, Beauman still spent much of the six years prior to the war playing polo, racing horses, hunting big game, fox hunting, fishing, and playing cricket while stationed first in South Africa and then back in England.[22] These were not inexpensive pursuits.

Though some sporting activities continued in an unsanctioned manner on the Western front, mess bills decreased hugely.[23] More than one volunteer officer found in the war the chance for the commission he could not have afforded in peacetime. For these men, war provided a career opportunity as well as a venue for patriotism. As Captain Harry Rice wrote to his younger brother, Charles, "I always had one ambition and that was to be a soldier so no matter what has happened between whiles I am a soldier now. Perhaps better off than I should have been if I had been allowed to join as a Tommy all those years ago – we'd not the opportunity or wherewithal etc for my being other than a tommy."[24] With the war, however, he was not only an officer but climbing up the command structure. Rice later told his brother that he planned to stay in the army after the war, if he survived, "and they keep me."[25] This was not an insignificant caveat. Though the officer corps became increasingly egalitarian

[20] Farwell, *Kipling's Army*, p. 81.

[21] Corp. J. H. Leigh to Mrs. L. Hayman, February 15, 1916: Mrs. L. Hayman, IWM-DD 88/51/1.

[22] Beauman, *Then a Soldier*, pp. 18–24.

[23] Some sportsmen, however, found new opportunities, however illicit. See Anthony Buxton, *Sport in Peace and War* (1920). Neville Lytton commented that "how on earth any British officer managed to get so much of it in France and Belgium I cannot imagine": "Sport," *London Mercury*, 4, 22 (August 1921), p. 445. Cyril Falls commented that "Major Buxton was a cavalryman and had the fortune to enjoy long periods of rest and training in regions unscarred by warfare": Falls, *War Books: A Critical Guide* (London: Peter Davies, 1930), p. 186.

[24] H. P. Rice to C. J. Rice, January 28, 1916: C. J. Rice, IWM-DD PP/MCR/116.

[25] H. P. Rice to C. J. Rice, June 10, 1917: C. J. Rice, IWM-DD PP/MCR/116.

throughout the war, rivalries between the regulars on one hand and the reserve forces of the Territorial Army and the recruits in Kitchener's New Army on the other were far from insignificant. Captain A. M. Lupton, in a letter to his sister Bess, described a shouting match between his men and a Kitchener's battery over which was the "real army." Lupton explained that "they are jealous as can be and have been very near a row. It is really very comic in two branches of the same army."[26] To the work-oriented professionals of the regular forces, however, the volunteers who filled Lord Kitchener's new battalions after August 1914 were not in the "same army" because they did not have the same experience, training, and attitude. Captain Joseph Maclean, in the Territorials, found relations difficult with regular army officers, who "are a pretty snobbish lot and simply tolerate us."[27]

The regulars' antagonism toward non-professionals started well before the war, and is illustrated by Lord Kitchener's consistent contempt for the Territorial troops. The Yeomanry and Volunteers who served in the Boer War had been widely criticized at the time. This animosity was subsequently directed toward the Territorials, even though they were founded in order to resolve the problems exposed in South Africa.[28] (Kitchener, for example, never trusted the Territorials, which is why he incorporated his New Army into an expansion of the existing regimental system.)[29] When the volunteers began to arrive in the trenches in 1915, the regulars who had survived the bloodbath of autumn 1914 had little confidence in the amateur soldiers. They were resented for not being professionals, and for their very eagerness. As one officer complained, members of Kitchener's army "think they are going to end the war in a fortnight."[30] Regulars did not think patriotism was an adequate substitute for professionalism, and desire could not replace skill. The War

---

[26] Arthur Michael Lupton to Elizabeth Lupton, June 23, 1915: Capt. A. M. Lupton, Peter Liddle 1914–1918 Personal Experience Archive, University of Leeds (hereafter PL) General.

[27] Joseph B. Maclean to Alex Maclean, June 10, 1917: Capt. J. B. Maclean, PL General.

[28] Reader, *Duty's Call*, p. 14; Ian Beckett, "The Territorial Force," in Beckett and Simpson, *Nation in Arms*, p. 143.

[29] Regular army regiments were expanded from two battalions to as many as fifteen or so. See Barnett, *Britain and Her Army*, p. 378. See also Martin Middlebrook, *Your Country Needs You! From Six to Sixty-Five Divisions* (Barnsley: Leo Cooper, 2000). Kitchener is reported to have told Violet Asquith, in comparing the volunteers to the Territorials, that "I prefer men who know nothing to those who have been taught a smattering of the wrong thing": quoted in Peter Simkins, *Kitchener's Army: The Raising of the New Armies, 1914–1916* (Manchester: Manchester University Press, 1988), p. 41. See also Beckett, "The Territorial Force," p. 131.

[30] E. C. Barton, undated letter c. June–August 1915: quoted in Clive Hughes, "The New Armies," in Beckett and Simpson, *Nation in Arms*, p. 112; see also Simpson, "Officers," p. 75.

Office was sufficiently concerned about both the military and social capabilities of some of these new officers, often derogatorily referred to as "temporary gentlemen," that it published a series of informational pamphlets that included titles like *The Making of an Officer* and *Customs of the Army.*[31]

In some ways, professional identity transcended patriotic nationalism. Regular soldiers often exhibited a powerful respect for other professional soldiers, friend or foe. They described themselves as a fraternity of men whose work was war, and they could respect and admire each other when that work was performed well. Regular soldiers were not, generally speaking, concerned with treaty systems or whether the war was "just." That was the business of the politicians, who had clearly settled the matter by declaring war. Immediately after the Armistice, General Sir John French, who had commanded the British forces on the continent in the early phases of the conflict, wrote that "soldiers should have no politics."[32] Unlike the prototypical volunteer officers with their enthusiasm for saving civilization, this seems to have been the attitude exhibited by many regular officers. Colonel Fred Hardman embodied this perspective when he wrote to his wife from the Dardanelles. He complained of mismanagement during the battle of Gallipoli, but concluded, "we shall do our best. It is not for us to reason why, we must go on and see it through."[33] General French, who had exchanged Christmas gifts with his opposing counterpart General Christiaan Beyers during the Boer War, argued that soldiers "should cultivate a freemasonry of their own and, emulating the knights of old, should honour a brave enemy only second to a comrade."[34] Soldiers of different nations thus became almost comparable to a guild, sharing respect for the skills of a profession in a closed community.

This professional attitude may go far to explain the famous Christmas Truce. On December 25, 1914, troops throughout much of the Anglo-German front line in Belgium and France were quiet, and there was some open fraternization in No Man's Land. Soldiers and officers met between the trenches and exchanged food, postcards, souvenirs, and reputedly played a soccer match.[35] The historian Modris Eksteins argued that the fraternization was based on the idea that war was a game, all in

---

[31] Simpson, "Officers," pp. 76–77.   [32] Quoted in Farwell, *Kipling's Army*, p. 110.

[33] Col. Fred Hardman to his wife, May 21, 1915: Ernest Sanger, *Letters from Two World Wars: A Social History of English Attitudes to War 1914–1945* (Phoenix Mill, UK: Alan Sutton, 1993), pp. 42–43.

[34] Farwell, *Kipling's Army*, pp. 111, 110. See also Reader, *Duty's Call*, pp. 25–26.

[35] Modris Eksteins discusses variations in the stories about the match, which many soldiers seem to have heard about, but in which no one actually seems to have played: Eksteins, *Rites of Spring: The Great War and the Birth of the Modern Age* (New York: Doubleday, 1990 [1989]), p. 113.

fun, combined with the British attitude of sportsmanship; he also suggested that the presence of reservists in the lines, with families at home,
contributed to the fraternization.[36] I would argue instead that French's
"freemasonry" – or what Ian Hamilton called "the Chivalry of Arms" –
contributed to the Christmas Truce. Reservists were in the trenches, but
they were still dominated by regular army soldiers in regular army battalions. The volunteers who were fighting the war for a cause rather than
because it was their job were still in the training camps at home. On
the first Christmas Day of the Great War, the professional soldiers, both
British and German, exchanged common courtesies and mutual respect.
An attitude of work, rather than service, made the fraternization possible. By December 1915, the surviving regulars had been overwhelmed in
the trenches by more idealistic volunteers, who had also been subjected
to a barrage of anti-German propaganda. The General Staff issued orders to ensure that fraternization did not recur, but this was unnecessary.
The conditions had changed, the soldiers had changed, the war had advanced, and there was little interest in befriending the enemy among the
more service-oriented junior officers controlling the front lines.[37]

The prewar professionals, however, were not the only soldiers who
thought of the military in terms of work. A significant number of men in
the ranks who entered the army even after the outbreak of war shared the
regulars' attitude. Though ideas about service may have motivated enlistment, they were frequently translated, once in uniform, into a language of
work. Soldiers, both volunteers and conscripts (and the quasi-volunteers
of the Derby Scheme) often referred to the war as a job that had to be accomplished. Though the line between the ideals of service and attitudes
of work was not always clear cut, the prevalence of talk about a "job"
among enlisted soldiers is distinctive. G. F. Wilby wrote optimistically to
his fiancée in the spring of 1916 that he "d[id]n't think this job can last
much longer." Wilby also referred to a recently conscripted friend who
"doesn't care for his job, too many drills and parades, and he says it is
almost impossible to get leave."[38] The typical military activities were perceived as unpleasant aspects of a new work position. Horace Bruckshaw,
an enlisted volunteer, chafed with impatience while waiting on a troop-
ship off Gallipoli, and complainingly asked his diary, "Why do they not
get at the job we have come out for." Later, in misery on the peninsula,

---

[36] Ecksteins, *Rites of Spring*, pp. 110, 123–125, 116.

[37] Occasional localized cease-fires were observed around the holidays in subsequent years,
but never on the scale of 1914. See Tony Ashworth, *Trench Warfare, 1914–1918: The Live
and Let Live System* (New York: Holmes and Maier, 1980).

[38] G. F. Wilby to Ethel Baxter, May 30, 1916, May 13, 1916: G. F. Wilby, IWM-DD
78/31/1.

he still maintained his workmanlike attitude. He explained that "We are absolutely fed up with this life although the job has got to be done."[39]

The British government, in fact, anticipated this work identity among the ranks from early in the war. They knew that to recruit the "respectable" male workers into the army would require more than an appeal to patriotism and the ideals of service. Though pay rates for civilian jobs seem to have had little effect in the first weeks of the war, by the autumn, when a decreased labor pool was raising wages for those who stayed, there was a clear relation.[40] Similarly, many men would join the army only if they were confident that their dependents were being appropriately cared for by the state. As a result, before the middle of August 1914 Prime Minister Asquith had announced separation allowances for all military wives. This acknowledgment of the need for a family wage for workers who became soldiers was explicitly connected to labor organizations, and when conscription of married men was implemented, the Workers' National Committee successfully lobbied to raise the allowances further.[41]

Many soldiers clearly identified their wartime military service as the job they had to do while the country was at war. Ilana Bet-El has argued persuasively that conscripts' "identity as soldiers was that of workers in uniform, whose job description was that of fighting." Despite the course of the war, "their perception therefore remained that of civilians hired to do a job of work, which was fighting a war on behalf of their country."[42] Because she studied the writings only of conscripts, however, Bet-El was not in a position to see that this phenomenon was not limited to them, but was typical of a larger group of men in the army. G. F. Wilby, stationed in South Africa, complained of a lengthy stay in Durban before following the rest of his company to German East Africa. As he wrote to his fiancée, "I am still having a nice time of it – but one feels as though it is a waste of time, doing nothing here. I would much rather be at work, and know

---

[39] April 12, 1915, July 4, 1915: Horace Bruckshaw (Martin Middlebrook, ed.), *The Diaries of Private Horace Bruckshaw, 1915–1916* (London: Scolar Press, 1979), pp. 23, 60.

[40] Simkins, *Kitchener's Army*, pp. 111, 203. High civilian wages had a stronger effect than low ones in wartime, though it was clear that army service at times provided better conditions and easier labor for some working-class men. Denis Winter, in *Death's Men: Soldiers of the Great War* (London: Penguin, 1979 [1978]), makes the argument for army service as an alternative to destitution rather than a patriotic reaction more strongly (pp. 33–34).

[41] Susan Pedersen, "Gender, Welfare, and Citizenship in Britain During the Great War," *American Historical Review*, 95, 4 (October 1990), p. 989.

[42] Ilana Bet-El, "Experience into Identity: The Writings of British Conscript Soldiers, 1916–1918" (unpublished Ph.D. thesis, University College London, 1991), pp. 245, 281–282.

that I was doing a bit to help this rotten job to a finish."[43] For these men, war was as much a task as a cause.

The idea of military service as work included the use of the language, and even techniques, of industrial action. Conditions in camps were rough immediately following the outbreak of war, as the military system was not prepared to handle the flood of recruits. While most new soldiers were initially patient, this tolerance wore thin when conditions failed to improve over several months. There were demonstrations, protests, and even strikes among the Welsh miner recruits stationed at Seaford.[44] Industrial action was part of the work experience for many new soldiers, and they tried to bring it with them to their new jobs in the military. Ian Hay, in his best-selling novel *The First Hundred Thousand*, humorously described the situation of Scottish industrial workers who volunteered for Kitchener's Army:

In the Army we appear to be nobody. We are expected to stand stiffly at attention when addressed by an officer; even to call him "sir" – an honour to which our previous employer has been a stranger. . . . The NCO's are almost as bad. If you answer a sergeant as you would a foreman, you are impertinent; if you argue with him, as all good Scotsmen must, you are insubordinate; if you endeavour to drive a collective bargain with him, you are mutinous; and you are reminded that upon active service mutiny is punishable by death. It is all very unusual and upsetting.[45]

Though Hay surely intended his readers to smile, the predicament was real. Many soldiers still saw themselves as workers, but the rules, as well as the job, had changed. Years of fighting experience did not change this attitude. Sergeant William Rigden described the "'strikes' amongst the men" which followed the Armistice:

for they were perfectly fed up with any sort of drill [as the war was over] and were all anxious to get back into "civvy" life. Several times not a soul appeared on parade as a protest. Another time, some thousands of men marched round and round the Commandant's house when they ought to have been on parade. And I'm blessed if I could blame them.

---

[43] G. F. Wilby to Ethel Baxter, May 29, 1917: G. F. Wilby, IWM-DD 78/3/1.

[44] Simkins, *Kitchener's Army*, pp. 243–244; Ian Beckett, "The Nation in Arms, 1914–1918," in Beckett and Simpson, *Nation in Arms*, pp. 22–23; Peter Simkins, "Soldiers and Civilians: Billeting in Britain and France," in Beckett and Simpson, *Nation in Arms*, p. 171. See also G. D. Sheffield, *Leadership in the Trenches: Officer–Man Relations, Morale and Discipline in the British Army in the Era of the First World War* (New York: St. Martin's Press, 2000).

[45] Ian Hay, *The First Hundred Thousand: Being the Unofficial Chronicle of a Unit of "K(1)"* (Edinburgh and London: William Blackwood and Sons, 1916 [5th edn.; orig. pub. 1915]), p. 15; see also pp. 28, 154.

If winning the war was the "job" that these soldiers felt they were in uniform to complete, then the Armistice symbolized its accomplishment. They saw no reason, therefore, to cooperate further with military activities and restrictions. Rigden himself was more than sympathetic; in January 1919 he was posted to Aldershot "but point-blank refused to go, indignantly stating I was expecting to be demobilised at any moment." He concluded proudly, "I didn't go, either."[46] It is hard to imagine that a regular soldier would have been pleased with this defiance of the command structure. With the war won, though, these worker-soldiers did not feel any further obligation to the requirements of the military, and there were a series of industrial-style protests demanding demobilization.[47] The job was done.

The military and society: women, work, and class

Some men in the ranks found it was possible to flout military convention and even military orders. This level of control, however, could not be exhibited by members of the women's auxiliary military organizations, though many of them also saw their war efforts as work. There were some attempts at comparable industrial action, but they were much more limited in scope, and quickly controlled. At least twice, women in the WRAF threatened to go on strike in protest over missing bonuses and uniforms. These attempts, however, were diffused merely by organization officials speaking to the women and promising that the omissions would be remedied.[48] These women were probably the most closely monitored war workers. The formation of these organizations in 1917 and 1918 accelerated the debate over women in "military" uniforms begun with the private paramilitary organizations of 1914–1915.

It may seem easy to group together the early volunteer organizations and the official auxiliary military organizations that came later. In fact, however, they differed in important ways. Both consisted of women wearing quasi-military uniforms and being trained in some form of parade and marching, and so became associated in the popular mind with "women soldiers." Social position, motivations, and ideas about gender roles and war service, however, were significantly and fundamentally different. The so-called upper-class Amazons of the Women's Volunteer Reserve (WVR) were, primarily, a small subgroup of service-minded volunteers who wanted a more militaristic venue for their contributions to the war

---

[46] December 1918–January 1919: Sgt. William A. Rigden, PL General.

[47] Beckett, "Nation in Arms," p. 25.

[48] Violet Douglas-Pennant, *Under the Search-Light: A Record of a Great Scandal* (London: George Allen and Unwin, 1922), pp. 35, 120–121.

effort.[49] The women who joined the ranks of the official auxiliaries, how-ever, brought an attitude of work to their patriotic commitment that was comparable to that of men in the ranks of the army, including the inter-est in financial details. This attitude also created problems in the pub-lic reception of women in military uniforms, though these "khaki girls" would face different charges from those that had been levied against their service-oriented predecessors in uniform.

As the women's military auxiliaries were sponsored by the War Office, they benefited early on from concerted efforts to create public support. In contrast to the negative debate members of groups like the WVR aroused in letters to the *Morning Post*, initial reaction to the official women's aux-iliary military services, two years later, was at first generally temperate. Two years of intervening war, two years of popular acceptance of women working in new fields (especially the large numbers who entered industry and particularly munitions), a year of becoming accustomed to male con-scription and the realization that if women filled base jobs then men could be freed for combat positions – these factors all led to a more ready ac-ceptance of women's military organizations. It helped, too, that they were now officially sanctioned and not operated by elite volunteers.[50] Initially, the need to get specific jobs done for the propagation of the war effort made the new women's auxiliaries popularly acceptable, and helped them to attract women more interested in work than in service (figure 1.1). Ironically, however, the women hired to do those very jobs would later be condemned for their "failure" to be sufficiently motivated by the "higher" calling of service to the country. Necessary as these women might be, much of the population continued to be distrustful of them, whether or not they were sanctioned by the government. The very image of a woman as a soldier, or even a pseudo-soldier, undermined the fundamental con-ception of men fighting a war on behalf of women at home (figure 1.2). Couched in a language redolent of class divisions, women in military uniforms, now paid workers rather than volunteers, were the subject of popular efforts to control the gendered threat they represented against existing conceptions of masculinity, femininity, and society.

Much of the population, in fact, continued to be distrustful of the idea of women in military uniform, whether or not sanctioned by the

---

[49] See Arthur Marwick, *The Deluge: British Society and the First World War* (New York: Norton, 1965), p. 88.

[50] The Women's Volunteer Reserve was headed by the Marchioness of Londonderry, though she disapproved of the military aspects. See her memoir, *Retrospect* (London, 1938). See also Krisztina Robert, "Gender, Class, and Patriotism: Women's Paramil-itary Units in First World War Britain," *International History Review*, 19, 1 (February 1997), pp. 52–65.

Figure 1.1 WAAC waitresses serving officers.

Figure 1.2 WAAC bakers in France, holding loaves of bread as rifles.

War Office. The WAAC, WRNS, and WRAF sought "educated" women to act as pseudo-officers, and women of the working classes to fill the "ranks." These women were paid, and found in the war an opportunity for new and often attractive work at wages frequently higher than those they were able to earn as civilians.[51] Officials discussed the use of actual military titles of rank but ultimately rejected the idea as being inappropriate for the women's services. This maintained another level of distinction between the men serving in the military proper and women who belonged to the auxiliary counterparts.[52] The women, though in uniform and under the command of the military, were not, in fact, really soldiers. Dorothy Loveday, an educated woman who joined the ranks of the WAAC as a driver, wrote to her former teacher that "Having begun by calling them officers they are now trying to change it to 'Forewomen and Administrators.'" Her administrator "was at College and is attractive and interesting"; her roommate in the ranks "has been a dressmaker."[53]

The minority of women who became "officers" may have been motivated by a call to service, but their need for financial remuneration made earlier options like volunteer nursing either less attractive or entirely impossible. In this, they were like the military officers for whom the war made commissions economically feasible. Dorothy Pickford, for example, was a WAAC administrator (i.e., "officer") who planned to leave the corps following the end of the war, but wrote her sister that "supposing I was obliged to earn my living I should stay."[54] Salaries were reasonable partly because many of the candidates whom officials considered ideal were already committed to other forms of war work. Women also needed to be enticed into the new and unfamiliar services, especially given the animosity often expressed toward females in military uniforms. The leaders of the new auxiliary military services tried to change this image of the uniform in order to attract women "officers," who were recruited through a special "Professional Services Bureau" at the Ministry of Labour. Violet Douglas-Pennant, who ran the WRAF during its first months, devoted considerable effort to choosing fabric and design before she was satisfied with the final design.

The majority of women in the auxiliary services, however, like the majority of men in the army, came from the working classes. They had

[51] See Lamm, "Emily Goes to War."

[52] See J. M. Cowper, *A Short History of Queen Mary's Army Auxiliary Corps* (privately pub. by the Women's Royal Army Corps Association, [1967]), p. 22; Gould, "Women's Military Services," p. 123.

[53] Dorothy Loveday to Miss Robertson, dated only "Friday": Miss Dorothy Loveday, PL Women.

[54] Dorothy Pickford to her sister Molly, December 19, 1918: Hon. D. F. Pickford, IWM-DD Con Shelf.

previous experience with paid labor, and cared that organizations like the WAAC gave them new work opportunities at higher wages than those available in traditional venues like domestic service. Female enlistment rates did not increase dramatically, in fact, until the higher-paid jobs in industry began to vanish under the Ministry of Munitions' 1917–1918 cutbacks.[55] In the public eye, however, this work orientation counted against the women. Only patriotism – not personal benefit – was a safe motivation for challenging prewar gender mores. Working-class women in uniform were therefore perceived as dangerous to the social order, a criticism often expressed in sexual and behavioral terms. The "morality" of women in the military auxiliaries was constantly under question; it is no coincidence that WAAC discharge forms gave ratings for both "work" and "personal character."[56] Sexual danger was a means of representing the social threat of these very public women.

Improper behavior, then, was one of the key criticisms of the WAACs, who were often compared negatively to other – less threatening – war workers. Peggy Bate, a member of the Women's Legion who drove for the War Office, made clear that she was not a WAAC. "Let me at once explain," she wrote to her fiancé, "that to ask one of my Squad if she is a Waac [sic] is rather like asking a Guardsman if he's in a labour corps!" She concluded, "We are the Women's Legion ... and of course the most superior thing you could dream of." Bate was defending her position as middle class in contrast to the predominantly working-class WAACs; she was making a distinction between war service and war work. While the WAACs were often associated with men in the ranks of the army, Bate thought of herself more as an officer, like her fiancé. She even compared her salary, uniform, and living expenses (unfavorably) to those of a "masculine subaltern," as if there were another, feminine, kind; this helped her distinguish herself from the working women of the WAAC.[57] Dorothy Loveday confirmed the tensions with the Women's Legion from the WAAC side. WAACs driving in London were asked either to join the Women's Legion if they wished to stay in London or to volunteer for overseas duty. Though Loveday chose the second option, she reported of the Women's Legion members that "the ones I have met ... think themselves very above the Wacks [sic] and are furious at having such riff-raff put into their corps."[58]

[55] Lamm, "Emily Goes to War," pp. 378–388.
[56] See, for example, discharge papers of Miss M. I. Gilmore, IWM-DD 83/6/1; Miss J. G. Lambert, PL Women.
[57] Peggy Bate to "Brett" Brettell, January 30, 1918, January 15, 1917: Lieut. F. A. Brettell, IWM-DD PP/MCR/169.
[58] Loveday had already been passed for foreign service; Dorothy Loveday to Miss Robertson, December 30, 1917: Miss Dorothy Loveday, PL Women.

Their increased independence created the space for criticism. Loveday heard the rumors of large numbers of "war babies" among the WAACs and attributed them to inadequate supervision. She described a subdepot "where four girls, under 20 and not of a reliable type, work together with four men, in charge of a sergeant. The place is very out of the way and isn't always visited by an officer . . . the door is kept shut." When Loveday entered the building, she "found the sergeant with a girl on either knee and we all had tea and another sergeant came in and a girl immediately sat on his knee." Despite what she presented as promiscuous behavior, Loveday discovered that much of the scandal was in fact just speculation. In less than a month she reported that "the number of girls sent back from France has now dwindled from 200 (rumour) to 8 (official)."[59]

Loveday thought that the military uniform was key to relaxed relations between the sexes. She was irritated that "once we are in uniform any Tommy thinks he can make advances. It's very annoying not being able to move without being spoken to." Though she was not responsive to the interest expressed in her by soldiers, other WAACs in her company were, and Loveday still believed that the uniform was the source of the behavior. "Why does uniform have such an odd effect," she asked in another letter, "the girls (just like the men) at once try to pick up with some one. Much more abandonedly than the girls on munition work did, though they are very much the same class." She admitted that perhaps only a minority of the women behaved the way she was describing, "but they are giving all the dogs a bad name." Loveday blamed the lack of discipline, and argued that class relations were essential to this dynamic. "Girls who want to stay out [late], just do it, they say it is worth it," she wrote, "they are used to work and fatigues are nothing to them." Because so many WAACs came from domestic service, "scrubbing floors" was just another kind of work rather than a punishment, and the "officers know it isn't any good" as a disciplinary tool.[60] Again, because the majority of WAACs approached their war effort in terms of work rather than service, they were left open to criticism.

The auxiliary military organizations were sometimes praised, but qualified in careful ways that were still about maintaining a conservative social hierarchy. The popular propagandist Ethel Alec-Tweedie, who had herself hoped to train informally with a paramilitary organization in the early days of the war, echoed the government's patriotic tone. She wrote of the WAAC and WRNS that "no praise can be too high for these bodies of

[59] Dorothy Loveday to Miss Robertson, January 14, 1918, February 6, 1918, undated [first page missing] but probably January 1918: Miss Dorothy Loveday, PL Women.

[60] Dorothy Loveday to Miss Robertson, undated [first page missing] but probably January 1918, February 6, 1918, January 31, 1918: Miss Dorothy Loveday, PL Women.

women."[61] The WAAC also received some positive attention in the press, but such articles were often heavily class- and gender-weighted. One piece was told from the point of view of an American pilot, who could not say enough of how he appreciated the efforts of the WAACs. The women were described, however, as "the daughter of a theatrical manager" and "a young war widow who was counting the hours till she could reach her small son." In reality, the majority of WAACs were single women who had left work in domestic service or industry. In the last line of the article, the pilot added "*it's not only their work we admire, either!*"[62] WAACs could not be positively portrayed merely for the important work they were doing as army auxiliaries. Instead, they had to be described in socially acceptable and especially physically attractive terms. The emphasis here reassured the reader that the subjects of the article were above all *women*, and remained so despite their occupation as paramilitary war workers.

There was also a reverse side to this image of attractiveness and desirability. Working-class women, dressed in army-style uniforms and working in the traditionally male-identified war zone (even if behind the lines), were socially dangerous. That danger was often described in terms of sexual misconduct, or its potential. Unfounded rumors were rampant, with perhaps the most popular concerning the number of pregnant WAACs alleged to have been sent home or to special maternity facilities. In an effort to redeem the reputation of the WAAC, both state and church offered official approval. Minister of Labour G. H. Roberts spoke out in February 1918 in favor of the women's service. The Archbishop of Canterbury followed with a statement of support, based on his encounters with them the previous summer.[63]

As public feeling remained quite unsettled, a commission was appointed by the War Office in March 1918 to assess the work and behavior of the WAACs. This commission, which included both Violet Markham and the Independent Labour Party organizer Julia Varley as members, reported that they had found "a healthy, cheerful, self-respecting body of hard-working women, conscious of their position as links in the great chain of the Nation's purpose, and zealous in its service." The commission also found that the service women were resentful of the denigration of their characters, though the scandal itself had no real effect on recruitment rates.[64] Dorothy Pickford wrote to her sister about the commission's

[61] Ethel Alec-Tweedie, *Women and Soldiers* (London: John Lane, [1918]), p. 127.

[62] Hilda M. Love, "America and the 'WAACs,'" newspaper clipping [no publication information]: Miss A. Essington-Nelson, IWM-DD 86/48/1.

[63] Cowper, *Short History*, p. 43.

[64] See Cowper, *Short History*, pp. 42–51 (quotation, p. 45); see also Lamm, "Emily Goes to War," pp. 386–387.

visit, and confirmed that the overwhelming reaction of the women in her unit was that they were "furious that a word should be said against them." Pickford did not think much of the investigatory process, but also felt that the problem was not one of "good behavior" as an absolute, but of differing class-based expectations. The WAACs had their own moral code. It might be different from that of other English people, but they kept to it, and were not likely to consider it necessary to change. Pickford, a middle-class veteran of Girls' Club philanthropic work, argued that based on her previous experiences "the behaviour is exceedingly good."[65] This was not enough, however, for many members of the general public, who continued to question WAAC morality. As a racy cartoon in the *Sporting Times* asked, "Would you rather have a slap in the eye or a WAAC on the knee?"[66]

Dorothy Pickford, the WAAC administrator, articulated many of the class issues raised in criticism of women in the ranks. One of her difficulties lay in her newly acquired awareness of the private lives of her workers. The war forced working-class lives into her conscious perception, as it did for the rest of middle-class society; she was unsure of how to react. Even in her philanthropic work, she was accustomed to the physical segregation of working-class recreation. Pickford wrote to her sister that it "still strikes me as funny here to see all my household staff smoking about the place when they are off duty. I suppose one's own servants all do, but they are never seen, and here when they are not on duty they are as much at liberty to do as they please as anyone."[67] Even though the workers were her subordinates but not her employees, Pickford still thought of them as "my household staff," and it is clear that she had never given much, if any, thought to the private lives of her servants before. They were a distinct population to her, domestic workers, so it was striking to a woman in her socioeconomic position that they should have the same liberties "as anyone." Pickford's letter (unintentionally) provides a potent explanation for women's motivations beyond patriotism in leaving domestic service and joining the WAAC, and the workers may have enjoyed the newfound opportunities to flaunt their independence and identity in front of her. The work was clearly more attractive than that which many of them had left.

[65] Dorothy Pickford to her sister Molly, March 14, 1918: Hon. D. F. Pickford, IWM-DD Con Shelf.

[66] Quoted in David Mitchell, *Monstrous Regiment: The Story of the Women of the First World War* (New York: Macmillan, 1965), p. 226.

[67] Dorothy Pickford to her sister Molly, February 24, 1918: Hon. D. F. Pickford, IWM-DD Con Shelf.

Some WAAC postings had fewer difficulties. Margaret Gibson, an administrator, wrote from France that a "small camp of motor drivers ... are in tents divided from us by a barbed wire fence, our girls go over and play tennis with them sometimes (with the non Coms [sic] of course)."[68] Class parallels between the WAACs and the soldiers were obvious, "of course." Gladys Parker, one of the few working-class WAACs whose contemporary reactions are available, wrote home from her post in France of a positive social life with few negative aspects. "Life out here is grand – so far," she told a friend, "it is just like a glorious long holiday."[69] A description of a "holiday," however, is far from the idea of service described by other participants. Women were not in France on holiday, critics argued, but to serve the need of the nation. Women of the working classes were simply not trusted, especially under the exceptional conditions of military camp life in France. If they were trustworthy, after all, then perhaps they would have to be given more responsibility in civilian life.

Dorothy Loveday found herself in the center of class conflicts because she was in a contradictory social position. By virtue of her education, she was a peer of the administrators rather than her fellow workers. Her status as a driver, however, kept her in the ranks – often, ironically, with women of considerably more elite backgrounds than her own. Automobiles were still very much the privilege of the wealthy, and efforts to recruit experienced drivers therefore focused on higher levels of the social hierarchy than did attempts to attract clerks, waitresses, and telephonists. Loveday resented these socially elevated women as much as she disapproved of many of the working-class recruits. She complained, for example, that the mess line went very slowly, as "most of the people who are educated think it's their natural right to thrust themselves in and get served first."[70] She believed that a lack of discipline was at the root of the problems with the Corps:

There are two more drivers today, a "Lady" and an "Hon." They are all so funny about discipline, and say nothing would make them call officers "Sir" and stand to attention when spoken to. They wouldn't do it to any man. Isn't it an extraordinary attitude. I can understand the rank and file of the Wacks [sic] objecting to saying "Mam" [sic] because they are a different class and they think it marks it, but the ... drivers here could afford to, their potted dignity won't allow it I suppose.

---

[68] Margaret Annabella Campbell Gibson to her sister May, September 16, 1917: Mrs. M. A. C. Gibson, PL Women.

[69] Gladys Parker to Mildred, August 3, 1917: H. L. Currall, PL General.

[70] Dorothy Loveday to Miss Robertson, dated only "Friday": Miss Dorothy Loveday, PL Women.

Loveday failed to grasp the gender and class dynamics. To those new drivers, expressing subordinance to men who were most probably their social inferiors was inconceivable because such behavior would *mask* the very differences that Loveday realized the working-class women were reluctant to *mark*.[71]

The official efforts to redeem the reputation of the WAAC continued. Queen Mary gave her name to the Corps in April 1918. The change was officially in recognition "of the good services rendered by the WAAC both at home and abroad... and especially of the distinction which it earned in France during the recent fighting on the Western Front."[72] During the German advance in the spring of 1918, a number of WAACs were killed when a bomb fell on their trench shelter. Some WAACs were awarded the Military Medal.[73] WAACs who were killed in that attack (like all women serving in the various support organizations and hospitals behind the lines of combat who died of any cause) were buried with full military honors, in military cemeteries, alongside soldiers. All of them were on "active service." Risk of life and limb in combat, however, was essential to the image of the soldier-patriot; its existence excused the differences among orientations toward work and service among men, and allowed them all to be cloaked within a class-minimizing language of patriotism. Despite the limited number of casualties in the WAAC in the spring of 1918, this blanket approval could not apply to them as they were not facing comparable risks.

The Women's Royal Naval Service (WRNS) and Women's Royal Air Force (WRAF), founded after the WAAC and smaller both in membership and scope, suffered from some of the same associations. Because they were less in the public eye, however, they had an easier time. Ultimately, they were awarded a patriotic stamp of approval from governmental and military quarters. Katharine Furse, who served as the first commandant of the WRNS, initially encountered resistance from the Admiralty. However, her ambitions to make the WRNS respectful of the traditions of the Royal Navy – within gendered limitations, of course – ultimately

---

[71] Dorothy Loveday to Miss Robertson, January 31, 1918, dated "December 16th about" [1917], February 9, 1918: Miss Dorothy Loveday, PL Women.

[72] Official announcement of the change from "Women's Army Auxiliary Corps" to "Queen Mary's Army Auxiliary Corps," April 9, 1918: quoted in Mitchell, *Monstrous Regiment*, p. 227. To avoid confusion, I refer to the organization by its original title, by which it is best remembered.

[73] See, for example, the papers of Mrs. M. A. C. Gibson, PL Women. The administrators, as well as the forewoman, were given the Military Medal even though that was usually reserved for members of the ranks. Not being commissioned officers, they could not be given the Military Cross. Also, since the Military Medal could be given only for bravery in the field, it was seen as a more appropriate choice than a civilian award like the MBE. See also Cowper, *Short History*, pp. 53–54.

bore fruit. As Charles Walker of the Admiralty wrote to Furse, "the way you have caught on to the true Navy spirit is one of the secrets of the extraordinary success of the WRNS."[74] Eric Geddes, First Lord of the Admiralty, wrote even more strongly that:

Of all the women's Services which the War has brought into being, there is none which in my opinion has attained the general high standard and the absolute absence from reproach of any kind which the WRNS has maintained throughout... Their work, general deportment, conduct and business-like smartness have won for them a place in the heart of the Navy which few of us foresaw when the Service was started.[75]

The WRNS, of course, involved only about seven thousand women late in the war. Still, they were praised by the Admiralty for who they were rather than the work they did. Geddes singled out their social behavior – "general deportment, conduct, and business-like smartness" – rather than their tangible contribution to the war effort. Their clerical duties and driving were summed up simply as "work." This differentiation between conduct and productivity was clear in the WRAF as well, where one of the primary duties of the woman commandant was responsibility for discipline and behavior.[76]

Efforts to provide validity for all the women's uniformed services included royal visits of inspection by the king, the queen, and Princess Mary. This connection with royal approval was further reinforced in June 1918, when the silver wedding anniversary of the king and queen was celebrated by a "Procession of Homage" of women war workers. When viewing the parade, however, Princess Mary wore the uniform of the Voluntary Aid Detachments, or volunteer nurses, rather than that of any of the women's military organizations.[77] A princess could be a VAD, but not a WAAC.

As the royal uniform perhaps made clear, the women were not the equivalent of soldiers, despite the suggestiveness of such symbolic gestures. Most WAACs who died while serving the country as members of the organization died from influenza in 1918–1919, rather than from any combat-related events.[78] (It was even safer, statistically, to serve in the WRNS; they suffered their first casualty in October 1918, when a ship

[74] Charles Walker to Dame Katharine Furse, November 16, 1918: Dame Katharine Furse, PL Women.
[75] E. Geddes to Dame Katharine Furse, November 18, 1918: Dame Katharine Furse, PL Women.
[76] Douglas-Pennant, *Search-Light*, p. 3.   [77] Cowper, *Short History*, pp. 56–57.
[78] Cowper, *Short History*, p. 63.

crossing between Ireland and England was torpedoed.)[79] To be a WAAC was not, in fact, like being in the army, and members of both organizations were aware of this, despite official efforts to suggest otherwise. Dorothy Pickford wrote that discipline in the WAAC was much milder than discipline in the real military forces, and men from the army often would not enforce such rules as were available to penalize the women.[80] One WAAC recorded in an official diary her approval of the new WAAC area controller for Boulogne. She was "a useful sort of person . . . not steeped in this appalling military attitude for women."[81] Dorothy Pickford had similar priorities, making it clear that her family was as important as the work she was doing in France.[82]

Similarly, Peggy Bate, who often compared herself to a soldier in her letters to her officer-fiancé, maintained that she loved him more than honor (rather than the traditional reversed formula). "That's the worst of girls you see," she explained, "they haven't got a keen enough sense of duty." Lieut. Brettell agreed with her, becoming upset when Bate was poorly treated on an assignment and suggesting that she leave, since, as a woman, her personal happiness was more important than her potential contribution to the war effort.[83] No matter the titles, the decorations, or the efforts of the War Office and the royal family, women were essentially separate from the military, and most of the public at large was far more comfortable thinking of them in those terms. Because of their work and especially because of their sex, they could not truly serve in uniform.

Men, the army, and service

All Britons, male and female, were exposed to the ideal of service: representations of patriotism, sacrifice, glory, and honor pervaded popular literature and poetry both in the Edwardian period and especially after the war started.[84] Readers of all ages and both sexes were influenced by works

---

[79] M. H. Fletcher, *The WRNS: A History of the Women's Royal Naval Service* (London: B. T. Batsford, 1989), p. 23.

[80] Dorothy Pickford to her sister Molly, March 14, 1918: Hon. D. F. Pickford, IWM-DD Con Shelf.

[81] War diary entry for July 25, Mrs. Gill, WAAC GHQ, quoted in Cowper, *Short History*, p. 31.

[82] Dorothy Pickford to her sister Molly, February 4, 1918, October 17, 1918: Hon. D. F. Pickford, IWM-DD Con Shelf.

[83] Peggy Bate to "Brett" Brettell, March 28, 1918, Brettell to Bate, undated [late May 1918?]: Lieut. F. A. Brettell, IWM-DD PP/MCR/169.

[84] This subject is well-trod territory among the secondary literature. See, for example, Beckett and Simpson, *Nation in Arms*; Ecksteins, *Rites of Spring*; Mark Girouard, *The*

like the poetry anthology *Lyra Heroica*, published in 1891 and still in print during the war. In the Preface, W. E. Henley explained the purpose of the collection: "To set forth, as only art can, the beauty and the joy of living, the beauty and the blessedness of death, the glory of battle and adventure, the nobility of devotion – to a cause, an ideal, a passion even – the dignity of resistance, the sacred quality of patriotism."[85] Poetry, of course, is the genre that came to be associated with the soldiers of the Great War. Though only a tiny minority during the war read the now-familiar harsh verses of Owen, Sassoon, and their fellows, poetry was indeed a great source of inspiration to many. Howard Nevill, on the Mine Carrier *Ramillies*, was far from the only reader who thought a new Kipling poem was "really good."[86] When John McCrae's famous verse, "In Flanders Fields," was published, it was widely embraced. Frank Ennor, who eventually served as a lieutenant in the army, included a newspaper clipping of it in his memory album.[87]

For Ennor, like many other young men, it was not enough merely to be employed in necessary war work: the country demanded that he become a soldier. Ennor originally worked on the war loan at the Bank of England and had considerable difficulty leaving to apply for a commission because his job was "protected," but ultimately succeeded.[88] The challenge that "In Flanders Fields" offered, to "Take up our quarrel with the foe: / To you from failing hands we throw / The torch; be yours to hold it high," was met by a multitude of volunteers, some of whom responded in verse themselves. The writer R. E. Vernède, an older volunteer who served as second lieutenant in the Third Battalion of the Rifle Brigade before being killed in April 1917, explained his hopes for himself in national crisis:

> All that a man might ask thou hast given me, England,
> Yet grant thou one thing more:
> That now when envious foes would spoil thy splendour,

Return to Camelot: Chivalry and the English Gentleman (New Haven and London: Yale University Press, 1981); Hynes, *War Imagined*; Peter Parker, *The Old Lie: The Great War and the Public School Ethos* (London: Constable, 1987); Reader, *Duty's Call*; Robert Wohl, *The Generation of 1914* (Cambridge, MA: Harvard University Press, 1979).

[85] Quoted in Reader, *Duty's Call*, p. 54.

[86] W. Howard Nevill to his mother, September 3, 1914: Commander W. H. Nevill, IWM-DD Con Shelf.

[87] Lieut. F. H. Ennor, IWM-DD 86/28/2. See John McCrae, "In Flanders Fields," in Jon Silkin (ed.), *The Penguin Book of First World War Poetry* (London: Penguin, 1979, 1981), p. 85.

[88] Frank Ennor to Kathleen La Fontaine, July 16, 1915, August 31, 1915, September 28, 1915, October 6, 1915, undated [1915], January 2, 1916, July 11, 1916: Lieut. F. H. Ennor, IWM-DD 86/28/1.

Unversed in arms, a dreamer such as I,
May in thy ranks be deemed not all unworthy,
England, for thee to die.[89]

Vernède explicitly acknowledged the gendered nature of the wartime call: it is, by definition, "all that a man might ask," not merely any patriot. This in turn contributed to the definition of masculinity. If military service was "all" a man asked, then a male who did not enter the army could not be truly a man.

Prose, too, was powerful and popular. In 1914–1915, for example, writing under the pseudonym "The Junior Sub" (junior subaltern, or lowest commissioned rank in the army), the journalist John Hay Beith published a series of fictional essays in *Blackwood's Magazine*. They were an example of the kind of unofficial propaganda that was so generally widespread at the time. The pieces recounted humorously, yet touchingly, the process of turning a mob of Scottish volunteers into part of Kitchener's New Army. In December 1915, the essays were collected and published as *The First Hundred Thousand*, by "Ian Hay, 'The Junior Sub.'" The title referred to Kitchener's original call for volunteers, and the book was extremely successful, going through numerous reprints in 1916, and followed in 1917 with *Carrying On: After the First Hundred Thousand*.

It was effective popular propaganda, as it matched the national mood. Bill Nevill, who posthumously symbolized the epitome of English sporting patriotism and self-sacrifice by kicking one of the legendary footballs in the first attacking wave at the Battle of the Somme, wrote home that Hay's book was "the best thing I've seen."[90] Though the stories were all lightly told – one volunteer nurse working in France, in recommending it to her father, called the book "most amusing" – underneath the humor was a serious message about the quality of the troops and the importance of what they were doing.[91] It was the institution of the military, rather than its wartime necessity, that was being gently mocked. Hay made clear how the motivations of volunteer soldiers – young officers and men in the ranks – should be perceived. The book opened with a poem "K(1),"

---

[89] Quoted prior to the Introduction of P. D. Ravenscroft (Antony Bird, ed.), *Unversed in Arms: A Subaltern on the Western Front. The First World War Diary of P. D. Ravenscroft MC* (Swindon: Crowood, 1990). Bird mistakenly gives the date of Vernède's death as May 8, 1917; in fact he died of wounds on April 9, 1917. See also R. E. Vernède, *Letters to His Wife* (London: W. Collins Sons, 1917).

[90] Bill Nevill to "All" [his family], January 27, 1916: Capt. W. P. Nevill, IWM-DD Con Shelf. For more on Nevill and the footballs, see Fussell, *Great War*, pp. 27–28.

[91] Eleanora Pemberton to her father, April 9, 1916: Miss E. B. Pemberton, IWM-DD 85/33/1.

which started self-deprecatingly, but concluded:

> And now to-day has come along.
> With rifle, haversack, and pack,
> We're off, a hundred thousand strong.
> And – some of us will not come back.
>
> But all we ask, if that befall,
> Is this. Within your hearts be writ
> This single-line memorial: –
> *He did his duty – and his bit!* [92]

That was what was most important in soldiers, Hay was telling the nation: they responded to the call of their country. Even though most soldiers in the ranks, volunteers or otherwise, saw their contributions as work, they were still given the popular stamp of approval through a language of service.

For officers, Hay elaborated further on the service ideal. Much of the story centered on Bobby Little, a prototypical young and innocent junior officer. One evening all the officers of the company were sitting in a dugout in the front line, having a jocular conversation about why they were each in the army. Little, however, did not join in the teasing. As Hay explained to his readers:

In all this general symposium there had been no word of the spur which was inciting him – and doubtless the others – along the present weary and monotonous path; and on the whole he was glad that it should be so. None of us care to talk, even privately, about the Dream of Honour and the Hope of Glory. The only difference between Bobby and the others was that while they could cover up their aspirations with a jest, Bobby must say all that was in his heart, or keep silent. So he held his peace. [93]

Through Bobby Little's thoughts, Hay made it clear that it was not just the young and idealistic, but all Britons who were motivated by honor and glory, even though they failed to state such emotions explicitly. In fact, he suggested, it was those who felt them most deeply who were least able to articulate them. All volunteer soldiers were swept into the fold of patriotism, however their own language may have varied. As Arthur Graeme West, a young officer who came to oppose the war, wrote: "Every man, woman, and child is taught to regard [the soldier] as a hero." [94] It was service, not work, that made him one.

---

[92] Hay, *First Hundred Thousand*, no page number.

[93] Hay, *First Hundred Thousand*, pp. 127–128.

[94] "Officers and the War," September 11, 1916: Arthur Graeme West, *Diary of a Dead Officer: Being the Posthumous Papers of Arthur Graeme West* (London: Imperial War Museum Department of Printed Books, 1991), p. 55.

This imagery was not restricted to men with a predisposition toward imaginative writing. Many soldiers did, in fact, talk about honor and the glory of patriotic sacrifice for their country, their empire, and its history. Edwin Vaughan, a young officer on his way to the front for the first time, recorded in his diary: "at last, I was actually on my way to France, to war and excitement – to death or glory, or both." He explained that "my mind was filled with a confusion of Boer War and other martial pictures."[95] Soldiers at Gallipoli were exhorted by Major-General M. G. Aylmer Hunter-Weston that "in Nelson's time it was 'England.' Now it is the whole British Empire which expects that each man will do his duty."[96] These connections of the current war to past conflicts were not unusual, though they often went further back to more mythic contexts. By the time of *Carrying On – After the First Hundred Thousand*, Bobby Little, now a temporary captain, had found words to explain part of what inspired him. Hay described Little, who was not "indeed a student of literature at all," at night "re-quoting to himself, for the hundredth time," Henry V's famous speech. Bobby Little, according to Hay, "was the sort of person who would thoroughly have enjoyed the Battle of Agincourt."[97] Many men also used the medieval imagery of King Arthur and his knights. Looking still further back, Second Lieutenant A. D. Gillespie appealed to ideas of epic manhood when he told his family that he associated casualties – even those close to his heart – with "all the men who had been killed in battle – Hector and Achilles and all the heroes of long ago."[98]

Paul Fussell, in *The Great War and Modern Memory*, argued for the importance of "high diction" in soldiers' letters, of the pervasive ideals of glory and honor.[99] Heroic imagery also could be used very lightly, as when one young officer wrote from France to his sister that that the "warrior is resting from war's alarms in his dugout & making a pig of himself" with the care package she had sent him.[100] Even this flippant reference, however, demonstrated its very pervasiveness. Heroic patriotism was more likely, however, to be used in a serious context, as in the farewell letter a second lieutenant sent his parents the night before he

---

[95] January 4, 1917: Edwin Campion Vaughan, *Some Desperate Glory: The World War I Diary of a British Officer, 1917* (New York: Simon and Schuster, 1981), p. 1.

[96] Quoted in April 22, 1915, Bruckshaw, *Diaries*, p. 27.

[97] Ian Hay, *Carrying On – After the First Hundred Thousand* (Edinburgh and London: William Blackwood & Sons, 1917), p. 184. Fussell, in *Great War*, discusses other examples of how references to *Henry V* relate to what he terms "high diction"; see pp. 198–199.

[98] A. D. Gillespie to his family, May 5, 1915: Sanger, *Letters*, p. 28.

[99] Fussell, *Great War*, especially pp. 21–23.

[100] D. O. Barnett to his sister, January 31, 1915 (postcard): Lieut. D. O. Barnett, IWM-DD 67/196/1.

was killed in the beginning of the Battle of the Somme. Jack Engall wrote home that the "day has almost dawned when I shall really do my little bit in the cause of civilization." He concluded, "I have a strong feeling that I shall come through safely; but... I could not wish for a finer death; and you, dear Mother and Dad, will know that I died doing my duty to my God, my Country, and my King. I ask that you should look upon it as an honour that you have given a son for the sake of King and Country."[101]

This idea of honor in the death of a family member was not unique, and was shared by members of the military as well as civilians. After Bill Nevill was killed on the Somme, his brother Howard, a naval commander, wrote home that an acquaintance "came up to me and touched my mourning-band saying 'I think the only thing I can do is to congratulate you.' He had lost a brother himself, poor chap, earlier in the war and I thought it was quite the nicest thing he could have said."[102] In this representation, death in combat was not a subject for sympathy but for empathetic celebration. When R. E. Vernède died of wounds, G. K. Chesterton wrote a note about him for the magazine of St. Paul's School, which both had attended:

The death of Robert Ernest Vernède, who fell fighting as a Lieutenant of the Rifle Brigade in the great advance on the Western Front, while so heavy a loss for those of us who loved him, may well be felt by the many more who admired him as something like a gain; an addition or completion to that new and shining company of poets whose patriotism turned them into soldiers, and gave them a life and death more worthy of a legend; those poets who have become poems.[103]

Chesterton represented Vernède's patriotism as so essentially transformative that it rendered his death an improvement to his life. The dead patriot-poet, symbol of the best England had to offer, transcended humanity to achieve legendary status. As another wartime writer put it, the soldiers "have not died," but rather "they have slipped into immortality."[104] Through that patriotic death, Vernède and others like him also returned the lost manhood to England, restoring the purpose that many felt the country had lost at the fin-de-siècle.[105]

---

[101] Second Lieut. John Engall to his parents, June 30, 1916: Sanger, *Letters*, pp. 60–61.

[102] W. Howard Nevill to his family, August 9, 1916: Commander W. H. Nevill RNR, IWM-DD Con Shelf.

[103] G. K. Chesterton, the *Pauline* [1917], quoted in C. H. Vernède, "Introduction," in Vernède, *Letters*, p. xvi.

[104] Alec-Tweedie, *Women and Soldiers*, p. 84.

[105] For more on masculinity, purpose, and the fin-de-siècle in Britain, see, for example, Samuel Hynes, *The Edwardian Turn of Mind* (London: Pimlico, 1968); Jonathan Rose, *The Edwardian Temperament, 1895–1919* (Athens, OH: Ohio University Press, 1986); Elaine Showalter, *Sexual Anarchy: Gender and Culture at the Fin de Siècle* (New York: Viking, 1990); Wohl, *Generation of 1914*.

Much has been made of the role of public schools in allegedly bring-ing new purpose to Britain's young men. Whether or not the educational experience was successful in inculcating ideas of honor, loyalty, and patri-otism, the school certainly remained a strong presence among the newly commissioned junior officers who had often only recently left the drafty halls and competitive games fields. Meeting a fellow "old boy" created an instant bond; both Frank Ennor and Geoffrey Raven, for example, emphasized the importance of Uppingham in their lives.[106] Eton grad-uates serving in France even organized an Old Etonian dinner in 1916; according to one report, 180 men attended.[107] It was the perception of the public schools, however, rather than the institutions themselves, that influenced ideas about masculinity and service. As Donald Hankey ex-plained in one of his popular essays early in the war, people "who knew him had no doubt about the public-school boy; and when we read of his spirit, his courage, his smiling contempt of death, we told ourselves with pride that we knew it would be so with him."[108]

This was, however, a powerful burden to bear. Many young men felt an almost overwhelming obligation to live up to expectations under what were at best difficult circumstances. If a soldier, no matter the conditions, did not prove himself on the field of battle, then he was not just failing his country. He was also failing to demonstrate that he was, in fact, a man – at least by manhood's wartime definition. Graeme West was frightened not so much of being killed or wounded, but that "one may be called upon to bear or perform something to which one will find oneself inadequate."[109] Edwin Vaughan had similar fears after he heard of a fellow officer who faced an attack while leading the company. As Vaughan admitted to his diary,

I lay awake for hours, thinking that I might have been in the line myself during that barrage and attack... Then how would I have acquitted myself? I saw horrible pictures of myself lying dead in a shattered trench, or helplessly bleeding to death in a shell-hole, with no power to call for help. And not less terrible I saw myself on the road, panic-stricken.[110]

The pressures of living up to the image of the ideal soldier could be greater than the physical fears of combat; a "panic-stricken" soldier was

---

[106] F. H. Ennor to Kathleen, July 16, 1917: Lieut. F. H. Ennor, IWM-DD 86/28/1; Lieut. Geoffry Raven, PL General.

[107] Diary entry, June 4, 1916: Capt. C. E. Townley, PL General; Ravenscroft, *Unversed in Arms*, pp. 83–84.

[108] "The Cockney Warrior," in Donald Hankey, *A Student in Arms* (London: Andrew Melrose, 1917 [1916]), p. 92.

[109] Diary entry, September 20, 1916: West, *Dead Officer*, pp. 68–69.

[110] Diary entry, February 4, 1917: Vaughan, *Some Desperate Glory*, p. 23.

almost oxymoronic. W. H. R. Rivers, famed psychiatrist of "war neurosis," referred to "the conflict between the instinct of self-preservation and certain social standards of thought and conduct, according to which fear and its expression are regarded as reprehensible."[111] The pressures of the ideal of service required the suppression of what must be entirely human reactions. Panic could only belong to the demasculinized: women and civilians, those who had failed, for whatever reasons, to live up to the ideals of the soldier.[112]

This code of behavior, however, made it difficult for many men to admit to any worries about either adequate performance or danger to family members. The front lines were a theater where definitions of manhood were constantly being enacted.[113] Though Joseph Maclean told his brother that "at times I endure absolute mental agony," he was also quick to continue by reassuring him that it was always manageable. There were only "a few days of it at a time and it is only odd spots of that that we get a really bad time."[114] Similarly, Lieut. Barnett could only tell his sister about a day after several of his friends had been killed, when he "sat and shivered with excited and entirely irrational funk, which [he] could not account for," because he could also tell her that "now I'm better than I've ever been in my life."[115] His emotional distress seems entirely comprehensible now, but for the soldier of 1915, such behavior had to be presented as an aberration.

Barnett's caveat was more typical of most letters home from soldiers than was the initial concern. The "warriors" presented themselves to their families as not just fearless but happy and thriving. Early in his service in France, Barnett reassured his sister that "I'm having a priceless time and I think I'm getting better at it." Similarly, after an attack with high explosives (about which Barnett cautioned his sister not to tell their mother), he concluded, "I simply love all this tho' you may not believe it."[116] Similarly, while still in training, Bill Nevill told his mother that

---

[111] W. H. R. Rivers, "War Neurosis and Military Training," in *Instinct and the Unconscious*, quoted in Hynes, *War Imagined*, p. 177.

[112] As the historian Ilana Bet-El has pointed out, masculinity was socially redefined in wartime: "a real man = a patriot = a volunteer = a soldier": Bet-El, "Men and Soldiers," p. 74. For more on masculinity and soldiers, see Gullace, *Blood of Our Sons*; Joanna Bourke, *Dismembering the Male: Men's Bodies, Britain, and the Great War* (Chicago: University of Chicago Press, 1996).

[113] For more on the theater of war, see Paul Fussell, *The Great War and Modern Memory* (Oxford: Oxford University Press, 1975), ch. 6. On the performance of gender, see Judith Butler, *Gender Trouble: Feminism and the Subversion of Identity* (New York: Routledge, 1990).

[114] Joseph Maclean to Alex, November 4, 1917: Capt. Joseph B. Maclean, PL General.

[115] D. O. Barnett to his sister, March 19, 1915: Lieut. D. O. Barnett, IWM-DD 67/196/1.

[116] D. O. Barnett to his sister, undated [first page missing, but should be January 1915], February 4, 1915: Lieut. D. O. Barnett, IWM-DD 67/196/1.

he was "as happy as I ever have been in my life." In France, but not yet with combat experience, he continued to reassure her, calling service "the greatest fun imaginable;" he told the rest of the family that he was "desperately well and fit and happy." This satisfaction was not, however, merely a sign of his military inexperience. Even after months of service in the trenches, Nevill told his family, "I simply love the life out here honestly." His last letter, written three days before he was killed, concluded, "I'm as happy as ever."[117]

It would be dangerous to dismiss these statements by soldiers like Barnett and Nevill as mere reassurance aimed at worried family members at home. Certainly, some of these protective concerns were being exhibited when Barnett, writing to his parents, compared following the sound of shells with tracking "the swish of a duck's wings at flight," or when Nevill told his family that the shells themselves were "most awfully pretty to watch, very like an ordinary regatta display."[118] Clearly, the letters should not be treated as transparent windows into their authors' minds. Soldiers, like all letter writers, considered both their audiences and the conventions of the time. This does not mean, though, that we are free to assume an omnipotence of knowledge that is in fact circular in its reasoning. Through much of the post-1918 era, the voice of wartime agony has been given special status at the expense of all other narratives. The soldier's story, in fact, became one of anguish and disillusionment, perpetuated by its primacy in important works like Paul Fussell's *The Great War and Modern Memory* and Samuel Hynes's *A War Imagined*.[119] As a result, we think that because we know how soldiers experienced the war, we know which texts to treat with respect, and which to dismiss as intentionally obfuscating. This knowledge of the war "experience," though, comes from privileging certain (often retrospective) texts. We need also to listen to the voices that had other stories to tell, and not automatically dismiss them.

Statements of contentment should be taken seriously, too, for another reason. They actually were, in fact, an appropriate convention; they were believable by their intended audience. Within a society where the idea of service was so highly valued for specific social classes, happiness in uniform was a real possibility, not simply a self-delusion. This ideal affected not just how soldiers portrayed the war to non-combatants, but how they

---

[117] Bill Nevill to his family, July 27, 1915, to his mother, August 1, 1915, to All, August 3, 1915, to his sister Else, June 28, 1916: Capt. W. P. Nevill, IWM-DD Con Shelf.

[118] D. O. Barnett to his parents, February 2, 1915: Lieut. D. O. Barnett, IWM-DD 67/196/1; Bill Nevill to his family, August 12, 1915: Capt. W. P. Nevill, IWM-DD Con Shelf.

[119] See ch. 5, "The Soldier's Story: Publishing and the Postwar Years," in this book.

understood their own war experiences themselves. They worked within the terms available to them. Without diminishing the terrors of trench bombardment or the total horrifics of mass advance into direct machine gun fire (though this was not, fortunately, a frequent occurrence), we must acknowledge and give credence to other portrayals of the war experience which are not uniformly negative. R. B. Talbot Kelly, who served as a gunner in France, wrote to his sister during the Battle of the Somme. He described the horrors of seeing "the awful dead in every shellhole and on every doorstep, with their smashed-in faces and their bayonet wounds; or blown to pieces by shellfire or bombed at the entrance to their dugouts." He followed this hellish description, though, by asserting that "still I was glad I was a soldier and would not exchange my experience for anything in the world, for war is surely a terrible but wonderful thing!" He concluded, "remember you have a lucky brother . . . one who is to be envied not pitied."[120] Here, Talbot Kelly's imagery is vivid and horrible, even though it is intended for a non-combatant; his sister, though a civilian and a woman, is not being spared the horrors of war (as has so often been argued by Fussell and others). More than that, the violent details were accompanied by continued enthusiasm, suggesting that a grasp of the horrors of the war did not necessarily lead to disillusionment. It was possible to have lost innocence yet not reject the war.

Finding fulfillment in wartime was an experience not just possible but easy for many to imagine during the war. Eleanora Pemberton, a volunteer nurse serving in France, corresponded with her mother in England. Roger Pemberton, her brother, was a lieutenant in the Oxfordshire and Buckinghamshire Light Infantry, and Eleanora was enjoying his letters:

I am so very much struck by his present attitude of mind which appears to me to be so very much healthier, happier and more expansive and genial than ever before. How strange it would be if it needed a war of this magnitude to make him find his particular corner in life as he really seems to have done. . . . he seems to have found his vocation and I am so very glad.[121]

When she wrote this letter, Roger had not yet faced combat. Yet that is not the point; what is significant is that satisfaction in the military was readily conceivable in wartime, both to soldiers and civilians. The fulfilled soldier was a very available identity. Certainly, this idea was more prevalent in the earlier years of the war, or among soldiers, like Roger Pemberton,

---

[120] R. B. Talbot Kelly to his sister "Tiny," [summer 1916]: quoted in "Editor's Introduction," by R. G. Loosmore, in R. B. Talbot Kelly, *A Subaltern's Odyssey: Memoirs of the Great War 1915–1917* (London: William Kimber, 1980), p. 19.

[121] Eleanora Pemberton to her mother, February 27, 1915: Miss E. B. Pemberton, IWM-DD 85/33/1.

without significant combat experience. Though it did decrease, however, it clearly did not vanish, and was a much stronger presence throughout the war than has been usually credited. Service could lead to fulfillment as well as disillusionment.

If being a soldier could make a man happy, then he was often especially interested in the regular army. Many volunteers admired the professionals, and wanted contact with the institutions of the prewar military because participation in them conferred the much-desired status of "soldier." Simultaneously, however, they criticized the discipline and tradition that were part of the very fabric of those institutions. Military discipline required civilians to make adjustments, and many of them never became comfortable with these changes. If traditions did not seem directly related to the war effort, then they were often described by volunteers as being beyond their definitions of patriotic contribution, and therefore unnecessary. Many soldiers were particularly uncomfortable with the implementation of military discipline, and P. D. Ravenscroft is highly unusual in his repeated service on field courts martial.[122] More typically, middle-class WAAC Dorothy Loveday echoed the sentiments of many a new officer when she wrote to her former headmistress that she hated "the trapped feeling" of the military rules and punishments.[123]

In a popular essay, a young volunteer officer named Donald Hankey jokingly suggested, from the civilian point of view, that traditional military discipline was an "ancient religion . . . [with] its mysteries, its hierarchy, its dogmas and its ritual."[124] Hankey elaborated further on the relationship between volunteer officers and the graduates of the military academies in an essay called "The Army and the Universities: A Study of Educational Values." "In the end," Hankey wrote, "both types found they had had something to learn from the other." He continued:

In the routine of the barrack and the trench the University man learnt the value of punctuality and a high sense of duty. He found it very hard to work when he felt inclined to meditate, to perform punctiliously duties of which he did not see the necessity but only the inconvenience. Yet time showed that the military code was not simply arbitrary and irritating, as it appeared at first, but essential to efficiency. So, too, the professional soldier saw that the psychological interests and broad human sympathies of the University man had their uses in helping to maintain a good spirit.[125]

---

[122] Diary entry, January 26, 1917, for example: Ravenscroft, *Unversed in Arms*, p. 68.
[123] Dorothy Loveday to Miss Robertson, undated ["Friday," 1918]: Miss Dorothy Loveday, PL Women.
[124] "An Experiment in Democracy," in Hankey, *Student in Arms*, p. 30.
[125] "The Army and the Universities: A Study of Educational Values," in Hankey, *Student in Arms*, pp. 167–168.

This, however, was a public attempt at smoothing over differences in order to present a unified effort. Private complaints from volunteer officers about the "inconveniences" of the established system were more frequent than Hankey's ultimate acceptance of military quirks, and the professional appreciation of the volunteers' intellectual capacities is remarkably absent from personal papers left by regulars. Hankey's essays, however, were published for a popular audience during the war. They were meant to be supportive of the country's military efforts, even while poking reasonably gentle fun. In a similar vein, Ian Hay described the good fortune of his Kitchener battalion being located in the line next to "the old regiment." The colonel called it "a really happy thought on the part of the authorities," and claimed that "the old hands took our boys to their bosoms at once, and showed them the ropes."[126] Hay left no room to imagine conflict among the older and newer troops on the verge of battle, or any differences in the critical definition of the man who was a true soldier. This portrayal masked real tensions between the professional and the patriotic – between work and service.

Women and soldiers: service, uniforms, and identity

Given the high status of the military figure in wartime, it should not be surprising that some women attempted to appropriate the identity of soldier for themselves, with varying, and generally limited, degrees of success. Though it is not difficult to understand why the persona of the ultimate patriot was attractive to many women, the fundamental role of masculinity in that definition foreordained their failure to achieve it. Women in khaki, even serving food, potentially undermined these images of manhood by diluting the associations between the uniform and the risk of death. At the same time, of course, women in khaki were redefining femininity as active rather than passive, presenting themselves as participants in defense rather than as the defended. Attempts to contain both aspects of social erosion made wartime praise for service beyond the reach of most female members of military organizations.

The paramilitary efforts of women early in the war, which were somewhat regimentally minded, met with considerable resistance. Ethel Alec-Tweedie blithely attempted to organize her own unit. "If Lord Kitchener would lend a sergeant two or three times a week for an hour," she wrote, "we would drill under him, and then drill ourselves, so as to get fit for *work of any kind.*" Not surprisingly, her offer was rebuffed by the War

---

[126] Hay, *First Hundred Thousand*, p. 207.

Office.[127] Others were more successful. Sylvia Pankhurst remembered the Women's Volunteer Reserve among the organizations that sprang up early in the war, "its members uniformed, drilled, saluting their officers, preparing to play their part at the Front."[128] Beatrice Leslie similarly described the WVR as being organized "on a strictly military basis," with the titles of army rank assigned from the "Colonel-in-Chief" down to "recruits." While Leslie praised the volunteers, she was careful to maintain an essential femininity in her descriptions of the women involved in this inherently masculine activity. While "many girls were eager to practice shooting," she reassured the readers of this popular propaganda that "of course they would never, in any circumstances, carry fire-arms themselves."[129] Lady Londonderry, who took charge of the WVR, also looked for ways to make her organization more socially acceptable. She made it clear that she considered its name to be inappropriately militaristic, and hastened to assure skeptical audiences that she was not creating "a military force of warlike Amazons." In the summer of 1915, Lady Londonderry found an appropriately feminine task within the military structure, and began the placement of women cooks at army bases.[130] Other women, however, like the controversial khaki-clad marchers, saw their paramilitary activities in a different light from their leader. Some (generally socially elite) women were not interested in the work, but in the service, with all its military connotations.

Winnifred Adair-Roberts was one of these women. After learning that "practically everyone I knew had joined the war in some capacity or another," she became the captain of "A" Company in the Women's Volunteer Reserve.[131] She took the practice of her "military" duties very seriously, especially the importance of parade, and regretted when the number of new "recruits" without experience prevented any "invigorating drill."[132] Adair-Roberts fell out with senior ranking officers in the

[127] She felt vindicated later by the formation of the WAAC: Alec-Tweedie, *Women and Soldiers*, pp. 9–10 (emphasis in original). Later, she also offered to organize women to fight in the air and in the trenches: pp. 26–27.

[128] Sylvia Pankhurst, *The Home Front: A Mirror to Life in England During the Great War* (London: The Cresset Library, 1987 [1932]), p. 38. See also Peter Calahan, *Belgian Refugee Relief in England During the Great War* (New York: Garland, 1982), p. 333.

[129] Beatrice P. Leslie, "Fresh Activities at Home," in Jennie Randolph Churchill (ed.), *Women's War Work* (London: C. Arthur Pearson, 1916), pp. 26–27.

[130] This scheme expanded significantly, and the women were eventually incorporated into the newly founded WAAC in 1917. See Barbara McLaren, *Women of the War* (London: Hodder and Stoughton, 1917), pp. 110–112.

[131] Winnifred Adair-Roberts, narrative of her Swiss "holiday" in August 1914, p. 36: Miss W. Adair-Roberts, IWM-DD 89/20/1.

[132] Winnifred Adair-Roberts, official reports for A Company, WVR: Miss W. Adair-Roberts, IWM-DD 89/20/1.

organization, and ultimately resigned from the WVR, taking approximately half her company with her to be newly formed into an independent "Captain Roberts' Company." She argued that this was the only way to maintain the military standards she considered essential to their efforts, and fulfill the ideals of service. Ironically, one of the women in the old company decided that it was the very strictures of the military that prevented her from following Adair-Roberts. A member named Reeves explained her own actions to her much-admired former captain in an emotional letter:

I know that if I were my brother instead of myself, and were in the Army where you can't resign, I know then that I'd have to go on with the work I was doing . . . I know that he would go on . . . the soldiers have as bad as this to face every day . . . and I hope I shall be able to pass the test and do the work even when all the joy's gone.[133]

If men could not leave the army, then Reeves said that she could not resign from the WVR, and the reason for attempting what she was doing was more important than her enjoyment of it. She wrote about obligation and the desire to measure up to expectations of performance, no matter the conditions, just as volunteer soldiers like her brother might have. Adair-Roberts and Reeves were each using the idea of service to justify their actions. For Reeves, though, the comparison to her brother – a *real* soldier – was the trump card of authenticity.

Another WVR member used even more heavily weighted imagery when she explained to Captain Roberts why she had decided not to resign. Tingle, who held non-commissioned rank in A Company, sadly pondered the limited number of women who were likely to attend the first post-split meeting, and wrote that she understood "a little bit how a boy we know felt a little while ago when he came out of a [battle]. His Battn. went up 800 and came out 2 hours afterwards 200."[134] Tingle presented those women who had resigned as casualties of combat, and herself as one of the lonely survivors. The very safety from the risks of battle was what precluded any legitimization of the women's paramilitary organizations, making this comparison deeply problematic. Women could not fight, women should not fight, women did not fight.

When "A Woman" wrote her angry letter to the *Morning Post*, she was very clear that it was the khaki uniforms in particular that she objected to. By putting on clothes that looked like men's, the women were losing

---

[133] Reeves to Winnifred Adair-Roberts, October 20, 1915: Miss W. Adair-Roberts, IWM-DD 89/20/1.

[134] Tingle to Winnifred Adair-Roberts, October 25, 1915: Miss W. Adair-Roberts, IWM-DD 89/20/1.

their own gender: because "clothes exercise an enormous influence on the mind," the corps members "assumed mannish attitudes, stood with legs apart while they smote their riding boots with their whips, and looked like self-conscious and not very attractive boys."[135] It was this aspect of her complaint that particularly resonated with other correspondents. They, too, were dismayed by "the ridiculous masquerades of women in khaki" who created a "feminine parody of the men who are dying by the thousands in the field."[136] The marchers were "dressing themselves like men and so burlesquing their sex," in an effort to "ape the Army" just at the time when women should "do nothing that will make [them] mannish."[137] It was, in fact, "entirely unnecessary" for a woman's uniform to be khaki, particularly as it "sets out to reproduce almost exactly the uniform of an officer holding the King's commission."[138]

The only thing that all correspondents seemed to agree on was the symbolic power of the uniform. Isabel Hampden Margesson, in her defense of khaki uniforms and especially those worn by the Women's Volunteer Reserve, wrote that "their uniform stands now for patriotism and efficiency," and it should be "understood as an outward and visible sign of service."[139] It was indeed about service, for women as well as men. As "Yet Another Woman" explained, "these ladies adopting a khaki uniform denotes that they are as patriotic as their brothers in the trenches who have also cast off mufti to don khaki, the symbol of true love of country."[140] Margesson explained further than "the uniform of the soldier has come during this year to stand for efficiency acquired by training and by submission to the irksomeness of discipline for the sake of patriotism." For these very reasons it was embraced by the WVR, who wore khaki as a sign of their knowledge that "patriotism involves self-denial, discipline, and courage, of no mean order."[141] A WVR member argued that the uniform was not "an imitation of a soldier's garb," but instead "an emblem of service" because "the habits of discipline, *esprit de corps*, and self-respect learned at drill are as valuable to the girl cadet as to her brother."[142]

The problem, though, was that this was the territory of men, and sisters and brothers were not the same. When "A Woman" wrote again, she clarified that some uniforms (like those worn by nurses) were more

---

[135] Letter by "A Woman," *Morning Post*, July 16, 1915, p. 6.
[136] Letter by "Another Woman," *Morning Post*, July 19, 1915, p. 9.
[137] Letter by "Matron," *Morning Post*, July 19, 1915, p. 9; letter by May Rickett, *Morning Post*, July 20, 1915, p. 8.
[138] Letter by "A Man," *Morning Post*, July 22, 1915, p. 5.
[139] Letter by Isabel Hampden Margesson, *Morning Post*, July 19, 1915, p. 9.
[140] Letter by "Yet Another Woman," *Morning Post*, July 21, 1915, p. 5.
[141] Letter by Isabel Hampden Margesson, *Morning Post*, July 26, 1915, p. 4.
[142] Letter by "E. B. Jayne, Private WVR," *Morning Post*, July 26, 1915, p. 4.

than acceptable, but that the heart of the problem was "women wearing soldiers' uniforms." This was because "they can never be soldiers, and all the drill and marching in the world will never make soldiers of them."[143] Again, it was only "a parody (and in the opinion of many a ridiculous parody) of the uniform worn by the King's soldiers, who are necessarily *men*."[144] Their claims to service could not be equal, so the women were only "playing at soldiers."[145]

This was true even when the woman wearing khaki was not herself a paramilitary; for a women to dress in clothing associated with men was really a move from the private world out into the public one. "Public women," of course, had long been closely connected with ideas about prostitution. When Peggy Bate planned to borrow a lieutenant's tunic for an "entertainment" early in the war, she was forced to drop the idea in the face of public shock. She grumbled to her boyfriend, Lieut. F. Austen Brettell, that "some people are nasty dirty minded rotters . . . it's utterly absurd cos I show less of myself in that than anything." In particular, there was "not a curve visible anywhere and my legs are one mass of knickers and puttee." Bate coded her gender transgression as sexual transgression. Popular aversion, however, was even more complex. The costume was disconcerting to her community not just because it overexposed her sexuality, but because it denied her femininity. Bate could not be allowed to symbolically violate the role of a young woman, especially in wartime. Dressing as a soldier, and therefore taking on an essentially masculine role, would have precluded her womanly identity as one of the "defended." Bate enjoyed the attention and assumed a certain air of martyrdom. Whether she really felt the same public restrictions or merely wanted her boyfriend to think that she did, she demonstrated the pervasiveness of this culture by writing to Brettell that in discouraging her from facing social condemnation he had "voiced the scruples [she had] been fighting down within [her]self for the past week."[146]

For women and men both, the line between the ideas of service and work was often shaded, yet distinctions persistently remained. Bill Nevill had been studying at Cambridge when the war started and was planning on a career as a schoolmaster. He then wholeheartedly embraced soldiering and the masculine identity it offered him (in stark contrast to teaching school). Ultimately, he requested a regular commission. Though he joined the army out of patriotism, he could also talk about it in terms

[143] Letter by "A Woman," *Morning Post*, July 21, 1915, p. 5.

[144] Letter by "Civilian," *Morning Post*, July 21, 1915, p. 5 (emphasis in original).

[145] Letter by Violet Markham, *Morning Post*, July 22, 1915, p. 5.

[146] Peggy Bate to "Brett" Brettell, undated ["Thurs. eve"; 1915]: Lieut. F. A. Brettell, IWM-DD PP/MCR/169.

of work, and specifically as a career. The war offered an economic opportunity as well as a patriotic one; he expected that by the time the conflict was over, he would be sufficiently senior in rank that he could live on his army pay.[147] In taking such a practical view of his military service, Nevill sounded a great deal like many of the regular army officers he admired. Nevill is remembered, however, not for his career planning but for the glory and self-sacrifice embodied in his actions at the Somme. The ideal of service has proved stronger than the reality of work in stories of First World War soldiers.

The military served as a nexus for the articulation of attitudes about idealized war service in Britain between 1914 and 1918. For men, particularly younger men, active service in the army (preferably in the trenches of France) came to epitomize the fulfillment of the country's call in need. Some soldiers approached their military commitment with the romance of service, while others saw their time in khaki as a form of work (whether for the duration only or leading to long-term professional fulfillment). The sweeping language of patriotism smoothed over real differences among the populations of men serving in the army. Women in military organizations told a different story. The imagery of work, especially when combined with highly gendered fears about women, military uniforms, and higher wages, emphasized class differences rather than glossing over them. Soldiers were patriots, whatever attitude they brought to their efforts. Working women, in contrast, were by definition cheapened. Women in military uniforms, whatever their motivations, were fundamentally disturbing to wartime definitions of both femininity and masculinity. Such threats needed to be contained to preserve the society for which the soldiers were fighting and dying, and popular efforts to do so regularly employed a powerful language of class distinction and criticism, often articulated through images of sexual danger.

Female participation, however, was also necessary and once it was clear that the conflict would not be resolved in a matter of months, the War Office actively recruited women. While the more elite service-minded women in the early years of the war who marched in khaki uniforms with groups like the Women's Volunteer Reserve had been condemned, the official groups formed toward the end of the war were described in militaristic terms and their members given many of the benefits and honors of soldiers. This approach on the part of the authorities suggested a belief that women would respond most readily to the patriotic language of service. In fact, many of them saw their war efforts as work on behalf of

---

[147] Bill Nevill to his family, September 13, 1915, September 15, 1915: Capt. W. P. Nevill, IWM-DD Con Shelf.

the nation, but work nonetheless. This opened them to significant social criticism.

While the soldier, and particularly the volunteer, was the single symbol of the patriotic male, his popular female counterpart served not in paramilitary organizations, but in the hospitals. Both sides of the debate in *The Morning Post* recognized this, and Margesson asked rhetorically if nursing was "to be the women's only expression of patriotism, and the nurses' uniform the only one of value?" She, of course, felt that "this war has revealed a far wider field for women's activities, all indispensably in the country's service."[148] The majority opinion, however, lay with a "Civilian," who argued that for women to dress like soldiers was as ridiculous as for men to dress like nurses. The writer was specific: "Nurses' uniform is honoured when it is worn by women who are nurses, soldiers' uniform is honoured when it is worn by men who are soldiers; but neither is honoured when it is worn by persons who have no just claim to it, or to whom it is from the very nature of things unsuitable."[149] The obvious ridiculousness of such male gender transgressions made a powerful argument against women who were, "from the very nature of things," unsuitable to the military. To find the women who were given the accolades awarded to the soldiers in the fields, we must look away from the khaki girls and toward the hospital wards, where different battles between ideas of work and service were fought.

[148] Letter by Isabel Hampden Margesson, *Morning Post*, July 19, 1915, p. 9.
[149] Letter by "Civilian," *Morning Post*, July 21, 1915, p. 5.

2 The healing of her men: amateur and professional hospital workers

The Imperial War Museum was founded in early 1917, long before British victory in the war was clear. Women's contributions to the national effort were identified from the beginning as one of the fields of collection.[1] Representatives of the subcommittee on "Women's Work" therefore approached Dr. Flora Murray of the Military Hospital at Endell Street in London. Murray and Dr. Louisa Garrett Anderson had formed the Women's Hospital Corps and, with the French Red Cross, opened hospitals in Paris and Wimereux early in the war. After successful cooperation with British military and medical authorities overseas, they were asked to open the Endell Street facility, the only hospital operating under the auspices of the War Office to be staffed entirely by women.[2] Murray refused to cooperate with the museum committee, "because she wished her hospital to be considered purely professionally as a military hospital and not as women's war work."[3]

This was not just rhetoric of women's equality from someone who described herself as "one of Mrs. Pankhurst's lot," but reflected the new emphasis on professionalism that had developed in the preceding fifty years.[4] The distinction that Murray drew between "women's war work" on the one hand and claims for professional status on the other was an

---

[1] On the foundation and early days of the Imperial War Museum, see Joan Evans, *The Conways: A History of Three Generations* (London: Museum Press, 1966), pp. 227–235, 249–250.

[2] See Flora Murray, *Women as Army Surgeons: Being the History of the Women's Hospital Corps in Paris, Wimereux, and Endell Street, September 1914–October 1919* (London: Hodder & Stoughton, [1920]).

[3] Arthur Marwick, *Women at War, 1914–1918* (London: Fontana/Imperial War Museum, 1977), p. 150. Marwick confuses Dr. Louisa Garrett Anderson with her more famous mother, Dr. Elizabeth Garrett Anderson. Denise Riley argues for the Second World War that "women's war work, even when presented as the result of their collective heroic capacity, was seen as work done by *women*": Riley, "Some Peculiarities of Social Policy Concerning Women in Wartime and Postwar Britain," in Margaret Higonnet, et al. (eds.), *Behind the Lines: Gender and the Two World Wars* (New Haven: Yale University Press, 1989), p. 269.

[4] Murray, *Army Surgeons*, p. 134. For more on professionalization, see Harold Perkin, *The Rise of Professional Society: England Since 1880* (London: Routledge, 1989), and

---

59

important subtext on several levels to the work going on in wartime hospital wards. Once again, conceptions of work were in tension with visions of service. In hospitals, the ideologies were in particularly close quarters, creating frequent conflict between ideals of professionalism and voluntary service. Women doctors, many of whom had connections to the prewar suffrage movements, wanted popular acceptance as the peers of their male counterparts. They offered their services to the War Office, and, when they were initially rebuffed, they found support elsewhere. They also wanted status within the Royal Army Medical Corps (RAMC), an official branch of the army whose members held military rank, as recognition for their qualifications. The military, however, strongly resisted their attempts.

Women doctors also had to distinguish themselves from the best-known female medical practitioners: nurses. Trained nurses, too, were making an argument for professional status. Nursing was considered exclusively and "naturally" the work of women, and those women who had trained as nurses were not disputing that association. They wanted, however, to establish nursing as a profession rather than a calling, one that required significant and consistent training, and was worthy of payment and respect. Primarily middle-class daughters of professional men who could not afford to support them if they did not marry, the nurses were staking their claims for a new socially acceptable work environment for gentlewomen. Nursing as a profession was itself a product of the latter half of the nineteenth century, and was not yet regulated by universal qualifications. The First World War provided an opportunity to strengthen the nurses' argument about the utility and uniqueness of the skills they had to offer (particularly in a time of national crisis).

Trained nurses, in turn, felt threatened by the other large population of women working in hospitals: the untrained volunteers. Usually members of Voluntary Aid Detachments, and called VADs, these women were often (though not exclusively) of a more elite socioeconomic background than that of the trained women.[5] They primarily saw amateur hospital nursing as their patriotic service to the country in wartime, their parallel efforts to their brothers who might be serving as subalterns with the BEF. They often sounded like the service-minded volunteers in the army. As

Roy MacLeod (ed.), *Government and Expertise: Specialists, Administrators and Professionals, 1860–1919* (Cambridge: Cambridge University Press, 1988). Perkin argues that "the more prestigious occupations, chiefly the clergy, law and medicine, laid claim to the exclusive label of 'profession,' which came to mean an occupation which so effectively controlled its labour market that it never had to behave like a trade union" (p. 23).

[5] A "VAD" was technically the detachment itself; its members, however, referred to themselves and were regularly referred to as VADs.

they had little or no experience in hospital work prior to the war, their presence undermined the argument the professionals were making that extensive training was necessary to nursing work. This threat, combined with different class backgrounds and ideas about work and service, led to significant conflicts in the wards.

Hospitals, then, were not merely the site for the healing – or deaths – of the war's wounded and sick. They were also the locus for struggles for professional recognition, with women doctors seeking status equivalent to that of men and trained nurses seeking status as practitioners at all. In a time of high nationalism, concerns about work standards and job identity were often read as unpatriotic, leading to conflict among people doing similar work but imagining it differently. Here, the concept of the social construction of work is critical. What seemed like the same tangible tasks could have entirely different meanings to the people performing them. The work itself, as well as how it was done, was key to how women doctors and trained nurses saw their contributions to the war effort. For the VADs, however, the wards were their trenches, where they served the nation as the female equivalent of volunteer soldiers. They, too, had changed their lives when the country asked. Three distinct populations of women each sought to define their work in ways that meshed with their own social background and professional identity. They were engaged in ongoing battles over professionalization and a conservative vision of the British social order.

Defining a profession: women doctors

Women doctors, despite their extensive training, faced a difficult struggle for acceptance in wartime hospitals. Their level of education even compounded their problems, as many people still found professional qualifications for women socially disturbing. Female doctors had to prove their competence in a male-dominated field to a gender-divided society, and they found an opportunity in a period dominated by images of masculinity. Dr. Beatrice Harraden, of the Endell Street Hospital, wrote that the Women's Hospital Corps:

had a double responsibility all through [the war]: firstly, for the lives and welfare of the soldiers entrusted to their care, and secondly, for the demonstration of women's efficiency and vindication of the confidence placed in their professional and administrative abilities. If they had failed to satisfy the Authorities even in the slightest detail, there is not much doubt but that the charge of the Hospital would have been handed over to a man, and that more than one military official would have had the joy and triumph of saying: "There – I told you so."[6]

---

[6] Beatrice Harraden, "Preface," in Murray, *Army Surgeons*, p. viii.

It was a heavy burden, being responsible for all aspects of running a hospital as well as the status of women in the profession. Contemporary writers also illuminated this double tension. Barbara McLaren declared that "Dr. Garrett Anderson and Dr. Flora Murray have contributed one of the finest pages to the annals of women's work during the war, and by their success have greatly advanced the position of women in the medical world."[7] Though she wrote supportively, McLaren continued to view the doctors' efforts through the lens of war work performed explicitly by women, rather than simply as work on behalf of the national effort. Jennie Randolph Churchill also recognized the war as bringing a "new epoch for women," in which "women doctors are filling the gaps in the medical profession, and are certainly doing their work admirably."[8] Churchill still portrayed women doctors as outside the mainstream of medicine, however, by describing them as replacing absent men rather than as professionals in their own right.

Flora Murray herself identified "the great professional opportunities naturally arising" from their "military work." When war broke out, she explained, women doctors

knew instinctively that the time had come when great and novel demands would be made upon them ... It was inconceivable that in a war of such magnitude women doctors should not join in the care of the sick and wounded, but it was obvious that prejudice would stand in their way. Their training and their sympathies fitted them for such work; they knew and could trust their own capacity; but they had yet to make their opportunity.[9]

For them, the war was more than an international crisis. It was also that chance they had been hoping to find to demonstrate professional capability.

This perspective was not distinctive to members of the Women's Hospital Corps. Dr. Elsie Inglis, founder of the Scottish Women's Hospitals, expanded on Murray's theme of participation by medical women when she addressed Millicent Fawcett's October 1914 meeting on "What Women Can Do To Help Win the War." "I cannot think of anything more calculated to bring home to men the fact that women can help intelligently in any kind of work," Inglis told the large gathering.[10] As Inglis's biographer later explained, "she saw a chance to kill three birds with one stone

---

[7] Barbara McLaren, *Women of the War* (London: Hodder and Stoughton, 1917), p. 1.
[8] Jennie Randolph Churchill, "Preface," in Churchill (ed.), *Women's War Work* (London: C. Arthur Pearson, 1916), p. 11.
[9] Murray, *Army Surgeons*, p. 4.
[10] Quoted in Margot Lawrence, *Shadow of Swords: A Biography of Elsie Inglis* (London: Michael Joseph, 1971), p. 102.

[through war work]: to serve the nation, demonstrate women's fitness for the vote, and advance the claim of medical women to do general work and not only gynaecology and paediatrics."[11] Article after article in *The Times* proclaimed the "dearth of doctors" and the "depletion of the medical profession" through the first year of the war.[12] Supporters of women medical practitioners used this proclaimed shortage as an opportunity to lobby for their importance, present and future.[13] The birth-control opponent Mary Scharlieb, writing from an address on Harley Street, described herself as having "an experience of medical life now verging on 40 years." She hoped that "when this urgent demand for women doctors is realized by the public many women of good birth, education, and ability will be desirous of entering the medical profession." She was careful to couch her advocacy in socially acceptable terms, however. Medicine, she felt, was for those women who did not expect "the most natural and desirable condition of life" – marriage. Scharlieb offered the hospitals in the war zone "officered entirely by women" as proof that "women are capable of rendering efficient professional aid."[14] Howard Marsh, professor of surgery at Cambridge, responded with qualified support from the perspective of his "experience exceeding, instead of verging upon, Mrs. Scharlieb's 40 years." He only acknowledged "many departments in medicine in which qualified women doctors can render perfectly adequate services," particularly "in public health, in hospitals for women and children, in women's wards of the large general hospitals, in missions, and often in general practice."[15] He was not advocating surgery or the more specialized branches of the profession, and made no mention of the women's war hospitals.

In 1914, women doctors clearly still had far to go to gain popular acceptance. Medicine had become increasingly professionalized in the second half of the nineteenth century, with male doctors fighting to create and maintain status as the sole trained practitioners of the science – rather than the art – of healing.[16] This defense of exclusive access to scientific

---

[11] Lawrence, *Shadow*, p. 99. Most women doctors specialized in the treatment of children and women; see Anne Digby, *Making a Medical Living: Doctors and Patients in the English Market for Medicine, 1720–1911* (Cambridge: Cambridge University Press, 1994), p. 293.

[12] See *The Times*, November 25, 1914, 11d; January 7, 1915, 7d; March 11, 1915, 5b; June 2, 1915, 9c.

[13] See *The Times*, December 10, 1914, 11c; January 22, 1915, 35b; January 25, 1915, 11c; May 22, 1915, 5c; May 25, 1915, 9d.

[14] Letter by Mary Scharlieb, "Women Doctors and the War," *The Times*, December 5, 1914, 9d.

[15] Letter by Howard Marsh, "Women Doctors and the War," *The Times*, December 8, 1914, 9d. Marsh's use of the title "Mrs." was a courtesy.

[16] See Noel Parry and José Parry, *The Rise of the Medical Profession: A Study of Collective Social Mobility* (London: Croom Helm, 1976). See also W. J. Reader, *Professional Men: The*

and medical advances in the later Victorian period led to animosity toward both women seeking qualification as doctors and nurses seeking greater professional status.[17] The medical profession raised significant barriers to entry by women, including refusing both education and licensing. Louisa Garrett Anderson's mother, Elizabeth, was licensed by the Apothecaries' Society, but the provision permitting this was changed soon thereafter.[18] The situation was particularly difficult in England and Scotland. The first female practicing physician in Britain, Elizabeth Blackwell, studied medicine in the United States. Several other early women doctors in Britain trained at the University of Dublin and the University of Paris. Most frustrating for women who wished to enter the medical profession, the University of Edinburgh originally trained women, but then refused to certify them through examinations. Ultimately, the London School of Medicine for Women was founded in 1874, and gradually strengthened its position as a facility to train women through hospital affiliations.[19] Even at that facility, however, gender played a fundamental role in training. Women had to learn not just to be doctors, but to be just like male doctors; they needed to conform to the norm rather than redefine the profession. As Elizabeth Garrett Anderson told one class of female medical students, "the first thing that women must learn is to behave like gentlemen."[20]

Financially speaking, women doctors by the outbreak of the First World War were at the apex of the hierarchy of paid working women.[21] Inside the profession, however, their position was still marginalized, and women doctors continued to battle their image as "strong-minded women" rather than female practitioners of medicine.[22] When Elsie Inglis, in autumn 1914, offered a completely (female) staffed and provisioned hospital unit

---

Rise of the Professional Classes in Nineteenth-Century England (London: Weidenfeld and Nicolson, 1966), pp. 175–179.

[17] For example, male doctors argued at different times that both female doctors and nurses would lower the status of the physicians and decrease fees. See Parry and Parry, *Medical Profession*, pp. 175, 185; Digby, *Medical Living*, pp. 290–292. Alternately, male doctors argued against female doctors because allowing women to practice medicine would critically decrease the number of women willing to enter nursing, even though nurses were also frequently disparaged. See Judith Moore, *A Zeal for Responsibility: The Struggle for Professional Nursing in Victorian England, 1868–1883* (Athens: University of Georgia Press, 1988), especially p. 47.

[18] The 1815 act had used "persons" rather than being sex-specific. See Parry and Parry, *Medical Profession*, p. 174; Reader, *Professional Men*, p. 175.

[19] See E. Moberly Bell, *Storming the Citadel: The Rise of the Woman Doctor* (London: Constable, 1953), especially chs. 6 and 8.

[20] Quoted in Digby, *Medical Living*, p. 295.

[21] Ruth Adam, *A Woman's Place 1910–1975* (London: Chatto and Windus, 1975), p. 19.

[22] Mary Poovey, *Uneven Developments: The Ideological Work of Gender in Mid-Victorian England* (Chicago: University of Chicago Press, 1988), pp. 173–176. See also Reader, *Professional Men*, p. 178.

to the British War Office she was told that her services were not needed.[23] Later in the war, Inglis reflected that "ordinary male disbelief in our capacity cannot be argued away. *It can only be worked away.*"[24] Work, explicitly, was her solution, so war was an opportunity for much more than national service. Rebuffed by the British War Office, she promptly offered her hospital to the French and Serbian governments, and was accepted. The first Scottish Women's Hospital opened at the former monastery in Royaumont in early 1915, followed by facilities in Serbia. Inglis died of illness contracted in Serbia, and contemporary reaction to her death illustrated the dilemma facing women doctors, by emphasizing selfless contribution over professionalism. Ethel Alec-Tweedie declared that "there is no name more worthy of honour than that of Dr. Elsie Inglis ... this brave woman literally laid down her life on the field of battle."[25] McLaren similarly emphasized selfless contribution over professionalism when describing Inglis, who worked "without any thought of recompense, without vainglory, and without any other motive than the desire to help and heal."[26] Contrary to her concerted efforts to redefine the image of the woman doctor, Inglis was remembered as a nurturer, not a professional.

The Women's Hospital Corps ultimately operated the Endell Street Hospital (as they had the Wimereux facility) under the auspices of the British War Office. Their initial hospital in Paris, however, like Inglis's unit, was a part of the French Red Cross system. Both hospital organizations were initially closely connected with the women's suffrage movement in Britain, though with two different factions within it.[27] Elsie Inglis was co-founder of the Scottish Women's Suffrage Federation, and the Scottish Women's Hospitals received a significant portion

---

[23] According to an often-repeated story, she was reportedly told, "My good lady, go home and sit still": see Lawrence, *Shadow*, p. 98; Arthur Marwick, *The Deluge: British Society and the First World War* (New York: Norton, 1965), p. 89; Nicola Beauman, *A Very Great Profession: The Woman's Novel 1914–1939* (London: Virago, 1983), p. 16. See also Eva Shaw McLaren, *A History of the Scottish Women's Hospitals* (London: Hodder and Stoughton, 1919), p. 5; David Mitchell, *Monstrous Regiment: The Story of the Women of the First World War* (New York: Macmillan, 1965), p. 178; Moberly Bell, *Storming the Citadel*, p. 152; Eileen Crofton, *The Women of Royaumont: A Scottish Women's Hospital on the Western Front* (East Linton: Tuckwell Press, 1997); Leah Leneman, *Elsie Inglis: Founder of Battlefield Hospitals Run Entirely by Women* (Edinburgh: Edinburgh National Museums of Scotland, 1998); and H. P. Tait, *Dr. Elsie Maud Inglis, 1864–1917: A Great Lady Doctor* (Leith: Bridgland Press, [1965]).

[24] Quoted in Mitchell, *Monstrous Regiment*, p. 181.

[25] Ethel Alec-Tweedie, *Women and Soldiers* (London: John Lane, [1918]), p. 130.

[26] McLaren, *Women of the War*, p. 23.

[27] See Moberly Bell, *Storming the Citadel*, p. 152. For more on the connections between women doctors and the suffrage movement during the war, see Nicoletta F. Gullace, *"The Blood of Our Sons": Men, Women, and the Renegotiation of British Citizenship During the Great War* (New York: Palgrave Macmillan, 2002), pp. 151–155.

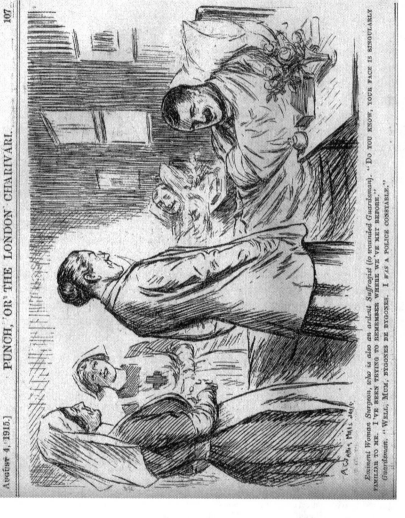

Figure 2.1 "Eminent woman surgeon" and Guardsman: *Punch*, 4 August 1915 (Wallis Mills).

of their initial funding from the constitutionalist National Union of Women's Suffrage Societies (NUWSS). Inglis, however, refused Millicent Fawcett's suggestion to include the word "suffrage" in the name of the organization, for the sake of broader appeal; she did, though, adopt the NUWSS colors in addition to the Union Jack.[28] On the other side of the suffrage fence, Flora Murray and Louisa Garrett Anderson of the Women's Hospital Corps were both members of the more activist Women's Social and Political Union (WSPU). The doctors adopted WSPU colors for the hospital, as well as its motto, "Deeds not Words."[29] These differing approaches to the struggle for suffrage were perhaps further reflected in the actions of the two organizations at the beginning of the war. Inglis, the constitutionalist, did not turn to the French authorities until she had first been refused by British officials. Murray and Garrett Anderson, however, felt that their history as "militant suffragists" gave them enough negative experience with the Home Office to expect rejection from the War Office, as "one government department is very like another." The French were known to be understaffed and undersupplied, so "they turned their attention where the need was great," without making any overtures to the British.[30]

Though the popular association of the Scottish Women's Hospitals with the NUWSS decreased significantly during the war, militancy remained important for the Women's Hospital Corps. Beatrice Harraden argued that "Endell Street represented work for the country and work for the woman movement combined." Similarly, Flora Murray suggested that the "long years of struggle for the Enfranchisement of Women ... had done much to educate women in citizenship and public duty." She also credited the militant movement with having "taught [women] discipline and organization ... shown them new possibilities in themselves, and ... inspired them with confidence in each other."[31] *Punch*, however, presented an alternative view. In a cartoon published in 1915 (figure 2.1), the caption under a picture of a woman doctor bandaging a patient in a hospital presented a conservative perspective:

Eminent Woman Surgeon, who is also an ardent Suffragist (to wounded Guardsman): "Do you know, your face is singularly familiar to me. I've been trying to remember where we've met before."
Guardsman: "Well, Mum, bygones be bygones. I *was* a police constable."[32]

---

[28] See Lawrence, *Shadow*, pp. 100, 102. A non-suffragist friend of Inglis's sent money for the hospitals with a note that stated, "I am glad you are doing something useful at last": McLaren, *Scottish Women's Hospitals*, p. 8.

[29] Murray, *Army Surgeons*, pp. 55–56.   [30] Murray, *Army Surgeons*, pp. 4–5.

[31] Murray, *Army Surgeons*, pp. x, 3–4.

[32] *Punch*, 149 (August 4, 1915), p. 107. Marwick, in *Women at War*, p. 35, identifies the cartoon as "probably referring to Dr. Louisa Garrett-Anderson's [sic] Endell Street Hospital."

This was no mere humorous invention, but seems to have been based on a real occurrence. Murray wrote that at their hospital in Wimereux "a suffragist friend met and recognized a wounded policeman. She claimed his acquaintance. 'I remember you,' she said. 'You arrested me in Whitehall.' 'I wouldn't have mentioned it, Miss,' he replied with embarrassment. 'We'll let bygones be bygones.'"[33] Though in the Wimereux version recognition was mutual, Murray's suffragist friend maintained control by acknowledging it first, placing the former policeman without prompting. Here the soldier was embarrassed by the recognition. *Punch*'s Guardsman, in contrast, edified the "Eminent Woman Surgeon," supported by the laughter of a watching patient and Red Cross workers. Though both sides were presented as cooperating in wartime (in contrast to their more acrimonious history), the power dynamics were reversed in the two accounts.

The complicated position of women within the medical profession was further compounded at the outbreak of war by their position (or lack thereof) relative to the military. In 1914, the only women who had official status were the small number of wives "on the strength."[34] Male doctors joined the Royal Army Medical Corps (RAMC) and were commissioned as officers. This, itself, was a relatively recent achievement; fifty years earlier doctors were not included in the lists of commissions published in the *London Gazette*, which suggested that they were not considered "real" officers. The modern RAMC, in fact, was not founded until 1898.[35] Women doctors, even those working in War Office-sanctioned military hospitals (which they were invited to do in 1916), were denied this newly won status and authority.[36] Their sex trumped their professional qualifications. Dr. Florence Stoney, for example, was described as working "on an equal footing with the men [at Fulham Military Hospital], except that she holds no military rank."[37] Technically, women doctors had no real authority over the male orderlies they supervised in the wards,

---

[33] Murray, *Army Surgeons*, p. 100. The encounter is also discussed in Mitchell, *Monstrous Regiment*, but Mitchell identifies the suffragist as a nurse (p. 191).

[34] Only a strictly limited number of enlisted soldiers were permitted to marry during their service; these women were therefore the wives "on the strength." Of course, other soldiers married unofficially, but were not eligible for the allowance and travel and lodging privileges. See Susan Pedersen, "Gender, Welfare, and Citizenship in Britain During the Great War," *American Historical Review*, 95, 4 (October 1990).

[35] Reader, *Professional Men*, p. 65; Edward M. Spiers, *The Army and Society 1815–1914* (London: Longman, 1980), p. 160; Maj. R. Money Barnes, *The British Army of 1914: Its History, Uniforms, & Contemporary Continental Armies* (London: Seeley Service & Co., 1968), pp. 276–277. See also Ian R. Whitehead, *Doctors in the Great War* (London: Leo Cooper, 1999).

[36] See Moberly Bell, *Storming the Citadel*, p. 166.

[37] McLaren, *Women of the War*, p. 43.

who were enlisted members of the army. Jane Walker, president of the Medical Women's Federation, explained the complexities of the situation in 1918. As she wrote to *The Times*, women doctors "have found that, working without rank among a body of men where the whole discipline depends on badge and rank, they have not the authority necessary for carrying out their duties, the authority which they unquestionably have in civilian hospitals."[38] Their lack of military status undermined their professional credibility and, Walker argued, their effectiveness as practitioners suffered in turn.

At the Endell Street hospital, the doctors "were not commissioned, but they were graded as lieutenants, captains, majors or lieut.-colonel, and each one drew the pay and allowances, under Royal Pay Warrant, of her respective rank." This compromise was possible, however, because the facility was entirely run by the women themselves. At other hospitals, the status of women doctors could be more tenuous. One, stationed in East Africa, reported that "her position had been excellent under a CO who allowed her to wear a captain's badge of rank, but that his successor had ordered her to remove it, and she was therefore a discredited person in the hospital to which she was posted."[39] Similarly, Dr. Edith Guest wrote from a military hospital in Egypt that "although we are senior in service to many of the men here . . . they all – however young and inexperienced – rank above us, and any youngster will take precedence of us even if we serve for ten years." She concluded that "the longer one serves, the more galling this becomes."[40] Walker, in her letter, acknowledged that "recently the War Office gave medical women serving abroad the right to wear uniform, but . . . many medical women have written to say that uniform without rank means nothing, and that it will only serve to emphasize the position of inferiority in which they are at present placed."[41] These were vivid, daily reminders of women's still-tenuous position as doctors.

Walker wrote her letter to *The Times* to protest the lack of official status for medical women serving in military hospitals. A question had been asked in Parliament on the subject, but Financial Secretary to the War Office Forster alleged that women doctors received the same

---

[38] Letter from Jane Walker, "Medical Women in the Army: Disabilities on Service," *The Times*, July 4, 1918, 13c. See also Leah Leneman, "Medical Women in the First World War: Ranking Nowhere," *British Medical Journal*, 307 (December 18–25, 1993), p. 1593. For more on the efforts for commissions by male doctors as well as the tensions that arose in wartime hospitals because female doctors were not commissioned or uniformed, see Whitehead, *Doctors in the Great War*, especially pp. 112–115.

[39] Murray, *Army Surgeons*, pp. 160, 240.

[40] Quoted in Leneman, "Medical Women," p. 1592.

[41] Letter from Jane Walker, "Medical Women in the Army: Disabilities on Service," *The Times*, July 4, 1918, 13c.

remuneration as their military counterparts, and concluded bluntly that "it is not proposed to grant commissions to women doctors."[42] Walker responded not only to express her dismay at the decision but to disprove the allegations of equal treatment and pay. She described the "growing indignation of medical women that the War Office, while continuing to ask more and more from them, persists in treating them as inferior to the men who are doing the same work, and with whom in civil life they are on a professional equality." Each woman doctor knew of these inequities from "her own bitter experience."[43] The work was the same, but the meaning put on it in wartime was not. At the highest governmental levels, who was doing it proved to be more important than what was being done.

The pressures of war were released by the Armistice in November 1918. With the support of both the Medical Women's Federation and the British Medical Association, Garrett Anderson and Murray then petitioned the War Office directly for military rank for women doctors. They were refused, though Murray reported that "it was interesting to find that many individual officers could see no objection to rank being held by women."[44] Winston Churchill, writing for the War Office, argued that commissions could not granted to women because they were not actually performing the same work as male doctors – they could neither serve near the trenches nor lecture on venereal diseases. He concluded that women doctors had "filled a very real need, and by their untiring devotion to duty, and their willingness at all times to perform any duty for which they were fitted have earned the gratitude of all ranks." His caveat, "for which they were fitted," demonstrated the ongoing power of gender over professional qualification: their status as women was more important than their position as doctors. As Churchill concluded, "the grants of Commissions to medical Women cannot be entertained nor can they be demobilised with commissioned Rank in order to provide a precedent should any future emergency necessitate their employment."[45] He invoked the service-oriented idea of exceptional work "for the duration" rather than the work-oriented perspective of professional achievement in

---

[42] "Women Army Doctors," *The Times*, July 3, 1918, 10c.

[43] Letter from Jane Walker, "Medical Women in the Army: Disabilities on Service," *The Times*, July 4, 1918, 13c.

[44] Murray, *Army Surgeons*, p. 241. For American women doctors "the only reward we can receive is … to be buried in Arlington Cemetery." See Mary Roth Walsh, *"Doctors Wanted: No Women Need Apply": Sexual Barriers in the Medical Profession, 1835–1975* (New Haven: Yale University Press, 1977), pp. 218–219.

[45] Quoted in Leneman, "Medical Women," p. 1594. See also the use of similar arguments to prevent higher wages for women in factory work, discussed in ch. 4 below.

order to deny the women doctors official status, either retrospectively or as a precedent for the future.

With the intransigence of the War Office clear, the two women doctors took their campaign to Parliament again, pursuing commissions as well as the right to be assessed at the Service Rate by the Income Tax Commission. There was some initial support from members of Parliament, and the tax concession was ultimately granted. The issue of military commissions, however, was never allowed to come to a vote. According to Flora Murray, at the beginning of the war "every woman in the land accepted her duty and her responsibility, and recognised at once that if the war was to be won it must be won by the whole nation, and by the common effort of all her children." She repeatedly described women doctors in wartime as professionals demonstrating their capabilities. She pointed out that the hospital in Paris "gave women doctors an opportunity of showing their capacity for surgery under war conditions," and called it "one of the outstanding pieces of work done by women in those first months of war." She also emphasized that, at the Endell Street facility, from the "professional point of view, the work which came into the hospital was excellent: it was varied and full of interest, and it gave women an exceptional opportunity in the field of surgery."[46] The support of the British Medical Association in the immediate post-Armistice efforts for commissions demonstrated an increased degree of recognition from within the profession. The complete resistance on the part of military authorities, however, as well as Parliament's silence, showed that the professional victory was far from complete.

Establishing a profession: trained nurses

The working situation was in some ways even more difficult for nurses during the war than it was for women doctors. Not only did they lack official status within the hierarchy of the military, they also had no official recognition as a trained profession. In the second half of the nineteenth century, since the highly publicized and highly mythologized voyage of Florence Nightingale to the Crimea, there had been a great debate over who should nurse, what nursing should be, and how to define the role of the nurse in the hospital and in medical care. Many doctors, including the editorial board of the *Lancet*, strongly opposed the professionalization of nursing. Nurses were to have no autonomy so they did not need any special knowledge or recognition. The historian Judith Moore argues that "medical men and surgeons . . . had a strong wish to retain the 'servants'

---

[46] Murray, *Army Surgeons*, pp. 3, 112, 160.

the *Lancet* so frequently assured them they deserved and little or no wish to replace them with nurses claiming to be trained."[47] For some doctors, the fear was both professional and economic. If nurses were given the official status of being "trained," then, as one explained, "patients might send for the nurse when they might otherwise send for the doctor because you can get a nurse for very little and the doctor's fee is higher."[48] Women doctors, who needed to differentiate themselves, were not universally supportive of the professional claims of nurses, especially early on. Elizabeth Garrett Anderson, for example, argued that it was difficult to distinguish between a nurse and a domestic servant, as both seemed focused on cleanliness.[49] This position, however, became increasingly untenable. Growing awareness of hygiene and public health issues, the professionalization of medicine as a whole, and the interest in nursing as paid employment from a new and respectable female population all brought about a major shift in the status of the hospital nurse.

This shift in status in the late nineteenth century was directly connected to a reconceptualization of nursing work, as illustrated by *The Story of the Growth of Nursing as an Art, a Vocation, and a Profession*, a book published in the interwar period. According to its author, Agnes Pavey, nursing was an art from "The Dawn of History to the Fourth Century AD," a vocation from "The Beginning of Christianity to about 1850 AD," and now a profession from "About 1850 AD to the Present Time."[50] Toward the end of the nineteenth century, nursing was increasingly coming to be seen in the popular mind as a profession, and was referred to repeatedly that way. New books were published on the subject. Nursing was now something that could be learned, indeed, that had to be learned; it was no longer perceived as the innate gift of women (though women alone were usually believed to be capable of it). As H. C. O'Neill and Edith Barnett stated in 1888, "it is commonly and justly coming to be held that nursing in all its branches is a career for educated women."[51] These authors were, perhaps, a bit ahead of popular perceptions, but they marked the changes already well underway.

It was not an easy battle for change, however, as women attempted to stake out a purview of female power within the male-dominated medical

---

[47] Moore, *Zeal for Responsibility*, p. 56.
[48] Quoted in Parry and Parry, *Medical Profession*, p. 185.
[49] Martha Vicinus, *Independent Women: Work and Community for Single Women 1850–1920* (Chicago: University of Chicago Press, 1985), p. 111.
[50] Agnes E. Pavey, *The Story of the Growth of Nursing as an Art, a Vocation, and a Profession* (London: Faber and Faber, 1938), table of contents.
[51] H. C. O'Neill and Edith A. Barnett, *Our Nurses and the Work They Have to Do* (London: Ward, Lock, and Co., 1888), p. 2.

hierarchy.[52] Class concerns also continued to inform almost all developments of professional nursing. Not only did trained nurses have to fight the *Lancet* and its followers, they also had to contend with Nightingale herself. Nightingale was strongly opposed to the concept of nursing as a "profession" rather than a vocation, and used the term in a pejorative sense at least as late as 1895.[53] She was convinced that such an approach would cheapen what should be seen as a calling or a vocation, and thus compromise standards of care. She was also opposed to the involvement of the middle classes, O'Neill and Barnett's "educated women." Instead, Nightingale argued that staff nurses should come from the class of "yeoman's daughters," with "ladies" as supervisory sisters; there was no opportunity for promotion from one group to the other. Training, to her, was inappropriate if overly academic. Instead she described nursing as "an art to be acquired by practice and discipline – a training of moral fibre – not a mere gathering of expertise."[54]

Nightingale's class distinctions, however, could not withstand the ideas and efforts of the many women of the so-called respectable classes who nonetheless had to earn their living: the new nurses themselves. Neither the daughters of "yeomen" nor upper-class ladies, trained nurses usually came from families who were considered middle class but who were without the financial resources to support unmarried daughters.[55] Their fathers were often doctors, military officers, solicitors, or similar professionals, and their options for work were limited.[56] Nightingale made nursing respectable, and then the respectable women whose employment it became took over its direction. These were women like Emily MacManus: "Time was moving on, and I had to think of my future ... Nurses seemed

---

[52] See Vicinus, *Independent Women*, p. 119.

[53] Monica Baly, *Florence Nightingale and the Nursing Legacy* (London: Croom Helm, 1986), p. 199.

[54] Baly, *Nightingale Legacy*, p. 52.

[55] See Vicinus, *Independent Women*, pp. 96–97; and Anne Summers, *Angels and Citizens: British Women as Military Nurses 1854–1914* (London: Routledge, 1988), p. 228.

[56] Vicinus, *Independent Women*, pp. 96–97. The social status of women entering the nursing profession was a subject of great concern and debate; see also Baly, *Nightingale Legacy*; Christopher J. Maggs, *The Origins of General Nursing* (London: Croom Helm, 1983); and Moore, *Zeal for Responsibility*. Summers documented that "the largest social category of the 466 candidates for admission [to Queen Alexandra's Imperial Military Nursing Service] between 1902 and 1914 comprised the 54 daughters of clerics, both Anglican and nonconformist; the next largest group was the 41 daughters of military officers; 35 candidates had fathers who were civilian medical practitioners. Nine women had fathers in whose occupations these categories overlapped: they were army medical officers, or naval surgeons, or army chaplains. Five women had fathers in the Indian Civil Service, four in the Mercantile Marine. Among the many other fathers' professions listed in the records were landowners, solicitors, War Office clerks, and officers of the police, customs, and inland revenue": Summers, *Angels and Citizens*, p. 228.

to be able to go where other people could not." The daughter of a doctor, with two aunts who also became nurses, MacManus used her nursing training to travel and gain a wide variety of experiences, eventually becoming matron of Guy's Hospital in London. The first student nurse she met was the daughter of a solicitor; her matron "came from a well-known family of soldiers, sailors, doctors, lawyers and the like."[57] In the late nineteenth century, these women wanted to turn nursing into a respectable profession for themselves. It would offer them a secure means of self-support. As an added attraction, it also frequently provided opportunities for the excitement of travel and new experiences.

There were no universal standards for training or status that defined a woman of any class as a recognized practitioner. The creation of nursing as a distinct profession, therefore, required the involvement of specific activities performed in set ways. Nightingale had concentrated on "the development of character and of self-discipline with moral training."[58] By the turn of the century, training for professional nurses was rigorous and difficult. New textbooks were written by nurses themselves that emphasized time and timing, precision and punctuality, positioning and regularity, as related to medical advances in asepsis and technique. Training was challenging, involving hard work and low pay. Programs at the major voluntary hospitals lasted for three years, and competition to enter could be stiff. During those three years, and especially during the first one, probationer nurses performed most of the hard cleaning and carrying work of the ward, and were closely overseen by staff nurses, supervising Sisters, and hospital Matrons. In addition to the medical aspects of nursing, they learned the rules of uniform, practice, and behavior by which a trained nurse could be recognized among her peers, including how to interact with the patients. As Maisie Bowcott recalled, Matron taught them to "treat them well, look after them well, but eyes down and remember they have womenfolk of their own."[59] All sexuality, of course, had to be repressed. Not only were ankles hidden, but the nurse's capelet was designed to disguise the curves of her breasts. Talking to patients was generally discouraged; it was considered time lost from other duties.[60] Trained nurses walked a fine line between the traditional role of women caretakers and that of qualified professionals. Care for the sick had long been the province of women within the family context. To

[57] Emily E. P. MacManus, *Matron of Guy's* (London: Andrew Melrose, 1956), pp. 31, 33, 42.

[58] Baly, *Nightingale Legacy*, p. 25.

[59] Quoted in Lyn Macdonald, *The Roses of No Man's Land* (London: Michael Joseph, 1980), p. 113.

[60] Maggs, *General Nursing*, p. 125. See also Vicinus, *Independent Women*, p. 107.

guard their trained status, nurses had to redefine themselves within a gendered paradox. They were qualified to do their work because they were women, but they also had to minimize perception of their sex in order to be perceived as professionals, who might be considered masculine in their financial independence. The idea that nursing was inherently and naturally the work of women was clearly a double-edged sword, simultaneously providing validation and requiring denial in order to confirm the nurses' professional qualifications.

This redefinition of nursing, however, led to its significant growth, until only teachers were a larger women's professional group.[61] Though nurses were increasingly seen as both worthwhile and necessary, they still had no official professional status. After lengthy in-fighting among the nurses, a Select Committee on Registration recommended a Register of Nurses kept by a state-appointed body, which would regulate the content and duration of training programs.[62] Parliament, however, did not act on this recommendation until after the First World War, and the Nurses Act, providing regulations for training, registration, and administration of the professional body, became law on December 23, 1919.[63] Before such official recognition, many nurses felt that the only way to maintain their status was by strict adherence to formal training and discipline: nurses were trying to prove that they were the only ones who could do their work properly.[64]

[61] Adam, *Woman's Place*, p. 27.

[62] For several perspectives on the internal battles over registration, see Vicinus, *Independent Women*; Adam, *Woman's Place*; Maggs, *General Nursing*; Moore, *Zeal for Responsibility*; Pavey, *Growth of Nursing*; Baly, *Nightingale Legacy*; Summers, *Angels and Citizens*; and Gerald Bowman, *The Lamp and the Book: The Story of the RCN 1916–1966* (London: Queen Anne Press, 1967).

[63] Bowman, *Lamp*, p. 56.

[64] Nursing was coming to be seen as a profession through an interactive relation between education and status, defining a "discipline" in the Foucauldian double sense. For a useful interpretation of Foucault's analysis of professions, discipline, and medical discourse, see Jan Goldstein, "Foucault Among the Sociologists: The Disciplines and the History of the Professions," *History and Theory*, 23 (May 1984). Goldstein's analysis is based primarily on Michel Foucault, *Discipline and Punish: The Birth of the Prison*. Medical discourses are, of course, a frequent subject of Foucault's examination; see especially "The Politics of Health in the Eighteenth Century," in Foucault (Colin Gordon, ed.), *Power/Knowledge: Selected Interviews and Other Writings 1972–1977* (New York: Pantheon, 1980). Though Foucault's value judgment about the merits of the process of professionalization would probably have differed from that of many of the nurses involved, his work is helpful in understanding the professionalization dynamic of nurses in Britain in this period. However, as Goldstein points out ("Foucault Among the Sociologists," p. 192), the fit with his disciplinary model is not perfect, owing to the considerably reduced role of the state as "police" as compared to France, the usual focus of Foucault's analysis. In the British case, the state responded by recognizing professional status that had already been discursively acknowledged, rather than working to

This position was even further complicated for military nurses. Members of Queen Alexandra's Imperial Military Nursing Service (QAIMNS) usually trained at the military hospital at Netley, but most members of the QAIMNS Reserve and the Territorial Forces Nursing Service trained at civilian hospitals, which merely felt like military institutions. This connection was due primarily to the influence of Nightingale and her *Subsidiary Notes – The Introduction of Female Nursing into Military Hospitals in Peace and War*, published in 1858. Many of its recommendations were adapted in training programs, leading to a blending of terminology and approach and giving a military air even to civilian hospitals.[65] Thus O'Neill and Barnett wrote in 1888, "nurses are soldiers, and it is a noble thing to fight in all causes."[66] Some nurses, however, were more soldiers than others were. Or, in reality, the problem was that they were not. Like women doctors, military nurses – even those in the official military services – had no official position within the army and navy command hierarchies. They were subject to the RAMC but had no real authority. They wanted such recognition, though they did not pursue it as actively or directly as the women doctors did. Nurses therefore considered it critical to demonstrate their importance to the institution of the military hospital.[67]

Trained nurses were also subdivided into separate and politically important categories. The official military nurses belonged to the QAIMNS. They served in military hospitals in peacetime as well as in war, and had a distinctive uniform: all trained nurses wore a small cape or "tippet" over their dresses, and those of QAIMNS nurses were solid scarlet, reminiscent of the dress uniforms of the soldiers. The increasing popular expectation that war would break out led to the Territorial and Reserve Forces Act of 1907, which created both a trained civilian army to supplement the professional forces and the Territorial Forces Nursing Service (TFNS). A QAIMNS Reserve was founded at the same time, recruiting from the ranks of civilian nurses, and nurses who volunteered for work in military hospitals after the outbreak of the First World War were made members of the QAIMNS-R. They, along with the TFNS, wore grey tippets with scarlet trim, so the difference between them and the Regular military nurses was immediately apparent to all observers (and frequently

---

enunciate such discourses, as in France. This official reluctance about public validation was almost certainly compounded by gender issues, since giving status to a population of women had powerful ramifications within the existing social order. This is an issue generally overlooked by Foucault. For more on power, knowledge, and resistance, see Foucault, *The History of Sexuality: An Introduction, Volume I* (New York: Random House, 1978), especially ch. 2, "Method," of part IV, "The Deployment of Sexuality," pp. 92–96, 99–102.

[65] Baly, *Nightingale Legacy*, p. 22.   [66] O'Neill and Barnett, *Our Nurses*, pp. 10–11.
[67] Summers, *Angels and Citizens*, pp. 175, 178.

resented by the reserve nurses themselves). In photographs, like that of the nursing staff of a military hospital behind the lines in France, the different tippets are clearly visible (figure 2.2). Rivalries between the TFNS and the QAIMNS-R could be strong as well, and based on professional capabilities. "The organization of the TFNS is *sublime*," one nurse reported the Matron of the Boulogne Area saying, "I get a batch of Sisters out; I look at them; and if they are Territorials I heave a sigh of relief. I know that their uniform is correct, their papers are in order, they have enough money, and *they know what to do*."[68] Her use of emphasis made her point clear. It was not just that TFNS nurses were capable people, but they were, above all, well-trained professionals. They "knew what to do."

Military nurses faced a challenge from another direction: popular ideas about the amateur nurse in wartime. Though Nightingale's work in the Crimea ultimately led to the creation of a military nursing service, it also established a cultural memory of ladies of leisure dashing off to the battlefields. During the Boer War, in turn, many philanthropically minded but untrained women had independently established themselves as "nurses." Because of this, as Anne Summers has argued, "the contest was now seen as one between professional nurses and rank amateurs." The inexperience of the Boer War amateurs, however, could be used to the trained nurses' advantage by underlining the professional status and competence of the regulars. In the same vein, the trained nursing community was far from hostile to the establishment of the Volunteer Aid Detachments in 1909. Initially, volunteers were expected to learn first aid skills but not to be "nurses"; instead they were to replace positions usually filled by able-bodied men, to free them for active combat. The VADs, therefore, were not originally perceived as a threat to nursing sisters, and many professionals became involved in the Detachments.[69] The contrast to the amateurs threw the value of their own extensive training into sharp relief. When war broke out in August 1914, then, trained nurses were certainly motivated by varied forms of patriotism, but for them, like the women doctors, the war was a special opportunity for work. As the official *Territorial Force Nursing Service Guide for Members of the Service* pointed out, during triage when floods of urgent patients would arrive at hospitals at once, "a trained nurse proves her worth."[70] It was in response

---

[68] January 5, [1916]: Miss Alice Slythe, Peter Liddle 1914–1918 Personal Experience Archive, University of Leeds (hereafter PL) Women (emphasis in original).

[69] Summers, *Angels and Citizens*, pp. 208, 263.

[70] Imperial War Museum Women at Work Collection (hereafter IWM-WWC) BRC 25 2/10.

Figure 2.2 British nurses in France, showing both the solid red tippets of the regular QAIMNS and the grey and red tippets of the QAIMNS Reserve.

to this ideology that a Sister would write from the front: "It's perfectly wonderful our being here, and we are all most happy in having our heart's desire – real hard work where we are really needed."[71] Even within the ubiquitous patriotism of a work of popular propaganda, the emphasis was still on work and professional capabilities.

One after another, trained nurses signed up for duty where they could utilize and display their professional skills. They were not generally a population whose education and social background encouraged personal writing, but many used journals to record what they considered to be exceptional experiences. Though not all nurses' reactions to their war work sounded like pro-war propaganda, the overall tone is one of routine work done under exceptional circumstances. Nurses who were serving in exotic locales kept diaries that sounded more like travelogues than accounts of patriotic effort. E. Campbell, on the hospital ship *Devanha*, kept a combination diary/autograph book, in the back of which is a watercolor of a nurse on deck, leaning back on a big pillow as she reclines in a deck chair with one foot on a bench, book in hand. The caption asks, "Who wouldn't be a Sister?"[72] Mary Brown, on the same ship, recorded more about dinners and letter-writing and how "queer" the "natives" were than about her work. When she did discuss nursing wounded soldiers, she was very matter-of-fact, even when the circumstances were horrific. She was not using her diary to contemplate her role in the war effort. Her only use of explicitly patriotic language, in fact, was ironic: when she was seasick in the rough waters of the Mediterranean, she wrote that after multiple attempts to dress, she vomited, or "gave up a bit more for my country."[73]

M. Clarke, a naval nurse on the hospital ship *Plassy*, was initially somewhat more enthusiastic. After the Battle of Jutland in 1916, she wrote, "I am thankful, and more than thankful, that we happened to be here and got all the work." Other nurses agreed with her assessment, apparently. A week later she reported that the Sisters from another hospital ship "were very envious of us having all the wounded." The work of nursing connected them to the propagation of the war. When she changed ships, however, and served in the Mediterranean, she lost some of her interest in the patriotic nature of her work, and rarely mentioned the war at all. In January 1917, she complained that "I hope I shall get a softer job next

71 See Grace Ellison, "Nursing at the French Front," in Gilbert Stone (ed.), *Women War Workers: Accounts Contributed by Representative Workers of the Work Done by Women in the More Important Branches of War Employment* (New York: Thomas Y. Crowell, [1917]), p. 183.
72 Miss E. Campbell, Imperial War Museum Department of Documents (hereafter IWM-DD) 88/51/1.
73 March 10, [1915]: Miss M. A. Brown, IWM-DD 88/7/1.

time, not that I mind work, but it is rather unfair, why one should have all the work while others are doing their own sewing all day long." Yet she, too, often mentioned writing letters and sewing during her shifts. She found time, while on duty, to make a black dress skirt, some new underclothes, and to cut out a combination pattern. A week later, her work load did not seem oppressive: "I have been on duty all day, but not busy, so I have been fixing up a fancy dress to wear at a small dance here to-night. I am going as a pierrette."[74]

Minnie Foster, a TFNS nurse stationed near Salonika, wrote home that it was not possible to become interested in the work as the patients were only in her care for one night. Primarily, however, she complained about her physical surroundings and sent very specific requests for things to be sent out to her, including film, white canvas shoes, and size six grey wool gloves to wear with her uniform.[75] Similarly, Sister M. A. Rice, in Alexandria, wrote a complaining letter home to her younger brother Charles. She concluded, "I am glad to be having this experience in a way, but I do get so tired in the heat of the day. I enjoy going out in the evening very much more and as I have a lot of friends here I am rarely indoors."[76] Her social life, rather than her contribution to the war effort, dominated her personal record. Trained nurses certainly considered their war work to be important, and saw themselves as patriots, but this was not the driving motivation in their lives as they described them in personal writings, unlike some other (more service-oriented) populations.

Their preference in location also illustrates this difference. France was considered the most desirable locale for service by many idealistically minded volunteers, male and female. Nurse F. Scott, however, on her way to a hospital in Serbia, reminded her friends that "as you know I have always wanted Serbia much more than France, firstly because the work is much better, they have no trained nurses and very few Drs." Under these circumstances she could clearly demonstrate her professional worth. Yet she too found conditions to be more important than ongoing commitment to the war. Six weeks later she wrote that "of course I can stay here as long as I like, but I don't intend staying after the 1st week of May. I do not think it wise for English nurses to stay here longer than 3 m[onths] at a time." Why? Because "summer will be dreadfully hot and trying, even now when the sun shines it is real hot."[77] These nurses

[74] June 4, 1916, June 11, 1916, January 22, 1917, November 13, 1916, and January 30, 1917: Miss M. Clarke, IWM-DD 84/46/1.
[75] August 20, 1917, and others: Miss M. G. Foster, IWM-DD 84/34/1.
[76] Sister M. A. Rice to Charles Rice, June 14, 1915: C. J. Rice, IWM-DD PP/MCR/116.
[77] F. Scott to "Syd & Girls," January 26, 1915, F. Scott to "Aggie & Connie," March 10, [1915]: Miss F. Scott, IWM-DD 77/15/1.

were not identifying with soldiers, who had no control over their working conditions. War had certainly changed the nature of a nurse's job, but perhaps not fundamentally so. Throughout the texts written by trained nurses during the war there is an aspect of "doing one's bit" but perhaps not *over*doing it.

Some of that difference in attitude may be a function of the duration of the war. Violetta Thurstan wrote that following the outbreak of war "nurses trained and untrained were besieging the War Office demanding to be sent to the front." She took that deluge as an opportunity to argue for the importance of registration as a means of quality differentiation: "Surely after this lesson the Bill for State Registration of Trained Nurses cannot be ignored or held up much longer."[78] For Sister Jentie Paterson, in France in the autumn of 1914, it was exciting to be closer to the front than any other nurses "except those on the trains which have penetrated to within a mile or two of the lines." She reported that "one such train was under fire while they were moving in the wounded and they are the 1st sisters to be specially commended, – we are dying for our turn next." Paterson sounded a typical note of patriotic recruitment when she condemned men who failed to join the army. As she wrote home in December 1914 (in a letter which was reprinted in the *Glasgow Citizen*), "We out here cannot understand how any self-respecting man, not required for home affairs, can remain in civilian garb." Even early in the war, though, family obligations were more important to Paterson than helping soldiers. On leave in February 1915, she learned that her sister Isbel, the mother of a small son, was both ill and pregnant again. Paterson then wired to the War Office requesting permission to stay in England with her sister. She was refused, and informed that she could not break her commitment unless she herself were sick. Paterson recorded in her journal that "I suppose they are quite right still it seems hard. My only sister and not with her when she requires it!"[79] The needs of one civilian family member still carried more weight with her than those of the wounded soldiers she was trained to nurse.

The war, in fact, could get in the way of professional skill. Nurse M. B. Peterkin preferred to care for soldiers who were ill rather than those who were wounded, as the "work is much more interesting, and

[78] Violetta Thurstan, *Field Hospital and Flying Column: Being the Journal of an English Nursing Sister in Belgium and Russia* (London: G. P. Putnam's Sons, 1915), pp. 2–3.

[79] Jentie Paterson to "Martha," November 16, 1914; "Glasgow Highlanders at the Front – Their Baptism of Fire," *Glasgow Citizen*, December 9, 1914; February 18, 1915. Paterson offered her services to the War Office on August 3, 1914, and joined the contingent from Guy's Hospital on August 7, 1914. She was in France by the end of the month, though was disappointed to be told that "none are to get to the front": August 7, 1914: Sister J. Paterson, IWM-DD 90/10/1.

is *real* nursing."[80] M. M. James insisted to her diary that she would not mind the hard work and long hours "if only I could feel that the [patients] were getting properly looked after." However, she wrote, "they aren't, nor fed either. And we slave from morning till night but there aren't enough of us." The work was problematic not because it was hard, but because she was not able to complete it to the standards she had been taught to consider minimal. Two weeks later she was more satisfied with the "best day I've had so far. Heaps of work but time to do it." Work was James's primary orientation rather than national service. She recorded in her diary that "our comic papers now are the *Nursing Mirror* & *N[ursing] Times*. We read them aloud at meals. They do so slop over with sickly sentiment about the 'brave women at the front' and so on."[81]

Challenging work was important not just for personal fulfillment but for public perception, and at least one nurse felt that her commitment to the war effort would be measured by the difficulties of her situation. Alice Slythe recorded in her diary that she had laughed with a fellow nurse about admitting "only about 36" new patients that day, because "it really didn't seem anything to talk about, and yet only a week ago we should have been overcome at the prospect of 20." When the work tapered off, she was both frustrated and embarrassed, as she showed in a verse she wrote in a friend's autograph album. After discussing all the cleaning they had done for lack of soldiers to nurse, she concluded:

> But this is not the work that wins the praise
> Of cheering crowds adown triumphal ways,
> And should the war end *now*, I shall not dare
> To show my face – just yet – in Angleterre!

If there were no unreasonable demands, then the nurse could not cloak herself in the mantle of indispensability. Slythe regretfully concluded the first volume of her diary by writing that she was ashamed that it was "far from being what you would expect of an Active Service Diary – it is simply an account on the surface, of a pleasant summer holiday." Yet, though she thought "of course it *ought* to run 'Called up at 2 a.m. dressed 50 cases; swallowed a cup of cold water; motored 3 miles up the line; dressed 70 more; slept 10 minutes on a haystack,'" her journal was far more typical of those kept by trained nurses during the First World War than perhaps she realized at the time.[82]

---

[80] March 9, 1915: Miss M. B. Peterkin, IWM-DD 77/60/1 (emphasis in original).

[81] November 7, 1914, November 18, 1914, December 23, 1914: Miss M. M. James, PL Women.

[82] May 27, 1915, [June] 10, [1915], [July] 14, [1915]: Miss Alice Slythe, PL Women.

Though nurses generally represented their needs as subordinate to those of the soldiers (even if their private actions at times belied those claims), this did not mean that they were without a sense of their own professional importance. Alice Slythe's diary shows some of the problems trained nurses encountered in their relations with doctors of the RAMC. With their doubly tenuous position, both professionally and militarily, trained nurses had little power to help themselves in conflicts. When Slythe was working at a Casualty Clearing Station, this often difficult situation reached crisis proportions:

I don't want this diary disfigured by local disturbances (there have been many) but well, there was once a hot-water bottle burn (not in my ward, Deo Gratias!) endless courts of inquiry were held, etc. and endless footling rules put up and approved Army fashion. We were all thoroughly tired of the subject, so when a perfect new list of regulations appeared including the order that if a patient needed a hot water bottle the order for its use must be written and signed by a Medical Officer, it was time to strike! So we struck, and the whole collection [of nurses] have resigned . . . I do hope we don't have to leave . . . but no nurse on earth would sit down under a thing like that.

Here, Slythe's language is closely related to that of the work-oriented en-listed soldiers, who also resorted to the techniques of industrial action during the war. She did not want to "disfigure" her diary with personal spats, but this conflict was much more than that. Their competence and training had been called into question. When faced with a total lack of confidence in their professional capabilities, the nurses had no power to maneuver or bargain. The only option available to them was mass resig-nation, though its ultimate ineffectiveness was perhaps foreshadowed by Slythe's hope that she and her colleagues would not be required to leave. The situation was investigated by the chief matron of all British nurses in France, and "Miss McCarthy came down, strafed the CO no end . . . said we acted perfectly rightly, she was very sorry for us, but thought the best thing would be to move us all."[83] Their judgment and competence were supported at the same time as their powerlessness was confirmed.

Of course, not all relations between trained nurses and doctors were so disastrous, but they were often strained. M. E. Goldthorp found that "people do not realize that we are all trained, there is one Sister here who has been [Operating] Theatre Sister in a large Hospital, also Sister of a large Medical Ward, she helped with this new [doctor], and first as she had started her lunch she was asked 'if she had washed her hands?'!"[84] Clearly,

[83] August 7, [1916], August 9–10, 1916: Miss Alice Slythe, PL Women.
[84] [January] 21, [1915], [January] 17, [1915], March 15, [1915]: Miss M. E. Goldthorp, PL Women.

some doctors still did not place much confidence in nursing training in the days before registration. In 1915, the condescension long exhibited by the *Lancet* was still in evidence. Many nurse–doctor relationships, though, were obviously cooperative. M. M. James recorded that her new medical officer was "a decent sort – not looking for work but ready to see anything I want him to."[85] Most obviously, of course, work was accomplished in the hospitals. The power, however, was almost entirely on the side of the doctors, which both parties knew.

Doctors were the final authorities, but trained nurses ran the wards. These responsibilities necessitated training; as one of them wrote, "it is not only medical and surgical nursing that is learnt in a hospital ward, it is discipline, endurance, making the best of adverse circumstances, and above all the knowledge of mankind. These are the qualities that are needed at the front, and they cannot be imparted in a few bandaging classes or instructions in First Aid."[86] This was a not very thinly veiled attack on the group of women called VADs, who usually had no training other than First Aid and Home Nursing certificates and little or no experience. During the war, however, they were placed in military hospitals to supplement the trained nurses. The change was another of the unforeseen results of modern warfare: as casualties were higher than expected, nursing staffs were not large enough to meet the need. Advances in defensive military technology, most particularly the machine gun, led to a much longer, drawn-out war with greater casualties, frequently in massive rushes, than facilities could manage. One nurse described the chaos in her hospital in France in early November 1914, writing in frustration, "This is really not nursing. I don't know what it is."[87] The matron of the 3rd London General Hospital reported that she had only 40 percent of the nurses she was entitled to according to the War Office schedule; to ease this crisis, VADs were placed in the badly understaffed military hospitals.[88]

The government found care-givers where it could, and the eager volunteers entered the wards of both civilian and military hospitals. Given the tentative professional position of the trained nurses, however, it is not surprising that VADs were not welcomed with open arms. In December 1914, the National Council of Trained Nurses of Great Britain passed a unanimous resolution "expressing unqualified disapproval of the present organization of the nursing of sick and wounded soldiers in military auxiliary hospitals at home and abroad," which they sent to the

[85] November 18, 1914: Miss M. M. James, PL Women.
[86] Thurstan, *Field Hospital*, p. 4.
[87] November 5, 1914: Miss M. M. James, PL Women.
[88] McLaren, *Women and the War*, pp. 87–88.

secretary for war and the press.[89] When this resolution was published in *The Times*, it drew a critical response from Lord Knutsford, articulating what was certainly a popular opinion. He asserted that untrained nurses were not being sent out by the War Office, the Red Cross, or the Order of St. John's. He acknowledged some early private citizens who might have set themselves up as nurses, but insisted that they had been identified and removed. Then he came to the crux of the matter: perhaps the complaint was that in some hospitals there were women working "who only had an elementary course of training under the Red Cross or St. John Ambulance" – i.e., VADs. "This is true," he wrote, "but why complain?" Their presence was not inappropriate because they were working under trained supervision, and "in most hospitals there are more untrained probationers than trained nurses," even in peacetime. They should also be supported because "these women are giving their services free at a time of national emergency."[90] Their very voluntarism stood in their favor as war workers, no matter the concerns of the trained professionals.

This support for the VADs drew two responses from the nursing community. Elizabeth Haldane of the Territorial Force Nursing Service hastened to assure Lord Knutsford that her organization consisted only of women who had completed "three years' training in recognized general hospitals," who should not be confused with the volunteers just because they were connected to the Territorial Forces.[91] More forcefully, Ethel Fenwick, long-time nursing advocate and president of the National Council of Trained Nurses, explained that she wanted to answer Knutsford's letter but was precluded from doing so as she was now participating in an investigation by the director-general of the Army Medical Service. She stood her ground, however, reaffirming "the opinion held by the members of our council that, when sick and wounded, it is the duty of a grateful country to provide our soldiers with thoroughly skilled nursing, and to rigorously exclude amateurs from attendance upon them."[92] The line between the trained professional and the amateur volunteer was clearly drawn. The presence of VADs working in the wards seemed to suggest both that long training programs were not necessary to make a competent nurse, and that nursing work was not a profession worthy of financial payment. These tensions were increased as the volunteers were often from a more comfortable socioeconomic background, and seemed convinced that interest, enthusiasm, and patriotic commitment could make them

---

[89] "Dangers of Untrained Nurses," *The Times*, December 10, 1914, 11c.
[90] Letter from Lord Knutsford, "Untrained Nurses," *The Times*, December 14, 1914, 9e.
[91] Letter from Elizabeth Haldane, "Territorial Nursing," *The Times*, December 18, 1914, 9d.
[92] Letter from Ethel Fenwick, "Untrained Nursing," *The Times*, December 15, 1914, 9c.

nurses. If hard work were equal to training, what would that mean for the battle for registration and professional recognition? The very presence of the VADs raised dangerous questions.

Voluntary service: VADs

The volunteer nurses who flooded into the wards in wartime were making an even loftier argument than claims of professionalism: they saw themselves as the female counterparts to soldiers. They were the most culturally successful in their proposition, because they were not, at heart, dangerous to contemporary gender hierarchies. This was true even though VAD work gave young women the opportunity to live away from home, in difficult circumstances, surrounded by the exposed bodies of men. It did not seem to matter that supervision, particularly overseas, was far less strict than under the parental roof. What mattered in the public eye was that these middle-class daughters, like their brothers, were serving the country as volunteers. Soldiers and VADs were both described as having volunteered to change their lives for a greater cause – but explicitly only for the duration. The potential social danger in the new circumstances of the VADs was contained because the service was both self-sacrificial and explicitly temporary.

Women learned the ideals of service the same ways their brothers did. Ideas about nationalism, patriotism, and empire centered actively on men, leaving only passive, often nurturing roles for women. As a result, many middle-class young women appropriated the more interesting male role for themselves, at least emotionally; often this meant living vicariously through their brothers and friends. These young men and women responded to the same stimuli at least partly because they increasingly shared similar educational backgrounds. As VAD Kate Finzi argued, the younger generation would make better war workers because they had "the public school *esprit de corps*, which characterises the modern girls, and which has taught them to play for their side or institution, and not for their own ends."[93] The outbreak of war, however, brought this appropriation to a sudden and jolting halt. The brothers, as a class, were joining the army; suddenly, what were their sisters to do? The ramifications of not being male were brought home in a new, powerful, and frustrating way.[94]

---

[93] Kate John Finzi, *Eighteen Months in the War Zone: A Record of a Woman's Work on the Western Front* (London: Cassell and Co., 1916), p. 250.

[94] On brother–sister relationships, see Angela Woollacott, "Sisters and Brothers in Arms: Family, Class, and Gendering in World War I Britain," in Miriam Cooke and Angela Woollacott (eds.), *Gendering War Talk* (Princeton: Princeton University Press, 1993); and Judith Meyers, "'Comrade-Twin': Brothers and Doubles in the World War I Prose of

Women could help refugees, they could knit for the troops, they could comfort and support, but they could not be the central figure of war: the soldier. For many women without real work experience, voluntary nursing seemed to be the answer. It was a deep-rooted parallel: more than one contemporary observer watched small children playing, boys as soldiers and girls as nurses.[95] The girls were often not just nurses, but explicitly VADs, with red crosses clear on their chests; the public thought of the volunteer rather than the professional (see figure 2.3). For the men who joined Kitchener's Army and the women who became VADs, it seemed a logical progression.

Just as soldiering was the best response a young man could make to the country's call, volunteer nursing was portrayed as the ideal war work for socially privileged young women. Nursing was widely acceptable for its traditional female associations, but for the VADs it meant more: it was their symbolic battlefront, and the hospital served as their trench. Amy Nevill steeled herself against the difficult conditions in a field hospital by reminding herself that the soldiers had to live in terrible conditions in the trenches (though she added the caveat that at least the men were not forced to work in cotton frocks).[96] Ruth Manning discovered when home on leave that she was "looked upon as a heroine." Her aunt asked the VADs in the family to wear their uniforms to dinner, as soldiers would. These young men and women, thus dressed, were visible signs of patriotic service. Manning also worked through hard times by direct comparison to the soldiers, invoking the famous recruiting slogan that your "King and Country need you" to keep herself motivated.[97]

Amateur hospital service and military service were repeatedly compared in both men's and women's wartime writings. The gender constraints remained clear, though. Being a VAD was the best way for a young middle-class woman to serve, as joining the army was for a man, but though parallel, they remained fundamentally unequal. Thekla Bowser's propagandistic book, *The Story of British VAD Work in the Great War*, described the work "performed in humbleness of spirit and true gratitude by those who are denied the greater honour of joining the King's fighting

May Sinclair, Katherine Anne Porter, Vera Brittain, Rebecca West, and Virginia Woolf" (Ph.D. dissertation, University of Washington, 1985).

[95] Peter H. Liddle, *Voices of War: Front Line and Home Front 1914–1918* (London: Leo Cooper, 1988), p. 84. See also Mary Frances Billington, *The Roll-Call of Serving Women: A Record of Woman's Work for Combatants and Sufferers in the Great War* (London: The Religious Tract Society, 1915), p. 194.

[96] Amy Nevill to her parents, March 8, 1916: Miss A. A. Nevill, IWM-DD Con Shelf.

[97] Diary entries, June 15, 1915, April 24, 1917, August 17, 1915: Miss R. B. Manning, IWM-DD 80/21/1.

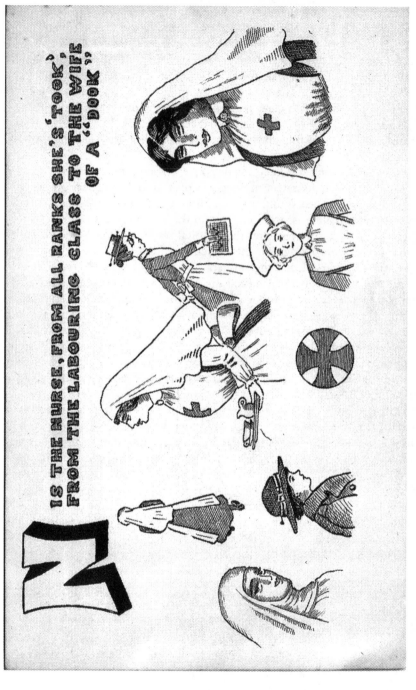

Figure 2.3 "'N' is the Nurse" cartoon, though the large red cross makes her clearly a VAD.

forces."[98] Still, men were often particularly supportive and understanding of women's decisions to serve as VADs. Frank Ennor initially had a hard time enlisting because he was doing "essential" work on the war loan at the Bank of England. After considerable effort, he finally succeeded in joining up. Lieut. Ennor reminded his future wife, Kathleen, of those comparable frustrations after she became a VAD. He told her "I am sure you just feel easier in your conscience now you have made a start. I know you must have felt all along as I did when at the wretched Bank of England, it's a rotten feeling isn't it?"[99] Similarly, George Puckle, a soldier, told his sister Phyllis, a VAD, that she "must be very glad to feel [she was] really doing something now."[100] When Amy Nevill was having difficulty being posted to a hospital in France, her brother Bill, a young officer in the trenches, wrote her that he had also been forced to wait for several months for his overseas posting, and could "sympathise."[101]

The language parallels commonly extended to the terminology of the army organizations themselves. VAD Elsie Ogilvie wrote to her friend Rhoda about the day they "set off together to join the BEF," as if she were a soldier with the British Expeditionary Force instead of a VAD nurse in a military hospital.[102] Ruth Manning referred to the anniversary of her first day of hospital work as dating from when "I first entered the Army."[103] Repeatedly, volunteer nursing was identified with military service rather than with a medical profession. This comparison came through in popular literature as well; Bobby Little of *The First Hundred Thousand* averred that VADs were like second lieutenants, "the people who do all the hard work and get no limelight."[104]

This idea that men and women alike were called to serve the country in wartime was common in descriptions of volunteer nursing. Olive Dent wrote in her 1917 book, *A VAD in France*, that she had become a volunteer nurse because "defence was a man's job, and I, unfortunately, was a woman... And yet the New Army of men would need a New Army of nurses. Why not go and learn to be a nurse while the Kitchener men were learning to be soldiers?"[105] It was the efforts of men and women

[98] Thekla Bowser, *The Story of British VAD Work in the Great War* (London: A. Melrose, 1917 [2nd edn.]), p. 35.

[99] F. H. Ennor to Kathleen La Fontaine, December 31, 1916: Lieut. F. H. Ennor, IWM-DD 86/28/1.

[100] George Puckle to Phyllis Puckle, June 10, 1915: Miss Phyllis Puckle, PL Women.

[101] Bill Nevill to Amy Nevill, September 8, 1915: Capt. W. P. Nevill, IWM-DD Con Shelf.

[102] Elsie Maxwell Ogilvie to Rhoda, January 1916: Mrs. Elsie M. Carlisle, PL Women.

[103] May 19, 1917: Miss R. B. Manning, IWM-DD 80/21/1.

[104] Ian Hay, *The First Hundred Thousand: Being the Unofficial Chronicle of a Unit of "K(1)"* (Edinburgh and London: William Blackwood and Sons, 1916 [5th edn.]), p. 310.

[105] Olive Dent, *A VAD in France* (London: Grant Richards, 1917), pp. 14–15.

together that were portrayed as leading to ultimate victory. A patient at the First Eastern Hospital published a poem in the hospital's magazine that concluded:

> It's a pill for Mr. Kaiser,
> And sadly him it vexes
> When he full well knows
> That his toughest foes
> Win war by BOTH the sexes.[106]

Men and women were presented as working together for victory, in an effort the Germans could not match. The women in such a portrayal of joint effort were, of course, not soldiers themselves but working in hospitals.

South Hampstead High School, a girls' public day school, implied a similar parallel when it started "a Roll of Honour for King and Country." This was a list, "on which are inscribed from time to time the names of near relatives of members of the School who are on active service, and of those who are nursing abroad under the Red Cross Society."[107] Most "Rolls of Honour" were records of casualties, but, by making it a record of service, they could to include women as well as men. Only women working in hospitals for the Red Cross, however, and not those engaged in other forms of war work, were explicitly included along with the soldiers.

The strength of this idea of equivalent service was reinforced through official channels. VADs were issued with identity disks, similar to those of soldiers. Katharine Furse, VAD commandant, used a parallel language repeatedly in communications both with the volunteers and with government officials and other agencies. The most striking example was a letter given to every VAD overseas, which she closely modeled on one Lord Kitchener had written for all members of the British Expeditionary Force in 1914. Furse considered this military source to be so important that she quoted both the original and her adaptation in their entireties in her memoir. Kitchener's text provided validation for her own: the relation of the letters justified her portrayal of the relation of the men in the trenches and the women volunteers in the wards. Furse made key gendered amendments: where the troops were exhorted by Kitchener to do their duty "bravely," the VADs were called on to do theirs "loyally." In addition to the "courage," "energy," and "patience" required for soldiers, nurses needed "humility" and "determination." Both were reminded that the "honour" of their respective organizations rested on

---

[106] "To Our Fairer Sex," by "Birdseed, Ward 7": *First Eastern Hospital Gazette*, vol. 2, April 11, 1916: Miss R. B. Manning, IWM-DD 80/21/1.
[107] *South Hampstead High School Magazine*, no. 27, November 1914, p. 4.

each individual's conduct, which in both cases should present "an example of discipline and perfect steadiness," though "under fire" for the men, and "of character" for the women. For soldiers, of course, combat behavior was most important. Women could only offer unimpeachable morality. While the soldiers were to "maintain the most friendly relations with those whom you are helping in this struggle," the VADs were told only to be "courteous"; Furse and her staff may have been worried about the consequences of young women being too "friendly." Where the troops needed only be "considerate," the volunteer nurses had to be "unselfish." The two letters then diverged significantly. Kitchener's note concluded with a warning against looting, and against French wine and women, as duty could not be fulfilled "unless your health is sound." The VADs' letter went on for several paragraphs, commending humility, compliance, patience, and generosity – especially to the Red Cross. There was a much stronger emphasis on religious imagery, including the addition of a specially written "Red Cross Prayer" on the back. Both the letter and the prayer explicitly articulated the idea of volunteer nursing as displaced labor for those fighting in the trenches. Ultimately, the VADs were told to ask God to "Teach us no task can be too great, no work too small, for those who die or suffer pain for us and for their Country."[108]

The prayer was appropriate, as at times the tasks were certainly great, and at other times, the work was indeed small. The official VAD Joint War Committee Reports, published in 1921, claimed that the volunteers were not "entrusted with trained nurse's work except on occasions when the emergency was so great that no other course was open."[109] This may have been the official policy, but such a condition of emergency seems to have been an almost constant occurrence in field and stationary hospitals in France. It was not the case at home, however. VADs working in Red Cross auxiliary hospitals in England complained of the lack of responsible work, and those in British military hospitals often claimed that the trained nurses with whom they worked would not trust them with anything other than rudimentary duties (except in times of crisis). Those VADs working in France, though, not only performed skilled tasks but even supervised entire wards.

Dorothy Field, for example, was pleased when she was transferred to a tent with twenty-eight beds at No. 10 General Hospital in France, as

---

[108] Katharine Furse, *Hearts and Pomegranates: The Story of Forty-Five Years 1875–1920* (London: Peter Davies, 1940), pp. 333–335. Furse's appropriation of "character" for women was itself a potentially startling linkage; see especially Stefan Collini, *Public Moralists: Political Thought and Intellectual Life in Britain 1850–1930* (Oxford: Clarendon, 1991), pp. 91–118.

[109] *Red Cross Society and the Order of St. John, Joint War Committee Reports 1914–1918 (1921)*, p. 80: British Red Cross Society Archive, Barnett Hill, Guildford (hereafter BRCS).

there she was "more or less running [her] own show."[110] Katia Freshfield, similarly, was in charge of "thirty to forty patients," and had developed a system with the trained nurse who was nominally in charge. The VAD called it "a capital plan by which we have a code through which she knows if I really want her or am only sending for form's sake."[111] Amy Nevill was put on night duty, and she "like[d] it tremendously," because she was "in charge of two surgical wards."[112] Winifred Kenyon even assisted a doctor in surgery because there was no trained nurse available.[113] This was the kind of work many VADs seemed to like. They wanted what they saw as "real" wartime nursing: surgical rather than medical, as wounded soldiers were emotionally closer to the war effort than those who were merely ill. This was quite different from the trained nurses who often considered medical nursing more "real" than the patch-up work of the surgical wards. VAD Eleanora Pemberton agreed that the desirable work was "really...nursing wounded," and she was pleased that she had real responsibility in the wards so much more quickly than she would have had in a hospital in England.[114]

Family relationships and obligations, however, were the one aspect of their lives that most clearly differentiated the VADs from soldiers. They did not face any serious punishments for leaving their work, and they were socially obligated to consider the needs of their families. Most VADs were under contract, and signed on for duty in six-month increments. The contracts, however, could be and were broken, though the Red Cross was sometimes difficult about reposting a woman who had done so. It was more common for a VAD to leave at the end of her contract because her family felt that she had been away from home long enough. The call of the "daughter at home" could be powerful indeed. Katharine Furse acknowledged that in one particular group, forty-seven of fifty-nine VADs went home after the completion of their first six months in France, though her correspondent felt that parents were slowly adjusting to the idea that there would not necessarily be "one daughter at home."[115] Family constraints

---

[110] Dolly Field to her parents, February 9, 1916: Miss D. Field, IWM-DD 91/27/1.

[111] Diary entry, January 1917: Miss K. Freshfield, PL Women.

[112] Amy Nevill to her parents, December 27, 1915 [section dated January 4, 1916]: Miss A. A. Nevill, IWM-DD Con Shelf.

[113] August 6, 1915: Miss W. L. Kenyon, IWM-DD 84/24/1.

[114] Eleanora Pemberton to her brother Tom, October 23, 1914; to her father, November 2, 1914: Miss E. B. Pemberton, IWM-DD 85/33/1. See also Evelyn Proctor to her mother, January 10, [1918]: Miss E. H. Proctor, IWM-DD 88/16/1; Gwen Ware, *"A Rose in Picardy": The Diaries of Gwen Ware, 1916–1918* (Farnham and District Museum Society Pamphlet, 1984), BRCS; March 14, 1915, June 6, 1915: Miss W. L. Kenyon, IWM-DD 84/24/1.

[115] Mary Campion to Katharine Furse, April 22, 1917: Dame Katharine Furse, PL Women.

continued to be a high priority for many of the VADs, however. After several years of work, Eleanora Pemberton decided that "I really think I shall have to be home [for father's birthday] next year, war or no war."[116] Her commitment, apparently, was not as indefinite as the conflict. Evelyn Proctor enjoyed her work in France and wanted to continue beyond her six months. She still deferred to her mother, however, telling her that the decision "rests entirely with you," though Proctor added persuasively that "nearly everyone manages a little more time."[117] Phyllis Goodliff took a more direct approach. She informed her mother, "I have just been asked if I am willing to sign on again for another six months and without the least hesitation have said I am as I am determined to see this show through to the end if I can, and you haven't said anything about wanting me back in England."[118] Goodliff made her own decision, but it was justified by her mother's previous failure to offer any opposition. Even in wartime, VADs felt a powerful sense of conflicting duties between service to their families and service to the country.

Family responsibilities were overcome by appeals that equated VADs and soldiers. Mrs. Alphonse Courlander argued in 1917 that officials who had first belittled the VADs later changed their minds, as "scoffing at amateur nurses went out of fashion when a new amateur army became a great factor in the war."[119] In a memorandum entitled "What We Want Included in the National Service Appeal to Women to Join Voluntary Aid Detachments," Katharine Furse wrote that "the daughters are wanted by the Country as well as the sons. All who can afford to work without pay should do so for the sake of the country – giving all they have to give for the men who have risked everything in order to save their Country."[120] Young women, like young men, were needed for the national effort. At the same time as Furse posited this parity, however, the gender hierarchy was maintained by her assertion of an intermediate step. The VADs were not serving the country directly, but doing so by helping the true risk-takers, the soldiers.

In late 1917, Furse made the link between the women she led and fighting men explicit. Though other women were doing important work, she wrote in particular about those who have "shared in the honour of our men in facing danger and [the] many [who] have thereby sacrificed

[116] Eleanora Pemberton to her father, May 23, 1917: Miss E. B. Pemberton, IWM-DD 85/33/1.
[117] Evelyn Proctor to her mother, dated only Tuesday [October 1917]: Miss E. H. Proctor, IWM-DD 88/16/1.
[118] Phyllis Goodliff to her mother, August 9, 1918: Miss P. E. Goodliff, IWM-DD 88/51/1.
[119] Mrs. Alphonse Courlander, "The VAD Nurse," in Stone, *Women War Workers*, p. 207.
[120] IWM-WWC BRC 10 1/1.

their lives and their health in the Service of the Sick and Wounded."[121]
The comparison to soldiers in the allegedly shared danger legitimized
the women's efforts. Though VADs tried to claim this parity of service
with soldiers for themselves, the fact remained that the work itself, with
its concomitant dangers (such as they were), was also being performed
by professional nurses, as Furse wrote. Though elsewhere very critical of
the trained nursing corps, when it came to the risks inherent in serving
near the front, Furse was obliged to acknowledge the nurses (though she
ignored women doctors entirely). Their differences in orientation toward
their work, however, led to conflict in the hospitals.

Wars in the wards

Captain Geoffrey Wait, in Rouen following a hospitalization, decided that
he had figured out the different women workers. He wrote to his mother
in 1916, "I know all the different type of VADs and sisters now. I know
all these little quarrels and grievances. Sisters don't like VADs because
they are untrained (?) [sic], frivolous etc. VADs don't like sisters because
they are dull, boring and never give them any responsible work to do,
only [treating them as] glorified housemaids."[122] Wait recognized from
his conversations in the wards that the issue of being "untrained" was
central to the clashes, even though he did not understand what it meant.
In contrast, propagandistic works like *The Story of British VAD Work in
the Great War* claimed that:

Trained Sisters have learned to appreciate the work of VAD members and freely
acknowledge that they could not possibly manage without them; whilst on the part
of the members they give respect and willing obedience to the skilled women who
have spent years in acquiring their knowledge of nursing. There is wonderfully
little friction, considering the enormous numbers of people who have been thrown
to work together suddenly, under somewhat difficult circumstances.[123]

The very force of these assertions of amity practically suggests the
contrary. It was, indeed, far from the reality in many wards. The
conflicts among British women working in hospitals during the First
World War illustrate a special circumstance where people who had different class identities were trying to occupy the same cultural space.
The trained nurses and the volunteers were both attempting to define the role of the nurse in wartime. In an unusual twist, the group

---

[121] IWM/WWC BRC 10 2/14.
[122] Geoffrey Wait to his mother, December 22, 1916: Capt. Geoffrey K. Wait MC, PL
General.
[123] Bowser, *British VAD Work*, p. 175.

considered lower on the socioeconomic scale was in the position of authority. This reversal of traditional hierarchical roles often exacerbated the confrontations.

Titles were extremely important to trained nurses; "Sister" was earned after lengthy difficult work, and those who had it or expected to earn it were often highly resistant to it being applied generally to VADs. A letter to the *British Journal of Nursing* from a Sister with ten years of experience complained that in her hospital "the untrained commandant – a girl young enough to be my daughter – insists on all the volunteers being called 'Sister.'"[124] At another Red Cross auxiliary hospital, the volunteers along with the sole trained nurse were all referred to as Sister, as it sounded, to the VADs, "so much nicer than nurse."[125] This distinction that was clear to the trained nurses, and understood if not appreciated by the VADs, was often ignored by doctors and incomprehensible to patients and visitors. Though rules about titles were generally more strictly enforced in hospitals in England, it proved impossible to keep patients at military hospitals in France from referring to all of their women caregivers as "Sisters." The situation varied more widely at auxiliary hospitals, which were run by Red Cross volunteers. At the humorous extreme, a magazine of comic sketches put together by staff at the VAD headquarters at Devonshire House satirically described the commandant of an auxiliary hospital, where "the VADs all wear Army sister's caps... [and] are called 'Sister.'" When asked what the actual Sisters were then called, she responded, "You mean the trained nurses? O, I haven't any. I find they always make things so difficult."[126]

The differing perceptions of the women in the hospitals themselves were recorded at the highest levels. Katharine Furse, VAD commandant, wrote a memorandum in 1916 about the process of placing volunteers in civilian hospitals. Though she described most VAD members as happy, the primary complaint she recorded was "Want of encouragement on the part of the trained nurses," resulting in some VADs being restricted to menial cleaning duties, no matter how much or what kinds of experience the volunteers might have had in previous hospital work.[127] In a further collection of specific complaints, Furse became even more direct, referring to "Intolerance on the part of matrons, sisters, and trained nurses."[128] She also wrote to her sister Madge that "the trained nurses

[124] Quoted in Adam, *Woman's Place*, p. 56.
[125] Journal entry, pp. 3–4: Miss M. Denys-Burton, IWM-DD 92/22/1.
[126] "The JC Room at Work; or, Not as Others See Us," one of "Two Short Plays" from "The Playhouse, Picadilly, Saturday, 7th December, 1918," in *The Devonshire House Book*. *VAD HQS*: Mrs. E. E. Quinlan, IWM-DD P348.
[127] IWM-WWC BRC 10 2/10.   [128] IWM-WWC BRC 10 3/3.

and some of the auxiliary hospitals do need all the criticism that can be brought to bear on them. I often feel a fool in my position for I have little power to look after my people but it is not for want of asking for it and if an enquiry be held I can produce plenty of evidence."[129]

Furse was not merely recording the complaints that came to her, but was clearly sympathetic to them, and drafted a detailed memo on "Foundations of the Present Difficulties in VAD Service." Of the eleven problems she cited, eight were criticisms of nursing training methods, selection of nurses for military hospitals, or the behavior of nurses and matrons toward volunteers. Furse invoked class issues by citing the "Trades Union feeling among trained Nurses involving jealousy of the untrained women." She also condemned the very nature of the professionals' qualifications: "present methods of training schools tend to kill individuality and to dwarf all interest in things outside the Profession...result[ing] in a general narrowing instead of expansion of the woman's mind." She claimed that much of the problem was related to the strain on hospital resources that the war had created. There were insufficient of "the best type" of trained nurses for the military demand (the very phenomenon that led to the widespread placement of VADs in hospitals). As a result, members of "the dregs of the Nursing Profession" were now serving in hospitals, some of whom were "money-seeking...and in many cases put[ting] their own interests in front of the good of the Sick and Wounded." Though Furse included disclaimers ("There are, of course, hundreds of exceptions"), only one item from her list of problems, "'Discipline' misinterpreted as 'Bullying'" (the only entry on which Furse did not expand with detail), held the VADs in any way responsible for the conflict.[130]

Trained nurses, of course, brought a different point of view to the conflict. The "Report of an Advisory Committee Appointed by the Army Council to Enquire into the Supply of Nurses," written in November 1916, provided a contrasting interpretation. This Advisory Committee was quite controversial, as it originally included Furse but no nurses. After an outcry, it was reconstituted with numerous senior members of the trained nursing community.[131] According to the report, while the nurses had "not always been fairly treated by untrained commandants" who operated the auxiliary Red Cross hospitals, VADs had only "complained." The professionals had actually been treated badly, the language suggested, while perhaps the volunteers were merely whining without basis. The volunteers exhibited "the inevitable tendency of the amateur

[129] Katharine Furse to Madge, May 2, 1917: Dame Katharine Furse, PL Women.
[130] IWM-WWC BRC 10 4/8.   [131] Furse, *Hearts and Pomegranates*, pp. 345–346.

to be impatient," so the skilled professional therefore had a "natural aversion . . . from trusting anything but simplest duties" to VADs, characterized as "beginner[s]." The clear implication was that nurses had the best interests of the patients in mind, and any limitations they placed on volunteers were necessary to ensure quality of care. The untrained volunteers, not understanding what nursing really involved, then misinterpreted the restrictions and "complained." In fact, the committee considered that the relative dearth of problems was "a great testimony to the devotion and unselfishness of the general body of nurses engaged."[132] This failed to explain the vast majority of problems by not addressing those occurring in military hospitals (where there could be no "untrained commandants"), or the number of cases by late 1916, more than two years into the war, when most VADs were no longer "beginner[s]." The report, though perhaps not as one-sided as the sweeping condemnation offered by Furse, made the terms clear, however. The conflict was between "the amateur" and "the professional."

As a result of these tensions, the caliber of work and the atmosphere in which it was performed depended almost entirely on personal relations between the VADs and the trained nurses. Volunteer Daisy Spickett maintained that work was "a nightmare" when "Sister always ordered you to do things and made beastly remarks all the time," but "when they are nice you do twice as much and get plenty of amusement out of it." She described the "Compleat VAD" as one who "goes where she is told to go, does what she is asked to do and produces any thing she is told to get by hook or by crook!"[133] A 1916 edition of the *First Eastern General [Hospital] Gazette* offered a humorous set of rules called "The VAD's Companion, Or Hints on Etiquette for Those in Military Hospitals." It began:

1. The mind should be a receptive blank until something is required, when an intelligent grasp of the subject should be immediately shown. Do not let it distress you that it is impossible to be both as ignorant and as intelligent as is expected of you.
2. Do all your own work cheerfully – and as much of the nurses' as possible.
3. Remember you should always have heard before the name of everything that is wanted, and always know where it is kept.
4. When a patient calls "Sister" do not hear.
5. If the [Medical Officer] calls you "Nurse" try not to look pleased.
6. Do not confuse yourself with the Nursing Staff . . .[134]

132 IWM-WWC BRC 25 0/4.
133 Daisy Spickett to her mother and Hilary, undated [1917]: Miss D. C. Spickett, IWM-DD 76/24/1.
134 *First Eastern General Gazette*, vol. 2, April 11, 1916: Miss R. B. Manning, IWM-DD 80/21/1.

All the key issues were being satirized: training, titles, status, and relations with patients and doctors.

Relations between the VADs and the trained nurses were often the subject of humor, usually biased in favor of the volunteers, as in the *Evening Standard*:

> The Hive was made for the bees;
> The bees make all the honey;
> The VADs do all the work;
> The Sisters get the money![135]

The satire, here, was double edged. The professionals, who had worked hard to turn nursing into a respectable career, were being criticized not only for their working procedures, but for their very paid status. Again, as with soldiers, the volunteer in wartime was lauded to the exclusion of the skilled professional. In the public eye, the nurses were not following careers, but instead were practically profiteers for benefiting from the war. (The same kinds of arguments would be used to argue against the wages being paid to women in industry.) Voluntarism allegedly guaranteed purely patriotic motivation, so a salary could be seen as calling intent into question. The qualified nurses were indeed in a very difficult position.

VADs spent more of their writing time complaining about relations with trained nurses than the reverse; the professionals, in fact, were most likely not to mention the volunteers at all. This seems especially to be the case in personal writings, though certainly there was significant criticism in the nursing press and from official nursing organizations. The vast majority of diaries kept and correspondence available from trained nurses, however, were written by women stationed in military hospitals overseas, whether in the Middle East or France. There is much less personal documentation available for trained nurses working in Red Cross hospitals inside the United Kingdom, and there is no doubt that those hospitals, run by volunteers, were often sites of conflict. Regular QAIMNS nurses also had fewer difficulties with VADs than did their civilian Reserve counterparts. This may have been a function of their backgrounds, as military nurses often came from more elite socioeconomic backgrounds than the civilian nurses who joined the military reserves in wartime did, and may therefore have felt less professionally threatened by the volunteers. A greater proportion of the regulars served overseas, as well, where decent relations with the VADs who stayed were often necessary for any semblance of

---

[135] *Evening Standard*, May 19, 1917, quoted in Furse, *Hearts and Pomegranates*, p. 335; Furse described it as "a nonsense verse, but perhaps there was a glimmer of truth in it."

competent care for soldiers in urgent need. Overseas, as well, the women were without their home communities, and therefore spent even more time in each other's company. This level of familiarity and security left room for better relations. Conversely, convalescent hospitals were often located in converted private homes of the wealthy, and staffed primarily by the local daughters of the so-called best families. These hospitals were all directed by VAD commandants. Trained nurses were clearly living and working in the home territory of the elite volunteers, and were responsible to wealthy women rather than to qualified medical doctors. As most of these facilities were for rehabilitation, the patients generally were not even sufficiently ill for them to demonstrate the fundamental importance of their own training and skills.

Though negative accounts dominated personal writings, VADs did describe positive relations with at least some members of the trained nursing staffs. Ada Garland called the matron under whom she served on the hospital ship *Britannic* as being "as good as gold to us" and said she "treated us just like her children."[136] Amy Nevill also liked her nursing staff from the beginning, writing home from France that the Sister in charge of her ward "is so awfully good to me, and anyone more patient with an idiot it would be impossible to find."[137] Good relations could even extend into social venues: Dorothy Higgins had her Sister to tea and went on a picnic with her; and Daisy Spickett and her fellow VADs planned "Progressive Games" for her Sisters, who were pleased, and "seemed awfully nice."[138] Of course, some positive social relations were recorded by the nurses as well as by the volunteers. M. Clarke and a fellow nurse named Tarleton, stationed in Malta, repeatedly had tea and played tennis with a number of VADs.[139] M. E. Goldthorp found the well-traveled VAD posted to her ward an interesting companion. Though Goldthorp felt "so sorry" for a VAD thrust into hospital work as a convoy of wounded arrived – "she has never seen such sights" – the nurse had mixed feelings about the arrival of five additional Red Cross workers, telling her diary: "I do wish they had been trained." At the same time, she was pleased that the doctors were discovering the limitations of the VADs. One volunteer was put in charge

---

[136] Ada Garland, "Experience of a VAD from 18.5.1916," p. 2: Miss A. Garland, IWM-DD 77/57/1.

[137] Amy Nevill to her family, October 5, 1915; see also to her mother, September 30, 1915: Miss A. A. Nevill, IWM-DD Con Shelf.

[138] D. E. Higgins to her mother, "Sunday [February?] 27th", [1916], April 4, 1916: Miss D. E. Higgins, IWM-DD 86/73/1; Daisy Spickett to "My Darling Mother & Dad & Hilary," dated only "Sunday" [December 1915], and to her parents, December 15, 1915: Miss D. C. Spickett, IWM-DD 76/24/1.

[139] February 16, 1917, February 23, 1917, February 28, 1917, March 16, 1917, April 27, 1917: Miss M. Clarke, PL Women.

of a ward (which meant that Goldthorp had "to keep an eye on" that ward as well as her own) and the medical officers "find a great difference with the VAD because if they order an Inj[ection] of Morphia, they have to give it themselves."[140] VADs at times proved a potent argument for the importance of training.

Despite these limitations, nurses could find the VADs very useful. M. B. Peterkin was pleased that "5 VAD people have arrived, who, even if not fully trained, will be of considerable assistance in many ways"; and she was "thankful" that one of them was posted to her own overworked ward.[141] Similarly, Alice Slythe referred to the two VADs working at Lady Gifford's nurses' convalescent hospital in France as "treasures... who work like Trojans."[142] She was also critical, however, of what she saw as class-based presumption by the VADs in her hospital. She recorded in her diary the story of a VAD who had been given permission to observe a head surgery:

Well, my lady walked into the [operating] theatre, took a chair, and settled herself down and crossed her feet – !!! The Captain turned and *looked* at her. Anyone might have known what he meant, but she nodded and smiled at him. This was too much. He came across – he always walks very slowly – and said 'Sister, *please* let me put your chair where you will have a better view,' and put it himself, beside the anaesthetist!! Anybody else would have gone out and died, but she said 'Thank you *so* much,' and sat down, and he took off his gloves and scrubbed up again and put on another pair and started, and afterwards he said he had never met such nerve in his existence!!! (For even another surgeon coming to watch would never have dreamt of sitting!)[143]

Yet clearly the breach of etiquette of which the VAD was guilty was not so apparent as Slythe wished to present. The trained nurse still needed to explain that the behavior would have been inappropriate "even [for] another surgeon," and she prefaced the account with the disclaimer that "perhaps only the trained will quite appreciate it!"[144] This may be a case of ignorance combined with inappropriate social expectations (it might not have been at all unusual to the VAD to have a man seat her) rather than one of insolence, but the class differences that most probably caused the situation also led to its personalized interpretation. Ironically, the surgeon also demonstrated his ignorance of protocol in addressing the volunteer as "Sister," the title reserved in the trained nursing community for those nurses who had achieved supervisory status. Slythe overlooked that breach (even while recording it) in her efforts to place all the blame

---

[140] May 18, [1915], May 12, [1915], May 17, [1915]: Miss M. E. Goldthorp, PL Women.
[141] May 15, 1915: Miss M. B. Peterkin, IWM-DD 77/60/1.
[142] February 1, [1916]: Miss Alice Slythe, PL Women.
[143] [January] 23, [1916]: Miss Alice Slythe, PL Women.
[144] [January] 23, [1916]: Miss Alice Slythe, PL Women.

for the misunderstanding on the shoulders of the VAD. Her account clearly positioned the trained nurse as the knowledgeable and competent hospital worker, despite adverse circumstances. The VAD was at best uninformed, and at worst a distraction from proper patient care.

Obviously, class perceptions played a critical role in these stories of conflict. Many VADs did consider the trained nurses, with less formal education and often less elite tastes, to be their social inferiors. Most VADs' descriptions of nurses were not generally as dehumanizing as Enid Bagnold's, who called them "so strange, so tricky, uncertain as collies."[145] Instead, they were merely condescending, as when Phyllis Puckle told her family that she liked a trained nurse despite "the trail of fallen H's" in her speech.[146]

The issue of potentially romantic relations with the men was also a source of class-based tension. After all, women, and especially women of the social class of the volunteers, rarely had the intimate physical access to men that was typical of the hospital ward. Because the majority of patients came from the ranks (they were both the majority of soldiers and had higher combat casualty rates than most officers), most VADs felt safe from connotations of inappropriate relations. The men were simply not conceivable as mates. Marjorie Denys-Burton, working in a convalescent hospital, was surprised and happy when she found she could enjoy a day's outing "with the groom, the gardener, a couple of miners, and a footman."[147] Winifred Kenyon was pleased that two VADs at her military hospital were "both ladies," and therefore "both good fun and nice with the men in the right way."[148] The problem, of course, from the VAD point of view, was that some of trained nurses were friendly in other than "the right way." Denys-Burton scornfully pointed out that the trained nurse in her hospital, who was (unwillingly) referred to as "Big Sister," considered "the better class men" from the ranks to be "choice 'partis' for her!"[149]

The most serious mutual criticisms about relations with soldier patients, however, stemmed from differing ideas about what the work meant. For the trained nurses, empathy was not only misplaced but also entirely inappropriate within hospital procedure. For the VADs, whose work in the hospitals was justified by their desire to serve the country, this orientation meant that though the nurses might understand the tasks that were required, they did not understand the actual process of caring

[145] Enid Bagnold, *A Diary Without Dates* (London: Virago, 1978 [1918]), p. 29.
[146] Phyllis Puckle to her mother, May 22, 1915: Miss Phyllis Puckle, PL Women.
[147] Undated entry [p. 17]: Miss M. Denys-Burton, IWM-DD 92/22/1.
[148] March 22, 1918: Miss W. L. Kenyon, IWM-DD 84/24/1.
[149] Undated entry [p. 16]: Miss M. Denys-Burton, IWM-DD 92/22/1.

for the patients. Mary Borden, who ran an English-staffed hospital serving the French army, accused her nurses of knowing their jobs, but not comprehending the men. To Borden, this was a significant lack. Since the nurses with their equipment and their procedures could not understand the men as anything other than patients, then they also could not understand the significance of their deaths.[150] As Enid Bagnold put it, sympathy was the VADs' métier, but the trained nurses' was "the running of the ward."[151]

The trained nurses had very different goals from the VADs: they wanted professional status, and believed that it could be achieved by demonstrating how important their work was, as performed only by trained nurses. Though the VADs represented a threat to that process, in the end, it dissipated. As *The Hospital* reported of the record of the Territorial Force Nursing Service,

> They preserved under all circumstances and difficulties a very high standard of nursing. This was expected of them, and the honour of the [nursing] schools was safe in their hands. But they proved equal to quite unaccustomed tasks . . . when we thank God for victory, let us thank him for the quality of British nurses.[152]

Having "proven" themselves under fire, they were rewarded with the creation of the state Register of Nurses after the war, guaranteeing the professional status that accompanied the uniform three-year training program. Yet this was not an unambiguous victory, either. Though the essential role of specific training and knowledge was officially recognized, the decisions defining qualification were removed from the hands of the nurses themselves and their governing body and taken over by the minister of health and the House of Commons.[153] In a single generation, however, their professional status was assured. When the Second World War broke out, the position – and necessity – of the trained nurse in hospital wards was entirely unquestioned.

The VADs had been suspect to the nurses because they potentially undermined ideas of professionalism. Though many VADs realized that the nurses perceived them as dangerous, they misunderstood why. VADs frequently suggested that conflict was rooted in fears over job competition after the war between professional and volunteers. This mistaken belief in fact contributed to further problems, as few VADs wished to continue hospital work in peacetime, and therefore thought that the nurses were ridiculous to worry about it. Most VADs were clear that hospital work

---

[150] Mary Borden, "Enfant de Malheur" and "Paraphernalia," in *The Forbidden Zone* (London: William Heinemann, 1929).
[151] Bagnold, *Diary Without Dates*, pp. 81–82.   [152] IWM-WWC BRC 25 2/7.
[153] Summers, *Angels and Citizens*, p. 290.

was only "for the duration," an attitude that made sense considering that the war, rather than the nursing, was their primary motivation.[154] The trained nurses, however, could not help but see these young women through different eyes. The ramifications of class differences, which made for often difficult relations between trained nurses and VADs, were real, but so were the threats to the status of nursing as a profession that they masked. Differing motivations, both relative to the war and especially to imagining the work itself, provided the foundation for the clashes. Trained nurses were not defying gender norms in their desire for official status within the military. Rather, they were trying to redefine those norms. They did not wish to be the counterparts of soldiers as the women doctors who sought equal status with the men in the RAMC did. They did not want to be female parallel soldiers as the VADs did. Instead, they only wanted to have the official nature of their involvement with the military in the war effort legitimated.

Among women hospital workers in the First World War, there was an inverse relationship between the level of training for specific war work and social acceptability. The same relationship also existed between training and depth of engagement with the war, and its role in self-defining work, experience, and identity. The greatest degree of social approval was re-served for those women who had changed their lives most in response to the demands of war. The VADs, therefore, who brought the fewest skills and limited or no training to the hospital wards, captured the popular imagination and were regularly used as the ideal symbols of women war workers. They made claims for parity with the soldiers, but only in highly gendered ways, and contingent on the nation's exceptional wartime cir-cumstances. Trained nurses, the vast majority of whom had completed grueling three-year programs to achieve their status, had a more difficult time. Their very professional status called their patriotism into ques-tion. As a result, they were often overlooked in popular accounts. When they were noticed, they won social approval because they consistently described their own position as subordinate to the soldiers. This conser-vative language negated the social threat the nurses otherwise represented by being financially independent. Nurses saw the war as a chance to put forward a claim to professional status in a way that was not socially dis-ruptive. Female doctors, the smallest and best trained of the three groups, had the hardest time achieving popular acceptance. Though they were identifying an opportunity like the one the trained nurses found, women

---

[154] Of the more than 120,000 members at the end of the war, only 129 pursued nursing through the VAD scholarship scheme, which ultimately funded training for a variety of positions for 557 women: *Joint War Committee Reports*, p. 203.

doctors were trying to do more with the moment. They wanted equivalent status to men in their profession, irrespective of the war. This was more seriously disturbing to ideas about relations between the sexes than any of the constructions of work offered by other women in the hospitals. Their efforts, not coincidentally, also met with the least success.

Trained nurses serving in military hospitals in the First World War were struggling to position themselves as uniquely competent professionals, possessing special skills to meet specific needs. Their status was threatened from above inside the medical profession, by (usually male) doctors interested in maintaining their own claims to the control of science and medicine. They were also fighting off a challenge, if an unintentional one, from below. The presence of the VADs working in the wards seemed to suggest both that long training programs were not necessary to make a competent nurse, and that nursing work was not a profession worthy of financial payment. In the tensions of war time, they encountered pressures from all around, in their difficult position relative to the military system. Middle-class female doctors, though with similar goals, were not allies in this process. They needed to differentiate themselves from nurses as women in medicine; they saw the war as an opportunity for professional work, but wanted to be seen as doctors utilizing their training, not women war workers. In some ways, however, the goals of the VADs were the loftiest. They expected to be perceived as responding to their country's call in the highest way they could, given their sex. Generally, they received this acclamation during the war itself. It meant a great deal to them, as their writings repeatedly show; much more than it did to other populations to whom it was sometimes applied, such as women working on the land and in the factories, and in other auxiliary war work. The position of these other workers was complicated in yet different ways.

3   Other armies: auxiliary war workers

"A Woman," whose irate letter to the *Morning Post* touched off the lengthy debate on the subject of women in military-style uniforms, wrote of her subjects that "if they cannot become nurses or ward maids in hospital, let them put on sunbonnets and print frocks and go make hay or pick fruit or make jam, or do the thousand and one things that women can do to help."[1] She was clearly defining gender-appropriate war work for women. Work in hospitals, performing the traditionally female tasks of nursing and nurturing, was best. If that was impossible, then women, appropriately attired, should turn to the land. By including jam-making along with haying, she made work on the land seem comparable to work in a kitchen garden. This, perhaps, was not inconceivably far from the kind of gardening that was a traditionally acceptable activity of leisured ladies. Work in the Women's Land Army, however, was a far cry from pruning one's roses, and the women who chose war work in agriculture were not, in general, from a leisured background. Most certainly, they did not wear "sunbonnets and print frocks." Instead, they wore clothing more appropriate to their heavy outdoor work, and the debate over breeches and skirts symbolized concerns about the "defeminization" of women land workers.

Volunteer work in hospitals was almost uniformly socially approved for young women; military-style organizations usually were not. Between these two extremes, however, women performed a wide variety of war work. Some worked full- or part-time in social or philanthropic work, on behalf of Belgian refugees, for example, or in the production of needed hospital supplies and "comforts" for soldiers. Women drove ambulances in Britain and on the continent. They also worked full-time on the land, replacing agricultural workers who were serving in the armed forces. Perhaps most famously, many women entered industry and worked in munitions factories. These wartime occupations can be placed along a spectrum of respectability, ranging from those that were consistent with

---

[1] Letter from "A Woman," *Morning Post*, July 16, 1915, p. 6.

cultural ideas about "women's work" to those that disrupted gendered
norms considerably. All these expectations were, of course, mitigated by
ideas about class position; what was considered appropriate for daughters
of "gentlemen" was not the same as for daughters of farmers or industrial workers. It was also generally true that the more service-oriented war
work was considered to be, the more socially acceptable it was. At the
other end, work-oriented efforts tended to be seen as more problematic.
For a woman to serve, after all, was not threatening to her subordinate
role in the existing social order. To work, however, suggested a position
within the realm of the public, one that might entail new forms of power
and, at a minimum, financial independence. These definitions were not
stable, though, and even service contained within it possibilities for subversion. Controversial work, conversely, was subject to extensive social
efforts to make it acceptable – even admirable – work for women, though
only "for the duration." Work, in fact, could be popularly translated into
service, partly defusing the threat that working women represented.

The First World War provided new opportunities for professional advancement, for women in particular, in a wide variety of venues. Educated
women began working in banks and government offices in significant
numbers for the first time, often with the expectation that their work
was not just temporary, but could continue into peacetime.[2] Other such
"professional" workers, of course, included doctors and nurses. Here,
however, I focus on work that was perceived as being explicitly for the war
effort, and not merely made possible by the absence of men who were in
the military. Almost any new work performed by women during the war
could be considered patriotic. A woman tram worker, for example, was
described as "doing her bit... She really is touched with red, white, and
blue paint."[3] I am looking, though, at specifically war-oriented work,

---

[2] Though women clerks were expected to continue after the war, they were still not considered to be on a career path like men's, as it was assumed they would leave the work upon
marriage. See, for example, Marie W. Seers, "Banking," in Gilbert Stone (ed.), *Women
War Workers: Accounts Contributed by Representative Workers of the Work Done by Women in
the More Important Branches of War Employment* (New York: Thomas Y. Crowell, [1917]),
especially pp. 87, 89–90; Laurie Magnus, *The Jubilee Book of the Girls' Public Day School
Trust 1873–1923* (Cambridge: Cambridge University Press, 1923), pp. 147–148, 154. The
history of *Brighton & Hove High School 1876–1952* (privately published, 1953; Archives
of the Girls' Public Day School Trust), recorded that during the war some alumnae "did
actual war work as VADs or helped to make munitions, but many more took the place
of men in banks, local government offices or in the various Ministries of London. From
this time onwards the records of Old Girls' careers became more numerous and varied"
(pp. 43–44). Arthur Marwick, in *The Deluge: British Society and the First World War* (New
York: Norton, 1965), refers to this phenomenon as "a central theme in the sociology of
women's employment in the twentieth century, the rise of the business girl" (p. 92).

[3] Kathleen Courlander, "'Fares, Please!,'" in Stone, *Women War Workers*, p. 113.

rather than all examples of women's work being given a patriotic stamp of approval.

War at leisure: the "comforteers"

Though married men were often expected to join the military, it was presumed that women would keep family obligations their top priority, despite the national crisis. There were, as one wartime author described, a "host of women who have too many home ties to give themselves entirely to war work."[4] These commitments did not excuse women with families from patriotic efforts, but they did significantly shift social expectations, and any woman who was perceived as prioritizing the war over her responsibilities to her children would have been roundly condemned. In August 1914, soon after the declaration of war, the women's magazine *The Lady* suggested an appropriate outlet for the patriotic energies of its readers. "The fact one cannot bear arms," claimed the journal, "does not excuse any one from helping their country's cause by fighting such foes as misery, pain and poverty."[5] Work on behalf of the needy, after all, had been considered the responsibility of socially elite women for centuries. By the second half of the nineteenth century, philanthropy was considered necessary on a part-time basis for most middle-class women, and socially acceptable full-time for many of them. Unpaid, of course, it was in fact the only full-time work that did not require a "lady" to risk her social status.[6]

Especially if it were locally based, such social work was considered an appropriate extension of women's influence over their own "sphere," the family. Even though it required leaving the home, it was not an invasion into the public, the domain (in this ideology) of men and defeminized women. This respectability made room for many women to find an acceptable sublimation of ambitions in social work because the effort was labeled as service. As men proved their citizenship in public venues, women – at least in the middle-class view – were responsible for demonstrating theirs through service to their families and, by extension, the needy in their communities. It was essential, however, that family

---

[4] Barbara McLaren, *Women of the War* (London: Hodder and Stoughton, 1917), p. 81.
[5] *The Lady*, August 13, 1914, quoted in Nicola Beauman, *A Very Great Profession: The Woman's Novel 1914–1939* (London: Virago, 1983), p. 16.
[6] See Jane Lewis, *Women and Social Action in Victorian and Edwardian England* (Aldershot: Edward Elgar, 1991), p. 2. See also Angela Woollacott, "From Moral to Professional Authority: Secularism, Social Work and Middle-Class Women's Self-Construction in World War I Britain," *Journal of Women's History*, 10, 2 (Summer 1998).

obligations were always placed above those of the community.[7] The outbreak of war did not change the expectation of social service for middle-class women; it merely shifted the objects of its focus. Before the war, women visited poor families, worked in girls' clubs, and worried about infant welfare. After August 1914, attention shifted to relief for Belgian refugees, the production of hospital supplies, and support for soldiers and their families. According to one observer, "in the first week of the war it is no exaggeration to say that there was hardly a woman in the kingdom who was not making something for the sick and wounded."[8] (One can only assume that she was excluding women of the working classes, who had considerable other demands on their time.) Gilbert Stone, in his essay "War Organizations for Women," included contact information for an impressive number of groups organizing such activities, including the Primrose League, the Union of Jewish Women, the Belgravia Workrooms and Supply Depot, Lady Smith-Dorrien's Hospital Bag Fund, and the "Disabled Soldiers' Aid Committee" of the Friends of the Poor.[9]

The work done by women through these organizations (and others) was varied. The Soldiers' and Sailors' Families Association, which before 1914 had focused on the needs of military wives "off the strength," took over much of the complicated work of administering military wives' pensions in the early phases of the war.[10] Women formed the majority (though not the leadership) of the myriad groups that sprang up immediately to help the Belgian refugees coming into England; they worked to find and furnish housing, to supply food, clothing, and medical attention when necessary, and ultimately to help find employment.[11] On a more informal level, Mrs. L. Gordon-Stables documented the work of "The Comforteers," who visited wounded soldiers in the wards, took them out for drives and on picnics, and to the theater and concerts. Class differences were always at the fore: Gordon-Stables cautioned that the ladies involved in these activities had to exercise tact in their relations with Tommies, or the soldiers might get the "wrong idea." She was confident, though, that the women's superior social skills would enable

---

[7] Lewis, *Women and Social Action*, pp. 2–3, 5, 11, 304, 309; see also Carol Dyhouse, *Girls Growing Up in Late Victorian and Edwardian England* (London: Routledge, 1981), p. 74.
[8] McLaren, *Women of the War*, p. 78.
[9] Stone, "War Organizations for Women," in Stone, *Women War Workers*, pp. 289–294, 298, 302–305.
[10] Susan Pedersen, "Gender, Welfare, and Citizenship in Britain During the Great War," *American Historical Review*, 95, 4 (October 1990), p. 292.
[11] See Peter Calahan, *Belgian Refugee Relief in England During the Great War* (New York: Garland, 1982), especially pp. 176–177.

them to handle any potentially awkward situations.[12] Many women took individual action, sending care packages to prisoners of war (known colloquially as "adopting" a POW), or knitting socks and mufflers to be sent to soldiers at the front, along with cigarettes and chocolate. A number of soldiers and sailors received letters from their former bible teacher, Mrs. Hayman, who took on the multiple correspondence as part of her contribution to the war effort. She also sent comfort packages to the front and to POW camps.[13]

In this way, the wartime conception of "family" was extended to include the varying tangible and intangible needs of military members and their families, as well as the civilian victims of the conflicts. Denis Barnett, a young volunteer officer, wrote enthusiastically in support for his sister's efforts for refugees under the auspices of the Croix Rouge.[14] Olive Dent, a VAD serving in France, hastened to reassure the knitters and other "comforteers" back in England, who might be chafing at their more tedious, less glamorous-seeming duties. "You are doing some of the most valuable war service," she wrote, "the comfort supplying department is as necessary to the Army Medical Service as the Commissariat or the Clothing Department is to the army in the field."[15] Similarly, a wartime author declared that the impressive output of the volunteers at the Central Workrooms showed "that women of the country, to whom more conspicuous service has been denied, have indeed achieved miracles of devoted industry."[16] They were serving domestically, but serving nonetheless. As service, their work was socially approved, if sometimes gently mocked for the results of excesses of enthusiasm (figure 3.1).

A few critics, however, questioned not the work itself but women's motivations for doing it, and in turn the quality that resulted. Women were accused of thrill-seeking at the expense of completing worthwhile work thoroughly, and of creating useless work in their eagerness to be in contact with the soldiers. Lieut. Col. T. H. Clayton-Nunn's comments articulated a prevalent attitude when he complained in his diary about the women who entered his hospital train in Southampton. "Two old ladies in short tweed dresses and thinking themselves young and comely were

---

[12] Mrs. L. Gordon-Stables, "The Comforteers," in Stone, *Women War Workers*, pp. 218–238; see especially pp. 228–230, 232.

[13] Mrs. L. Hayman, Imperial War Museum Department of Documents (hereafter IWM-DD) 88/51/1.

[14] Denis Barnett to his sister, June 22, 1915: Lieut. D. O. Barnett, IWM-DD 67/196/1. See also his sister's papers: Miss C. U. Barnett, IWM-DD Con Shelf.

[15] Olive Dent, *A VAD in France* (London: Grant Richards, 1917), p. 148.

[16] McLaren, *Women of the War*, p. 83.

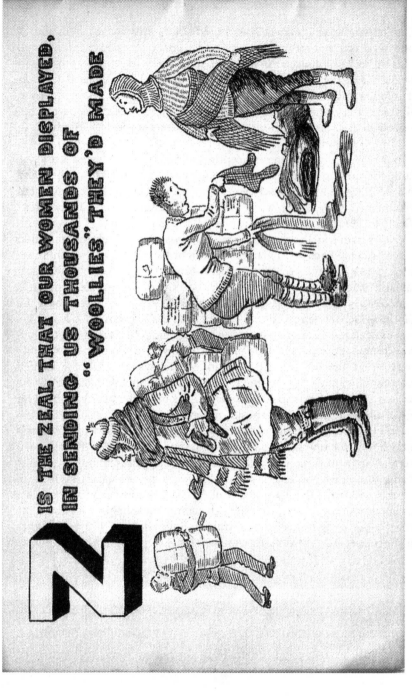

Figure 3.1 "'Z' is the Zeal That Our Women Displayed," showing the enthusiastic production of a variety of woolies.

going about giving chocolate and cigarettes to the officers and men," he wrote, and two others "parade[d] the length of the train soon after the start, giggling and saying to each patient, 'Glad to be back again, Eh!'" Clayton-Nunn responded in the negative, "which rather damped the situation." Though his tone may have been particularly acerbic, the sentiment behind his sarcastic conclusion that it was "useful good war work by moneyed ladies" was certainly shared by some.[17] Katharine Furse, for one, lamented that canteens, operating "on a bad economic basis," were "wasting thousands of women" workers who might be more usefully employed elsewhere.[18] This was not, perhaps, an entirely fair criticism. These women were not for the most part available for the kinds of full-time war work that occupied Furse. Instead, they had real obligations to their families at home, responsibilities that British society continued to value more than any more active contribution to the propagation of the war. Generally speaking, they were described, if with a smile, as doing just as they should be doing.

War at school: learning service

Part-time volunteer activities were not just the purview of married women or of adult daughters at home. They were also enthusiastically embraced by schoolgirls and their institutions, particularly ones aimed at the daughters of the middle classes. Students at private boys' schools were often preparing for commissions through membership in Officers' Training Corps. Similarly, the girls at schools like those founded and operated by the Girls' Public Day School Trust (GPDST) were eager to do their part, both in training for more active war work later and in the philanthropically minded activities they could already share with older women in their families and social circles.

These parallels should not be surprising. In the decades preceding the Great War, girls often received educations quite similar to, though separated from, those intended for their brothers. The GPDST, for example, was founded in the late 1880s with the explicit goal (as a leaflet later explained) "to provide for girls at moderate fees a Public School education as good as, or better than, their brothers enjoy."[19] These schools,

---

[17] Diary entry, April 11, 1916: Lieut. Col. T. H. Clayton-Nunn, Peter Liddle 1914–1918 Personal Experience Archive, Leeds (hereafter PL) General.

[18] Katharine Furse to Lord Selbourne, May 18, 1916: Dame Katharine Furse, PL Women. As Furse was interested in recruiting members to her own VAD organization, she was not an unbiased source.

[19] "The Girls' Public Day School Trust," printed leaflet, c. 1923: Girls' Public Day School Trust Central Archive, London (hereafter GPDST).

and others like them, aimed to instill in their students the same ethics of honor and patriotism that the boys' public schools were famed for. Their graduates therefore felt similarly eager to serve the country in wartime. For the girls, perhaps, it was even easier: they did not have to wait to enter the army, but could begin knitting scarves and making bandages immediately.

A double meaning of service – both philanthropically to those in need and patriotically to the country in its crisis – was made explicit to many of these schoolgirls. At Wimbledon High School, the headmistress, Miss Gavin, offered weekly talks on the progress of the war and the role of the school and its members in the nation's effort. As the *Wimbledon Boro' News* reported in its obituary of Gavin, every week "she gave a 'War talk' to the school, which was a masterly summary of the current events of the war; she was eager to interest the girls in active work."[20] At Blackheath High School, the headmistress, Miss Gadesden, urged the students to live up to her long-held ideal "that they should learn to love the duty of service to others." The school's history described her "passionate feeling that they must all take part in the war effort in some way."[21] R. M. Haig Brown, headmistress of Oxford High School, summed up this orientation in the address she delivered at the end of the summer term, 1918. "How would it be possible to say," she asked rhetorically, "that any educational aim that tends to produce such qualities as unselfishness, loyalty, *esprit de corps*, patriotism, width and generosity in thought and outlook, and an intelligent and understanding sympathy is not justified over and over."[22] Headmistresses universally labored to instill the concept of service in their young female charges.

This was more than an exercise in intangibles, however. As an organization, the GPDST reacted to the outbreak of war in 1914 in specific, concrete ways. It reinforced the commitment to patriotic war service on the institutional level that it was already inculcating on the individual level. The buildings at both Wimbledon and South Hampstead High Schools were on occasions used to billet troops during school holidays. Staff salaries were frozen, and tuition reduced for daughters of soldiers. School prizes consisted merely of certificates for the duration, a sacrifice the girls were called on to make in order to save the expense of the customary costly

[20] "Death of Miss Gavin: The Funeral Service," *Wimbledon Boro' News*, March 9, 1918: GPDST. See also Magnus, *Jubilee Book*, p. 133.
[21] K. M. Watts, *A History of Blackheath High School* (privately published, no date), p. 13: GPDST.
[22] R. M. Haig Brown, *Ad Lucem: Some Addresses* (London: Oxford University Press [Humphrey Milford], 1931), p. 115.

books. Many schools admitted Belgian refugees at little or no cost. They all participated in a wide variety of war work, often including Red Cross training, fundraising, and gardening.[23]

School activities were covered in the local press. The *Standard* recounted that at Brighton High School, in addition to raising money and making hospital supplies, the students had "adopted" a "Torpedo-Boat Destroyer," just as many older service-oriented women took on the responsibility for sending "comforts" to soldiers.[24] Bath High School and Streatham Hill High School were both actively involved in raising War Savings Certificates and the production of comforts.[25] At Blackheath High School, a portion of the playing fields was plowed over for gardening allotments; athletics for girls took second place to vegetable growing, in wartime. Students from the school also worked part-time in the canteen at the Woolwich munitions factory, sent the ubiquitous care parcels to soldiers and POWs, and, surprisingly, even did some factory work making compasses for airplanes.[26] The list goes on: many institutions, such as Sydenham High School, joined the Girls' Patriotic Union; others, like Oxford High School, were continuing a tradition begun during the Boer War when they mailed their parcels to the soldiers.[27] These kinds of activities were not unique to GPDST schools. Girls from Roedean and Wycombe Abbey, for example, spent part of their long holidays serving in the wards and offices of the Endell Street Hospital, run by the Women's

---

[23] See *Indicative Past: A Hundred Years of the Girls' Public Day School Trust* (London: For the Friends of the Girls' Public Day School Trust by George Allen & Unwin, 1971), pp. 119–120: GPDST.

[24] "War Work by Girls," *Standard*, February 16, 1916: GPDST.

[25] Magnus, *Jubilee Book*, pp. 87, 154.   [26] Watts, *Blackheath High School*, p. 13.

[27] *Sydenham High School 1887–1967* (privately published for the GPDST, no date), pp. 14–15; V. E. Stack, *Oxford High School 1875–1960* (Abingdon: For the GPDST, 1963), pp. 10, 12: GPDST. For similar records from other schools, see also *Wimbledon High School Centenary Magazine, 1880–1980* (privately published, no date), pp. 32–33; *A School Remembers: Sutton High School GPDST, 1884–1964* (privately published, no date), pp. 20, 62; Pamela R. Bodington, *The Kindling and the Flame: A Centenary Review of the History of South Hampstead High School* (privately published, no date), pp. 13, 30; *South Hampstead High School Magazine*, no. 27 (November 1914), pp. 3–5, no. 28 (November 1915), p. 8, no. 29 (November 1916), pp. 3–5, and 22, no. 30 (November 1917), pp. 4–5, no. 31 (November 1918), pp. 1 and 5; *Belvedere High School, Liverpool, GPDST, 1880–1980* (privately published, no date), pp. 10–11; *Nottingham High School for Girls, GPDST, 1875–1954* (privately published, no date), pp. 20–21; Hazel Bates and Anne A. M. Wells (eds.), *A History of Shrewsbury High School (Girls' Public Day School Trust) 1885–1960* (Shrewsbury: Wilding & Son, 1962), pp. 36–37; *Norwich High School 1875–1950* (Norwich: Goose Press, no date), pp. 32, 70–71, 73–76; Muriel Pike, *The Oak Tree: The Story of Putney High School, 1893–1960* (privately published, 1960), pp. 34–36; Olive Carter, *History of Gateshead High School 1876–1907 and Central Newcastle High School 1895–1955* (privately published, no date), p. 53; *Brighton & Hove High School 1876–1952* (privately published, no date), pp. 43–44 (all GPDST).

Hospital Corps.[28] While still within the safe confines of school days, these girls were eager to sample the responsibilities of more active participation. It gave them access to the excitement and fulfillment of war service. Socially, this was doubly acceptable. It was appropriate to the philanthropic traditions of their sex and socioeconomic position, as adapted to the aims of war service, and it was also safely performed under the official auspices of their schools.

War at the wheel: "fast" drivers

The position of women drivers, including ambulance drivers, was complex. This was especially true in France. The full-time effort contributed by these primarily socially elite young women was given the popular stamp of approval of war service. The outdoor, mechanical nature of their duties – previously performed exclusively by men – gave it simultaneously a subversive undertone of work. Being associated with hospitals and healing lent the drivers an aura of womanliness, which was partly countermanded by their connection with the masculinity of automobiles. Though one contemporary observer declared in a work of popular propaganda that "there is no more certain sign of the times than the sight of women in khaki uniforms and military badges driving Army motors and lorries," women driving cars often faced significant disapproval.[29] When Peggy Bate, for example, first began driving, she was forced to defend herself against accusations that she was "unwomanly, ungirlish... and that motor driving for girls was degrading."[30] Despite the protection of the hospital's reputation, ambulance drivers (especially those overseas) also had to deal with a reputation for being faster than their cars. One cartoon depicted the driver "in theory," dashing and tidy next to a sparkling, modern vehicle; "in popular fiction," rakishly attired and surrounded by a party; and "in reality," trudging through mud, muck, and rain (figure 3.2). The work was neither as romantic nor as exciting as its reputation.

Ambulance drivers had a reputation for being "sporting" women, former tomboys. Though some VADs and members of other organizations like the Women's Legion also worked with ambulances, most women drivers were members of the First Aid Nursing Yeomanry,

[28] Flora Murray, *Women as Army Surgeons: Being the History of the Women's Hospital Corps in Paris, Wimereux, and Endell Street, September 1914–October 1919* (London: Hodder & Stoughton, [1920]), pp. 250–251.

[29] McLaren, *Women of the War*, p. 136.

[30] Peggy Bate to "Brett" Brettell, dated only Wednesday [May 1916]. Brettell disagreed; Brettell to Bate, 25 May 1916: Lieut. F. A. Brettell, IWM-DD PP/MCR/169.

Figure 3.2 VAD ambulance driver "In Theory, In Popular Fiction, In Real Life" cartoon; Olive Mudie-Cooke lithograph, "With the VAD Convoys in France, Flanders and Italy" (Cambridge, circa 1920).

known – unironically – by their acronym as the FANY. The FANY was formed well before the outbreak of the war, and as members were required to be good horsewomen with their own mounts, the membership was economically and socially elite. A knowledge of rifle shooting was highly recommended in the organization's official *Gazette*. "Look how the women and children suffered in the Franco-Prussian war!," it exhorted in 1910, "look how they suffered in the mutiny! Remember Cawnpore!"[31] Daughters of the empire, motivated by the memory of the Mutiny, were being called upon to join the new organization and improve the transportation of wounded soldiers near the front beyond the dismal standards of the Boer War. In 1914, however, they still met with the same negative reaction from the War Office as had women doctors and their outfitted hospitals. As a result, they began their ambulance driving in the service of the Belgians.[32]

Members of the FANY were regularly described in unwomanly terms, and the drivers themselves often embraced this gender ambiguity. Their *Gazette* reprinted extracts from an article in *Vogue* about a visit to their camps in France. The author described the FANYs as having "a sort of splendid austerity, that pervades their look and their outlook, that spiritually works itself out in this determined sticking at the job, this avoidance

[31] Miss G. M. Nicholson, "Women & Sports: No. 1 – Miniature Rifle Shooting," *Women and War: Official Gazette of the 1st Aid NYC and Cadet Yeomanry*, 4 (October 1910): Mrs. E. F. Colston, PL Women.
[32] Letter to the Editor, *Women and War*, 5 (November 1910); A. H. Gamwell and P. Beauchamp Waddell, "The FANY," *Cavalry Journal*, 11, 41 (July 1921).

of any emotion that interferes with it, and in their bodies expresses itself in a disregard for appearances that one would never have thought to have found in human woman." The masculine comparison was explicit in the conclusion: "This at last is what it is to be as free as a man."[33] Other observers agreed. Antonio de Navarro, at the Scottish Women's Hospital at Royaumont, wrote about their "masculine livery," which meant that the drivers' "sex was not always evident to the wounded men." He euphemistically described how "constant open-air work had transformed the faces of these young women into pictures of vigorous health," which in turn contributed to the confused identification. He maintained, however, that the "sexless storm-clothes" merely hid "attractive revelations."[34] Their physical femininity had to be exposed in order to defuse any social threat suggested by their gender ambiguity. Olive Edis, a photographer for the Imperial War Museum, described the FANYs she met as "a very jolly type of good-class English girl...some of a decidedly sporting and masculine stamp – but so fresh and healthy and attractive."[35] "Healthy" seems to have been a frequent polite synonym for "masculine," or at least "unfeminine."

The women drivers did not reject this identity, but seemed to welcome it. Immediately after the war, P. B. Waddell (writing under the name "Pat Beauchamp") published the autobiographical *Fanny Goes to War*. She described with satisfaction the amazement of the local French citizens at their "manly Yeomanry uniform." She also repeatedly told stories of being mistaken for a man. She seemed proud of these errors, presenting them as resulting not just from her attire, but from her competence doing her work, including messier jobs like changing tires.[36] When Waddell was wounded, she found that her sex complicated hospital procedures near the combat zone, and "it was no good protesting that I had always wished I had been [a man]."[37] Similarly, Grace McDougall, the first of the group to serve in France, shared several stories of being mistaken for a man. Her response was to laugh "aloud with great delight."[38] McDougall

[33] "Extract from 'Vogue' May 1918: 'A Personal Impression of the FANY Camps in France,'" *First Aid Nursing Yeomanry Gazette*, Supplement for June 1918.

[34] Antonio de Navarro, *The Scottish Women's Hospital at the French Abbey of Royaumont* (London: George Allen & Unwin, 1917), pp. 134–135.

[35] Olive Edis, "The Record of a Journey to Photograph the British Women's Services Overseas Begun on Sunday March 2nd, 1919," p. 5: Miss O. Edis, IWM-DD 89/19/1.

[36] Pat Beauchamp [P. B. Waddell], *Fanny Goes to War* (London: John Murray, 1919), pp. 16, 124, 251.

[37] Beauchamp, *Fanny Goes to War*, pp. 261–262.

[38] Grace McDougall, *A Nurse at the War: Nursing Adventures in Belgium and France* (New York: Robert M. McBride, 1917), pp. 73, 75. The choice of "nurse" rather than "driver" for the title of her book demonstrates the culturally problematic connotations associated with women drivers, even in wartime.

described frustration when she and a colleague were removed from work with some troops because of their sex. "The fact that they bore themselves as men was of no avail," she wrote (in the third person) about her experience, "nor even that in consequence two men still lived whose breath had gone from their bodies." Sex roles were more valued than the conduct of the war, she suggested, "so an officer came with courteous but strict injunctions to escort them to GHQ."[39] Many FANYs wrote with glee about the gender confusion and the masculine freedom of movement their work gave them. They may, in fact, have welcomed the opportunity to "be a man" in some sense, as some of them had explicitly previously desired. Despite this, they were not attempting to stake out a public claim for themselves as equals to men, and especially not to the men in the trenches. The drivers talked about proving their capabilities in fields previously only associated with men, but this was safe to do because it was eventually revealed that women were actually performing the work. The unmasking was as important as the initial perceptual error.

To affirm their femininity, the drivers maintained the subordinate status of women war workers. When invalided back to France following the amputation of her leg, Waddell was placed in the WAAC ward at the Endell Street hospital. On Christmas day, she distanced herself from their celebrations. "I don't know what they toasted in the men's wards," she wrote, "but in the WAACs it was roughly, 'To the women of England, and the WAACs who would win the war, etc.' It seemed too bad to leave out the men who were in the trenches, so I drank one privately to them on my own."[40] (Waddell's social background was certainly different from that of the majority of WAACs, so her rejection of gender solidarity may also have been an expression of the power of class-based identity.) Unlike Flora Murray, the FANYs were more than content to be included in the Women's Collection at the new Imperial War Museum. Their *Gazette* concluded that "it is fitting that permanent record of the work done by the FANYs should be handed down to posterity in the Women's Section of the National War Museum."[41] For McDougall, the war "proved to men that women can share men's dangers and privations and hardships and yet remain women."[42] These women described the excitement of acting like men, and receiving shares of both the corresponding freedom of movement and the praise for accomplishment. They offered socially titillating stories of being mistaken – at least briefly – for men. The social

---

[39] McDougall, *Nurse at the War*, p. 197.   [40] Beauchamp, *Fanny Goes to War*, p. 266.
[41] "Foreword," *First Aid Nursing Yeomanry Gazette*, 5, 3 (May 1917). The Imperial War Museum was originally called the National War Museum.
[42] McDougall, *Nurse at the War*, p. 78.

danger was minimized, however, as they were ultimately revealed to be women. Though their accounts were potentially disruptive, and they revelled in their transgressions quite pointedly, most FANYs still did not seem to want to undermine the existing gendered hierarchy. Their consistent subservience to men was far more powerful than their interest in doing masculine work; they enjoyed testing the limits of the system, but were not interested in changing the structure itself.

War on the land: agricultural soldiers

Though an army in name, women on the land were further from the actual conflict than any other group of war workers. They did not wear military uniforms, serve overseas, support the troops with munitions, or even have any direct contact with soldiers. Recruitment was challenging: work conditions were difficult, and the romance of war was distant. Their contributions were nonetheless necessary to enable more men to go on active military service and still ensure the food supply for the nation. The tensions between ideas of service and work for women laboring on the land were even more problematic than for the "fast" ambulance drivers, as most of them were without elevated social position to bolster their status. Yet the primarily working-class members of the Land Army were repeatedly appealed to on official levels – even more than other populations of women contributing to the war effort were – as female "soldiers," giving to their country on an comparable level to that of the men serving in the trenches. After all, they had joined the Women's Land Army, the first official organization to employ military terminology in its name. The president of the Board of Agriculture even averred late in 1916 that he was convinced that "the victory or defeat in this great War may be brought about on the cornfields and potato lands of Great Britain."[43] The language of essential service was used to outweigh the stolid work associations of heavy farm labor. It was surely aimed as much at middle-class opinion as at working-class recruits, in an effort to overcome the perceived social danger of women performing work traditionally associated with men. The cultural risk seemed all the greater because the women wore clothes that masked physical difference and permitted physical liberty. It was also safe to talk about these women as soldiers because it was so patently untrue: women working on the land were clearly not in the army, unlike the ambiguity of the khaki-clad members of the WAAC. The clothes were masculine, but not military; so,

---

[43] See Gladys Pott, "Women in Agriculture," in Mrs. H. Usborne, *Women's Work in War Time: A Handbook of Employments* (London: T. W. Laurie, [1917]), p. 117.

for them, association with the army from a safe distance made their un-womanly work socially acceptable. They were an army obviously in name only.

The opening paragraph of the *Women's Land Army Handbook* insisted on the parallel, however. It explained to members that "You are now in the Women's Land Army; serving your Country just like the Soldiers and Sailors, though in a different way. You have to grow food for them and for the whole Country and your work is quite as important as theirs."[44] The work (for pay, though admittedly low) that the women performed was transformed into service through this association. This imagery also showed itself vividly in the "Land Army Songs" that actually preceded the text. The first one specifically referred to parallel service by women and men, because "If war shall fall / Then each and all / Must help to bring peace nigh." Both sexes were responding to an equal call but for different yet comparable tasks:

> The men must take the swords,
>   And we must take the ploughs,
> Our Front is where the wheat grows fair,
>   Our Colours, orchard boughs.
> Our Front is where the wheat grows fair,
>   Our Colours, orchard boughs.[45]

Each sex had its obligations. Not only was the physical location of the "Front" invoked, but also the military tradition of regimental "Colours." The other "Land Army Song" included in the *Handbook* made its comparison to men in the army only through its choice of melody: it was meant to be sung "to the tune of 'The British Grenadiers.'" The lyrics of the song carried a different gendered message. They praised the women who "all are working" in different capacities, but all selflessly: "None ever dream of shirking / Or ask for fame or praise"; or even, perhaps, the glory of heroes.[46] This depiction of the women agricultural workers also significantly glossed over any issues of remuneration for the predominantly working-class women members. Land Army members were women doing physical work traditionally performed by men, made socially safe by patriotic militarism.

Similar imagery also appeared in other published sources. A book on women's war work published in 1917 included an essay on "Women in

[44] *Women's Land Army Handbook*, p. 5: Miss D. Ferrar, IWM-DD 92/30/1.
[45] "Land Army Song – To the Tune of 'Come Lasses and Lads,'" *Women's Land Army Handbook*.
[46] "Land Army Song – To the Tune of 'The British Grenadiers,'" *Women's Land Army Handbook*.

Agriculture" by Gladys Pott, a middle-class Land Army member. In it, she declared that:

In response to the Empire's call our men have been required to lay aside all individual claims and family interests, and face indescribable hardships, suffering and death . . . Are English women less prepared to shoulder their share of toil or endure petty hardships which are almost luxuries compared to the trials borne by our soldiers?[47]

All members of the Land Army were also given fancy certificates that read, "Every woman who helps in agriculture during the war is as truly serving her country as the man who is fighting in the trenches, on the sea, or in the air."[48] The parity with soldiers could not have been more explicit. It was an easy and safe reward to give to women doing wretchedly hard work because of the very real distance between the land workers and the serving army.

The concept of parallel service combined with the idea of hard but worthwhile work was used in recruiting efforts to the Land Army. Minister of Agriculture Prothero, speaking to "a great women's meeting" in London, emphasized the difficulties of the labor:

It is hard work – fatiguing, backaching, monotonous, dirty work in all sorts of weather. It is poorly paid, the accommodation is rough, and those who undertake it have to face physical discomforts. In all respects it is comparable to the work your men-folk are doing in the trenches at the front. It is not a case of "lilac sunbonnets." There is no romance in it; it is prose.[49]

Yet while Prothero was explicitly denying the romance of the labor, he was romantically invoking the image of work "comparable" to that of the soldiers – and not just soldiers in general, but specifically "your men-folk . . . in the trenches." This was a powerful emotional appeal on behalf of the Land Army, both to the women workers themselves and to society at large.

It was indeed a romantic appeal, as is illustrated by the use of almost identical language in the explicitly romantic novel, *The Land Girl's Love Story*, written by Berta Ruck in 1918 and published just after the end of the war. The fictional recruiting officer might have been using Prothero's talk as a model: "I have put before you the disadvantages of this life.

---

[47] Pott, "Women in Agriculture," pp. 125–126.

[48] See Sharon Ouditt, *Fighting Forces, Writing Women: Identity and Ideology in the First World War* (London: Routledge, 1994), p. 54.

[49] See McLaren, *Women of the War*, p. 102. The real "prose" of land work, overlooked by Prothero and others but mentioned by McLaren (p. 104), was that "in addition to their farm work, [most women land workers] do their own cooking and housework; therefore they are really doing a man's work outside, but without the prepared meal and the immediate rest that most men can look forward to after work."

Long hours. Hard work. Poor pay. After you get your board and lodging a shilling a day, perhaps. Very poor pay. But, girls – our boys at the Front are offering their lives for just that. Won't you offer your services for that – and for them?"[50] Here, wages were mentioned, but in such a way as to make their significance at best negligible. The women joining the Land Army were again explicitly compared to soldiers, and "now Trafalgar Square saw girls being recruited as, three years ago, it saw young men being asked why they were not in khaki."[51] This comparison was ubiquitous. F. I. Hildrick Smith, a middle-class land worker writing for her school magazine, addressed her readers with both practical and patriotic advice. "You haven't got to" ruin your hands, she told them, "one good nailbrush, one cake of soap, a pair of nail scissors, and a pot of vaseline – I need not tell you how to use them – and the soldiers are sacrificing far more than their hands, aren't they?"[52] She was reassuring her readers about the ease with which a safe femininity could be preserved within the seemingly masculine environs of agricultural work.

Patriotism, therefore, did not require the sacrifice of femininity, even on the land. In fact, Ruck's recruiting officer promised "a good complexion," though perhaps it was not "worth mentioning" in comparison to the "good conscience" the workers would have "to meet those lads when they return from fighting for you." When the heroine, Joan, met the recruiter, their physical differences were made explicit: "Government office clerk and Land Girl. She, in smock and breeches, radiated rosy health; I, wearing my blue costume, Frenchy blouse, flower-wreathed hat and Louis-heeled shoes, wilted in limpness and pallor." Repeatedly, the novel compared the health of a land worker to the poor physical state of an office worker. Joan had been toiling in an unpleasant and unventilated "rabbit warren" at Whitehall, in a job that "was described as 'thundering good for a girl.'" This work made her, however, "a plain and weary girl, with ten years added to her actual age. A slim, stooping figure that moved without zest. Eyes without brightness. Hair ditto." Once she had been on the land a few weeks, she metamorphosed into "a straight and supple body, all conscious of the Jest of living. Limbs rounded and firm. Face joyous, glowing, and clean-skinned under the tan. Hair glossy and full of gleams; eyes bright as the morning, with the atmosphere of sunshine and clean airs all round me. A new self, in fact, made by a new life." This transformation was not unique, Joan averred; in fact, "thousands of girls

[50] Berta Ruck, *The Land Girl's Love Story* (New York: Dodd, Mead and Company, 1919), p. 18. See also Ouditt's discussion in *Fighting Forces, Writing Women*.

[51] Ruck, *Land Girl*, p. 18.

[52] F. I. Hildrick Smith, in *Queen Mary's High School Magazine* (1916), p. 5: Miss E. T. Rubery, IWM-DD 85/7/1.

all over the country at this moment can show the same miracle."[53] Land work, here, actually enhanced femininity.

Hildrick Smith and Ruck were both participating in the discussion over whether work on the land was appropriate for women. The terms of this debate brought out clear concerns over gender and class threats, as represented through the female body and sexuality. Despite the reassuring imagery offered by "A Woman," sunbonnets were in fact not practical. She was correct, however, that clothing was symbolically charged, and it was a particularly sensitive issue in land work, which by its nature necessitated recourse to attire that was repeatedly described as "masculine" (figure 3.3). The *Land Army Handbook* reminded members to save frills for days off duty and keep the uniform "workmanlike." It also cautioned that though "you are doing a man's work and so you are dressed rather like a man," workers were still women. They had to "remember that just because you wear a smock and breeches you should take care to behave like an English girl who expects chivalry and respect from everyone she meets." Again, the values of a "traditional" English society were being emphasized in circumstances that threatened to undermine them. The ideal land worker, the *Handbook* continued, would make people "admire your independence and your modesty, your frankness and enthusiasm; [and] show them that an English girl who is working for her Country on the land is the best sort of girl."[54] She was not dangerous to the social order; in fact, she supported it. Hildrick Smith agreed. "You can have breeches," she explained, "but do wear a coat over them. Don't try to be a man if you are doing man's work. Please [stay] womanly."[55] Similarly, Gladys Pott suggested a "very short skirt or tunic" over "thick stockings and heavy boots, with gaiters or puttees, [and] knickerbockers."[56] The skirt was the necessary element, preserving the essential appearance of womanliness despite the circumstances, its very presence testifying to the true nature and preferences of its wearer. Ruck's fictionalized account defused the threat of clothing by putting its defense in the mouth of the most socially elite character. Sybil's voice was "that of what was once called 'the governing class,'" a "country-house girl" who had "never been away from home before without a maid." She explained to Joan that "when you're on a man's job you've got to dress the part, not just for

---

[53] Ruck, *Land Girl*, pp. 19, 20, 7.   [54] *Land Army Handbook*, p. 5.
[55] F. I. Hildrick Smith, in *Queen Mary's High School Magazine* (1916), p. 5: Miss E. T. Rubery, IWM-DD 85/7/1.
[56] Pott, "Women in Agriculture," p. 121.

Figure 3.3 Land Army members astride a fence, showing both leggings and skirted jackets.

the look of it, but for the use. A man works 'in the sweat of his brow' – and of his body. So he has got to have clothes he can sweat into comfortably – to put it frankly . . . Working as a man, you simply can't wear the clothes you wore when you were just sitting still as a girl!" The clothes did not make the wearers masculine, however, because of the way they fitted the body. Ruck's recruiting officer wore "the Land Girl's uniform that sets off a woman's shape as no other costume has done yet . . . Her fresh, light belted smock, with its green armlet and scarlet crown, looked cool as well as trim." More than that, "there was scarcely a girl in that camp who didn't look a thousand times more attractive in uniform than she did in an ordinary hat and frock. Uniform does manage to be always 'right' in a way that only the most successful 'other clothes' ever achieve."[57] Active women, despite their gender-masking clothing and occupation, were still presented as feminine, as measured by the attractiveness and shapeliness of their bodies. Since they were still fundamentally women, they did not represent undesired social change in a time of national crisis. Men were still men, and women were not.

Women without experience of paid labor were essential to the process of culturally transforming grinding agricultural work into sublime patriotic service. As Sharon Ouditt has argued, "if patriotism could be construed as a substitute for wages, then the land could be worked and the farmers need not lose much by it."[58] Popular propagandists at the time were aware of the challenge. Ruck therefore contrasted women in (Land Army) uniform to men who were not. One character confronted a group of locals who were laughing at the women's clothes: "'Making fun, were you, because we girls wear the breeches? A good job for the country that we do. As for you, it's a pity they can't take and make you,' raising her voice to a shout, 'wear petticoats!'"[59] Gladys Pott admitted that the difficult work on the land did not have the "glamour and attraction" of other war contributions, like "munition making, hospital nursing, [and] canteen management," which "all appear to be directly connected with Army organisation, and to be essential to the prosecution of the war." She considered this lack, however, all the more reason that "the girl of good education be prepared to put aside all personal prejudice and natural desire for the comforts of life and take up for the sake of her country what may be a rough and uncongenial task."[60] Ruck's heroine Joan joined up in a pique after being jilted by her lover, but realized from the example of her fellow recruits that she needed to serve in order to live up to the effort

[57] Ruck, *Land Girl*, pp. 35, 84, 63, 80, 18, 159.
[58] Ouditt, *Fighting Forces, Writing Women*, p. 53.
[59] Ruck, *Land Girl*, pp. 150–151.   [60] Pott, "Women in Agriculture," p. 125.

of her brothers who were serving or already killed in action.[61] Elaborating on the same theme, the wartime writer Barbara McLaren argued for the importance of service-oriented self-sacrifice by educated women:

It is unnecessary to state the reasons which bring an educated woman voluntarily to take up such a hard and exacting life ... only a deeply-rooted motive can be the compelling force, and there can be no finer form of patriotism than the unsensational performance of these strenuous tasks, far from the glamour and excitement of direct contact with the war. Not only in the fruits of her own labour, but by the force of her example, as one of the pioneers along a new road for women, [they each are] performing as fine a war service as any Englishwoman to-day.[62]

The repetition was clearly not "unnecessary," since McLaren proceeded despite her disclaimer. Women like Hildrick Smith were important because they embodied this image of the land worker. She was serving the nation through agriculture for the duration of the war, but not, so to speak, upsetting the social apple-cart in the process.[63]

The service-minded land worker appeared in Ruck's novel as well, which employed many of the same images of classlessness that were applied to the army and other forms of war work. Joan first thought the women were "a queer mixture," and the farmer at the training facility said "some were one thing and some another" but they were "good little workers, all." Sybil, whose home "boasted one of those other countless bedrooms where Queen Elizabeth had passed a night," slept next to Lil, "who had been maid-of-all-work in one of the million villas that are too small to house and feed a servant decently, but where a servant must be kept because one is kept in bigger houses." Their colleagues included "a girl from Somerville, a pickle-factory hand, a student of music, and Vic the Cockney." Vic was the widely acknowledged leader, but everyone benefited from the "wealth of new ideas [and] fresh outlooks on life gained by the inter-mingling of class with class." The parallel to the alleged conditions in the trenches was explicit, as Joan concluded that "Kitchener's First Army was not more of a medley of types!" In case the reader missed the comparison, it was repeated. When her training was complete and Joan prepared to leave the camp for her first posting, Ruck had Joan think about how "I had found sisters of every class and kind. Now I had to leave them all ... with the chance that we should never meet again! It's the fate that breaks up so many a cheery mess, both in the Army and the Land Army!"[64]

[61] Ruck, *Land Girl*, pp. 85–86.   [62] McLaren, *Women of the War*, p. 16.

[63] F. I. Hildrick Smith, in *Queen Mary's High School Magazine* (1916), pp. 5–6: Miss E. T. Rubery, IWM-DD 85/7/1.

[64] Ruck, *Land Girl*, pp. 35, 63, 84–85, 200.

In its efforts to attract women to the difficult labor and comparatively low pay of land work, the Ministry of Agriculture repeatedly used comparative imagery. The military parallels created therefore bordered on the extreme. There was a Roll of Honour for deaths resulting from farm accidents (as there was for combat-related casualties), and a record of Distinguished Service in the Land Army structured like the official Mentioned in Dispatches.[65] There was a medal awarded "to commemorate... service during the Threshing Season 1918–1919" by the War Agricultural Executive Committee of the County of Kent.[66] The Food Production Department reminded members of the Land Army that "British women, just like British men, know how to face difficulties."[67] The more obviously women were not soldiers, the safer it was to describe them that way to soothe popular anxiety.

The results of the unofficial campaign to present Land Army workers in a positive social light were mixed, however. Howard Nevill, a naval officer, approved of his friends Hilda and May going on the land. In contrast, Lieut. Frank Ennor was glad his future wife Kathleen became a VAD instead, as he did not want her to become "somewhat muscular in the arms."[68] Again, disapproval was being expressed in terms of women's bodies; Ennor was not comfortable with the woman with whom he was romantically involved being in any way less feminine. Katharine Furse, though certainly not without an agenda of her own as the VAD commandant, also resisted the recruiting efforts to attract women onto the land: she denigrated it as "hoe[ing] turnips." Furse felt strongly that "it is a pity to tell our women that they are more needed on the land than in the hospitals."[69] Most would have agreed with her preference for healing over farming when it came to war work for women.

This ongoing popular resistance made for propaganda efforts that were an awkward mix of class-based language. Patriotism and military parallels were intended to appeal to upper- and middle-class women (who even in a small minority would lend the work a greater degree of social approval). In reality, however, women land workers, especially as the war progressed, were overwhelmingly accustomed to paid manual labor. In this, land army work was similar to the munitions industry, which was subject to

---

[65] Ouditt, *Fighting Forces, Writing Women*, p. 56.

[66] See letter from F. J. Heron Maxwell, Helen Rice, and F. S. W. Cornwallis to Miss M. Britton: Mrs. M. Harrold, IWM-DD 86/20/1.

[67] Food Production Department to Miss D. Ferrar, July 1918: Miss D. Ferrar, IWM-DD 92/30/1.

[68] Howard Nevill to his family, April 19, 1917: Commander W. H. Nevill RNR, IWM-DD Con Shelf; Frank Ennor to Kathleen La Fontaine, July 16, 1917: Lieut. F. H. Ennor, IWM-DD 86/28/1.

[69] Katharine Furse to Lord Selbourne, May 18, 1916: Dame Katharine Furse, PL Women.

propaganda campaigns emphasizing the "lady munitionette." One socially privileged land worker, Ina Scott, found an additional parallel; she
wrote that her work was satisfying even though unpleasant because "one
is doing what is really necessary." She explained that the "stimulating
feeling is not easy to explain, only we felt that here we were really achieving something – something as tangible as making munitions, although we
had to wait to see the result."[70]

War in the factories: "Tommy's sister"

Scott's enthusiasm for the patriotic value of munitions work was not universal, however. Firmly grounded in the realm of industrial labor, it was
difficult to construe factory work as uplifting service to the nation. It
was also distinct because men and women were both doing effectively
the same kinds of work.[71] Munitions production involved more women
than any other sector of war work, yet men remained central to the factories and retained both power and skilled jobs through union activity.
Women workers were praised for their heterogeneity, as munitions was
portrayed as the ultimate class melting pot. They were also celebrated
for their determination, putting up with strenuous work under difficult
conditions in the name of the war effort. Simultaneously, however, they
were condemned for earning wages described as unreasonably high and
for spending the money on consumer luxuries like jewelry and fur coats;
a broader critique of consumerism and the choices women made was
often expressed through a focus on their bodies. For women, munitions
was always considered "war work," but for men, for whom the option of
serving in the military was technically available (it could in reality have
been difficult for a man skilled in a protected industry to leave his job),
the patriotic approval was muted. Women, after all, were supposed to
be working only "for the duration," while men in the factories expected
to remain there in peacetime. The temporality associated with women's
efforts in industry left room to praise their patriotic effort without acknowledging that the vast majority had a history of paid labor and would
continue to work for compensation, even if not in munitions, after the
war. Once again, the idea that work was only "for the duration" helped
diffuse the threat these women represented by entering a relatively well-
paid, traditionally male-dominated sphere. Tensions continued just below

[70] Ina Scott, "The Land," in Stone, *Women War Workers*, p. 57.
[71] Medicine is the other obvious example where men and women were performing the
same war-related tasks. However, as it required extensive training, it was not an option
to anyone seeking "war work," but instead created the professional tensions between
men and women discussed in ch. 2.

the patriotic surface, however, and emerged regularly in criticisms of the women workers, their behavior, and their attitudes.

Though not technically an "army" like the women who worked in agriculture, nor an official military organization like the WAAC, women munitions workers were still regularly described as the female parallels to the men in the trenches. As with the Land Army, this was a relatively safe way to try to defuse the masculine associations of the work they were doing, since they were not, of course, actually soldiers. Barbara McLaren called for "public recognition [of] the great army of women munition workers," who "are working for the country as vitally as the soldiers."[72] Ethel Alec-Tweedie even referred to the female munitions worker as "a soldier-woman."[73] The equation was widespread. As a famous recruiting poster urged, "These women are doing their bit – Learn to make munitions." In the foreground, a woman pulls a factory coverall on over her clothes, her hair already tucked under a cap. In the background, her counterpart – the soldier – waves goodbye as he walks out of the factory, rifle on his shoulder (figure 3.4). They were each "doing their bit," in gender-appropriate ways. This concept, however, spread well beyond official propaganda. Ian Hay's Major Wagstaffe, in *Carrying On*, sequel to the best-selling *The First Hundred Thousand*, spoke very positively about female munitions workers.[74] The *Daily Chronicle* maintained that "The nation's debt to these heroic women, many of whom have lost their husbands in the war, is so great that it may even be likened to the debt which the nation owes to its soldiers and seamen."[75] Though comparing workers to soldiers did the double job of attracting women to the factories while easing public concern about their presence there, it was still not an easy process. The article in the *Daily Chronicle* suggested that the women were working because their husbands had been killed: they worked not for money, or independence, or even pride in the work, but because of patriotism, self-sacrifice, and personal loss. The work was tied entirely to war in this view; none of the women in the article would have had any need or interest to continue industrial work in peacetime.

Working-class women, however, predominated, and class-based tensions certainly existed in the factory, even though it was almost inevitably described as a class melting pot. These depictions did not accurately

---

[72] McLaren, *Women of the War*, pp. 54, 29.

[73] Ethel Alec-Tweedie, *Women and Soldiers* (London: John Lane, [1918]), p. 34.

[74] Ian Hay, *Carrying On – After the First Hundred Thousand* (Edinburgh and London: William Blackwood and Sons, 1917), pp. 311–312.

[75] *Daily Chronicle*, August 16, 1918, quoted in Gail Braybon, *Women Workers in the First World War* (London: Croom Helm, 1981), p. 159.

Figure 3.4 Recruiting poster: "These Women Are Doing Their Bit –
Learn to Make Munitions."

reflect the real populations of women working in munitions factories during the war, who overwhelmingly had experience with paid labor (whether
in other factories, domestic service, or other manual labor).[76] Instead,

[76] The authoritative sources on munitions workers are Angela Woollacott, *On Her Their
Lives Depend: Munitions Workers in the Great War* (Berkeley: University of California

they displayed both the social tensions that surrounded these women and the cultural efforts to ease them in the name of the national crisis. One inveterate self-appointed observer of society, Ethel Alec-Tweedie, described "every class" working together: "well-educated ladies... parlour-maids... the usual factory hands."[77] Naomi Loughnan, one of the minority of "educated" munitions workers, averred that "we are all on a level, Duchesses or coster-girls," at least "inside the gates." She maintained, in keeping with popular propaganda, that "we come face to face with every kind of class, and each one of these classes has something to learn from the others."[78] Another middle-class factory worker, Monica Cosens, offered an equally diverse list, and claimed this was representative not just of her own factory, but of those throughout the country.[79] Similarly, Barbara McLaren wrote of "a soldier's wife from a city tenement, a vigorous daughter of the Empire from a lonely Rhodesian farm, a graduate from Girton, and a scion of one of the old aristocratic families of England."[80] The factory was clearly an appropriate place for women, L. K. Yates explained: "social status, so stiff a barrier in this country in prewar days, was forgotten in the factory, as in the trenches, and they were all working together as happily as the members of a united family."[81] Only a cause as great as the nation's need could unite women of such diverse social positions. Perhaps most importantly, they functioned together as a "family," rather than a more dangerous unit of industrial organization like a union.

Cosens clearly identified her own efforts with those of the soldiers.[82] She began a wartime account of her experience in the munitions factory with a chapter entitled "Enlistment." She wrote, "Oh, I wanted – wanted more than anything else in the world to become a 'Miss Tommy Atkins' in

Press, 1994); Deborah Thom, *Nice Girls and Rude Girls: Women Workers in World War I* (London: I. B. Tauris, 1998); and Laura Lee Downs, *Manufacturing Inequality: Gender Division in the French and British Metalworking Industries, 1914–1939* (Ithaca: Cornell University Press, 1995).

[77] Alec-Tweedie, *Women and Soldiers*, pp. 31–32.

[78] Naomi Loughnan, "Munition Work," in Stone, *Women War Workers*, pp. 28, 25.

[79] Monica Cosens, *Lloyd George's Munition Girls* (London: Hutchinson, [1916]), pp. 116–117.

[80] McLaren, *Women of the War*, p. 52.

[81] L. Keyser Yates, *The Woman's Part: A Record of Munitions Work* (London: Hodder and Stoughton, 1918), p. 9.

[82] Scholars have recently emphasized the similar positions of munitions workers and soldiers. Woollacott argues that health risks and even deaths (suffered fortunately by only a minority of workers, despite dangerous working conditions) were "sacrifices comparable to those of soldiers." Because of the Munitions of War Act of 1915, workers "experienced a system that was military-like in its restrictions and enforcement." See Woollacott, *Lives Depend*, especially pp. 15, 58, 88, 90, 194. My question is different; I am concerned with perceptions of war work, as articulated both by the workers and in response to them.

Lloyd George's army of Shell-workers."[83] Though women working in factories were alleged to be members of all strata of society, when the workers were compared to the army it was always the enlisted men who were discussed. Women munitions workers were referred to as "Miss Tommy Atkins" or "Tommy's sisters," making them parallel to the men serving in the ranks. Cosens even argued that the perception was reciprocal. When the wounded soldiers from the local Red Cross auxiliary hospital picked primroses and sent them to the women's munitions canteen, Cosens effused that in that action "was real proof that Mr. Tommy Atkins thought about us. It made us feel we were sharing the war with him. It drew us together, and we felt for the first time we were working *with* our soldiers and not *for* them."[84] Certainly, this is not the only possible conclusion to draw from men presenting women with flowers (which certainly could not have been entirely unusual). The action could also be read as reinforcing traditional gender roles through gallantry, for example. For Cosens, however, it was a powerful validation of her role in the war effort.

Descriptions of munitions work often centered on references to soldiers. Naomi Loughnan explained in 1917 that the "dark winter mornings are cold and comfortless, but thousands of men are out in the open trenches, and the constant remembrance of them stifles our groans." She elaborated, placing women clearly below men in the army in the hierarchy of patriotic effort:

Whatever sacrifice we make of wearied bodies, brains dulled by interminable night-shifts, of roughened hands, and faces robbed of their soft curves, it is, after all, so small a thing ... Men in their prime ... are offering up their very lives. And those boys with Life, all glorious and untried, spread before them at their feet, are turning a smiling face to Death. We cannot boast – there is nothing to boast about – but we can volunteer for the Danger Buildings.

Loughnan explained that she was "sick of frivolling," and "wanted to do something big and hard, because of our boys and of England." The final motivation, however, was provided by "the dreaded telegram [that] came at last ... [so] we gave up talking and made our way to the lowest level – the gates of the nearest ammunition factory."[85] She justified an action that might, in other contexts, be construed as unwomanly by making explicit the central role of the war in motivating her. She was working in munitions, in this account, as her way of mourning for a soldier.

---

[83] Cosens, *Munition Girls*, p. 7. She also regularly referred to working-class women munitions workers as "Khaki girls."

[84] Cosens, *Munition Girls*, pp. 67–68 (emphasis in original).

[85] Loughnan, "Munition Work," pp. 29, 40–41, 38–39.

Most munitions workers did come from the working classes, if not from Loughnan's "lowest level." According to the 1917 records of the Gretna factory, of every hundred workers "thirty-six had formerly been in domestic service, twenty had lived at home, fifteen had already worked in munitions elsewhere, twelve had worked in other kinds of factories, five had been shop assistants, and the remaining twelve had been laundry workers, farmhands, dressmakers, schoolteachers, or clerks."[86] This, of course, is not how they were popularly portrayed. Loughnan presented munitions as providing a distinctly class-based call to arms. "Educated" women had to prove their superiority to working women, and their right to stand with the men in the army. Patriotism and idealism alone were acceptable motivations for munitions work, according to Loughnan; she ignored the need for financial support that working-class female munitions workers might have experienced, condemning it as work "for the sake of mammon," effectively grouping them with war profiteers. Loughnan did not describe herself as working for the war, which involved pay and therefore personal benefit, but instead as serving the country, giving herself and therefore identifying herself as "worthy."[87] She left no room for anyone who was not financially independent to reach the highest ranks of patriotic sacrifice.

Expectations like these exacerbated class tensions among the women working in munitions, however masked in the popular representations. Even Monica Cosens, who portrayed life in the factory in almost universally positive terms, was forced to admit to misunderstandings. Though individually women were friendly, she wrote, "*en masse* there is a certain spirit of rivalry between them... They accuse each other of things neither would dream of doing." Though at first Cosens "did not like the look of [her] companions," within a week she said she "had grown to like them, then to appreciate them, and finally to love them." Despite her remarkably rapid affection, however, she was mocked for the luxury of her fur-lined gloves, as was a "War Volunteer" companion who placed a newspaper over a dirty bench before seating herself.[88] Such declarations of difference in both circumstances and standards must not have been appreciated by most of their coworkers.

Middle-class munitions workers like Loughnan and Cosens, however, argued that distinctions went deeper than attitudes toward dirt on the job or luxuries. They suggested that class differences illuminated fundamental distinctions in attitudes toward the war. While Loughnan felt

[86] Woollacott, *Lives Depend*, p. 22; see also pp. 19–20. The statistics are drawn from IWM Women's Work Collection, Mun. 14/8.
[87] Loughnan, "Munition Work," p. 34.
[88] Cosens, *Munition Girls*, pp. 114, 18, 51, 113–114.

that her "stern sense of duty" was her "only weapon of defence" against sleep on long night shifts, "ordinary factory hands have little to help keep them awake [because] they lack interest in their work because of the undeveloped state of their imaginations." This, she wrote, was because "they do not definitely connect the work they are doing with the trenches."[89] She condemned them for thinking primarily of the work and not the war. Similarly, Cosens described some women clustered around a current newspaper, and concluded that as "they look eager, excited, pleased . . . there [must have] been a great victory." When she joined the group, however, she discovered that the workers were discussing "the portrait of a new cinema star," and concluded that they were "queer, [because] their work is so vital to the war, and yet how that war is progressing is to them a secondary thought."[90] This was, of course, not the right attitude toward the propagation of the war, and further evidence of working-class women's inherent unreliability in the context of the war effort.

Women working in munitions factories, across the class spectrum, clearly supported the war being fought.[91] This was not sufficient, however, for a more service-minded worker like Naomi Loughnan. She, along with much of the public, argued that the motivation for doing the work was as important as the work itself. Workers had to understand *why*, in a patriotic sense, they were working, and not value the income they gained from it – a standard that revealed a deep class bias. If workers did not conform to this cultural expectation, they were publicly condemned. To make this point more clearly, Loughnan related, condescendingly, the story of a "girl, with a face growing sadder and paler as the days went by because no news came from France of her 'boy' who was missing." When the worker was "gently urged to work harder and not go to sleep so often," however, she "answered, with angry indignation: 'Why should I work any harder? My mother is satisfied with what I takes home of a Saturday.'"[92] Her alleged failure to associate her production with the fate of her soldier friend was used as a means of condemning her very presence in the factory; Loughnan entirely fails to consider any other interpretations – based on war weariness or profound sadness, for example – of the comment. This was not a unique criticism; women workers at Woolwich Arsenal were also accused of working short weeks because they thought

---

[89] Loughnan, "Munition Work," pp. 32–33.   [90] Cosens, *Munition Girls*, pp. 80–81.

[91] As Woollacott argues, "whether or not they kept informed about the particular events of the war, women munitions workers believed themselves vitally involved in the war effort": Woollacott, *Lives Depend*, pp. 199–200.

[92] Loughnan, "Munition Work," p. 33.

only of their pay. In their case, credit for increasing working hours was given to Lillian Barker, lady superintendent of the factory. She was said to have explained to the women how much the munitions they failed to make on their extra days off might mean "to Tommy in a tight corner."[93] Patriotism as a motivation defused the social threat of their interest in their own socioeconomic welfare.

Because many leisured women would not commit the time and effort to full employment, Lady Moir and Lady Cowan formed the Women Relief Munition Workers' Organisation in 1915 to work weekends at the Vickers factory. This was part-time work, replacing the regular staff on their off days. Socioeconomically privileged women could work fewer hours than the regular workers, and still be presented as contributing to the operation of the factory at full capacity. Ideally, however, from the government perspective, these women would join the regular factory shifts. The official rationale behind these recruiting efforts (which were not overwhelmingly successful) was that "educated" women would learn the new tasks more quickly, despite their lack of experience. The subtext, however, was that women who saw their time in the factories as service to the nation rather than as a new work opportunity would not resist being displaced from their jobs by returning soldiers at the war's end, as working-class women might.[94] Equally important, women who saw their work as temporary would not be interested in the labor unions. They were ultimately safe industrial laborers. It was this hope that led Ethel Alec-Tweedie to claim that female workers in the factories "have put strikers to shame."[95]

Naomi Loughnan argued that returning soldiers should remember that "the women competing with him are no blacklegs, but the daughters and the widows for the most part of those comrades who died by his side on the battlefields."[96] They were not merely soldiers' wives, they were widows. Rather than trusting to such generosity – perhaps not identifying with the description – many women became union members themselves. This trend began in the prewar years, but accelerated dramatically during the war as radically increased numbers of women became involved in industrial work. Union membership, however, was more critical for men in munitions. Shops could be closed in practice if not in technicality. G. F. Wilby, in the army, wrote to his fiancée about their friend Spicer who had gone into munitions. "Anything to dodge the Army I expect," Wilby wrote critically. Some months later, however, Spicer discovered that the

[93] McLaren, *Women of the War*, p. 11.   [94] See Woollacott, *Lives Depend*, pp. 180, 40.
[95] Alec-Tweedie, *Women and Soldiers*, pp. 23–24.
[96] Loughnan, "Munition Work," pp. 319–320.

factory work had its drawbacks as well. Wilby reported that "he is having a very miserable and lonely time of it, as nobody will talk to him or mix with him at all, just because he doesn't belong to the Trade-Union."[97] A man, unlike one of the new women workers, was much more likely to remain permanently at the factory. His presence outside the union, therefore, potentially weakened the efforts for higher wages and better conditions that relied on a unified shop floor. Women outside the union fold, however, did not present as serious a problem. Correspondingly, they were at times treated with a friendly condescension by the men in the factories. Monica Cosens expected animosity and "contemptuous tolerance" but reported "no irritability nor impatience." Secure in their superiority of skill, she claimed the men "never made you feel they were expecting you to do more than you were, but rather the other way, that they had not expected you to pick up the working of the machine as quickly as you had." Cosens also had worried about her ability to face "perhaps injustice and insolence from a class of men by whom I had always been treated with deference, but who were now to be my masters, and if necessary would hold the rein tight."[98] Naomi Loughnan put it even more starkly: "as long as we do exactly what we are told and do not attempt to use our brains, we give entire satisfaction, and are treated as nice, good children." It was a tenuous truce, however, as "any swerving from the easy path prepared for us by our males arouses the most scathing contempt in their manly bosoms."[99] From the pens of middle-class women, however, it would be surprising to find uniformly positive portraits of men in the factories. Those accolades were reserved for the men in uniform.

Union membership, in any case, did not protect women from discrimination inside the industry. The historian Deborah Thom has pointed out that women workers were considered "substitutes" or "dilutees" even when they were in fact extra workers, necessitated by the increased demands of the war.[100] Women were always by definition only filling the

---

[97] G. F. Wilby to Ethel Baxter, April 28, 1916, January 18, 1917: G. F. Wilby, IWM-DD 78/31/1. Men in the army, however, often chose to condemn trade union activity in wartime. See, for example, Ian Hay, *The First Hundred Thousand: Being the Unofficial Chronicle of a Unit of "K(1)"* (Edinburgh and London: William Blackwood and Sons, 1916), pp. 237, 310; Hay, *Carrying On*, pp. 181–183; diary entry, September 3, 1915, Horace Bruckshaw (Martin Middlebrook, ed.), *The Diaries of Private Horace Bruckshaw, 1915–1916* (London: Scolar Press, 1979), p. 76.

[98] Cosens, *Munition Girls*, pp. 96–97, 8.   [99] Loughnan, "Munition Work," pp. 35–36.

[100] Deborah Thom, "Women and Work in Wartime Britain," in Richard Wall and Jay Winter (eds.), *The Upheaval of War: Family, Work and Welfare in Europe, 1914–1918* (Cambridge: Cambridge University Press, 1988), p. 304. For a different kind of account of the battle for equal pay, see Sylvia Pankhurst's 1932 memoir, *Homefront: A Mirror to Life in England During the First World War* (London: The Cresset Library, 1987 [1932]).

slots of the missing soldiers, who would one day return and take over their "own" jobs. Though the Ministry of Munitions ordered women to be paid the same rates for the same work, numerous evasions resulted in significant differentials in wage rates. The simplest way to avoid the restrictions from the Ministry was to reconstitute job descriptions: if a woman was not doing the identical combination of tasks that the man had previously performed, then the wage rate could be adjusted. Similarly, some jobs were redesigned to include a minimal amount of heavy physical labor to exclude women from equal pay. In April 1918, male workers in the national shell factories earned on average £4 6s 6d per week, while they earned £4 14s 8d per week in the national projectile factories. Comparable wage rates for women were £2 2s 4d and £2 16s 8d respectively.[101]

Yet, despite these differentials, the issue of women's wages in the munitions factories was at the center of negative perceptions of the workers. Certainly many women were earning more money than they had previously, particularly if they had been in domestic service, but even if they had been in industrial work. Women's earnings were not usually portrayed as payment for work performed. Instead, they were frequently considered excessive money being spent in a reckless manner on the women workers' bodies, with fur coats, lavish underclothes, and jewelry often given as examples of profligacy. The women were accused of being self-indulgent in their consumerism, and one contemporary observer referred to an "orgy of silver bags and chiffons," and asserted that more money was being spent on "clothes, especially underclothes," in 1917 than 1915, primarily at "second, third, and fourth-class shops."[102] In this portrayal, not only were women workers being profligate, they were also not even buying quality goods, showing further their inability to be responsible for their disposable income. As with the representations of working-class women in the WAAC, the ghost of the prostitute, whose decorated but diseased body was always seen as a social danger, haunted these critical descriptions.

Some concerns were also expressed about elevated male wages, but not to the degree or with the virulence of the debate about women's.[103] Munitions work brought women new physical liberties, including

---

[101] Woollacott, *Lives Depend*, pp. 115, 305. See also Braybon, *Women Workers*, p. 167.

[102] Alec-Tweedie, *Women and Soldiers*, pp. 77, 67. See also Nicoletta F. Gullace, *"The Blood of Our Sons": Men, Women, and the Renegotiation of British Citizenship During the Great War* (New York: Palgrave Macmillan, 2002), pp. 158–165.

[103] See especially Angela Woollacott, "Dressed to Kill: Clothes, Cultural Meaning and First World War Munitions Workers," in Moira Donald and Linda Hurcombe (eds.), *Representations of Gender from Prehistory to the Present* (New York: St. Martin's Press, 2000). See also Claire Culleton, "Gender-Charged Munitions: The Language of World War I Munitions Reports," *Women's Studies International Forum*, 11, 2 (1988).

freedom to travel, live away from home, and work fewer hours in less supervised circumstances than domestic service. The idea of young un-married women (who were the culprits depicted, despite the presence of married women and mothers in the factories) enjoying both these free-doms and higher wages seemed threatening to English society. As Carol Dyhouse has argued, "wage-earning is believed to buy [working-class girls] a premature and socially undesirable independence. Further there is a strong assumption . . . that financial independence and sexual precoc-ity go hand in hand."[104] Seeking out creature comforts while the men suffered in the trenches was portrayed as particularly unpatriotic.

As it did not go away, this negative image continued to be countered by varied efforts to demonstrate the patriotic commitment of the very nec-essary women munitions workers. Monica Cosens argued against "the idea that some people have that Lloyd George's girls only work for the sake of the wages." Though "of course, they could not afford to give their services," Cosens continued, "they might find other work nearer home, less heavy and less irksome." The women did not choose an easier al-ternative because "they realize munitions are vital to the conclusion of the War, and they want to help by making them, no matter what discom-forts they are called upon to bear."[105] By reassuring her readers that the working-class women were closely connected emotionally to their homes and families, Cosens was arguing that the workers, despite their new liv-ing circumstances and financial independence, were good women and good citizens, not reckless spenders, excitement seekers, or prostitutes. Similarly, Minnie, the heroine of "A Story of Munition Life" (serialized in *The Limit* factory magazine), told her sweetheart that she probably would not have holidays to match his leave. She was not just starting a job, but was responding to a higher call: "I'm going to do real work now – Munitions are wanted dreadfully."[106] Both man and woman would be subjected to the demands of their war contribution, with the dictates of army and factory equally beyond their control. Here, as in other efforts to present munitions workers as patriots, the "heroism" and "morale" of women in the factories were compared with that of men in the field.

In another popular account, a parlormaid renounced much more than seems realistic. Her fiancé was "amongst the first batch of the New Army who went to the front." Before he left for France, she reassured him that

[104] Dyhouse, *Girls Growing Up*, p. 113. See especially Angela Woollacott, "'Khaki Fever' and Its Control: Gender, Class, Age and Sexual Morality on the British Homefront in World War I," *Journal of Contemporary History*, 29 (April 1994).

[105] Cosens, *Munition Girls*, pp. 119–120.

[106] "Minnie Phelps: A Story of Munitions Life. Chapter II," in *The Limit*, 4 (October 1918): R. Seale, IWM-DD 76/103/1.

"you are off to do your bit, God bless you, and you will be constantly in my thoughts and my prayers." She had news however: "I am going to spring a mine upon you, not a German mine, old chap, but a truly British one. While you are at the front firing shells, I am going into a munition factory to make shells." The parallels could hardly have been clearer. Not only did her factory work correspond to his military service, but her actions were also "truly British." Perhaps reflecting the middle-class perspective of the author of the piece, she told him that she knew that "the job will not be as well paid as domestic service, it will not be as comfortable as domestic service." Even though "it will be much harder work," she was looking forward to it because "it will be my bit, and every time you fire your gun you can remember I am helping to make the shells." Her soldier fiancé was supportive of her efforts, praising her with "well done, my girl, it is splendid of you."[107]

Propaganda, however, did not reflect society; it was most necessary when it most contradicted expectations. Popular texts were full of references to how attractive and feminine the women factory workers appeared. Yates described the "rows of graceful women and girls" in a fuse shop; Alec-Tweedie admired "trim and smart" workers in khaki; and McLaren claimed that "visitors are struck by the high proportion of good looks, even of beauty."[108] Many men were less sympathetic to the idea of the women they loved working in munitions factories, however, and the very repetition of such representations showed the strength of the idea that munitions production was masculinizing. G. F. Wilby wrote from his military post in East Africa to his fiancée Ethel Baxter, a barmaid in London, to discourage her from taking on munitions work. "Whatever you do," he told her, "don't go on Munitions or anything in that line." His concerns were explicitly about gender roles: "just fill a Woman's position and remain a woman, – don't develop into one of those 'things' that are doing men's work." He did not want his view of British society to change: "I want to return and find the same loveable little woman that I left behind." This feared change, in turn, would jeopardize their very relationship, as "I love you because of your womanly little ways and nature." For Wilby, maintaining a gender hierarchy was more important than one woman's potential role in the war effort, so he told Baxter, "don't spoil yourself by carrying on with a man's work, [as] it's not necessary."[109] The heavy labor involved in being a barmaid was

---

[107] Alec-Tweedie, *Women and Soldiers*, pp. 28–29.
[108] Yates, *Woman's Part*, p. 24; Alec-Tweedie, *Women and Soldiers*, p. 30; McLaren, *Women of the War*, p. 11.
[109] G. F. Wilby to Ethel Baxter, August 18, 1918: G. F. Wilby, IWM-DD 78/31/1.

appropriate to a working-class woman, but factory work was dangerously mannish.

Wilby's feelings on the subject did not change when he heard that Baxter had indeed gone into munitions. He wrote that he was "not at all pleased about it, – in fact [he was] very cross." He explained that he did not like "[his] little girl helping to make shells to blot out human lives... [she wasn't] made for such a thing, – [she was] really made to bring lives into the World." Though Wilby continued to assert that "the only reason" he disapproved of Baxter's work "was because [he] thought [she] might develop coarse, manly ways," she remained unworried.[110] Though outsiders may have identified the women by the work they were doing, they did not themselves. Munitions was work, not service; it was not fundamental to who they were and did not jeopardize their self-identification as women.

Service, however, was socially safer than work. Industry officials (along with some writers) therefore argued successfully for the placement of middle-class women as superintendents in factories. Their job was to control the large numbers of working-class women by supervising their "welfare," as had been previously done in the United States. The oversight was always presented as benefiting the workers, who were often freed of the original responsibility for their behavior. Just as in the prewar Girls' Clubs, the socially elite lady reformer was called for to improve both the moral and physical atmosphere of the factory.[111] As Alec-Tweedie argued, "the best sort of forewomen – and they may have from 100 to 400 girls under them – are better-class ladies." She had the experience to do the job, even though she had never previously worked for pay: "the aristocrat who is accustomed to rule a large household has learnt to rule in a sympathetic way. Her girls respect her, love her, follow her." This proved still another way to compare women in factories to enlisted men in the trenches: Alec-Tweedie declared that, "like Tommy, they prefer not to follow their own class." She presented a mutually beneficial relationship – "The lady rubs the rough edges off the factory hand, and the factory hand teaches the lady a new side of life" – but the imbalance was still clear, as "cleanliness, tidy hair, and more polite speech invariably follow

---

110 G. F. Wilby to Ethel Baxter, October 3, 1918: G. F. Wilby, IWM-DD 78/31/1. In Ethel (Baxter) Wilby's 1984 typescript memoir, she recalled that "people didn't think much of munitions girls, but they had to do it. I thought I was doing the right thing, but evidently I shouldn't have and my husband wrote and said, 'A nice girl like you was meant to produce, not to kill'": Mrs. E. Wilby, IWM-DD 92/49/1.

111 See Angela Woollacott, "Maternalism, Professionalism and Industrial Welfare Supervisors in World War I Britain," *Women's History Review*, 3 (March 1994); Downs, *Manufacturing Inequality*.

the lady."[112] Again, criticism went beyond deportment to a focus on workers' bodies: the "rough edges" consisted not just of poor manners but of unacceptable personal hygiene and insufficient attention to appearance.

The two-sided responsibility for both social control and improvement of conditions was explicit in a description of the lady superintendent (as the women chief welfare supervisors were called) at the munitions factory at Gretna. Mabel Cotterell's "wise administration" was credited not just with "a marked improvement... in health and physique, which good food, clean housing, and regular employment have brought the workers," but also with giving the women "a greater regard for truth, honesty, and duty."[113] To be sure, some of the reforms thus instituted led to safer working conditions and more pleasant amenities.[114] The justification for their institution, however, was often paternalistic toward the working-class objects of the reforms. As Lloyd George, then minister of munitions, declared, "the workers of today are the mothers of tomorrow," so "in a war of workshops the women of Britain were needed to save Britain; it was for Britain to protect them."[115] Echoing the same sentiment, Ethel Alec-Tweedie argued for welfare improvements in the factories because they would boost productivity, and because the women workers "are the potential mothers of the race for which we are now fighting."[116] By invoking the future maternal role of the women in the factories, this imagery worked to subvert the specter of the independent, masculinized – or promiscuous – female worker. Sexuality was safely contained within maternalism.[117] It also further emphasized the idea of unusual work only "for the duration," after which the women would revert to the traditional responsibilities of motherhood. The middle-class "lady" supervisors were a key part of this process of subversion, and a clear example of the culturally expressed need for social control over physically and financially independent working women. They also paralleled the traditional relationship between mistress and servant.

---

[112] Alec-Tweedie, *Women and Soldiers*, p. 18. See also similar claims in Mary Frances Billington, *The Roll-Call of Serving Women: A Record of Woman's Work for Combatants and Sufferers in the Great War* (London: The Religious Tract Society, 1915), p. 207; and McLaren, *Women of the War*, p. 52.

[113] McLaren, *Women of the War*, p. 13.

[114] See, for example, Dorothea Proud's discussion of "Welfare Work" in Stone, *Women War Workers*, pp. 239–253.

[115] Yates, *Woman's Part*, p. 37.

[116] Alec-Tweedie, *Women and Soldiers*, pp. 20–21.

[117] On maternalism, see especially Susan R. Grayzel, *Women's Identities at War: Gender, Motherhood, and Politics in Britain and France During the First World War* (Chapel Hill: University of North Carolina Press, 1999).

War in the household: servants, service, and the social order

Much of the tension about the newfound independence of working-class women was articulated through discussion of the so-called servant problem, both during and immediately following the war. As Eleanora Pemberton, a VAD, sympathetically asked her mother in 1916, "are all the servants making munitions?"[118] Contemporary estimates suggested that somewhere between 100,000 and 400,000 women left domestic service for new wartime jobs in 1914–1918.[119] The First World War was certainly not the beginning of middle-class concern about the dearth and quality of servants, but it was one point when debate crystallized around specific, seemingly identifiable causes. Women were leaving posts in private homes for the opportunities newly open to them, whether in munitions, in the army auxiliaries, on the land, or even taking tickets on the trams. The middle-class households that had increasing difficulties hiring the staff to which they were accustomed viewed this exodus with little sympathy. Ethel Alec-Tweedie discussed at length what she presented as the insensitivity of wartime domestic servants. They remained, she averred, selfishly unaware of the new financial restrictions on their employers; they also failed to grasp that taking care of the household of a woman doing canteen or hospital work was their "bit of war work, and . . . a real help to the country."[120] Working-class women who left domestic service for munitions work were praised as a group; as individuals, however, they were frequently condemned for "selfish" behavior in searching for higher wages, better conditions, or more interesting work when another parlormaid could not easily be found.

The ongoing discussion about the so-called servant problem acted as a way to articulate middle-class tensions in wartime British society over the newfound independence of many working-class women. It was, of

---

[118] Eleanora Pemberton to her mother, undated [received April 12, 1916]: Miss E. B. Pemberton, IWM-DD 85/33/1.

[119] Woollacott, *Lives Depend*, p. 183; Gareth Griffiths, *Women's Factory Work in World War I* (Phoenix Mill, UK: Alan Sutton, 1991), pp. 13–14. Griffiths also points out the increasing mean age of domestic servants, which, along with its decline as a percentage of employed women, suggests that new female workers were not entering the field at comparable rates to previous generations. The number of women entering munitions is difficult to assess, as different official industrial categories included munitions production in addition to other kinds of work, but it seems to be somewhere on the rough order of one million. See Woollacott, *Lives Depend*, p. 18; Griffiths, *Women's Factory Work*, p. 13; Richard Wall, "English and German Families and the First World War, 1914–1918," in Wall and Winter, *Upheaval of War*, p. 56; Thom, "Women and Work," p. 304.

[120] Ethel Alec-Tweedie, in *English Review*, April 1916, quoted in Alec-Tweedie, *Women and Soldiers*, pp. 41–42.

course, universally demeaning to the humanity of the women workers in question. Peggy Bate, for example, helped her recently married sister Trix set up a new flat in London. Bate admitted to her sweetheart in a letter that though they had established relations "with laundry men butchers bakers etc.," they had "absolutely failed to procure a maid," as "such things are unknown quantities since the war work for girls craze."[121] Bate herself was involved with war work, and became a driver with the Women's Legion. She repeatedly described her efforts as important to the war. When working-class women became unavailable as servants, however, then war work in the middle-class perception became a "craze" rather than appropriate behavior.

Middle-class expectations after the Armistice suggest that efforts to contain the perceived threat of working women in wartime were in fact partly successful. Since the exodus of servants during the war years was associated with the "the war work for girls craze" rather than the actual conditions of domestic service, many middle-class wives expected a re-turn to employment in private homes after the conclusion of the war. To facilitate the process, several training schemes were instigated by of-ficial agencies. Violet Markham led one effort; her Central Committee on Women's Training and Employment gave skills experience to almost 100,000 women, the majority for domestic service.[122] In another, as an offshoot of a program established by the Ministry of Labour to train "war brides" in the wifely arts they might not have learned while working in munitions factories, unmarried women were to be resettled into domes-tic service.[123] Woolwich Arsenal also organized a program to provide training in the domestic skills which might have been forgotten or never learned by its former women workers, with the intent of making them either better wives or better servants. This program was part of the gen-eral movement to return women to the household, whether to their own or someone else's. Advertising for the venture therefore described it as a new "call" to British women, "not to make shells or fill them so that a ruthless country can be destroyed but a call to help renew the homes of England, to sew and to mend, to cook and to clean and to rear babies in health and happiness."[124] The former munitions workers were supposed to be retrained in femininity and motherhood, revoking the threat of their independence in the war years.

Katharine Furse, who after her departure from the Voluntary Aid Detachments became the original commandant of the Women's Royal

[121] Peggy Bate to F. A. Brettell, December 25, 1915: Lieut. F. A. Brettell, IWM-DD PP/MCR/169.
[122] Lewis, *Women and Social Action*, p. 263.   [123] Woollacott, *Lives Depend*, pp. 154–155.
[124] Thom, "Women and Work," p. 314.

Naval Service, also organized a scheme to aid in the placement of enlisted-level women (or "ratings") as servants. This plan, however, met with luke-warm approval at best. Furse submitted a memo to all WRNS officers to determine the cause of the resistance:

If any ratings will write their views shortly for my information I shall be delighted to have their advice and help. I am very keen to find out exactly what is objected to in ordinary Domestic Service and how we could make it more attractive so that women who may otherwise be out of work shall profit by good conditions in private houses.[125]

What Furse discovered was that the majority of former domestic servants, having experienced work that paid better, treated them with greater re-spect, and gave them more free time and less supervision, refused to return to their earlier conditions and demanded recognition of what they had accomplished. In recognition of the changed circumstances, by September 1919 Furse was writing to her sister Madge about a dis-traught friend who "can't get a servant because it's a dull place." Furse herself thought that the WRNS were better people for having done war work, and that their expectations had shifted. Her realization of change was still limited, however, as after the war she still thought the solution could be found in making "people" – i.e., working people – "more un-selfish," which unfortunately could not be done in time to "save" the friend in need of domestic help.[126]

This resistance to domestic service was costly for many women, as a job offer of any sort jeopardized their eligibility for the out-of-work benefit. Despite this threat, however, large numbers of them refused the work. Most of the women who did return to household service attempted to set new conditions. Not only did they demand higher wages, but also they much preferred to live out, and if required to live in insisted on more time off. Some of the middle-class fears of the effect of the war on working-class women were indeed realized. The prevalent idea of "for the duration" did mean that women's work that would not have been con-sidered appropriate prior to 1914 became exceptional effort on behalf of the war needs, rather than a new long-term trend. However, it ultimately failed to completely contain the threat that such wartime working women had represented, as the changes in their postwar behavior and demands demonstrated. Their enforced departure from the factories did not lead to their return to domestic service.

---

[125] Draft for Remarks, February 8, 1919: Dame Katharine Furse, PL Women.
[126] Katharine Furse to Madge Vaughan, September 2, 1919: Dame Katharine Furse, PL Women.

This "crisis" over war workers and servants showed the efforts that went into making work that was not traditionally considered appropriate for women seem acceptable for the duration of the war. To achieve this, popular ideology translated work into service. This shift, however, could not entirely defuse the threatening image of the independent working woman that lay just underneath the patriotic patina (and frequently broke through the surface). Women's war contributions outside paramilitary organizations and hospitals fell on a spectrum of accustomed acceptability. Those who chose predominantly part-time efforts on behalf of Belgian refugees or soldiers' and sailors' families, or who knit or sewed for hospital supply depots, were complying with a well-established tradition of social intervention on the part of middle-class women. They were far from controversial, even if they were occasionally mocked for their enthusiasm. Such work was clearly service-oriented, in a distinct combination of philanthropy and patriotism. The work also seemed inherently feminine, and it was consistent with the existing class order in its hierarchical approach. At the other pole, the "masculine" efforts of women in munitions factories were even more socially problematic than women farm workers. These working-class women were concerned with issues of pay and conditions as well as the needs of the country, and they represented a double threat. They made incursions into worlds of work usually explicitly associated with men. Their increasing financial independence also seemed to undermine class hierarchies. Attempts at controlling such perceived dangers ranged from the addition of middle-class workers who were appealed to on account of their patriotism to the social supervision of "lady welfare superintendents." The failures of such efforts were visible through the widespread condemnation of munitions workers' alleged profligacy and immorality.

In between these two extremes, however, there was some room for subversion of gender and class expectations. Some women discovered space within the bounds of traditionally feminine work for considerable personal freedom. Schoolgirls sometimes found an opportunity for experimentation with other kinds of work, at times away from home, while still maintaining the umbrella of acceptability provided by their schools' supervision. Single women had similar new opportunities, sheltered by the auspices of charitable organizations. Women who worked in canteens overseas illustrate this phenomenon. They were involved in the preparation and presentation of food, along with the provision of civil and polite company: eminently the work of women at home. Moreover, most of the canteens in France were operated by religious organizations like the YMCA and the Church Army, whose chaperonage was beyond question and whose very image imparted a certain selfless, hard-working, and pure air to the occupation. The work itself was often drudgery, and the atmosphere could be difficult, as there were tensions among and between the different sponsoring organizations, which cooperated with each other only loosely.[127] The volunteer workers, however, primarily approached the labor with much the same attitude as many of the VADs: like Kate Finzi, they reveled in the problems. "The difficulties at first were many," she wrote, "a fact which considerably enhanced the joy of the work."[128] They were serving and interacting with the soldiers, they were living in interesting locations away from home, and even the church groups did not provide anything close to the supervision that was commonplace for a "daughter at home." Because canteening did not require the long-term commitment of VAD nursing, and because the work seemed more genteel and better chaperoned, women who traveled to France did not appear to be crossing many gendered and classed boundaries. Yet within that space they found room for considerable independence and adventure. Some of them did not return to England permanently until after the war was over; some even traveled with the canteens to Germany following the army after the Armistice. These were new opportunities indeed.

One family, even, could encompass many of the self-revising strands of wartime British society. The spectrum of attitudes toward war work for both women and men across class barriers, from VAD work to WRNS, from canteening to part-time philanthropy, from servants leaving households to soldiers in the trenches, are all illustrated by the story of one family at war: the Beales of Standen.

---

[127] See, for example, Mary Campion to Katharine Furse, April 22, 1917: Dame Katharine Furse, PL Women. See also Kit Beale and Irene Rathbone, discussed in chs. 4 and 6.

[128] Kate John Finzi, *Eighteen Months in the War Zone: A Record of a Woman's Work on the Western Front* (London: Cassell and Co., 1916), p. 45.

4   A family at war: the Beales of Standen

In August 1915, Helen Beale – unmarried, soon to turn thirty, and the youngest daughter of an affluent professional family – left for France to work as a VAD at 26 General (Military) Hospital with the British Expeditionary Force. In peacetime, a single woman of her social position would not have considered independent travel away from the responsibilities and protections of home. War, however, drastically changed the rules and expectations. "I can't tell you how very noble I think it was to face the unknown by yourself as you are doing," Sylvia Beale wrote to her sister-in-law Helen; "but it must be an immense satisfaction to feel you have fitted yourself to do what every woman in the country would wish to be doing now if she had the knowledge. I mean, there is nothing a woman could help the country more in doing than mending its men."[1]

Helen Beale served in her local Red Cross hospital and in military hospitals in London and France before becoming an "officer" in the new Women's Royal Naval Service (WRNS) in 1918. Much of her family was active in the war effort in varying ways, ranging from service in the military to amateur nursing to involvement in munitions production to part-time volunteer work. The Beale family is not unique in this breadth of war service, nor, of course, in its vision of women as "menders of men." What makes this family particularly fascinating historically, however, is the depth of documentation they left behind them. The Beales were a close family, and reacted to their wartime separations with regular and detailed correspondence, most of which they then kept. Helen Beale, her mother, and her sister Maggie all wrote frequently to each other. Helen also kept the letters she received from other family members and close friends, bringing them home with her from her different postings. This process was aided by the Beales' continuous residence at Standen, their family house outside East Grinstead, in Sussex. Helen Beale never married, and remained at Standen for the rest of her life. When she died in

---

[1] Sylvia Beale to Helen Beale, August 16, 1915: Beale Family Papers, Cobnor Cottage, Chidham, Chichester (hereafter BP).

1972, and the estate became a National Trust property, her correspondence was packed away in suitcases, and only recently rediscovered by a family member.[2] This impressive collection of letters offers a rare opportunity to investigate how the First World War affected a successful professional family, and how they dealt with the interactions of family responsibilities and ideas about war service.

The correspondence is particularly revealing about the concept of service, as the Beales frequently applied it to their own family members. Their references to work are more peripheral, and come primarily in their discussions of servants and their wider circle of acquaintance. All of the Beales, male and female, expressed in varying degrees a sense of obligation that they considered both appropriate to their class position and a necessary and honorable reaction to what they patriotically saw as a just war. The Beale men echoed the popular perception that service as a soldier was the only acceptable effort for men to make on behalf of the nation. The younger men joined the military, and even older men with managerial positions in protected industries worried that they should. Women gave their efforts to a variety of non-combatant services, ranging from full-time work in hospitals to part-time volunteering at supply depots, and including canteening, "adopting" prisoners of war, household economizing, and serving in one of the women's auxiliary military services. All these forms of war work were explicitly and repeatedly described as service to the country. Peacetime occupations (including philanthropy) were displaced, at least initially. For the Beale women at the center of this correspondence, choices about the kind of service they could offer were strongly influenced by opinions voiced within the family, as well as the perceived needs of the home.

The Beale family papers offer a case study of the key ways gender and class were implicated in expectations about work and service in the First World War. Their views both for themselves and for others reflected the social mores of their day. Though working-class participation in the war was considered admirable in the aggregate, they often described individual examples of servants leaving as desertion of work obligations to their employers. They considered that working-class women were not "serving" in the same way they applied that language to themselves and their social peers. Similarly, the Beales showed little understanding of the claims for professional status that paid nurses were making.

Both James Beale and his wife Margaret Field came from well-known and socially powerful non-conformist families in Birmingham. James was

[2] I am extremely grateful to the late Mrs. Joan Edom, niece of Helen Beale and daughter of Sydney Beale, for the generous access she permitted me to her family's papers, as well as for our discussions and her letters.

a successful solicitor in the family firm of Beale & Co., which in the middle of the nineteenth century became involved in highly profitable work for the Midland Railway. They moved to London in 1868 for the construction of the Midland terminus at St. Pancras. Their seven children were born there between 1871 and 1885, the first four in Gordon Square, and the remaining three after the family moved to Holland Park, Kensington. In the early 1890s James Beale, like many of his contemporaries, decided to spend some of his accumulated wealth on a house in the country. He settled on a location outside East Grinstead, in the Sussex Weald. The house, Standen, built in 1892–1894, was designed by the great Arts and Crafts architect Philip Webb, and furnished by the firm of William Morris.[3]

James Beale died in 1912. When the First World War broke out, his widow Margaret was living at Standen with her two unmarried daughters, Maggie and Helen, and their substantial staff. The oldest child, Amy, had married Edgar Worthington in 1902. She had four children and was living in London. John, or Jack, as he was known, was also in London with his wife Daisy and their four children, and working at the family firm. Sydney was an army officer who would serve at Gallipoli and in Egypt. He had recently married Margaret Crookshank, daughter of a neighboring family, and they had also established themselves in the city. Dorothy lived in London too, with her husband Harold Brown and their six children. Sam and his wife Sylvia were further afield, living in Edinburgh, but visited Standen for holidays and remained closely connected to the family.

Helen, the youngest of the Beale children, was twenty-nine years old when she left for France in 1915. She and her older sister Maggie had joined their local Voluntary Aid Detachment in 1911, in the early stages of the organization (figure 4.1).[4] For Helen and Maggie Beale, being a VAD before the war was not a significant commitment. It meant classes leading to First Aid and Home Nursing Certificates, and Helen also spent a week observing nursing in the wards and the operating theaters, learning hospital routines.

The sixteen or more Beale cousins who contributed to the war effort exemplified the variety of opportunities British men and women of the

---

[3] This combination of architect and design firm led to Standen's inclusion in the National Trust, despite its relative lack of age. See the National Trust publication *Standen, West Sussex* (London, 1993); Mark Girouard, "Standen," in *The Victorian Country House* (New Haven, CT, 1979); Dan Klein, "Standen: An Early Paradise," *Connoisseur*, 208 (December 1981); and Lawrence Weaver, "Standen," *Country Life*, 27 (May 1910).

[4] Helen Beale's Certificate of Discharge from Voluntary Aid Detachment 68, Sussex, dated January 30, 1918, records service June 1911–January 20, 1918.

Figure 4.1 Helen Beale and Maggie Beale in VAD uniforms; the comment is from their brother Sam Beale.

middle classes had in the First World War.[5] Following the outbreak of war, both Helen and Maggie worked in their local Red Cross Auxiliary

[5] When Bill Beale was killed in action, Maggie wrote to Helen that he had been "quite the most promising of the 16 cousins who joined." This probably refers only to men in the military; a significant number of women in the family also did war work (Margaret S. Beale to Helen Beale, March 16, 1916, BP).

Hospital. Helen then made the decision to commit to nursing full-time. Maggie continued to nurse part-time, but as the war progressed became more active with her prewar interest in infant welfare, a shift that clearly illustrates the way women of her social position saw war work as a crisis-specific extension of their peacetime philanthropic endeavors. Like many other financially secure women, Maggie, Margaret, and Dorothy all considered household economizing to be an important contribution to the war effort. To help her neighbors with war economies, Maggie even organized frugal cookery classes in East Grinstead (though they were not well attended). Several of the married daughters and daughters-in-law, including Sylvia, Amy, and Daisy, did part-time volunteer work, primarily making hospital supplies and "comforts" for soldiers. More unusually, Sydney's wife Margaret trained in massage (which became modern physical therapy) and worked at a London hospital. She continued to work part-time after the birth of her daughter Joan in 1917, though she left the hospital after her husband was invalided home in 1918, before the Armistice. The married women of the Beale family also discussed in some detail the experiences of their servants, who were leaving their posts for newly opened war opportunities. As domestic servants became increasingly difficult to find, this was the subject of much frustrated discussion. Younger female cousins and friends of the family also contributed to the war effort: Kit Beale worked in YMCA canteens first in France and then in Germany after the war, Sybil Field and Winifred Burt were VADs in England and France, and the Hoare sisters served as VADs in England, France, and Serbia as well as doing YMCA canteen and rest camp work.

Among the men in the family, Sydney Beale, a regular army officer, served in the Middle East. The other brothers and brothers-in-law, who ranged in age from thirty-three to fifty-eight, were working in protected industries. Still, Sam Beale and Harold Brown both grappled with strong feelings that they ought to enlist, demonstrating the power of the idea that military service was the only acceptable war work for men. Younger, unmarried male cousins volunteered for the military. Bill Beale was killed and Sydney Field and Walter Field were wounded while with the infantry in France; Mark Field was luckier in the artillery. Dick Bell-Davies became one of the first aviators, and was awarded the Victoria Cross, Britain's highest military honor.

When Helen decided to do hospital work in France, she had widespread support from her family. This was partly contingent, however, on her older sister Maggie's presence at home to care for their widowed mother, and also on their mother's continuing good health. Though Helen had responsibilities as a "daughter at home," they were sufficiently eased by the national crisis to allow her to serve overseas, provided that the family situation did not degenerate in any way. Sylvia, therefore, was far from the only family member to write approving letters during those early days in France. Another sister-in-law, Daisy Beale, wrote that "it must be very satisfactory in these days to be giving all your time to a definite job you know there is a need for." Helen's cousin Bill, serving in the army, wished her "all luck in the new job" and thought that she would "enjoy the life all right." Sybil Field, a cousin who was serving as a VAD in an Auxiliary Hospital, "env[ied] [Helen] feeling in the thick of things; and being so useful"; Elsie Field and Winifred Beale also wrote of "envy" of Helen's job.[6] Helen's work for the nation far outweighed her status as a single woman living away from home, and garnered her widely articulated social approval with no hint of condemnation.

Relatives often considered Helen's individual efforts to be symbolic of greater family contributions to the war effort. Dorothy wrote that she felt "an enormous amount of reflected glory" from her sister's hospital work. Helen's mother Margaret wrote that she felt herself "patriotic [in] undertaking to do without you for six months," the duration of a VAD overseas contract. She made the sacrifice patriotically, "as it is about the most I can manage for my country [so] I am going to do it as cheerfully as may be." A week later she reported how proud Helen's uncle was of the younger generation: he mentioned not only Helen's nursing but also her cousin Kit who was working in France with the YMCA along with family members serving in the military. The uncle used the symbolic parity of men's and women's war work, emphasizing the different but equal contributions of both his nieces and his nephews. Similarly, after a cousin was awarded the Military Cross, Margaret reported to Helen that "Uncle Ted is delighted about Walter's M.X. It *is* nice for them."[7] Walter's high combat honor reflected well not just on him but on the whole family, and was seen as a family achievement in addition to a personal one. The medal was a public acknowledgment of Walter's appropriate response to the war, since only a soldier could earn it. Both men and women who were fulfilling their obligations to the nation in wartime reflected positively on their parents.

Ideas about gender, however, frequently broke down the seeming comparability of men's and women's war work. The opposition between serving the family and serving the nation was one of the key points of conflict.

---

[6] Daisy Beale to Helen Beale, August 13, 1915; William Beale to Helen Beale, August 15, 1915; Sybil Field to Helen Beale, November 7, 1915; Elsie Field to Helen Beale, December 22, 1915; Winifred Beale to Helen Beale, August 19, 1915: BP.

[7] Dorothy Brown to Helen Beale, October 6, [1915]; Margaret A. Beale to Helen Beale, August 15, [1915]; Margaret A. Beale to Helen Beale, August 22, [1915]; Margaret A. Beale to Helen Beale, June 11, [1918]: BP.

This tension was best illustrated late in 1915, when Helen Beale had to decide whether to commit herself to an additional six months' service overseas. VADs sent to France served a probationary month, after which they were committed for six months if their work was satisfactory. At the end of that original obligation, they were asked to renew their contracts in six-month increments. If a VAD stayed at a military hospital, then often the leave she was technically due at the end of the first contract was delayed, as trained nurses had higher priority and all leave was regularly stopped for military reasons. Beale arrived in France in August, and by December the family was already debating whether she should stay on.

She described conflicted feelings about the best thing to do, making it clear that she wanted to see her family again, but also expressing strong convictions about service during the war. "One must do something to help along a little tiny bit over this beastly war," she maintained, "so if I did give this up I suppose after a bit I should have to be after some other job." She already had, however, what she (and many other people) considered the most attractive job: that of a VAD in France. As she explained, "I know and like this one in a good many respects and find it awfully interesting being out here." More than just her preference, she presented the issue of her utility: "one probably must be rather more useful after seven months of it." She confirmed this opinion through an outside authority because "Matron said in answer to one person who asked her whether we were really wanted to stay on that naturally she preferred to have the men handled by people who had been doing it for some time and not by raw new comers." Though her own preferences seemed quite clear, she still concluded that "altogether it is a problem."[8]

Beale presented the decision to stay as the right thing to do for the soldiers in the war, because if "one originally came out to help along and not only to 'see what it's like out here' it looks as though one ought to stay on for a second bit of time even though one might occasionally feel that a break or a change wd. be welcome!"[9] She clearly did not want to be seen as one of the adventure-seeking women sometimes criticized in the press. Because she was unsure of how best to resolve the tension between her preferred service to the nation and her assumed service to her family, she invoked the opinions of those in authority – the matron and trained nurses – in support of her remaining in France. Beale maintained, however, the importance of weighing seriously the needs of her family. Helen asked Maggie to interpret their mother's real opinion, as "that wd. be a real reason to help me settle what's best to do."[10]

[8] Helen Beale to Margaret A. Beale, December 11, 1915: BP.
[9] Helen Beale to Margaret S. Beale, January 10, 1916: BP.
[10] Helen Beale to Margaret S. Beale, January 10, 1916: BP.

In response, Margaret Beale repeatedly reassured her youngest daughter that the decision was her own. For her, both patriotism and her daughter's satisfaction were important. In December Margaret wrote that "you know *how glad* we should all be to have you, but I, at all events, am still more glad when I know that you are doing what you think it is right to do and what makes you happy."[11] She did seem worried that Helen might be working too hard, and that a rest might be in order. After thinking it over and discussing it with Maggie, however, Margaret wrote that "until this war is over I don't believe you would be happy to [stay at home] and I am thankful that I am not at present an invalid or so worn out as to make it the right thing for you to do that."[12] Under these circumstances, ideas about the needs of the nation could take precedence over the regularly perceived needs of the family.

Similarly, Maggie was supportive of her sister staying on in France and thought that nursing close to the front was particularly important work. She argued, however, that Helen should demand some leave before serving her second six months. "I don't think it would be shirking or slacking to do so," Maggie wrote, as "I think it will be quite useful to bring home to the authorities what the conditions of life of a VAD are. She is a person with a home with claims on her, and it is silly of them to ignore it." If Helen could not be guaranteed the opportunity to return to similar work, though, Maggie thought she was better off staying on. She should not risk losing such a desirable post, as she would not be happy working in an auxiliary hospital or doing ancillary work for an organization such as the YMCA. Other types of work, she argued, would be "rather a throwing away of all the knowledge you have acquired."[13]

Helen asked for the support of her brothers, as well. Sam Beale, four years older than Helen and the youngest of the brothers, wrote to her just before the family gathered for Christmas. Helen had an obligation, Sam suggested, and "if you feel you can stand the hard work, and enjoy anyhow most of the work [then] you will probably regret it if you do not sign on." He repeated this idea of responsibility, further emphasizing the sense of national service: "if you can stick it, as you know you can do it, I think you will regret in the future not having done what is so obviously in your hand to do." He acknowledged the competing demands of the family specifically in order to overcome them. His letter went on to reassure

---

[11] Margaret A. Beale to Helen Beale, December 19, [1915]: BP. See also Margaret A. Beale to Helen Beale, November 28, [1915] and December 19, [1915]: BP.
[12] Margaret A. Beale to Helen Beale, January 17, [1916]: BP.
[13] Margaret S. Beale to Helen Beale, January 14, 1916; Margaret S. Beale to Helen Beale, December 22, [1915]: BP.

Helen that their mother was fine and continued to be supportive of her working in France. As he wrote, "I don't think you need worry about Mother...she is more intensely proud to think that all her belongings are doing what they can." Similarly, Jack, the oldest of the Beale brothers at forty-one, told his sister Helen that "the arguments in favour of coming home are very strong but I expect in the end you will decide to stay on." He wrote not just of responsibility but of personal interest, emphasizing the appeal of VAD work overseas, suggesting that "any joy you would be likely to get at home – after a month or six weeks holiday – would be bound to seem rather pallid after active service."[14] Full-time war work was of primary importance; Jack also perceptively noted that it was more satisfying and exciting than staying home.

Only one member of the Beale family was willing to express any opposition to Helen's committing to an additional six months of service in France. Her sister Dorothy, thirty-six in 1915 and the mother of six, wrote that it would be "a great undertaking to sign on again without a good holiday in between." Dorothy was generally less supportive of the work as a necessary contribution to the war, and more put off by the hardships it entailed. As she wrote when Helen went on night duty, "I suppose possibly a sense of virtue and well doing helps but I don't believe that can go far compared to a good night's sleep and the prospect of so many weeks more of it must be oppressive indeed." She was more ready than the rest of the Beale clan to publicly place personal comfort ahead of national service. Dorothy later explained that she did "quite see all [Helen's] arguments and knew [she] would be feeling all that way, which was a good deal why [she] argued so fiercely the other way!" The tone of her letters, however, was quite different from that of the other family members, and revealed the often-overlooked mixed feelings many patriotic English men and women expressed about the war effort.[15] Dorothy would, of course, have expected a man to put up with the difficult circumstances of foreign service without needing a significant break (and without complaint). A woman, and especially one of Helen's (and Dorothy's) social position, however, was accustomed to certain creature comforts. Dorothy did not describe the war as sufficient justification for giving them up for any length of time.

This kind of family involvement in a woman's decision to commit to full-time war work away from home was not unique to Helen Beale,

[14] Sam Beale to Helen Beale, December 21, 1915; John Beale to Helen Beale, January 13, 1915 [sic – actually 1916]: BP. Helen turned thirty while serving in France.

[15] Dorothy Brown to Helen Beale, December 25, [1915], undated [autumn 1915], 9 January [1916], 26 January [1916]: BP.

though her case is the most thoroughly documented in the Beale letters. Other women connected to the clan preferred, at least initially, to avoid any possible separation from family. Sybil Hoare, a friend of the Beales, wrote of her plans to join her sisters with the YMCA at Le Havre. Hoare had been working at an auxiliary hospital in England, but hesitated to commit to nursing overseas. She said she was holding back because "I shouldn't like to leave Mother for so long, three months is bad enough." A cousin, Sybil Field, raised similar concerns. She was also a VAD, nursing in an auxiliary hospital when Helen went overseas. Field was envious of Beale's new position, but she too worried in writing about leaving her parents for such a long time and going somewhere alone. Time and experience made her bolder, however, and that winter Field decided to take an intermediate step, and went to serve in a military hospital in London. There she was living away from her family but still seeing them regularly. Her parents' acquiescence was critical to this decision, however. When she wrote to Helen that "I have at last taken the plunge, and decided to go off for six months somewhere," she explained that she could go to London because "Dad and Mother are willing to let me go." Field's aunt, Helen's mother Margaret, wrote of being "sorry for her parents having to do without her."[16] She herself, of course, was living without Helen. Margaret still had Maggie at home, though, while the Fields were now separated from their only daughter. This was clearly, however, a reciprocal relationship for many women and their parents. Not only were young women of the middle classes generally required to stay at home with their families, but many of them represented this circumstance as highly attractive and not to be given up lightly or easily. The war created opportunities for some women, but others articulated a more challenging sense of obligation.

Being a VAD in a big London military hospital proved to be quite different from work in a Red Cross auxiliary hospital. While adjusting to the changes, Sybil Field talked about her difficulties deciding whether she should apply to go to France, both because the work would be more intense and because the distance from her family would be so much greater. After three months in London, Field wrote to Beale that "for now I feel as if what little proper nursing I knew was all gone, so I oughtn't to try for abroad." She was more conflicted than this suggested, however, as she then immediately continued, "would you advise me to try for France?" The sticking point was not, in fact, about her self-perceived skill level, but

---

[16] Sybil Hoare to Helen Beale, December 6, [1915]; Sybil Field to Helen Beale, November 7, 1915; Sybil Field to Helen Beale, January 7, [1916]; Margaret A. Beale to Helen Beale, February 27, [1916]: BP.

because "as I stand it is possible to get to my folks once a month, whereas once in France there one sticks." Alternatively, Field considered leaving nursing to join the YMCA canteen in France where her cousin Kit Beale worked, as YMCA leave schedules were much more regular than those at military hospitals. Canteen work, however, did not have the cachet of volunteer nursing, and ultimately Field crossed the channel as a VAD. She remained in France, in fact, more or less continuously until after the Armistice.[17] Again, family expectations of an unmarried daughter shifted significantly in the face of wartime commitments.

Helen did indeed decide to remain in France for a second six months. She justified her decision by describing a sense of obligation to the men who had no choices like hers, as well as the idea of parity of service with them. "I can't help all the time feeling that it's a bit faint hearted not to go on when one has the opportunity of being treated just like they treat the male thing," she wrote; "it seems a bit weak somehow to give up and want more holiday and a change when they don't get it or get the chance of it."[18] If men could not go home for an indefinite period merely to see their families or because a break before returning to war service would be pleasant, then Helen Beale argued that she could not either. That rationale was certainly an appropriate justification for continuing where she apparently wanted to be. Similarly, when Sybil Field first decided to offer her services to a military hospital, she wrote to Helen that working part-time in an auxiliary hospital had made her feel "rather as a fit man might feel" who was avoiding combat service. Traditional daughter-at-home responsibilities were compounded by the men's war commitments, but though "it will be very dull for Mother . . . if I were a man I sh[ou]ld have gone long ago." The image Field used resonated sufficiently to Beale that she repeated it in a letter to her sister Maggie a few days later, adding "I know just what she means."[19]

The wartime association between hospital work and army service meant that the family frequently used military imagery to describe women. Helen Beale wrote of the trained civilian nurses who volunteered for the military nursing reserves after the war broke out as "Kitchener's Nurses," just as the men who joined the newly expanding military were "Kitchener's Army." The relationship between the two groups was consistent also. Just as the prewar army regulars considered themselves

[17] Sybil Field to Helen Beale, dated only "Sunday" but probably written in May 1916; Sybil Field to Helen Beale, March 20, 1918: BP.
[18] Helen Beale to Margaret S. Beale, January 10, 1916: BP.
[19] Helen Beale to Margaret A. Beale, December 11, 1915; Margaret A. Beale to Helen Beale, January 17, [1916]; Sybil Field to Helen Beale, January 7, [1916]; Helen Beale to Margaret S. Beale, January 10, 1916: BP.

inherently better than the new volunteer soldiers, Beale explained to her mother that the military nurses "consider themselves a bit superior to the others who are Kitchener's nurses, so to say."[20] There was a certain self-consciousness in the use of this language. When Beale was first nursing in an army hospital in Britain, for example, she wrote to Maggie of gathering her "kit (you see how military I am getting)."[21] Beale's descriptions of being on "active service" in France made explicit comparison to the experiences of soldiers. In her letters, she equated the physical difficulties of nursing in hastily constructed military hospitals with few amenities, and living in tents or drafty huts, with the hardships of life in the army. They were both "active service" in France, even if Etaples was not the front line, and women working in hospitals faced little real fear of death.[22] Though the hospitals lacked the most defining aspect of military active service – the risk of death – the women workers still reveled in the patriotic status that the rough conditions conferred on them.

The hardships were in fact desirable, as they suggested a greater closeness to the men in the trenches. About a month after her arrival at 26 General Hospital in France, Beale had an opportunity to visit another hospital, which had been installed in the Casino at Le Touquet. She found that it was not merely a more elegant structure than the one in which she worked, but also a more completely outfitted facility. She wrote her mother that she preferred the challenges of nursing in huts, however. The Casino "fortunately didn't make me want to leave this and be there." Despite the "charm and magnificence" of Le Touquet, Beale felt that 26 General "is 'active service' and that [other facility] is much more like being in a hospital at home and out of the world and war doings." The Casino was too much like being in England, while "here we really do feel in the thick of things."[23] Beale was not interested in the creature comforts that her sister Dorothy valued so highly. Facing physical hardships put Helen Beale amidst what she called "war doings." Similarly, she described a published account in the *Queen* magazine of a St. John's hospital near her in France. Though Beale said it might be interesting for her family to read the piece, she warned them that its subject

---

[20] Helen Beale to Margaret S. Beale, undated [August 1915]; Helen Beale to Margaret A. Beale, August 25, 1915: BP. In other contexts, as discussed in ch. 2, VADs were often compared to Kitchener's Army as the two amateur groups who volunteered to supplement the professionals.

[21] Helen Beale to Margaret S. Beale, February 10, 1915: BP.

[22] Helen Beale to Margaret S. Beale, November 13, 1915; Helen Beale to Margaret A. Beale, May 4, 1916; Helen Beale to Margaret A. Beale, May 14, 1916: BP.

[23] Helen Beale to Margaret A. Beale, September 17, 1915: BP.

was "far more swanky and less active servicy than we are."[24] The closer
the association to the army, the better.

The Beale family members, male and female, often described war work
by women in these military terms. Bill, in the infantry, advised his cousin
Helen on her arrival in France to "keep on the soft side of the Colour
Sergeant and ginger up the orderlies," as if she were in the army itself.
Helen described her sister-in-law Margaret as being "in the crack Massage
Corps," giving a military form to a civilian occupation. When Helen first
left for France, Jack's wife Daisy referred to her having her "orders";
brother Sam later also referred to Helen being "under orders." Sam,
a restricted civilian worker, was envious of the lack of choice she had.
Being at least representatively in the military, for him, meant "not having
to think whether what you are doing is the best thing to do or not."
His wife Sylvia, who also corresponded with Helen, took the linguistic
and symbolic army parallels yet further. Sylvia thought Helen must feel
gratified to be "the right man in the right place." Helen's niece Peggy
summed up the family support in her response to a school project "to
make sandbags or comforts" for the soldiers. Dorothy reported to Helen
that Peggy was "so proud" to be making something for her aunt in France,
because "it is for a nurse [i.e., VAD] which is just as good as a soldier."[25]
Here, the volunteer was simultaneously conflated with the professional
and equated with the army.

The imagery of parallel service, however, could not live up to the commitment it implied. Ultimately, it was her responsibility to her family that
brought Helen back to England when a soldier could not have returned.
Her mother Margaret became ill, and required surgery in July 1916.
Helen had committed to serve at 26 General until September, and the
family was adamant that Helen should not be worried or come home
early. They told Helen that Margaret was being well cared for, but Sam
did write, "if it is possible to refuse to sign on again, without any appearance of shirking, I think I should."[26] While her mother was still healthy,
Helen preferred to stay on in France, doing work she argued was important. As soon as her mother's health failed, however, her home role
as a care-giving daughter became paramount in her letters. "You see,"

[24] Helen Beale to Margaret S. Beale, November 18, 1915 (section dated November 20):
BP.
[25] Bill Beale to Helen Beale, August 15, 1915; Helen Beale to Margaret A. Beale, March 29,
1916; Daisy Beale to Helen Beale, August 13, 1915; Sam Beale to Helen Beale, undated
[spring 1916], October 21, 1915; Sylvia Beale to Helen Beale, November 7, [1915];
Harold Brown to Helen Beale, October 19, 1915; Dorothy Brown to Helen Beale, undated [early November 1915]: BP.
[26] Margaret S. Beale to Helen Beale, August 25, 1916; Sybil Field to Helen Beale,
March 23, 1919; Sam Beale to Helen Beale, July 26, 1916: BP.

she wrote, "I found after about a week's experience that stopping out here whilst you were not all right and well was just one of the things that couldn't be comfortably done." Patriotism was one thing, and family quite another, as "my staying here has always been contingent on you and Mag taking care of one another and though she is taking care of you I know, I want to come back and take care of her as well."[27] Beale requested permission to return to England a month early because of her mother's condition. This request was denied, however, and she did not arrive in England until September 11, 1916. That was the extent of the control the military organization had over her, however. The appeal of service overseas paled when compared to the needs of her mother.

Helen Beale returned to England in response to her mother's illness, despite her enviable position in France. When Sybil Field, in turn, considered returning home to spend some time with her family, she hesitated. Her mother was still supportive of her continuing the overseas work. At least as important, she wrote, was that she did not "think nursing in England after being out here [in France] [wa]s attractive."[28] France represented the war, the reason for her efforts, and the center of her new life. There was another reason, too, why Field did not want to come home. She wrote to Helen that she was enjoying the work she was doing. Field had been doing responsible nursing work, and she explained that "if I am still in the [operating] theatre, I shan't want to stop at all." Beale's friend and hut-mate in France, Dorothy Pring, described the same preferences. Pring continued to work as a VAD nurse, and late in the war wrote to Helen that "I was sent back to the [operating] theatre to my great joy. We had a wild time for about a fortnight, on duty all day with scarcely time to eat and then on to 11 or 12 o'clock each night." These hours exhilarated her. "Haven't I been lucky to get so much theatre work?," she asked, "I *do* love it so much."[29] Women of their social background might never have discovered that they had an affinity for the graphic medical work of operations. The surgery would also have seemed more interesting and worthwhile than the heavy cleaning and carrying which ward work often entailed. The contrast was even more starkly opposed to the social monotony, if safety, that was the hallmark of the life of the middle-class "daughter at home." It is also evocative of the ways in which many men continued to describe the exhilaration of trench service, even late in the

---

[27] Margaret A. Beale to Helen Beale, April 9, [1916]; Helen Beale to Margaret A. Beale, July 25, 1916: BP.
[28] Sybil Field to Helen Beale, March 20, 1918: BP.
[29] Sybil Field to Helen Beale, March 20, 1918; Dorothy Pring to Helen Beale, November 4, 1918: BP.

war; the graphic reality of warfare and the tragedies of 1916 were not necessarily a turning point in perceptions for either men or women.

The high level of responsibility Sybil Field and Dorothy Pring had was consistent with their location and experience: they had both been working for several years at busy military hospitals in France. Other VADs, of course, were not given such authority. As Field wrote to Helen Beale, "it does make all the difference in life, whether one's [S]ister is nice or not." VADs like Helen Beale sometimes found the rules for the proper running of a ward to be unnecessarily confining. Beale wrote to her mother of the frustrations of cleaning things that never stayed clean for long, and "sometimes it's a bit hard to see the connection between getting your beds all lined up *quite* straight and the corners of the counterpanes all *exactly* square and beating the Kaiser which is what we and the whole hospital are here for really!!" She then added, somewhat dubiously, that "all the same it must be good for the men to have to be so clean and finished in all their ways and methods and surroundings." Beale presented the hospital merely as part of the effort to win the war. For the professional nurses, however, a well-run ward was an end in itself, as well as being part of the treatment process. Yet though the Beale women were critical of the intransigent implementation of these rules, they also recognized adherence to them as the sign of a well-trained nurse. Maggie wrote to Helen about a "new stricter and more dignified" nurse at the Red Cross auxiliary hospital in East Grinstead, but added critically, "she hasn't much method."[30] Without "method," she could not be a good nurse as she must not have been well trained.

The Beale women, like other VADs, discovered that the amount of responsibility they had varied with the location and type of the hospital. Maggie complained about her auxiliary hospital in England that "from the nursing point of view the hospital is a complete frost," as "any intelligent char woman could do all I did." Her self-comparison with the lowest level of domestic servant demonstrated the class issues underlying Maggie's – and many other VADs' – dissatisfaction with the tasks assigned to them in the wards. They were not used to being at the bottom of any social hierarchy, and it did not sit well with them. The lack of responsibility, however, was usefully invoked by some women. Beale's friend Sybil Hoare, for example, wrote that "of course as you say, the work is mild, that is not exciting in any way, but I should hate that form of excitement."[31] Liberty and responsibility could be intimidating, and

---

[30] Sybil Field to Helen Beale, November 7, 1915; Helen Beale to Margaret A. Beale, March 22, 1916; Margaret S. Beale to Helen Beale, October 31, 1917: BP.

[31] Margaret S. Beale to Helen Beale, November 25, 1914; Sybil Hoare to Helen Beale, December 6, [1915]: BP.

by being self-effacing, she could justify her work without contributing to any social upheaval. Work for nursing VADs in the less stressful auxiliary hospitals ranged from cleaning and polishing – Maggie Beale's "brasses" were particularly admired by her night sister at East Grinstead – to changing dressings, applying hot plasters and other "fomentations," and taking temperatures.[32] It was unlikely, however, to become more responsible, as the patients were almost exclusively convalescents who were not in need of serious medical attention. There were almost no grounds to challenge its social acceptability.

Military hospitals in England, primarily located in London, were legendary for the problems between the volunteers and the professionals. Though floods of urgent casualties following major battles like the Somme in July 1916 could force responsibilities onto the volunteers, in normal conditions most trained nurses limited VAD tasks to those traditionally assigned to low-status probationers. These were jobs, for the most part, that the VADs considered more appropriate for the orderlies.[33] While Helen Beale was nursing in a London hospital early in the war, she reported that the Staff Nurse "treats us all as if we were about fifteen [years old] and very foolish and as though we had never done anything of any sort before in our lives . . . I don't think she will teach us very much really except the routine." From the nurse's perspective, these women of leisure might not seem to have accomplished much of significance. A year and a half later, Sybil Field had more serious problems at the 4th London General Hospital. Her staff nurse went beyond "offensive remarks cast out in the heat of the moment" and instead "used to tell the Sister things that weren't true, and talk about us to the men." In contrast, though, she respected her Sister, who was "beginning to unbend now." She was amused by being asked "if one can take a temperature or put on a fomentation etc." Yet given the wide variety of training (or lack thereof) that VADs received, and the highly variable work they did in auxiliary hospitals, it was hardly inappropriate for trained nurses to question the capabilities of individual VADs. It struck Field, however, as being "most particular."[34]

The women of the Beale family (and VADs in general) found the most responsible nursing work in military hospitals in France. This was partly

---

[32] Margaret S. Beale to Helen Beale, May 19, [1916]: BP.

[33] The conflicts between volunteers and professionals described in well-known narratives such as Vera Brittain's *Testament of Youth: An Autobiographical Study of the Years 1900–1925* (New York: Penguin, 1989 [1933]), Enid Bagnold's *A Diary Without Dates* (London: Virago, 1978 [1918]), and Irene Rathbone's *We That Were Young* (New York: The Feminist Press, 1989 [1932]) are almost all in military hospitals in England.

[34] Helen Beale to Margaret S. Beale, October 11, 1914; Sybil Field to Helen Beale, March 24, [1916]: BP.

a function of the exigencies of warfare: the hospitals were often overburdened and there could be little choice other than to allow the volunteers to dress wounds and perform important medical tasks that could not be left undone. It was also a function of time. More of the trained nurses overseas were military nurses and therefore more secure in their position relative to the volunteers. As they got to know the VADs better both individually and as a group, they were more willing to trust them with important work. Thus when Beale first arrived at 26 General Hospital in Etaples, in one of the earlier groups of VADs to arrive in France, she wrote home that she liked her Sister ("a real army one"). She said she was not using any of the nursing skills she had acquired, however. Her tasks consisted primarily of "beds and washings and all the usual things and . . . 'little dog fetch and carry' in the mornings whilst the dressings are being done."[35] Those first weeks and months in France were a necessary period of adaptation on both sides of the training divide. Though Beale described the atmosphere overseas as one more of caution than animosity in her letters home, she was a little more blunt in the diary she began upon arrival in France (it lasted for only one entry). She recorded that the "atmosphere is distinctly chilling; I say we are made to feel rather like pariahs and it is obvious that we are not to forget we are only VADs." There was a distinction, however, between personal and professional identities. "In the ward it is alright though," Beale wrote, "I am merely treated as rather an ineffectual housemaid at present though I do help with the dressings now and then and have been allowed to put on 2 [fomentations]."[36] As the volunteers demonstrated their willingness and usefulness, however, Beale reported home that "though the atmosphere suggests that we are somewhat of interlopers – at meals and so on – I think it is thawing . . . In my ward they are very pleasant and I think appreciative of one's efforts."[37] The breakthrough came in the wards, but by the end of the month relations had warmed enough for the nurses to invite the VADs to an off-hours party.[38]

The nurses, of course, were not the only ones making adjustments. The VADs also found they needed time to accustom themselves to the harder work under more difficult conditions that accompanied hospital life in France. Acknowledging this, Beale wrote home in October 1915 that "a little hard work is excellent for the constitution." Her professed motivation made the challenge worthwhile; if the work were not hard, it

---

[35] Helen Beale to Margaret S. Beale, undated [August 1915]: BP.
[36] Helen Beale to Margaret A. Beale, August 13, 1915; Helen Beale to Margaret S. Beale, undated [August 1915]; Helen Beale journal entry, August 17, [1915] [only entry]: BP.
[37] Helen Beale to Margaret A. Beale, August 18, 1915: BP.
[38] Helen Beale to Margaret A. Beale, August 27, 1915: BP.

would not have been as important. "It is a great time to be out here and a thing to remember for always and I wouldn't be missing it for anything," she told her family, "though it is rather a strain on one's nerves and temper sometimes."[39] The importance of her participation in the war far outweighed the discomforts, and was in fact justified by them. Beale recounted the physical exhaustion that accompanied the emotional strain of ward work overseas. In December she was moved from the surgical wards (where she had been working since she arrived in France) into the medical line. This meant that she was caring for the sick rather than the wounded. She wrote home that it was "really a relief after three and a half months of acute, or more or less acute, surgical cases, to be in a ward where nobody is very bad for a bit." She admitted that "it's been pretty anxious work at times these last two months, more so for us untrained people because one felt so uncertain sometimes whether there was reason to fuss or not." Her lack of knowledge and experience hindered her, as she was "very anxious not to neglect anything, yet one couldn't always be quite certain whether the thing was worth getting the professional eye in to see or not!" Beale described the negotiation of a delicate space between proper patient care and good relations with the trained nurses. The downside of the move to the less exacting ward, however, was that "anyhow now it's more housework that has to be done."[40]

Like most VADs, however, Beale preferred nursing the wounded, who were clearly the victims of the war. The "housework" also had its own share of problems, as Beale found it difficult to keep the ward up to the matron's standards of order and cleanliness. "With one orderly only who has all the fetchings and carryings to do," she told her family how she relied on "a constantly shifting set of convalescent patients to get to do the work." Unfortunately, the men "can't quite see what it matters about the tables and forms and trays all being scrubbed *every* day and the spoons etc kept shiny." Of course, Beale herself initially described similar difficulties comprehending the importance of nursing method. Eventually, however, she adapted to the workload and wrote of almost enjoying the long and tiring night shifts, as they involved more "real nursing" and less housework.[41]

Comfort with the work accompanied improved relations with the hospital staff, but Beale's letters also recounted the antagonism that at times existed between the volunteers and the professionals. When she first

[39] Helen Beale to Margaret A. Beale, October 3, [1915]: BP.
[40] Helen Beale to Margaret A. Beale, December 2, 1915: BP. It is worth noting Beale's usage of the "professional eye," demonstrating the Foucauldian concept of the power of the gaze of the authority figure in determining the patient's condition.
[41] Helen Beale to Margaret A. Beale, December 8, 1915, August 20, 1916: BP.

reported the difficult relations between trained nurses and VADs to her family, her mother responded that she was sure that Helen would "melt the stand off regular nurses." She then asked, "are many of them 'ladies'?"[42] This awareness of class underlay many of the differences in approach between the volunteers and the professionals. Though not all VADs were from socially elite backgrounds like the Beales and the Fields, the majority of them were financially secure or they would not have been in a position to volunteer full-time.[43] Though Sybil Field, after her arrival at the 4th London General Hospital, reported her roommates to be "jolly good sorts, though their speech betrays them," most of the non-professional war workers mentioned in the Beale papers are from more privileged backgrounds. When Helen described her hut-mate in France, Dorothy Pring, she explained that her family "must be very well off for she is used to hunting tremendously and doing all sorts of sporting things evidently." Beale went to school at Roedean, known for providing a somewhat sporting yet solid education to daughters of the elite, and repeatedly commented in her letters home on seeing fellow Old Roedeanians doing war work similar to hers. Beyond schoolmates, she found members of her social circle, like one volunteer nurse who lived near the Beales' London flat. She "knows the Bruces and Morses quite well," Beale wrote to her mother, "I have often met her at dances in 'the old days.'"[44]

The trained nurses, on the other hand, tended to be described in less socially complementary terms, by the Beales as well as by other VADs. Helen wrote to Maggie that the new Sister in her ward was a vast improvement over her predecessor, being a "lively and cheerful little article." She continued, however, that the nurse was "perhaps somewhat 'du peuple' but that is no harm! bonhomie and good temper are much more important than anything else out here." After all, there was a war on. Similarly, a "most oppressive" staff nurse was replaced by "a nice cheery, rather bourgeoise, little party... who generally refers to one as 'dear,' but who is a real good sort and a good worker which just makes

---

[42] Margaret A. Beale to Helen Beale, August 26, [1915]: BP.

[43] Beginning in 1915, VADs nursing full-time in military hospitals were paid a salary approximately half that of the trained nurses. This payment did allow more women to remain in hospitals, but as the vast majority of VADs began work in local, unpaid hospitals, significant self-selection had already occurred.

[44] See Sybil Field to Helen Beale, March 24, [1916]; Helen Beale to Margaret A. Beale, August 27, 1915; Helen Beale to Margaret S. Beale, October 3, 1914; Helen Beale to Margaret A. Beale, September 17, 1915; Helen Beale to Margaret S. Beale, November 25, 1915; Helen Beale to Margaret A. Beale, September 17, 1915, February 23, 1916; Margaret S. Beale to Helen Beale, August 25, 1915; Helen Beale to Margaret A. Beale, December 5, 1918: BP.

all the difference."[45] The tone of the description almost suggests that the nurse was professionally subordinate to Beale, rather than the other way around; the confidence of social status seemed to outweigh professional qualifications. When Beale, on night duty, was having difficulties with her supervising Sister, her mother wrote that she would "like to have the chance of telling [the trained nurse] what's what and how thankful she ought to be to be privileged to have you to help her." Similarly, Dorothy Brown wrote to remind her sister that "when you are not in hospital, you are not a humble little underling at all."[46] Despite the copious propaganda efforts to the contrary, socioeconomic position was far from being sublimated by patriotic commitment, and contributed significantly to the sense of self-worth displayed by so many volunteers. Beyond the social cues coming from home, Helen Beale clearly exhibited the privileges she assumed for herself during her first autumn in France. Most notably, she wore her furs when the temperature began to drop. She wrote to her sister Maggie that "I'm afraid it's thought a little swanky by some but it can't be helped!"[47] Discomfort in the name of the egalitarian hardships of "active service" went only so far.

These tensions between ideas about class and appropriate war work were clear when Helen Beale became an officer in the Women's Royal Naval Service (WRNS) at the start of 1918. The WRNS did not come into being until late in the war, and Beale encountered significant resistance when she decided to leave the Red Cross. The director of her local Voluntary Aid Detachment, Clare Blount, wrote that she understood Helen's frustration with the lack of opportunity for promotion and greater responsibility, typical of the complaints of many VADs. However, she continued, as "you must have gained a great deal of experience . . . it is a pity it should all be wasted and your energies turned in an absolutely new direction."[48] Service in one of the women's auxiliary military organizations did not carry the same automatic social approval as volunteer nursing, and the director exploited these perceptions in her efforts to keep Helen Beale from resigning from the detachment. Blount also sent Beale more strident and explicit criticism from M. Pelham, Red Cross County Director. Pelham, not mincing words, wrote to Blount that "we have no absolute power to prevent Miss H. Beale if she chooses to be so unpatriotic as to go." He belittled her commitment to the war, explaining that

[45] Helen Beale to Margaret S. Beale, October 24, 1915; Helen Beale to Margaret A. Beale, July 11, 1916: BP.
[46] Margaret A. Beale to Helen Beale, October 26, [1915]; Dorothy Brown to Helen Beale, January 9, [1916]; Margaret A. Beale to Helen Beale, January 17, [1916]: BP.
[47] Helen Beale to Margaret S. Beale, November 25, 1915: BP.
[48] Clare Blount to Helen Beale, January 8, 1918: BP.

"I do everything in my power to prevent Nurses leaving for other work as they are so badly wanted and if good nurses it is most undesirable that they should leave for more exciting work perhaps in the 'Wrens' [sic]."[49] Pelham and Blount took advantage of the prevailing popular unease with women in military uniforms in their (unsuccessful) efforts to keep Beale within the folds of the socially secure Red Cross.

Helen Beale crafted her response to these criticisms very carefully, using the officials' own language against them. She disputed that she was "acting unpatriotically or seeking excitement" because she "did not act on impulse but after quietly thinking out how [she] could turn such abilities as [she had] to the best advantage." She had been a VAD for a long time, and "in the 4th year of the war it seems to me one is bound to reconsider one's position and whether the work that one took up as emergency work at the beginning of the war is still the channel where one's abilities can give most in service to the country." Beale was confident that "In my case I am quite sure that it is not so." For years, Helen Beale and other VADs had argued that their experience in hospitals entitled them to greater responsibility in spite of their lack of formal nursing training. To further her new choice of war work, she reversed herself. In her letter, while continuing to assert her commitment to service to the nation, she argued that "I do not believe that 'experience' in nursing can ever take the place of real 'training.'" Agreeing with her former critics, she explained that "therefore I think that it is quite necessary that VADs should always be doing junior work to a certain extent however long their service has been." Beale herself, however, had more to offer, and "when there is a call for women to undertake positions of responsibility in other services and administrations – not in the nursing world – which their experiences and work before the war may have fitted them for and which their life in hospital since the war had greatly added to their experience then it seems to me that undoubtedly they sh[oul]d come forward and leave the ordinary VAD work to the younger members of the Detachment." She maintained that, despite the need for nurses, "it is clearly for each individual to decide for themselves where they can render the best service," and invoked male authority by adding that "my brothers – whose opinion I value much – urged me to undertake this new work."[50] Beale was redefining service for females of her class position by publicly preferring one of the uniformed women's military auxiliaries to volunteer nursing.

[49] Copy of letter from M. Pelham to Clare Blount, undated, enclosed with letter from Clare Blount to Helen Beale, January 8, 1918: BP.
[50] Draft of letter from Helen Beale to Clare Blount, undated: BP.

The Beale women as well as the men supported her change of war work. This general level of approval contrasted to the mainstream of popular wartime opinion of the auxiliary military organizations. The Beales's perspective, however, was rooted in frustration with the treatment VADs working in Britain received at least as much as with any approval of the auxiliary military organizations. Maggie wrote that the change was best for Helen. She added that she had seen that "more VADs are being begged for [but] on the whole I'm not surprised they are short!" Their mother stated supportively, "I am sorry they are trying to make your leaving VAD work difficult, but I am sure you are doing the right thing in taking up this other war work, so don't mind them." Dorothy, too, was sympathetic, and described the new work as "just exactly the right thing" for Helen, adding "what a comfort not to be still washing and shining up etc at the hospital!" Her distaste for manual labor had apparently not decreased with the duration of the war. Helen Beale, because she could not remain in a Voluntary Aid Detachment while she was a member of the Women's Royal Naval Service, was discharged in January 1918, after six and a half years of service. Blount requested that Beale return her badges.[51]

The transition from the VADs to the WRNS was difficult, but not illogical. Precedent had been already set at the highest level. Katharine Furse, the first commandant of the Voluntary Aid Detachments, left that post in 1917 and then took on the organization of the WRNS.[52] Furse looked among the VADs for the first WRNS officers, and Helen Beale was not the only one to make the move. Beale was unwilling to return to France because of the restriction it had placed on her mobility (even during a family crisis) and also because of the highly unreliable leave system. She also described feelings of frustration with the limited responsibility she was given, despite her years of experience, when she returned to nurse in England. In contrast, Beale presented a commission in the WRNS as an opportunity to contribute more significantly and independently to the war effort, with a level of responsibility more consonant with her social

---

[51] Margaret S. Beale to Helen Beale, January 8, 1918; Margaret A. Beale to Helen Beale, January 11, 1918; Dorothy Brown to Helen Beale, March 10, [1918]; Clare Blount to Helen Beale, January 18, 1918: BP.

[52] Clearly a very strong and dynamic woman, Furse also alienated a number of people within the wartime hierarchies. She resigned as a result of a political crisis over reorganization and coordination of women's (non-nursing) auxiliary service organizations, and was replaced at the Voluntary Aid Detachments by Lady Margaret Ampthill. Helen Beale admired Furse greatly, and wrote home after an official inspection that she was "a most wonderful person ... so splendidly big in her outlook and yet very human; as usual she made devoted adherents of all the people who hadn't known her at all before. It does make a big difference to have somebody like that at the head of the show": Helen Beale to Dorothy Brown, 21 April 1919: BP. See also Furse's autobiography, *Hearts and Pomegranates: The Story of Forty-Five Years 1875–1920* (London: Peter Davies, 1940).

position and abilities than hospital work had provided. As Sybil Field (still nursing in France) wrote to her cousin (now with the WRNS at Dover), "I expect you like being your own boss and running the show. Evidently a pleasant change from being a humble VAD."[53]

Not everyone, however, shared this declaration that social status like Helen Beale's matched well with the WRNS. Beale had difficulties finding more women whom she considered appropriate for officer status in the WRNS, difficulties that were closely implicated with perceptions of class, gender, and appropriate war work. Much of the concern was connected with issues of female military uniforms. The problems were exacerbated by the widespread negative reaction to the WAAC, particularly as it was expressed toward the working-class women who filled the "ranks." Helen Beale described much of the furor as ludicrous, even though she and her organization suffered from its ramifications. As she argued in a letter to her sister Dorothy, "the WAACs have made a very bad impression here [in Dover]." This was caused, she posited, by the "inevitable want of imagination and power of change of thought and circumstance which people, as you say, show so much." The blame lay less with the WAACs and more with the civilians, who "think it is dreadful to see girls in khaki walking out with a man." They did not realize, she continued, "until you rub their noses into it, that things must change in the fourth year of a War like this." According to Beale, "a little wholesome walk out together is probably a mutual benefit to both the girl and the man." Beale, in military uniform herself, still maintained that "I don't hold any particular brief for the khaki young woman." She argued, however, for the principle of war service when she wrote "I can't see why it should be considered quite all right for a little fluffy over-dressed female to walk out with a Tommy and not a girl who has deliberately given up the fluffiness."[54] Helen Beale was more ready than were many members of her socioeconomic class both to give women who joined the auxiliary military organizations credit for the work they were doing and also to acknowledge their position relative to their female "civilian" counterparts.

The Beale family seemed to associate Helen's new uniform with the elite traditions of the Royal Navy. Sybil Field wrote to Helen Beale requesting a photograph of her in her "swanky new togs," (figure 4.2), and Dorothy Brown jokingly worried that Helen would "become so imbued with the ways of high naval circles that you will feel the professional classes hardly suitable to know."[55] Beale, however, reported that some of

[53] Sybil Field to Helen Beale, March 20, 1918: BP.
[54] Helen Beale to Dorothy Brown, March 14, 1918: BP.
[55] Helen Beale to Dorothy Brown, February 21, 1918; Sybil Field to Helen Beale, March 20, 1918; Dorothy Brown to Helen Beale, February 28, [1918]: BP.

Figure 4.2 Helen Beale in her WRNS uniform, 1918.

the civilian women already working for the Navy had to be let go, as they refused to join the WRNS "because they don't want to tie themselves [down], or to wear the uniform provided or for some similar reason." The WRNS were also having difficulty finding women interested in being officers, as many women were already committed to other war work by 1918 and "all the superior and high class young women don't want to see themselves in [military] uniform."[56] WRNS officers had the advantage over many other forms of relatively socially acceptable war work, however, of a reasonable salary. As a result, Helen described them overall as "a sporting lot," many of whom "can't afford to be out of a job and very much prefer this present one to teaching or whatever it was that they did before."[57] This was a different population than the one that filled the membership rolls of the VAD.

Response to the new service in the Royal Navy itself was mixed. Beale described some officers as supportive, others as more resistant, but ultimately she said almost all were pleased with the work the WRNS did and were reluctant to lose them after the war. As she wrote to her mother just after the war ended, "the joke is that down here lots of the men in charge of the offices have been groaning at having to have women at all (what is the use of these people etc. etc.!) but when it comes to taking them away, they suddenly seem to become too valuable to part with!" By August 1919, some members of the Navy were lobbying for the continuance of the WRNS as a Reserve. That idea, however, was socially and politically problematic given the number of demobilized men looking for jobs.[58] The WRNS were a creation of the war work movement, and without that justification they were much more culturally problematic.

Returning soldiers were not the only job seekers, of course. The demobilized WRNS from the ranks were also looking for jobs after the war. Following 1918, many of them refused to return to domestic service, creating a new episode in the ongoing saga known as "the servant problem." After the Armistice, Beale repeatedly received requests from people hoping to hire demobilized WRNS. At first, Helen Beale also believed that the end of the war would solve the wartime scarcity of servants. She even wrote to her sister Dorothy that "in a few months' time there will be quite a good supply of girls wanting employment and . . . you'll be able to get maids again pretty easily." By May 1919, however, the supply of returning servants had failed to materialize. Margaret Beale wrote to her

[56] Helen Beale to Margaret A. Beale, February 17, 1918; Helen Beale to Dorothy Brown, March 14, 1918: BP.
[57] Helen Beale to Margaret A. Beale, December 16, 1918: BP.
[58] Helen Beale to Dorothy Brown, February 21, 1918; Helen Beale to Margaret A. Beale, January 21, 1919, August 14, 1919: BP.

daughter asking whether there might be "a kitchen maid for me amongst your staff." The same day, however, Helen reported the shortage to Maggie. Their sister-in-law Daisy, she wrote, "wondered (as a large number of people do, we find) whether we happened to have any demobilized Wrens available for her house-hold!" Helen was forced to tell her that "we haven't any." The situation was little better (from the hiring point of view) in September, when Beale had to tell her sister Amy that she was "very much afraid that [she couldn't] fit her out with any really nice demobilised Wrens suitable for her household." The requests were not just from her family, either. Beale wrote home that "we are having to turn ourselves into a kind of Mrs. Hunt's Registry Office for demobilised Wrens and have calls from distracted and vague officers – evidently put up to it by their wives – anxious to get hold of maids." The reality, though, was that Helen "was afraid [she didn't] know of a single suitable Wren to offer" either to the local ladies or to her family members.[59] Beale did not generally complain of the character of the women working for her and had previously seemed willing to offer references if possible, so her inability to find someone "suitable" must have stemmed from general lack of interest in domestic service rather than any problems with the women themselves.

Throughout the war, the difficulty in finding servants was merely an extension of the middle-class hardships to be tolerated "for the duration." In 1915, Margaret Beale sadly informed Helen of Sylvia's difficulties at home: "her Kate and Mary" were leaving domestic service to become tram conductors. "It seems a pity," she wrote, "but the money tempts them."[60] In this view, when working-class women found jobs that paid better, it reflected not their abilities but their weakness in the face of temptation. Similarly, another of the Beale daughters, Amy Worthington, was looking for new help because her "pretty Elsie and the housemaid both wish to leave to 'better' themselves somehow, which is a nuisance." The mistresses of these households seemed incapable of any empathy or comprehension of their servants' lives. Amy was in for a difficult search, in any case, as it appeared "to be almost impossible to find any but the grandest kind of butler or cook now." Dorothy took her domestic difficulties

[59] Helen Beale to Dorothy Brown, February 23, 1919; Margaret A. Beale to Helen Beale, May 7, [1919]; Helen Beale to Margaret S. Beale, May 7, 1919; Helen Beale to Margaret A. Beale, September 10, 1919, September 18, 1919; Margaret S. Beale to Helen Beale, September 21, 1919; Helen Beale to Dorothy Brown, October 14, 1919: BP.

[60] Margaret A. Beale to Helen Beale, December 27, [1915]: BP. Sylvia herself was a bit more sympathetic to her former employees' position; though she seemed to feel a bit put out that the women were leaving after six years' service with her, she reported to Helen that the wages were very high, which allowed for saving: Sylvia Beale to Helen Beale, December 12, 1915: BP.

the most personally, and wrote irately to Helen that "unluckily domestic troubles are beginning again already." Her "treasure of a . . . maid has
to be replaced, as she wished to go and 'district' nurse." The maid told
Brown she "always had meant to," but "it does not occur to her that
it was hardly fair not to warn me before she came." Apparently Brown
saw domestic service, ideally, as a lifelong commitment. Ironically, she
accused servants of thinking only of their own situations. In Brown's account, the maid was thinking solely of herself, and "she will go exactly
to the month and I shall probably be left with no one judging by other
people's experience."[61] For Brown, the needs of her family outweighed
any personal rights or professional interests on the part of her servants.

When it came to domestic help, patriotism could serve as either a hin-
drance or a justification from the middle-class perspective, depending on
the circumstances. Mason, the head gardener at Standen, was canvassed
as part of the Derby scheme of semi-voluntary conscription.[62] Margaret
Beale wrote to Helen that she didn't think he was a man "who ought to
go." She then clarified, "at least I don't want [him] to." This was because "I can't think how we are to get along without Mason." Earlier
that autumn, however, the departure of a less essential male employee –
the butler – had provided an opportunity for economy. "Wise is going
to make munitions!" Margaret wrote to Helen, "When I asked him if he
did not think he ought to do something for the war I found he had been
thinking of it and was quite ready to go." She felt gratified that "if he
succeeds in getting a job it is an easy way for me to economise." His departure for the factories was therefore presented as a double contribution
to the war effort – his and hers. Other domestic departures were more
problematic. Grace, a maid frequently mentioned in the correspondence
because she sewed much of Helen's kit for hospital service in France,
said she would leave if her wages were not raised. Maggie decided to let
her go rather than pay her more. At least as important, though, was that
"Mother and I don't see being dictated to." The issue was clearly not just
financial but also rooted in social relations between the classes. By her
next letter, Maggie was considering not replacing Grace when she left.
It would be a war economy: "we now wonder, in view of Sir Aukland

---

[61] Margaret A. Beale to Helen Beale, February 6, [1916], February 27, [1916]; Dorothy
Brown to Helen Beale, September 3, [1916]: BP.

[62] Lord Derby's scheme was an intermediate step between an all-volunteer army and the
institution of conscription. The government took the impetus to contact men of service-
able age to ask them to "attest" their willingness to serve, if called up; if they agreed,
then they were assigned a priority and inevitably called up for some sort of service. They
could refuse, but that required a positive action, rather than the passive refusal of not
going to a recruiting office. The plan was not particularly successful, and was followed
fairly rapidly by the implementation of conscription.

Geddes' announcement about 3 maids being enough for all, whether we ought to engage another maid [or not]! 9 for two sounds shocking!" She was, however, still planning on filling Grace's last days with the family sewing, asking Helen if there was anything she "badly want[ed] done."[63]

Dorothy Brown also took the approach of economizing on servants as her contribution to the war effort. Astoundingly, she had briefly (while discussing making carpet slippers for convalescents) proposed going into a factory to make munitions. She postponed any active plan until the winter curtains were done, however. Dorothy then decided that cutting back on one servant was the best solution for her, as "my metier is at home." As she explained it, "I would much sooner do housework than war work." Brown was less sympathetic to, though amused by, her daughter Dolly's war economy proposal. Dolly was reported as having told her mother, "You talk about saving money Mummy and then you waste it sending me to school where I learn only what I knew before." "All the same," Dorothy continued to her mother, "the school seems quite a success."[64] The carpet slippers Dorothy proposed along with the household economies were typical of war work for married women with children. Here, as elsewhere, the Beale clan were no exception. Amy Worthington sewed clothing and blankets for Belgian hospitals and for convalescent camps in Brittany and Normandy. Sylvia Beale worked at the new Hospital Supply Depot near her, making swabs, bandages, and other hospital necessities. She retained a sense of humor through the work, laughing at "the laboriously careful way we are taught to make them (the big [swabs] took fully 10 minutes each) when one thinks how many are got through in a day in hospital!"[65] Part-time work also left more control with the worker herself. Though unmarried, Maggie Beale was primarily responsible for the care of her mother and for running the household at Standen. She had much more power to set her nursing hours at the local auxiliary hospital than Helen would have dreamed of in a military hospital. Maggie also appreciated being profusely thanked for her contribution, particularly for the tiring night work.[66] Daisy Moss, a friend of Helen Beale's, "adopted" a POW after VAD nursing proved too hard for her; Sybil Field did as well.[67]

---

[63] Margaret A. Beale to Helen Beale, November 2, [1915], September 30, [1915]; Margaret S. Beale to Helen Beale, October 5, 1917, October 10, 1917: BP.

[64] Dorothy Brown to Helen Beale, September 24, [1915], October 6, [1915], March 24, [1916]; Margaret A. Beale to Helen Beale, October 26, [1915]: BP.

[65] Amy Worthington to Helen Beale, November 21, [1915?]; Sylvia Beale to Helen Beale, November 7, [1915]: BP.

[66] "There is nothing like making a fuss!," Maggie wrote to her sister: Margaret S. Beale to Helen Beale, May 3, [1916]: BP.

[67] Daisy Moss to Helen Beale, January 3, 1916; Sybil Field to Helen Beale, November 7, 1915: BP.

Margaret Beale sent packages to an enlisted POW, who came to see her and thank her personally after his release. After meeting him, Mrs. Beale sent him to have tea with the maids.[68] Her real contribution to the war effort though, she told Helen, was "as the mother of so many hard workers for their country."[69] She was content with their reflected glory.

Cutting back on a servant or two (where convenient) was an important "war economy" that the Beales considered necessary not merely for the war effort itself, but also to model patriotic behavior for others. This was a function of their position in the social hierarchy of their community. Maggie was particularly concerned with this, and wrote to Helen that, though "all classes ought to save," the elite had a special obligation. "We," Maggie wrote, need to be an "example to the working classes." On their own, "we are such a drop in the ocean now we hardly count, but the working classes as a whole are rolling in money, and according to their custom spending as fast as they get it." Beyond her questionable economics, workers were again condemned for the money they earned, because they did not use it in ways the financially elite saw as appropriate. "One can hardly persuade these people voluntarily to save," Maggie wrote, "when for the first time in their lives they are pretty well off! They don't see the necessity." The undercurrent of the social threat represented by a financially independent working class is vividly clear in this imagery. For the sake of example, Maggie wanted "to stitch a label" on her coat to say "this fur is 22 *yrs* old!" It was, of course, still a fur, a luxury beyond the reach of many people. She was concerned with more than mere example, however, and also organized economy cookery classes in town. Unfortunately, she reported, "none of the labouring class attend."[70] Class-based proselytizing, however well intentioned, was apparently not appreciated.

As an unmarried adult daughter of a certain social position, Maggie Beale was well established in charitable works of this nature. She had been particularly active in infant welfare work before 1914. The war was a high priority for her, however, and she adapted her interests to the exigencies of wartime. Beale became particularly interested in the "Fight for Right" society, headed by Gilbert Murray, Sir Henry Newbolt, Sir Francis Younghusband and Robert Bridges, which was "meant to bind together all non-combatants into a kind of army, to inspire and encourage and organise war work all over the country." Again, calling the workers an "army" – and thus comparing them implicitly to soldiers – legitimized wartime efforts on behalf of the nation. Helen was interested in the group

---

[68] Margaret A. Beale to Helen Beale, February 19, [1919]: BP.
[69] Margaret A. Beale to Helen Beale, July 26, [1918]: BP.
[70] Margaret S. Beale to Helen Beale, November 14, 1915: BP.

also, and wished one of the organizers could speak at her hospital in France. She hoped it would "shake us up and remind everybody that their own particular little nut and grievance or job etc. isn't all that important" because "it's awfully hard to keep on reminding yourself!" Helen Beale "couldn't help asking one little person who was feeling dreadfully ill-used and sorry for herself at lunch the other day all because her particular friend couldn't get her time off to match her own whether she knew that there was a big war on!" This service-oriented approach was successful: "she took it very nicely I must say and didn't make any more fuss."[71] Beale invoked the popular idea of self-sacrifice on behalf of the war effort to influence the behavior of her coworkers.

Neither Helen nor Maggie Beale showed much patience with people or organizations who seemed to be putting personal or political goals higher on their agenda than the war effort. This condemnation definitely included any groups that actively continued to advocate for women's suffrage. The Beales had little sympathy generally with the suffrage movement – Helen referred to *The Englishwoman* as "a suffrage publication [that] contains the usual sentimental and unconvincing sort of stuff" – but were particularly irritated by efforts on behalf of the female franchise while the war was going on.[72] Maggie related, with some glee, the story of a clash between the East Grinstead Women's Suffrage Society and the local War Work Association. "Wouldn't you have thought the War would have taught the EG suffrage folk not to be petty," she asked, "and to put national needs before Women's political rights?" She then proceeded to recount the misadventures of the suffrage society at a recent fundraising event:

Well they snubbed [the War Work Association] when they thought [the] scheme would fail, and now it is succeeding they come, hat in hand, to offer to join. So for the recent Red [Cross] Day's excitement they were asked to take charge of the sale of fruit cakes, jams etc. wh[ich] was part of the programme . . . If you please they shut the door between themselves and the other half where the other activities were on post and then stuck up their old Suffrage emblems all over the walls. Don't you call it mean? Now they have sent a pompous and obscure message to say they will co-operate with the War Work Ass[ociation] if "they may keep their individuality."[73]

Helen responded that she was "so amused to hear about the EG Suffrage ladies and the War Work Assoc." She argued they were missing the point of a country at war: "How childish they are to be sure – what wd their

[71] Margaret S. Beale to Helen Beale, February 2, 1916; Helen Beale to Margaret S. Beale, February 28, 1916: BP.

[72] Helen Beale to Margaret S. Beale, August 25, 1916: BP.

[73] Margaret S. Beale to Helen Beale, October 23, 1915: BP.

'individuality' be to them if Kaiser Bill was to be top dog I should like to know." The conflict between the groups continued, apparently. The following month Maggie expressed exasperation after the suffrage group complained that they had not been mentioned by name in the press accounts of the Red Cross Day events, and requested an immediate correction. The War Work Association replied with a certain smugness that the absence was not an oversight, as "the number of helpers [was] too great to make it possible to name them all." Maggie concluded, "I do not fancy they care for cooperation that is not well advertised in the local press!"[74]

The passage of partial suffrage for women in early 1918 was clearly not a significant event in the lives of the Beale women. Helen wrote to Maggie with some irritation that priorities still needed to be maintained. "I can't quite see what real good the Society for Propagating Knowledge of Politics for Ladies is going to do," she complained. "Let's win the war first say I." Maggie, though sharing some of Helen's concerns, attended a Women's Citizens Association Meeting. She did not find it useful, however, as it consisted of "endless speeches, to no particular point except jubilation over the Vote and the necessity for women caring about public things."[75] She continued to attend their meetings but discovered that the organizers were more enthusiastic than informed. Maggie, one of the less active-minded members, was the only one who knew that women had been eligible for election to local councils for some time.[76]

Though unsure about the place of women in politics, the Beales never publicly wavered about the place of men in war. Maggie Beale supported the Derby scheme of semi-voluntary conscription in principle, and wrote to Helen that its approach of "compulsion by consent" seemed to her "the only cheery circumstance."[77] She later asked "why can't they bring in universal service tomorrow?"[78] Their brother Sam also supported the Derby scheme, but a bit more cynically. He wrote to Helen that "Lord Derby's scheme strikes me as awfully good." He liked the plan because

[74] Helen Beale to Margaret S. Beale, October 29, 1915; Margaret S. Beale to Helen Beale, November 22, [1915]: BP.

[75] Helen Beale to Margaret S. Beale, February 25, 1918; Margaret S. Beale to Helen Beale, March 15, [1918]: BP.

[76] "Finally we decided on a study circle to try and inform ourselves more accurately": Margaret S. Beale to Helen Beale, December 11, [1918]: BP.

[77] Margaret S. Beale to Helen Beale, October 23, 1915: BP.

[78] In the same letter she also recounted her irritation with their driver and his wife "about their son. Kit [Beale, whose brother Bill had recently been killed] quite innocently said the severest things about those who don't go to fight, but shelter behind the ones who have more pluck, as she was being driven from the station. I was so pleased": Margaret S. Beale to Helen Beale, March 29, 1916: BP.

"as far as I can make out it is National Service less the legal compulsion, and illegal compulsion should be nearly as strong." He tapped the core of English liberalism when he argued that "as it is called voluntary everybody is pleased as can be, and will be able to say I told you so whatever happens."[79]

It seemed obvious to the Beales that young men should be fighting, and Sydney Beale and the unmarried male Beale cousins were all in the military. The crisis in the family came over whether Dorothy's husband Harold Brown, a father of four and well past the first bloom of youth, should attest his willingness to serve in the army under the Derby scheme. To the dismay of much of the family, Brown was seriously talking of attesting, as it was referred to.[80] Margaret Beale wrote to Helen that Brown had received a letter about the scheme at the same time as the gardener Mason. As with Mason, Mrs. Beale did not think that he "ought to go." She explained that "it will be wretched if [Harold] goes as a soldier, but he is very anxious to be doing something." Popular pressure for men to join the army could be incredibly strong, and Harold was not immune to the many messages that bombarded him in the press and on the streets. He was clearly conflicted about what he ought to do. He had been working nights on an anti-aircraft gun, but had been forced to stop because the authorities had "taken away our gun as being no good and they shew us no signs of giving us another." He had more time in bed now but perhaps no more sleep, as he argued that he "ought to be up and doing something." The uncertainty of his position seemed particularly troubling. As he told Helen, "I do wish the Government would back up and say whether they are going to call out all the men they want compulsorily." Compulsion would take the burden of decision off his shoulders, of course. A few weeks later he was still sounding uncomfortable with his home comforts (which, as Helen so well knew, were not consonant with ideas about "active service"). He wrote to his sister-in-law that he was "still off duty and . . . feeling that it is about time [he] got something to do again."[81]

Harold's wife Dorothy, in contrast, knew her mind. She certainly did not want him to leave, and made her feelings quite clear on the subject (as she had on the topic of Helen's staying on in France for an additional

---

[79] Sam Beale to Helen Beale, October 21, 1915: BP.

[80] For more on these social pressures, see Nicoletta F. Gullace, *"The Blood of Our Sons": Men, Women, and the Renegotiation of British Citizenship During the Great War* (New York: Palgrave Macmillan, 2002), especially ch. 5, "Conscription, Conscience, and the Travails of Male Citizenship."

[81] Margaret A. Beale to Helen Beale, November 2, [1915]; Harold Brown to Helen Beale, October 4, 1915, October 19, 1915: BP.

six months). Dorothy wrote to her youngest sister about the issue at some length, explaining that

[Harold] can't make up his mind what he ought to do now in the way of war work and has got the enlisting fever very badly. I don't think it will really come to that, as in his saner moments he feels it is more just what he would like at the moment than a really patriotic duty. The alternative seems to be shutting up the office and going into the Munitions office... I hate the idea of Harold doing it too, as I know how worried he will get and overdone and also there is the money question. I know he will be awfully sorry not to send the boys to public schools, but I don't see how we can... don't think I am worried about money matters though, because I am not in the slightest.[82]

Dorothy invoked the specter of jeopardizing the class status of their sons by denying them the education that was the hallmark of their social position. She did this in order to overcome the power of "patriotic" motivation when it seemed contrary to the interests of her family. In November, Harold was appointed to the Munitions Control Board. Maggie may have spoken for the family when she told Helen that she "hope[d] it [would] square his conscience as to enlisting."[83]

It seemed for a time that it had. Dorothy reported to Helen that "'enlisting' does not seem imminent at the moment and Harold is really very busy... really I think he is waiting to see the result of Lord D's campaign." More than that, she admitted that "also there has been somewhat of an outcry from a good many people at the idea of his going." Dorothy's concerns were persuasive, and she reported with relief to Helen that Harold had ultimately decided not to attest. "It was my doing as he was on the point of going yesterday," she wrote, "but I only hope it was right." Though she was primarily concerned with the well-being of their family, Dorothy still claimed "that he can do more for the country, as things are at present, out than in." Validating her own perspective by bringing in support from other people, she explained that "everyone he consulted said the same." Patriotic obligation was powerful, however, and "all the same his conscience would have made him if I had not urged him not to." Harold himself wrote to tell Helen of the great debates "as to whether I was or was not to become a Derby recruit." He explained with clear frustration that "it ended at the twelfth hour in my not joining although I am not at all sure that I ought not to have done so. Anyway it is settled now for better or worse but I find I get more and more restless all the time to be doing something a little more obviously useful than what I

[82] Dorothy Brown to Helen Beale, October 22, [1915]: BP.
[83] Margaret S. Beale to Helen Beale, November 22, [1915]: BP.

am doing."[84] He had difficulty justifying his sense of national obligation with his family responsibilities.

It was not the end of the story, however. Harold Brown, along with much of the rest of the eligible population, was offered a second chance to attest under the Derby scheme early in 1916. Dorothy still argued that he should not make himself available for enlistment, as did Maggie. Their brother Jack, though, thought it was the right thing for Harold to do, especially as in all likelihood he would not have to fight. After all the debates, Harold Brown attested to his willingness to serve his country under Lord Derby's enlistment scheme in January 1916. Dorothy wrote resignedly to Helen that she would "be amused that Harold ha[d] attested after all . . . when there was a chance of doing it again – he felt so bad at not having done it when the fatal day was passed." She still maintained that "of course the arguments against it remain just as strong as ever," but they were not sufficient. "Any way," she concluded, "he feels contented for the moment."[85]

Jack, however, and perhaps also Harold, understood the politics of the Derby Scheme correctly. Dorothy was extremely relieved in March when Harold was given a war badge and letter of exemption from active service "in the interests of the prosecution of the war." She told Helen that

Harold is very scoffing over it himself and says oh well it will postpone his going for a bit, but he thinks every blessed one will have to go before very long. Anyway as I point out to him it does not now rest with him, as if he did go in to the army he would only be commandeered at once for office work and he may just as well be doing that independently and making a little money for the community and incidentally his family at the same time.[86]

Harold ended up with the best of both worlds of obligation. He was safe at home with his family, but he also satisfied social demands. He responded to the wartime call for all men who could to join the military, the only acceptable form of service.

Though she argued strongly and worked hard to keep Harold away from active service, Dorothy was less tolerant of younger men who faced the front with anything less than enthusiasm. Her own husband was presented as an exception to the popular imagery of military service. Like most of her fellow citizens, though, she was stingy with any other aberrations. A cousin serving in the infantry, Walter Field, had been wounded in

---

[84] Dorothy Brown to Helen Beale, November 25, [1915], December 12, [1915]; Harold Brown to Helen Beale, December 17, 1915: BP.

[85] Margaret S. Beale to Helen Beale, January 20, 1916; Dorothy Brown to Helen Beale, January 26, 1916: BP.

[86] Dorothy Brown to Helen Beale, March 24, [1916]: BP.

battle. In December 1915, following his convalescence, he wrote to Helen Beale that he was "pretty nearly certain to be passed fit again" for active service. He thought he would not be sent out to France for some months, though, for which he was "not really very sorry," though he was bored. By February he had been approved and expected to leave for France within a couple of months. Dorothy Brown heard how depressed he was at the idea, as he had just lost his last good friend, reported missing. Her response to this was quite unsympathetic, especially given her recent efforts to keep her husband away from the front. She explained to Helen that "I hate to hear of them depressed at having to go, don't you? I met a young sub[altern] the other day, who said they had a grand time and he *did* enjoy it and he was in trenches only a few yards off the Germ[an]s." The eager soldier was a former master at her sons' school, and she found it "quite refreshing to hear anyone so enthusiastic."[87] Brown, like many civilians, needed soldiers to seem happy about their patriotic sacrifices. Action alone was insufficient; motivation and attitude, for men as well as for women, were key to the public portrait of the true patriot in wartime.

Helen Beale's response to Walter Field's impending return to France is lost, but she was certainly concerned in 1918 when another of the cousins, Sydney Field, was passed fit for active service again. Beale wrote that she was sorry to hear of it, as "it is perfect madness for him to go to the Front again." She was also "ever so sorry" to hear that the former family gardener Mason was wounded, but "one can't help feeling that he is lucky to have been able to get back to the base and the comparative comforts of hospital." Similarly, she felt that her brother Sydney Beale's situation was almost ideal: "quite well enough to be able to enjoy himself in a mild way and yet not so well that he could think of going back to Active Service yet . . . just the right sort of state to be in."[88] The years of conflict and her work in the wards had taken their toll on her expressions of war enthusiasm. Though still committed to the idea of service where possible, she was willing to consider "acceptable" ways to avoid actual combat, at least for members of her family and community.

Helen Beale had evidence of the costs of war from her family as well as from her work. Walter Field was not the only member of the clan to be depressed by his combat experience. Mark Field wrote to Beale after their cousin Bill was killed in action in early 1916. Mark Field, serving in the artillery, called the infantry the "suicide club," and wished for the peaceful laziness of prewar life, or at least home leave. He condemned and

[87] Walter Field to Helen Beale, December 20, 1915; Dorothy Brown to Helen Beale, February 9, [1916]: BP.

[88] Helen Beale to Margaret A. Beale, February 23, 1918, April 11, 1918, July 21, 1918: BP.

defended the war simultaneously, summarizing the ambiguous feelings of those who felt the general obligation of service to the nation at the same time as the emotional and physical drain of combat. He wrote that "the whole thing is so stupid – waste of lives, time, material and money all for practically nothing. Still we have them beat I have no doubt though the process is evil."[89] A necessary evil, he might have continued.

Field wrote to Beale that he "should hate to be killed as [he] enjoy[ed] life pretty well." He also wrote, "how young we shall all have to be after the war to hide our grey hairs shan't we, those of us who come thro'." His military service fundamentally changed the way he presented himself and his society. Some of the women in the family also found their lives changed in the postwar world. Maggie Beale, despite her resistance to the enthusiasms of the East Grinstead suffrage workers, found herself politically active on local committees. This was a new extension to the social welfare work with which she had been long involved. Sybil Field, after nursing on in France after the Armistice, decided to take some time off, at least until the autumn. Though she had thrived on the novelty of the work opportunities the war offered her, she slipped comfortably back into the prewar patterns that she had initially found so difficult to leave. As she wrote to her cousin Helen, "I'm doing such housekeeping as is necessary with our very able cook, looking after Mother, going on little walks, gardening when fine, and quite an amount of sewing, the regular daughter at home touch." Sybil Hoare, however, though originally even more leery of change, wrote differently about her demobilization. She told Maggie that she was "contemplating a trip to Ceylon, (just for fun with a friend)." With the war over, she described herself as needing something more to do than the home activities that had previously filled her life. Kit Beale deferred her return home to a house that was emptier since her brother's death in action. Instead, she continued her YMCA canteen work in Germany when the British army deployed there following the Armistice. Similarly, a friend of Helen Beale's from the WRNS was unsure about what she would do next, but insisted she "must do something or life will be so very empty."[90]

Helen Beale was not herself demobilized from the WRNS until almost a year after the war ended, as she was responsible for breaking up her unit. She returned to Standen, and was active in the organization of the Girl Guides. Following the deaths of her mother and her sister Maggie, she ran the large property at Standen alone until her own death in 1972.

[89] Mark Field to Helen Beale, April 4, 1916: BP.
[90] Mark Field to Helen Beale, April 4, 1916; Sybil Field to Helen Beale, March 23, 1919; Margaret S. Beale to Helen Beale, February 23, 1919; Q.S. [signed only with initials] to Helen Beale, dated January 5, 1918 [sic – actually 1919]: BP.

Family and service both remained central to her life. Her mother had once written her, "you do have varied experiences. I think some day when the war is over you must turn your letters into a book."[91] They were put away, though, and not rediscovered for more than seventy years. Now, they provide an invaluable opportunity for the interpretation of war work, as looked at through upper-middle class eyes. The Beales were articulate and prolific. They were also a close-knit family whose very respect for each other's opinions led to this wealth of materials. Through the letters of the members of the clan – particularly those of Margaret, Maggie, and Helen Beale – we can see how ideas of service to the country were important to both men and women of the leisured classes. The family did not universally apply this ideology to other members of the society, however, excluding trained nurses and domestic servants, for example. Ideas about gender were critical in how the Beales viewed the roles of men and women in wartime, but class was inextricable and just as important. Through one family, we see the nation at war.

[91] Margaret A. Beale to Helen Beale, February 22, [1918]: BP.

Part II

Memory and the war

5   The soldier's story: publishing and the postwar years

When *The Letters of Charles Sorley* was published, Orlo Williams wrote anonymously in the *Times Literary Supplement* that "on reading the title of this book many people, we fear, will exclaim with dismay, 'Another long book about a young hero-poet!'"[1] To modern readers, familiar with the better-known war texts of Robert Graves and Siegfried Sassoon, Edmund Blunden and Wilfred Owen, and even Rupert Brooke, Williams's concern resonates. Sorley's letters, however, were published in 1919, before any of those men other than Brooke were famous, and long before Graves's and Blunden's memoirs, Sassoon's prose texts, or the widespread publication of Owen's poetry. Already, too, in 1920, a review of Captain Wedgwood Benn's memoir, *In the Side Shows: Observations by a Flier on Five Fronts*, asked rhetorically, "who was not long ago surfeited with stories from the front?"[2] The same journal, later that year, referred to "the colossal pile of 'war-books'" already published.[3] Despite their abundance, however, these are not the books of the Great War which have proved the most culturally durable. Though the poetry of the war that was canonized in the anthologies dates almost exclusively from the war years themselves, the prose – both fiction and memoir – came a decade and more later, primarily in the period from 1927 to 1931. This was when Erich Maria Remarque and Edmund Blunden, Richard Aldington and Ernest Hemingway, and especially Robert Graves and Siegfried Sassoon published the texts that were hailed by some as "the truth about the war." At the same time, other people vehemently criticized the vivid pictures these writers drew and the meaning they seemed to imply.[4] These writers were at the center of what was perceived at the time to be a great debate over how books should

---

[1] [Orlo Williams,] "Charles Sorley," *Times Literary Supplement* (hereafter *TLS*), December 11, 1919, p. 726.
[2] "Politics and Economics," *London Mercury*, 1, 3 (January 1920), p. 353.
[3] "History and Biography," *London Mercury*, 1, 5 (March 1920), p. 606.
[4] For another perspective on the "war books controversy," see Samuel Hynes, *A War Imagined: The First World War and English Culture* (London: The Bodley Head, 1990), ch. 21, "The War Becomes Myth," pp. 423–463.

represent the war; this was, fundamentally, a contest about what the war itself meant. In 1914–1918, you were recognized in many social venues as a worthy (if not necessarily equal) participant in the war – whether you were a soldier, a VAD, a munitions worker, or a bandage roller. By the twentieth anniversary of the beginning of the conflict, however, the popular definition of culturally legitimate war experience had narrowed to that of the soldier in the trenches: young junior officers or possibly men in the ranks, preferably serving in France or Belgium, and almost certainly disillusioned. What might be called the "soldier's story" of the war had been created in memory, and had significantly hushed – though never entirely silenced – alternative views.

The 1920s, of course, were in many ways a difficult time in Britain. The promised "homes fit for heroes" failed to materialize, and though the average standard of living for those with jobs actually rose slightly, this was more than counterbalanced by the rising unemployment rate, particularly noticeable to society among returning veterans. Unemployment stood in the vicinity of 10 percent throughout the 1920s, rising to 16 percent in 1930 and 20 percent in the three following years, as the international economic situation further deteriorated.[5] John Maynard Keynes had added to the awareness of a burden by teaching the nation about the economic consequences of the peace on top of the price of war.[6] The war was a subtext to society; as Eric Leed has argued, this was when it was "framed, institutionalized, given ideological content, and relived in political action as well as fiction."[7] Literature was an essential part of this process; when, as Alison Light has shown, "readers could see themselves in an embattled and defended relation to the lost past but also, increasingly to the urgencies of the present. Such a cultural identity prided itself on being disenfranchised and dispossessed."[8] It was only the difficulties of the 1920s and after that created the disillusioned look back at war; it was not, for most people, a product of the war years themselves.

It was in 1928 that the floodgates opened and books about the war became all the rage. Edmund Blunden's *Undertones of War* was widely acclaimed for its new perspective. It was followed in relatively short order by soon-to-be-canonical texts like Robert Graves's *Good-bye to All That*,

---

[5] See Peter Clarke, *Hope and Glory: Britain 1900–1990* (London: Penguin, 1996), especially pp. 128–134, 146, 152.

[6] As Hynes argued, "Keynes offered his readers not only statistics but visions – of a stable prewar world that had been lost, and of a postwar world that was threatened and uncertain, and these visions surely contributed to the way in which Englishmen imagined their world – their history, and their immediate reality": *War Imagined*, p. 292.

[7] Eric Leed, *No Man's Land: Combat and Identity in World War I* (Cambridge: Cambridge University Press, 1979), p. xi.

[8] Alison Light, *Forever England: Femininity, Literature, and Conservatism Between the Wars* (London: Routledge, 1991), p. 47.

Siegfried Sassoou's Sherston trilogy, and the English translation of Erich Maria Remarque's *All Quiet on the Western Front*. There was also a plethora of lesser-known, less literary memoirs and novels. This abundence followed a number of years when publishers had been reluctant to take on titles about the war, though a few had appeared and some had even done very well. The new books, though, were acclaimed for offering a different perspective on the war and its effects on the men who had fought: the elusive "truth." Yet the disillusioned perspective discussed widely in the reviews is intriguing, both because it does not always seem to apply to the books it was attached to, and because it was not, in fact, entirely new. Its themes appeared in some ways throughout the decade; though, as close comparison reveals, much of the kind of disillusionment presented by the best-known authors was a postwar construct. These books were much more about life after the war than about the war itself. They were part of the construction of memory, not experience.

To assess the contest, I focus here on the publishing revolution of ten to fifteen years after the Armistice, when the war became not just a permitted topic after a decade of silence but an almost incessant one. Publishing – and in turn reviewing – were generally on the increase, and literary criticism was considered by many to be as much a site for political and personal battles as for formal evaluation.[9] Book reviews illuminate how war books were popularly received throughout the period, and editorial comments reveal changing British attitudes toward the war that had been fought and won, but at a heavy price. During what was known at the time as the "war books controversy," these conflicting visions – soon to be unified in a new history of the war – became particularly clear.

The steady trickle of silence

The "silence" of the 1920s on the subject of disillusionment has been frequently averred. Samuel Hynes declared that "for a period of nearly a decade, there was a curious imaginative silence about the greatest occurrence of recent history."[10] Modris Ecksteins claimed that "the war was buried" and that "few tackled the issue directly" until Remarque's huge

---

[9] D. L. LeMahieu identifies this as a period of "staggering increase in cultural supply": LeMahieu, *A Culture for Democracy: Mass Communication and the Cultivated Mind in Britain Between the Wars* (Oxford: Clarendon, 1988), especially pp. 130, 319–320, 332–333.

[10] Hynes, *War Imagined*, p. 423. Hynes maintained that "the silence is not merely an historian's after-the-fact creation: writers noticed it at the time, and speculated on its causes." The evidence he offers in support of this claim, however, is drawn either from the beginning of the decade (H. M. Tomlinson writing in 1920) or the end, during the flood (Eric Partridge in 1930 and the Annual Register in 1929) rather than during the "silence" itself.

success changed the literary landscape entirely.[11] Similarly, Robert Wohl wrote that though "the war poets had provided the theme [of] doomed youth led blindly to the slaughter by a cruel age," still "a decade passed before this theme was developed in prose in a systematic or sustained fashion."[12] In fact, however, the texts of disillusionment – and their critics – came steadily throughout the 1920s, though certainly not in as great a number as at the end of the decade. They did not capture much popular attention, though, making it much easier for them to be overlooked retrospectively.[13] The situation was not significantly different in 1921 than in 1928, at the beginning of the new flood: a few personal narratives, critical of the war and telling painful stories of horrors and disillusionment, appeared at both times. It was what came next that was so remarkable: the first period led to an ongoing trickle of stories of the war, and the second opened the floodgates of literary output and popular readership, and effectively rewrote the generally accepted history – and memory – of the war years themselves.

Novels and memoirs, in small but clearly noticeable numbers, began to be critical of the war soon after the Armistice. More than that, reviewers often responded to them as if the ideas of disillusionment they presented were deplorable but not entirely new or surprising. They were still very much a minority view, however, and they failed to trigger a more general cultural response, despite their visibility in the literary community. In the spring of 1921, Jeffery E. Jeffery's *Side Issues* appeared, for example. A collection of short stories alleged to be of greater interest for their content than their literary polish, "the ugliness of war and the injustices that accompany demobilization are set out with considerable effect and an evident attempt at fairness, though with a tendency toward rhetoric." H. O. Lee, writing anonymously in the *Times Literary Supplement*, continued that, though the case was perhaps overstated, Jeffery "is dealing with evils which are known to exist."[14] The reviewer in the *London Mercury* had less patience with Jeffery's perspective. Though he felt the collection deserved praise for being "well worth reading as an example of the feelings inspired in the young by the war and after, especially after," its technical shortcomings were a function of its very nature. The stories "are the fruit of bitter reflection," but instead of that being a positive attribute

---

[11] Modris Ecksteins, *Rites of Spring: The Great War and the Birth of the Modern Age* (New York: Doubleday, 1989), pp. 254–255.

[12] Robert Wohl, *The Generation of 1914* (Cambridge, MA: Harvard University Press, 1979), p. 105.

[13] For more on the literature of this period, see Rosa Maria Bracco, *Merchants of Hope: British Middlebrow Writers and the First World War, 1919–1939* (Oxford: Berg, 1993).

[14] [H. O. Lee,] "Side Issues," *TLS*, April 15, 1920, p. 242.

as it would seem later in the decade, "the author is still too near his own bitterness to work with the perfect freedom of an artist."[15] The reviewer was much more concerned with the lack of literary sophistication – with Jeffery's failures as an artist – than with the impact of their content, or their comment on the war just past.

An equally critical book provoked a more heated response. In 1914–1918, Neville Lytton served in the trenches, as a press censor, and with the General Staff. In 1921, he published his memoir of the war years as an indictment of almost everything he described. Reviewers felt that Lytton deserved praise because of his wartime commitment to allowing journalists access to truthful accounts of developments at the front, and especially for "such splendid attention to the 'real scouts' – the officers and men who stuck it in the trenches or the air, with unconquerable bravery or intelligent skill." This approval resonated of wartime attitudes, with their glorification of the common participant, doing his bit as only a Briton could to bring victory. In contrast, however, "it is to be regretted that he has joined the ranks of those who use their pens to air their personal grievances against their senior officers." Lytton, in fact, was "frank to the verge of ferocity in all his criticisms…As a censor of the Press he may have been successful; but as a censor of his own pages," the reviewer wrote, he was "deplorable." The clearest example was that "his attack upon his brigade commander" was "outrageous."[16] Other reviewers were less concerned with these issues of honor and also less surprised by Lytton's conclusions. Though an interesting book that was especially enlightening on the subject of the relations between propaganda, accuracy, and the press, it was otherwise a "rather belated book of reminiscences" – the war had been over for more than two years, after all. It told "the old familiar tale of mud and blood and bugs and rats, of heroism and funk and boredom, of 'strafing' colonels and stupid generals, and all the rest that it was our lot to endure or to read about for four-and-a-half years."[17] Clearly, as early as 1921 readers of a reasonably traditional (though new) literary journal like J. C. Squire's *London Mercury* – itself no proponent of modernism – were well informed about the basic conditions of trench warfare. The "mud and blood and bugs and rats" were known, but had not yet acquired the symbolic power with which they would later be imbued.

A review in 1922 of C. E. Montague's *Disenchantment* offers an argument for this paradox of awareness and interest. Its title clearly suggests it

[15] "Fiction," *London Mercury*, 2, 8 (June 1920), p. 237.

[16] [Cecil Headlam,] "The Press and the General Staff," *TLS*, April 28, 1921, p. 267.

[17] C. M. Lloyd, "Politics and Economics," *London Mercury*, 4, 22 (August 1921), p. 448.

as a forerunner of the soldier's story, and one reviewer at least pointed out that it did "not belie its title." Orlo Williams, writing anonymously in the *Times Literary Supplement*, offered that though "there is truth enough" in the book, he was "uncertain whether the digestion of these gloomy pages will be of great benefit to anybody." It was not a case of new information, for Montague "tells – what everybody knows – of incompetence and corruption in authority... of the hopelessly impersonal aspect of huge modern armies which destroys the ideal of a 'band of brothers,'... of the long, ghastly tedium which trench warfare involved, and of the death of the first dashing spirit in a fog of weariness and suspicion." The problem lay not in the war but in Montague himself; Williams wrote that "those who go so obviously to war in the spirit of romance are certain to suffer these disenchantments." Williams himself was a veteran but not of the trenches – he served as a major in the Middle East before finishing up in the War Office. His views had political undertones as well. Conservatives like Williams, as they anticipated the end of coalition government, were appropriating part of the new story of war emerging and using it to blame the declining Liberals. Montague had been a regular contributor to the *Manchester Guardian* for years, and the text of his book initially appeared there as a series of essays. Williams therefore used his review of the text to offer a political jibe. He presented a new perspective where initial realism protected soldiers – good soldiers and good men – from unnecessary and harmful disillusionment. If your expectations were appropriate from the beginning, and you "went to fight with loathing" but a knowledge of the necessity which impelled you, then you "were not so surprised."[18] This was the same idea Williams had used to praise Charles Sorley, the "young hero-poet," more than two years before. Sorley "felt, as thousands did, that the war itself was unmitigated evil, but that England was in it to ward off a greater evil." The fact that war was hell was not enough to condemn it. It was hell indeed, as anyone should know – Sorley's "whole soul revolted against war as such," which Williams found "not surprising" – but hell with a worthwhile purpose. Perhaps as important, "this feeling did not prevent [Sorley] from becoming a thorough soldier."[19]

Williams continued in this vein in his review of H. M. Tomlinson's *Waiting for Daylight*. He called the essays "stanzas in a complaint which is not now uncommon," and compared it directly to Montague's *Disenchantment*. Williams argued that the two books shared a "theme upon which so many attractive variations can be composed," and defined

---

[18] [Orlo Williams,] "Disenchantment," *TLS*, February 16, 1922, p. 106. Cyril Falls later offered a similar but more personally kind criticism: Falls, *War Books: A Critical Guide* (London: Peter Davies, 1930), p. 218.

[19] [Williams,] "Sorley," p. 726.

it: "the world by its own stupidity was plunged into dark night, and ... it is a long time waiting for the dawn." Again, Williams did not present the detailed knowledge of wartime conditions as anything new. Instead, he disagreed with Tomlinson's interpretation of their significance. "No reasonable person will assert that there is no ground for this complaint," the review continued, "but there will be many – even of those who suffered at heart as deeply as Mr. Tomlinson – who will refuse to admit that it is the only reasonable attitude." Williams went on to strike at what would be the heart of many of the future soldiers' stories (like Siegfried Sassoon's, for example), which were to draw much of their power from the contrast between prewar and postwar society (and blame the change on the war). "It will occur to [many] to ask," wrote Williams, "whether, after all, the world was so wonderful in July, 1914, that it can appear a kind of Arcadia in retrospect, and whether these lamentations do not lay an excessive emphasis on a horror that was transitory, though bad enough." Yes, the war was horrible, and it "tore these thoughtful, poetical souls unkindly from their roots, and groans not unnaturally went up." Williams reminded his readers, though, that "the five years of devastation were but a twinkle in eternity."[20]

Williams's final complaint was one that resonated throughout reviews of war books for the next decade. "Controversy is a good thing," he wrote, "but no man, least of all a contemplative man, is right to suppose that his particular discontents are universal. That our author takes his readers' attitude too much for granted is our chief criticism." As he concluded, "there are other points of view."[21] Superior ones, too, he was clearly implying, and politically wiser ones, as well. In a later review of Oliver Onions's *Peace in Our Time*, an uneven novel about the difficulties many soldiers faced trying to become members of postwar society, Williams expressed somewhat flippant concern that "readers of another nation would only too readily put down a part of [the protagonist's] misfortunes to certain radical defects in the British character on which Mr. Onions dwells a little too charitably."[22] This, too, foreshadowed much of the debate over the soldier's story of horror and disillusionment that would become so dominant. If things were so awful on the British side, the reviewers would ask, how did we ever win the war? If they were so awful on the German side – and several German novels were key to what came to be called the "war books controversy" – then why did it take four and a half years to beat them? Finally, these reviewers asked, how could

---

[20] [Orlo Williams,] "Waiting for Daylight," *TLS*, April 6, 1922, p. 225.
[21] [Williams,] "Waiting for Daylight," p. 225.
[22] [Orlo Williams,] "Peace in Our Time," *TLS*, October 25, 1923, p. 706.

undervaluing either the German challenge or British accomplishment be good for postwar society at home or abroad?

In contrast, texts that used literary skill and emotional power to approach the war more conventionally were likely to earn uniform praise from reviewers. In 1923 Rudyard Kipling came out with *The Irish Guards in the Great War*, his account of the regiment in which his son served and was killed. Both author and text garnered acclaim. "The true gold of Mr. Kipling is to be found unalloyed in this memorial to the Irish Guards; in erecting it he has erected his own," the *Times Literary Supplement* offered, "and he has sacrificed to his theme all his own prepossessions, as the Guardsmen whom he describes sacrificed themselves to their regiment." In doing so, Kipling told "the story of the war in the West."[23] Kenneth Pickhorn went even further in the *London Mercury*, claiming that Kipling had done a better job of capturing the realities of trench warfare than had any writer who had actually experienced it. Its success lay not just in "the effectiveness of the big scenes" but also in "the exactness of the proportion between battles and trench-holding and billets, between horror and endurance and cheerfulness." This issue of balance would also be at the heart of the war books controversy, as critics accused writers of focusing only on the horrible, compressing events that had in reality been interrupted and spread out in order to achieve a more powerful indictment of the war and its conditions. For Pickhorn in 1924, however, Kipling's book was "unsurpassed" as "a reproduction of the great experience of this generation."[24]

In any case, it still seemed (to critics as well as the broader public) like the wrong time to conclude the issue of how to represent – and therefore remember – the war. A novel based in the war, like Edith Wharton's *A Son at the Front*, could be simultaneously perceived as too early and too late, though reviewers seemed to agree that further time for retrospection would be necessary for a final judgment. Marjorie Grant Cook, in her anonymous review in the *Times Literary Supplement*, wrote that "a war novel may be thought dull, unnecessary at this time; but the pendulum swings back; and when the world is better adjusted this book will be seen to have its permanent value among the minor documents of the war." Though "it would seem inopportune to most writers to bring out a war book at this date," she was glad that "an artist" like Wharton had, and "no one can regret that she has done so."[25] She was wrong, though,

---

[23] [E. E. Mavrogordato,] "Mr. Kipling and the Irish Guards," *TLS*, April 19, 1923, p. 265. Mavrogordato (1870–1946), himself too old to have served in the war, was a barrister and wrote regularly for the *TLS* and on tennis and winter sports for *The Times*.

[24] Kenneth Pickhorn, "History," *London Mercury*, 10, 59 (September 1924), p. 558.

[25] [Marjorie Grant Cook,] "A Son at the Front," *TLS*, September 20, 1923, p. 618.

as apparently J. B. Priestley could. Though Wharton was "an admirable craftsman," and the book "well-planned and well-constructed and quietly and effectively written," it was still unsatisfying. "Perhaps it has arrived at the wrong moment," Priestley suggested, "and been produced either too late in the day or too early . . . pathos of this kind now seems a somewhat cheap trick." He felt the book was caught in a vacuum in the middle of something. Its topic "might have made for journalistic fiction a few years ago, and might make good social historical fiction some years hence; but to most of us at the moment it seems a blighting subject." Priestley was willing to concede that his was not the final word, however, though he was overly pessimistic about how long reevaluation of the war would take. "It is, however, much too early to pass a confident judgment on such a story as this," he wrote, "and if ten or twenty years of this peace leaves any of us alive, it will be interesting to see how it reads after that interval."[26] The moment for evaluating the war had apparently not yet arrived, and those authors who tried to do so had a hard time finding an interested audience.

Priestley was not long in changing his mind about the appropriateness of war novels in the mid-1920s, however. Just a few months later, Priestley wrote that Patrick Miller's *The Natural Man* was "the first war story I have read for some time," suggesting perhaps that he already felt that true "war stories" only concerned combat, and perhaps were only written by men.[27] The diversity of war experiences that had been supported during the 1914–1918 period was, literarily, on its narrowing way down to the trench. Priestly recounted the history of books about the war, from "patriotic rant" and "glorious adventure" on to "disillusion" where "sensitive young men [were] . . . plunged into mud and blood; and the army in actual combat was shown to be nothing but obscenity and slaughter, and out of it nothing but a stupid farce." This view – which sounds very much like the version that entered popular culture for good a few years later – was now in the past for the Priestley of 1924, as "Truth as usual waited for the noise and dust to subside before she made her

---

26 J. B. Priestley, "Fiction," *London Mercury*, 9, 49 (November 1923), pp. 102–103; Priestley's own writing career did not become successful until 1929, with the publication of *The Good Companions*.

27 Reviewers were often critical of war books by women, especially when they were concerned with soldiers and combat. When gender was masked, however, as with *The Victors*, by "Peter Deane" (Pamela Hinkson), they could receive more supportive reviews. See, for example, [Cecil Headlam,] "Down and Out," *TLS*, June 4, 1925, p. 378; and Falls, *War Books*, p. 270. Eric Partridge's positive notice even argued, with dramatic irony, that the book "exhibit[s] a rare and manly pity": Partridge, "The War Continues," *Window*, 1, 2 (April 1930), p. 72. See also Hugh Cecil's discussion of Deane in *The Flower of Battle: How Britain Wrote the Great War* (South Royalton, VT: Steerforth Press, 1996), pp. 315–341.

appearance," but "she shows her hand in this new book." It was not "*the* war story," however, as it separated its protagonist from "any kind of background of normal relationships and interests." So the public still had to wait for the Holy Grail of war book reviewers, "the story that will show both in conjunction, war experience and normal relationships and interests or at least the memory of them." Miller had, however, written "the war itself, actual experience at the front, presented vividly and realistically, made into a solid reality."[28]

Priestly was not alone in representing the evolution of war books as one away from disillusionment and toward truth, as exemplified by *The Natural Man*. Edgell Rickword, writing anonymously in the *Times Literary Supplement*, offered substantially the same view. Rickword was a political radical, who himself had served on the Western front and written anti-war poetry. "During the war and for some time afterwards," he wrote, "most of the best war books were, intentionally or not, propaganda for pacifism." They focused on "the shrinking of the sensitive mind from such an unexampled spectacle of horror." Miller, in contrast, "gives us a very fine study of the fighting man from a point of view which, though not all-embracing, comes nearer to the whole truth of war psychology than the cries of indignation and pain which were the first to reach expression."[29] According to the reviewers, then, "disillusionment" as a means of remembering the war had come early and already gone by 1924. In fact, of course, it was just about to come into its own.

The floodgates of controversy: drowning opposition

"It is curious to reflect that until about a couple of years ago," Cyril Falls wrote late in 1927, "readers treated books of personal memoirs of the war with some impatience and declared that the time for them was past." Now, however, he saw "an undoubted revival of interest in books of this character."[30] The floodgates of the "war books boom" – which developed into the "war books controversy" – were opening. The story of disillusionment had clearly been present for some time. Now, however, it would catch a new generation of readers and convince them, despite a hurricane of debate, of the significance of the war. The Great War was a great tragedy, all agreed, as everyone also agreed that it was important. Now, however, that relevance would come to rest not in potential political stability or economic safeguards, both of which many citizens of Britain were getting tired of waiting for or else were losing faith in. Instead, what

[28] J. B. Priestley, "Fiction," *London Mercury*, 10, 59 (September 1924), p. 540.
[29] [Edgell Rickword,] "The Natural Man," *TLS*, August 7, 1924, p. 488.
[30] [Cyril Falls,] "Two War Books," *TLS*, November 3, 1927, p. 776.

seemed to matter was the price paid by the individual young men who fought in the war and were wasted (either physically or psychologically) without purpose, by leaders who should have (or perhaps did) know better. The war was culturally important, now, not for what it had achieved, but for what it had cost. Resistance to this perspective of betrayal and disenchantment was vociferous but ultimately overwhelmed. The soldier's story became entrenched.

Things began quietly enough. An early review of Siegfried Sassoon's *Memoirs of a Fox-Hunting Man*, though extremely positive, did not even mention that the final section of the book was devoted to Sherston's early war service in France.[31] This seems remarkable in retrospect, as the contrast between the pastoral fox-hunting days and the horrors of the trench is now considered the heart of the novel. In fact, the review was not placed with other new fiction, much less other war books, but appeared next to a piece on E. W. Hendy's *The Lure of Bird Watching*, further emphasizing the focus on the pastoral. Another review only referred to the wartime section in order to compare Sassoon to Proust; a tea-dixie at the front served as Sherston's madeleine.[32] The subsequent trade edition quoted reviews from *The Observer, The Times, The Sunday Times*, the *London Mercury*, and Bohun Lynch in *Britannica*, none of which mentioned the war at all. The dust jacket notes only mentioned the "social revolution" that had taken place in England because of the war. A special limited edition of 300 copies only the next year, however, made the contrast explicit. William Nicholson's illustration for the front cover showed a chair with a hunting jacket draped over the back, and top hat, hunting breeches, two-tone boots and hunting stick all clearly visible. On the back cover, the image was repeated but the clothing had changed. Now an army jacket hung on the chair, joined by an officer's hat and boots, and a rifle leaned in place of the hunting stick (figures 5.1, 5.2). The fox hunter had become the soldier; now the book really was about the war.

As this evolution in packaging showed, things heated up quickly. Between the end of 1928 and late 1930, a new battle over the war was waged: the battle over representation and memory. Books about the war came fast and furious, and were often reviewed in groups. They were considered not just as individual texts, but as they related to each other (and to history). Much of the controversy was centered on British books: Edmund Blunden's *Undertones of War* (1928), Siegfried Sassoon's *Memoirs of a Fox-Hunting Man* (1928) and *Memoirs of an Infantry Officer* (1930), Robert

---

[31] [Cyril Falls,] "Memoirs of a Fox-Hunting Man," *TLS*, October 11, 1928, p. 727.
[32] J. M. Murry, "Memoirs of a Fox-Hunting Man," *New Adelphi*, 2, 3 (March–May 1929), pp. 261–262.

Figure 5.1 William Nicholson's front cover taken from the illustrated edition of Siegfried Sassoon's *Memoirs of a Fox-Hunting Man*.

Figure 5.2 William Nicholson's back cover taken from the illustrated edition of Siegfried Sassoon's *Memoirs of a Fox-Hunting Man.*

Graves's *Good-bye To All That* (1929), R. C. Sherriff's play, *Journey's End* (1929). Two American books were also important: E. E. Cummings's *The Enormous Room* (1928) and Ernest Hemingway's *A Farewell to Arms* (1929). German books, however, in many ways served as the trigger to the controversy, and much critical attention was centered not just on Erich Maria Remarque's *All Quiet on the Western Front* (1928) but also on Arnold Zweig's *The Case of Sergeant Grischa* (1928).

Zweig's novel appeared in English translation in 1928, and was immediately acclaimed. The "Sergeant Grischa" of the novel was an escaped Russian prisoner of war, who stole the papers of a deserter, was caught, and condemned to death in the deserter's place. Though his true identity was revealed, the Germans executed him nonetheless, as an example. J. C. Squire called it "the best war-novel which has yet appeared in any country."[33] Edward Shanks, a poet and literary critic who served in the infantry in 1914–1915 before being invalided out, went cautiously further, suggesting that if the projected sequels were as good, "Herr Zweig will have written the best war novel since Tolstoy."[34] Another reviewer thought it was "not only in itself an unusually good novel," but "also that extremely rare thing, a good war-novel; in fact, the one good war-novel that has ever come the reporter's way."[35] For Cyril Falls, it was "probably one of the ten best war-novels."[36]

Many of the now-canonical texts, too, were widely praised soon after they first appeared. The books seem to have been open to a broad variety of interpretations, and reviewers on both sides of the breaking controversy often liked them.[37] Few notices, for example, had anything but appreciation for Edmund Blunden's *Undertones of War*. It appeared just as the rush of war books was beginning, and, along with *All Quiet*, seemed to trigger the debate over how the war should be talked about. As one of the first of these new books, reviewers discussed how it was different from books that had come earlier. H. M. Tomlinson, echoing Blunden's own preface, declared that it was a book "by a ghost for other ghosts," so that "some readers will not know what it is all about; they will say so, not being ghosts, and seeing none."[38] This focus on a special,

---

[33] J. C. Squire, "Editorial Notes," *London Mercury*, 19, 110 (December 1928), p. 115.

[34] Edward Shanks, "Fiction," *London Mercury*, 19, 110 (December 1928), p. 208. See also Shanks, "Sergeant Grischa," *TLS*, December 6, 1928, p. 963. Shanks served in the 8th South Lancashires. He finished the war working in the War Office.

[35] Reader Reports, *Life & Letters*, 2, 10 (March 1929), p. 236.

[36] Falls, *War Books*, p. 303.

[37] This is, perhaps, a sign of the "conservative embracing of modernity" Light identifies in the interwar years: *Forever England*, especially pp. 10–11, 214–215.

[38] H. M. Tomlinson, "Undertones," *New Adelphi*, 2, 3 (March–May 1929), pp. 258–260. Tomlinson included, unchanged, several paragraphs of this review in "War Books," *Criterion*, 9, 36 (April 1930), pp. 415–416.

otherwise incomprehensible knowledge, only achieved by direct personal
experience, came for some to be the true test of the quality of the books,
and one of the hallmarks of the war book controversy. Whose truth should
be offered? Who was qualified to judge? Most reviewers were willing to
agree that Edmund Blunden, for one, was. J. C. Squire wrote that *Undertones* was "at once poetical and profoundly realistic in detail," and that it
"brings back the infantry man's war so vividly that it is difficult for the
reader to believe that he does not share each one of Mr. Blunden's memories." He concluded, "it is a masterpiece."[39] In a rather lonely dissent,
Henry Williamson wished the book had more "realism," as he termed it.
"Mr. Blunden writes with restraint," he wrote, "which is a necessary attitude for an artist; but too much restraint...may result in sterilization."
Williamson wanted from Blunden what Squire maintained he already
had: "the complaint, based upon desire, that persisted through two readings of this book was that all should have been recreated, so that a youth
reading might experience *exactly* what Second-Lieutenant Blunden experienced at the time." That was, however, "much to ask for; it is all;
a god-like task of creating." Though he wanted more from it, however,
Williamson concluded that "Mr. Blunden shows signs of the power one
longs to encounter in books, and finds so rarely."[40] Cyril Falls echoed the
general perception, however, when he wrote of the "beauty and pathos"
of *Undertones of War*, and declared that "it is probably the only single book
of its kind we have had in English which really reaches the stature of its
subject."[41] Similarly, Eric Partridge felt that it "is certainly the best of all
poets' records of the War," though it "has captured rather the pathos and
desolation of war than its futility and tragedy."[42] He also called it one of
the best "personal accounts" of the war.[43] With even less equivocation,
another reviewer called it "the most moving of English books of front-line
reminiscences."[44]

Robert Graves, too, came in for a fair share of praise (though not from
Blunden or Sassoon). The power and appeal of *Good-bye to All That* were
not based on strict veracity, and Graves himself soon admitted to over-
dramatizing and exaggeration (and scholars and veterans have both been
pulling his stories apart ever since). Some of the praise, therefore, seems

---

[39] J. C. Squire, "Editorial Notes," *London Mercury*, 19, 110 (December 1928), p. 115.
Squire himself did not serve in France.

[40] Henry Williamson, "Reality in War Literature," *London Mercury*, 19, 111 (January
1929), pp. 300–302.

[41] Falls, *War Books*, pp. 182–183.

[42] Eric Partridge, "The War Comes into Its Own," *Window*, 1, 1 (January 1930), p. 93.

[43] Partridge, "War Continues," p. 63.

[44] "The Garlands Wither," *TLS*, June 12, 1930, p. 485.

quite remarkable, as when Bonamy Dobree wrote of the "sort of objective vision, which Mr. Graves almost achieves." Dobree called the memoir "a declaration of courage," and thought it was "balanced," though he found "now and again . . . a touch of satire." (Many readers would consider that an understatement.) He was particularly pleased with Graves's general pro-militarism, which most reviewers overlooked by concentrating on the indictment of the Great War in particular. Dobree himself was a product of the Royal Military Academy at Woolwich, and had served as a regular officer in the Royal Field Artillery from 1910 to 1913. He rejoined the army in 1914, served in France and Palestine, and was Mentioned in Despatches before going on to a peacetime academic career in English literature. Dobree called Graves's memoir "partly a tribute to the Royal Welch, one of which that regiment may be proud," and was pleased that the author "did not despise the parade ground; for . . . he knew . . . that musketry drill is no mere bee in the regular's bonnet." The book, thus, was "a courageous appeal to his generation to put the past behind it and to go forward sadder but still hopeful, as individuals who have cast off cant."[45] It is hard to recognize in this review the book that would become one of the cornerstones of the soldier's story of disillusionment.

Cyril Falls, a military historian who was twice Mentioned in Despatches but spent much of his war service behind the front lines with the General Staff or as liaison to the French, also commented on Graves's admiration for the regimental system. He wrote that "his War scenes have been justly acclaimed to be excellent; they are, in fact, among the few in books of this nature which are of real historical value." For Falls, though, the memoir was more complicated, and more problematic. Graves's "attitude," he wrote, "leaves a disagreeable impression. One might gather that thousands of men instead of a few hundred were executed, and that suicides were as common as blackberries. He is, in short, another example of the 'intellectual' whose intelligence with regard to the War penetrates a much shorter distance than that of the plain man."[46]

This debate over who was best qualified to recapture the "experience" of the war – or over whose account was most universal, perhaps – ran throughout the controversy. When Cyril Falls praised Charles Douie's reminiscence, *The Weary Road*, for its positive portrayal of the capacity

[45] [Bonamy Dobree,] "An Autobiography," *TLS*, November 28, 1929, p. 991.
[46] Falls, *War Books*, p. 202. Falls was clearly uncomfortable with extremes; it is perhaps a telling detail that at the start of the Second World War, Falls and his sister wrote to *The Times* asking for more columns by "Mrs. Miniver" (the persona adopted by Jan Struther), as she would offer "the golden mean which provides the only true content . . . [and] we should also be assured on seeing her name in the headlines that we were to be neither harrowed, lectured, exhorted, nor repressed." See Light, *Forever England*, pp. 114–115.

and actions of British soldiers, he admitted that Douie could "not speak for the British soldier." Instead, Falls called him "a very fair spokesman of the young, well-educated temporary officer, though not of the type which Mr. Kipling calls the 'brittle intellectual.'"[47] This debate about the role of the man of thoughts, letters, and perhaps poetry, and his qualifications for representing anything typical, came up repeatedly. When Falls reviewed the anthology *Everyman at War* anonymously, he wrote that the narratives were "not the reminiscences of professional writers or men of any one type, class, or military calling... They *are* the war... almost all have the stamp of reality and hardly one has the air of exaggeration."[48] He made this point more explicitly in his own *War Books* bibliography. There, he declared that "the narrators are in no case professional writers, and, though some (but by no means all) lack literary skill, they are far more representative of the British Army, Navy, and Air Force, than any professional writer with his overcharged sensibilities and his inevitable reaction to literary influences and conventions."[49] Similarly, another reviewer declared that "the professional man of letters, with his acute sensibilities, is in many respects a bad witness to the effects of war upon his fellowmen." This was because "he does not seem able to assume the protection of that extra skin which, just as the hands of a manual worker grow callous to meet the wear of his toil, saved the majority of men from the worst anguish." He, too, contrasted the "professional writers" who had written "most of the gloomiest books" with the "unskilled contributors" to *Everyman at War*, who "bear their sufferings with far less complaint."[50] To be overly literary, in this view, was to be overly sensitive, and therefore blinded to a larger-scale accurate portrayal of the war.

Sometimes national prejudice was revealed in critical opinions. Cummings and Hemingway stimulated mixed responses, some of which seemed to be based in their American citizenship. Cyril Falls, for example, indicted *A Farewell to Arms* primarily because its protagonist failed to live up to standards of honorable behavior. He referred to "its 'hero'" as someone who "engages in conversations on various subjects with Italian officers, seduces an English girl serving as a nurse, and leaves his post to assist at the birth of her still-born baby and her death a little later." Falls dismissed the novel's importance entirely by concluding that he

---

[47] [Cyril Falls,] "A Symposium on War," *TLS*, November 21, 1929, p. 938.
[48] [Cyril Falls,] "Everyman at War," *TLS*, May 8, 1930, p. 382.
[49] Falls, *War Books*, p. 225.
[50] "Garlands," *TLS*, p. 486. (This anonymous reviewer has not been publicly identified. It is, however, unlikely to have been Falls, as his pieces were clearly marked in the TLS records. As war books by men were almost universally reviewed by men, I use masculine pronouns for convenience.)

"may well have misrepresented it," as he "found it quite impossible to finish."[51] Douglas Jerrold criticized the protagonist even more, as

> it is impossible to write of him with reasonable restraint. A man who breaks his engagements, deserts at the height of battle, and aids and abets the desertion with him of a nurse whom he has seduced, would on any reading not be a man I should care to meet except in circumstances which allowed me to say what I thought about him. When we add that this unspeakable cad is not a combat officer but an ambulance driver whose sole duty is to relieve suffering there is no more to say . . . To write his story without conveying or even hinting at any trace of weakness in his character, or any trace of wrong thinking in his philosophy, is, however, to write a lie, to sin against the Holy Ghost, and between those who cannot realise it and those who cannot do anything else there is a gulf not to be bridged.[52]

The war, for Jerrold, had clearly not changed or threatened his system of values; that it might have done so for anyone else was therefore apparently beyond his comprehension. Hemingway failed because he was not supporting the traditional English order of values.

The most violently divided opinion, however, was reserved for the German Erich Maria Remarque.[53] Desmond McCarthy claimed that "the great majority of those who have read *All Quiet on the Western Front* have regarded it as a most salutary book, strengthening aversion from war, [but] others have suspected the author of a desire to exploit horrors for their own sake."[54] Both these perspectives were clearly represented in book reviews. Herbert Read wrote that *All Quiet* "cannot be read for pleasure; it is terrible, almost unendurable, in its realism and pathos . . . it is the first completely satisfying expression in literature of the greatest event of our time." He called it "the greatest of all war books," and validated it – as others would condemn it – by the tests of personal history. "I have discussed it with men of all degrees, especially with those whose experience of the war was as complete as that of the author," he wrote; "I have tested it against my own memories; and always my conviction remains firm."[55] Those memories were extensive; Read was an officer with the Yorkshire Regiment in Belgium and France, was awarded both the Military Cross and the Distinguished Service Order, and was Mentioned in Despatches. In contrast, when indicting the entire school of war literature identified as following the lead of *All Quiet*, another reviewer agreed

[51] Falls, *War Books*, pp. 278–279.
[52] Douglas Jerrold, *The Lie About the War* (London: Faber and Faber, 1930), p. 34.
[53] For more on the reception accorded Remarque's novel, see especially Ecksteins, *Rites of Spring*.
[54] "The End of War?," *Life & Letters*, 3, 18 (November 1929), p. 400.
[55] Herbert Read, "A Lost Generation," *Nation & Athenaeum*, April 27, 1929, p. 116.

with this methodology for investigating the novel's validity, but not with the results of that process. "Apart from one's memories and from probabilities," he wrote, "there is only one method of arriving at the truth, and that is to ask one's friends for their views." So he did, and "questioned a great number of combatants, junior officers mostly but a fair proportion of them rank and file, and . . . not one has ever seen his own image or that of his comrades in a 'War book' of the type described."[56] Perhaps each reviewer chose his friends by their shared interpretations of the past.

A heated debate continued over how to read the book. Edward Shanks treated the novel (erroneously) as a memoir, "for there is no reason to attempt to separate [Remarque] from the narrator in his book." His criticism was centered on the narrowness of Remarque's portrayal, which contained "no lighter moments in the war."[57] Other reviewers, again, read it differently: "though his material is autobiographical, Remarque is a true novelist," one wrote. All Quiet was "a terrible document" that "sounds the same vivid, accusatory note as the finest of Siegfried Sassoon's early war poems."[58] Richard Rees, however, posited that it was "journalism rather than literature," and that "the reader's nerves are so violently assaulted that he almost loses his own power of reacting at all. The lesson of the book might be more easily learned if there were more contrast."[59] Reviewers could not even agree on the book's genre, much less its significance or quality.

Critics also argued about each other's views. Herbert Read, writing in T. S. Eliot's Criterion, recounted in disgust that J. C. Squire "has described it as the kind of book we shall be ashamed of having admired a year hence." Read wrote that he "would rather describe Mr. Squire as the kind of reviewer we shall all be ashamed to be seen reading a year hence if he continues to make such irresponsible statements." He accused Squire of "merely taking sides in a contemporary squabble."[60] They all were, of course. For some, it seemed to be a generational difference. When Robert Herring was reviewing the film version of All Quiet in 1930, he reflected on the controversy engendered by the novel. "I am tired of arguing about this book," he wrote; "I know what it means to me and to others like me." His argument then replicated one of the important characteristics of the story of disillusionment: the gap in understanding between young people and their parents' generation. "It would seem that we are wrong, if

[56] "Garlands," TLS, p. 486.
[57] Edward Shanks, "Fiction," London Mercury, 20, 115 (May 1929), p. 87.
[58] Readers' Reports, Life & Letters, 3, 14 (July 1929), p. 60.
[59] Richard Rees, "Second Thoughts About the War," New Adelphi, 2, 1 (September–November 1929), pp. 142–143.
[60] Herbert Read, "Books of the Quarter," Criterion, 9, 37 (July 1930), pp. 764–765.

we believe our elders," Herring continued, "but if we believe our elders, we are so often wrong that that makes no difference."[61] *All Quiet* seems to have resonated particularly with younger readers. This was perhaps especially true for those who came of age just after the war and who wanted to understand the experiences that had been so formative for their older brothers. *All Quiet* seemed to offer them a window into that shadowy time. They could, they felt, know what *really* happened.

In fact, much of the debate over how to represent the war often came down to the issues of "reality," or "documentation," or, most often, "truth." The books that best captured the war as lived, in the eyes of the reviewers, were the ones they liked best – though there was then a significant difference of opinion about success and failure as measured by this yardstick. Henry Williamson called his review essay "Reality in War Literature," and he praised E. E. Cummings's *The Enormous Room* as "a recreation of the first magnitude."[62] Charles Morgan liked R. C. Sherriff's play, *Journey's End* (though it failed to meet the requirements for "great tragedy"), because the story was told "with persuasive accuracy and minute observation of detail." It was, in fact, "a remarkably solid and satisfying transcription of life."[63] Eric Partridge, discussing Charles Edmonds's *A Subaltern's War*, read the book "more keenly" because their service records were similar, and "with delight I 'check up,' and what is more, find myself able to corroborate his statements."[64] The power here rests, not in the argument, but in the accuracy of the details. As H. M. Tomlinson wrote, "it is something, is it not, to be able to regard an object of art with an intimate knowledge of what it could portray? – for heaven help the writer, who, we will instance, puts a tin hat on a soldier at Neuve Chapelle, or doesn't know the difference between the various sorts of French mud."[65] Personal experience was essential not just for the author but for the critic; veracity of detail was all important for capturing the essence of the war. This approach, of course, valorized a particular kind of war role; as Samuel Hynes has pointed out, the Great War was the first modern conflict whose story came to be known through the words of people who could claim "the authority of direct experience."[66] That privileging, however, rests on the assumption that "experience" is consistent; as we have seen, this was far from the case. For Edmund Blunden, as for many, reality could even be fictional. He praised Richard Aldington's

---

[61] Robert Herring, "Movies and Talkies," *London Mercury*, 22, 130 (August 1930), p. 363.
[62] Williamson, "Reality," p. 300.
[63] [Charles Morgan,] "Three New Plays," *TLS*, February 14, 1929, p. 114.
[64] Partridge, "War Comes," p. 96.
[65] H. M. Tomlinson, "War Books," *Criterion*, 9, 36 (April 1930), p. 402.
[66] See Hynes, *War Imagined*, pp. 158–159.

Death of a Hero as a "record." Blunden explained that he used the word "deliberately, not denying the novelist his liberties of composition, but in order to draw attention to some of the closest and strongest narration of western Front warfare that has been produced."[67] The proof was in the details, not the dramatization; truth did not, in fact, have to be true.

These ideas of "reality" played directly into the debate over how to represent the war – as what, after all, was "reality"? When Cyril Falls reviewed *A Soldier's Diary of the Great War*, he reserved much of his comment for the disillusionist Introduction by Henry Williamson. "Evidently," Falls wrote, Williamson "feels that the stuff of the diary is not strong enough and does not sufficiently illustrate the horrors of war." The result was that Williamson "proceeds to rewrite the Ploegsteert scene, making of its dirty peacefulness something so ghastly that it would almost serve for the Salient." Falls allowed that "Mr. Williamson is entitled to his own opinions"; however, "he seems to have chosen an unhappy occasion to voice them here." The author of this diary, Falls recounted, turned down the chance to be transferred home because he "must see the show through while perfectly fit." For Williamson, Falls needled, "this must be . . . peculiarly infamous conduct."[68] This same text was being read differently by two participants in the war books controversy. Williamson and Falls were offering contrasting views of what "truth" meant in war books, because they were at fundamental odds over how the war itself and its combatants should be remembered.

Falls then made his perspective even clearer when he reviewed Charles Edmonds's *A Subaltern's War*. Falls liked the book very much, primarily, it would seem, because it offered "a strong protest against the tone and spirit of a great number of recent War books." Falls was diplomatic in his criticism, imputing to the authors of the books he criticized only the desire to avoid future wars, but he left no doubt where his sympathies lay. Edmonds presented himself as "representative of a large part of his generation" in rejecting the entirely negative view of the war that had become so prevalent, and Falls was "inclined to believe that his claim is in a measure just." It was not that Edmonds was making war seem less awful than it really was, as his account of Ypres was "as grim as almost any other that has been published." Reality remained the critical mode of evaluation. War was portrayed horribly because it was indeed horrible, but Edmonds "had, and claims for the majority of his fellows at the front, more spiritual toughness and less self-pity than most recent writers of War

[67] [Edmund Blunden,] "The War Generation," *TLS*, September 19, 1929, p. 713.
[68] [Cyril Falls,] "A War Diary," *TLS*, April 11, 1929, p. 285.

novels and reminiscences would lead us to suppose were general." The
support for this conclusion was again the gathering of data from fellow
veterans. "It is exactly the impression one gathers," Falls wrote, "from
discussion of these books with one's friends." Despite being "not likely to
make war appear any prettier than it is or the young to think more lightly
of it," Falls thought that Edmonds offered "a tribute to British spirit and
endurance," which was "timely at a moment when well-meaning writers
are unconsciously belittling them."[69] Falls later confirmed this opinion in
his own book. He wrote that "perhaps it is [Edmonds's] protest against
the tone and spirit of recent novels and journals dealing with the War
which gives his work its chief importance."[70]

Edmonds's argument about how to remember the war was in the "Essay
on Militarism" at the end of his book, which was itself the subject of much
critical attention. One reviewer wrote that the book was valuable because
"it puts forward the true soldier's point of view, and shows it as worthy
of respect." The "Essay on Militarism" was an important part of the
effort to counter the story of disillusionment, and was "most timely in its
protest." As a result, A Subaltern's War was "strongly recommended."[71]
Even Robert Graves called Edmonds's Epilogue "a well-intentioned essay
on militarism." Graves also thought it was "intended as a nasty hit against
'the disillusioned weaklings,'" like Henry Williamson. Edmonds, Graves
wrote, was "still war-minded," and could, even in 1929, write about "the
'yellow streak' of pacifism." As Graves presented it, Edmonds's chief
fault was documentary rather than philosophical: the accounts of battles
were not valuable "because of his unwillingness to mention the name of
his regiment, its recruiting district, the number of his brigade, or even
that of his division." More than that "he seems reticent about the really
shameful things that happened." Graves wrote therefore that he "cannot
like" the book.[72] This is ironic criticism, coming from an author who
identified his regiment, but acknowledged the inaccuracy of his details.

The Weary Road, by Charles Douie, also proved to be a lightning rod
for the debate over how to remember the war. For Cyril Falls, Douie's
book was not just a good war book; it was one whose author "makes a fine
stand for British character and wholesome patriotism." Falls contrasted
the narrative to some of the German books that had been recently translated, and whose "twist of perversion so common in German books on
the War will probably limit the sympathy of the average British reader."
Douie's attitude, however, was pure. In fact, "he knows now and knew

[69] [Cyril Falls,] "A Subaltern's War," TLS, July 25, 1929, p. 585.
[70] Falls, War Books, p. 194.
[71] "Books of the Quarter," Criterion, 9, 36 (April 1930), p. 575.
[72] Robert Graves, "More War Books," Nation & Athenaeum, August 10, 1929, p. 629.

then for what he served." Falls compared Douie to Blunden in "catching the spirit of the war" as well, again demonstrating the openness of these war texts to the interpretations that best served the arguments of their reviewers and readers. Douie was an effective addition to the arsenal of "protest against the tone of much recent War literature."[73] As the reference to "whole patriotism" shows, the war books controversy was alleged to be not merely about accuracy or misrepresentation, but about health and disease for the nation and its citizen-readers. Falls's *War Books* was described as "a signpost pointing, for the benefit of the bewildered, to where the healthy spots may be found and the paths that avoid the unhealthy."[74] Eric Partridge used a similar analogy when comparing books from different countries. "English books," he wrote, "are more healthy" than either the "sensational" German or "terrible and tragic" French texts. Perhaps as a result, "their authentic reminiscences are superior."[75] Authenticity – truth – was again the key issue. Most German war books "have gone wrong," Clennell Wilkinson agreed, "not from the right reasons, as in the case of our own 'mud-and-blood school,' but from wrong ones." (Wilkinson included both *All Quiet* and *Sergeant Grischa* in this group.) They were not portraying truth, but instead "they have deliberately commercialised horror and filth."[76] This was, they seemed to argue, a very un-English thing to do.

It was when reviewers considered the aggregate effect of these books (in conjunction with the less sophisticatedly literate ones that rapidly and in great numbers joined them) that some became greatly concerned. Others, at the same time, were quite gratified. Reviewers, as reviewers do, used the books to make their own arguments, and the texts proved remarkably pliant for these purposes. Richard Rees mildly criticized *Good-bye To All That* because Robert Graves was not "able or willing to tell a little more about himself and a little less about the events he took part in." More than half of the book, he pointed out, was about the war, "and much of it, of course, is of appalling interest, but much of it is confusing and uninformative – at any rate for one who did not have first-hand experience of the events he described." Graves, or Blunden, or Tomlinson might have argued that that was the point; Rees was simply not one of the "ghosts," so he could not understand. Rees, however, used Graves's memoir to make a different argument. It was a valuable book, he wrote, because it demonstrated that "religion and patriotism and the conventional mainstays of our self-respect wither like chaff in a furnace, but in

[73] [Falls,] "Symposium," p. 938.   [74] "Garlands," p. 485.
[75] Partridge, "War Comes," p. 90.
[76] Clennell Wilkinson, "Recent War Books," *London Mercury*, 21, 123 (January 1930), p. 238.

their place is forged the steel of human comradeship – in which alone is the hope of the future." He explained that "to the thinking man, whose eyes are free from the blinkers of social, religious, and patriotic prejudice, it is clear that the ordeal of the war was but a heightened and intensified parable of the ordeal of life in general."[77] He therefore used *Good-bye to All That* (as he also used *Death of a Hero, All Quiet on the Western Front*, and *Journey's End*) to argue that "the war was *not* a sudden thunderbolt hurled into a well-ordered society." Instead, "it was the outcome of a bad system, based on superstitious morality and unsound economics." Most importantly, we must "go still further and ask whether if rotten things happen to us, there may not, perhaps, be something rotten about the way we live."[78] The war was not exceptional, he claimed. It was merely the clearest symptom of a diseased society.

Rees's comments were more extreme than most, of course. Many reviewers, however, used the war books to make points about the strength or weakness of the British people, the British economy, and the future chance for peace. The past could be read – like a book, perhaps? – in order to understand where the nation was now, and where it was going. Cyril Falls argued that the negative "propaganda" (as it was frequently called) of disillusionment could not be accurate. The proof was in the British armies, which were composed of individual Britons who must have been stronger than they were being portrayed, and who "outlasted in morale and offensive vigour their opponents and some of their allies."[79] *A Subaltern's War* was a case in point. Edmonds demonstrated, Falls later wrote, "that ordinary men endured [the war] without becoming the shambling, woebegone spectres so often depicted." This was very important, because "these spectres would not have been victorious against the worst troops in the world."[80] The point was less about the war and more about the value and capacity of the British people. As J. C. W. Reith of the BBC, himself a wounded veteran, argued, "war is not all ruthless perversion and degradation... characteristics unrealized and unimagined are revealed, and decidedly not all of them are such as had better be left unprovoked."[81] Falls was happy to quote Douie that "the sight of a man who has lost his self-respect is far more repugnant than the sight of a brave man, dirty and bleeding."[82] For Edmund Blunden, by contrast, the blood and guts and horror were not just part of the picture, but were the whole purpose of the books. Telling the truth about the conditions of war was

[77] Richard Rees, "End of a World," *New Adelphi*, 3, 3 (March–May 1930), pp. 213–216.
[78] Rees, "Second Thoughts," pp. 144–145.   [79] [Falls], "Subaltern's War," p. 585.
[80] Falls, *War Books*, p. 194.
[81] Quoted in LeMahieu, *Culture for Democracy*, p. 144.
[82] [Falls,] "Symposium," p. 938.

the only way to look forward to a positive future. "It is in such documents," he wrote about Aldington, "where a 'clear light' falls upon the rusty wire and trodden bodies and yellow-faced reliefs ... that the hope of the future conscience largely dwells."[83] Looking back at the corpses was the only way to look forward to the future. These texts were not just novels and reminiscences: they were judgments on the British nation and people, past, present, and future. They were, as well, comments on masculinity; Falls, Edmonds, and their colleagues were defending against the idea of a domesticated (and therefore weak and unheroic) nation.[84]

Because these arguments were more about looking forward than looking back, most reviewers presented the "war books controversy" as a new phenomenon. One reviewer, unusually, as he identified "a reaction against the ideas and ideals with which we fought the Great War," also posited that "it is a mistake to suppose that it has appeared only in the last two years," as "the works of fiction and of personal reminiscence published between 1919 and 1927 had their full share of it."[85] This is, of course, true; the change which occurred in 1928–1930 was one of number rather than kind. In the midst of the torrent, however, most reviewers seemed to have forgotten this. Richard Rees wrote of the "ten years' silence about the war."[86] Cyril Falls, who had reviewed books throughout the 1920s himself, wrote that "until about two years ago no one wanted to hear about the War, or, if they did, the publishers and book-sellers had not realized the fact."[87] Clennell Wilkinson referred to "the publishers' dam" of the last decade being now "broken."[88] In response, review essays examining the span of publications and directly addressing the issue of a war books controversy began to appear in late 1929 and into 1930. Most of them, in fact, were published just as the flood itself was lessening.

Wilkinson, in an essay on "Recent War Books," started by defining his subject. He was not addressing military histories, or regimental records, or generals' memoirs of command, he said, but "books that purport to give a true account of [the war], or some corner of it." This category could include fiction: "call the book a novel and you have a free licence from your readers to crowd all your leading events into one day, or one week, at your will, and to arrange them in what seems the most suitable order." This was acceptable, though, because "they are real events – things personally experienced." The key to a war book, then, was not just a function of

---

[83] [Blunden,] "War Generation," p. 713.   [84] See Light, *Forever England*, pp. 7–10.
[85] "Garlands," p. 485.   [86] Rees, "Second Thoughts," p. 145.
[87] [Cyril Falls,] "Three Records of the War," *TLS*, October 31, 1929, p. 359.
[88] Clennell Wilkinson, "Biography and Memoirs," *London Mercury*, 21, 122 (December 1929), p. 187.

its purpose, but of its author's background. "Experience," especially in the trenches, was the primary credential an author needed. Wilkinson contemplated the relative publishing dearth of the 1920s and argued that it had been misconstrued. Pointing to the sales of adventure and mystery books with war settings, he declared that "it was not the war that the public was sick of, or war-books as such, but only the kind of war-books that were being served up to them." Looking back, Wilkinson professed to have been confused by some of the more negative texts, until he came to understand that they were not "reminiscences pure and simple," but anti-war "propaganda" rather than "history" or even "literature." "As such we must accept it," he wrote, and "if its effect is to postpone the next war every sane man among us will rejoice." Now, however, he and the public were looking for books that would help them understand the war – "to see it whole," he wrote. Edmund Blunden had succeeded in this, he thought. So, too, had Robert Graves.[89] While condemning the disillusionist books, Wilkinson praised two authors who have come to be associated most closely with that literary approach. These books clearly were initially open to wide-ranging interpretations. The soldier's story did not emerge fully developed from the war, or even from the war books boom. Its creation was a process, a product of a cultural debate.

The ideal for war books, the constant measure against which reviewers seemed to hold up their subjects, had two primary components: its message should be universal, and it should fall between the extremes of representation. Eric Partridge identified three types of authors of war books. First, there were "the optimists (very few, these optimists)" who "are inclined to be idealistic." There were also "the pessimists," who were "naturalist – even brutal." Finally, he discussed "the impartialists," who were "realistic in the best sense of the word . . . it is these last who have produced the best work."[90] His requirements were clear. War books should be realistic but not naturalist, impartial rather than optimistic or pessimistic. No one had any more patience with the enthusiastic and eager stories of the early war years. The war had indeed been horrific, everyone agreed. The debate instead was over the meaning (or lack thereof) of the horror, and so how best to remember it. This is why one reviewer liked Frederic Manning's *Her Privates We*, which "avoids the hysterical morbidity of some, and the still more destructive and demoralizing forced cheerfulness of others."[91] The real question, however, was about how to think about the present and future of British society. Was remembering horror in all its details the only protection against its repetition?

[89] Wilkinson, "War Books," pp. 238–241.   [90] Partridge, "War Comes," p. 104.
[91] P. Q., "Readers' Reports – War Novels," *Life & Letters*, 4, 22 (March 1930), p. 249.

Or did portraying soldiers as less than fully in control undermine future British strength? Because so many critics were looking for a more moderate approach, they managed the high-wire act of utilizing texts that might otherwise have seemed hard to reconcile with each other in support of their arguments. But they continued to search for the Great War's story – its *War and Peace*, as they called it more than once.

Eric Partridge was one of the critics on this quest. He served in the ranks with the Australian Expeditionary Force at Gallipoli and on the Western front before pursuing a literary career. Partridge included review essays on war books in each of the first two numbers of his new literary journal, *The Window*. Like many of his colleagues, he started with a chronology of the evolution of war books, finishing quite precisely: "by April 1929 in Germany, and by June in England, the Great War had come into its own." What this meant was that "men felt that they both could and must speak out and tell what they went through in 1914–1918; the public felt that they wanted to hear what those men had to say."[92] Partridge then proceeded to discuss and evaluate a considerable number of war books. By the second essay, three months later, he felt that the situation had changed: "I observe that war books have already become much less popular than they were in March–December 1929." However, he wrote, "the movement is against novels that falsify, against undistinguished memoirs, and perhaps against foreign as opposed to English books." Readers were becoming more critical and discerning, Partridge argued, but "there is still room for a war novel as good as *Her Privates We*." In Partridge's overview, his selection was remarkable for including women authors (in addition to the gender-masked Peter Deane). He wrote very positively of *Below the Watchtowers*, Margaret Skelton's homefront novel, as well as Mary Borden's sketches and stories of hospital life, *The Forbidden Zone*. He even found some friendly words for the much-criticized *It's a Great War*. Its author, Mary Lee, committed the double sins of being American and claiming that civilians had a more comprehensive view of the war than combatants could manage.[93]

The supply of new books was diminishing, but the furor surrounding the narratives already published was reaching its peak in early 1930. Review essays abounded, Cyril Falls published *War Books: A Critical Guide*, and Douglas Jerrold entered the fray with a polemic in the form of a pamphlet called *The Lie About the War* (so called in contrast to books that claimed to offer its "truth"). Especially in his Preface, Falls made

---

[92] Partridge, "War Comes," p. 104.
[93] Partridge, "War Continues," pp. 62–85. Falls, in contrast, wrote of Lee that "really, it is not the place of women to talk of mud ... [and] she is wholly mistaken in her notion that important books on the War must be written by women": Falls, *War Books*, p. 282.

explicit the perspective he had repeatedly implied in his book reviews of the preceding years. "As time goes on," he wrote, personal reminiscences have "become more and more critical of their own country's political and military leadership, more and more bitter in tone, more and more filled with loathing of war." Novels, if anything, were more extreme, following in the trail blazed by *All Quiet*. "The writers have set themselves, not to strip the war of its romance – for that was pretty well gone already," Falls explained, "but to prove that the Great War was engineered by knaves or fools on both sides, that the men who died in it were driven like beasts to the slaughter, and died like beasts, without their deaths helping any cause or doing any good." This case was supported by both false evidence and "the falsest of false evidence . . . by closing-up scenes and events which in themselves may be true." He explained what he meant:

Every sector becomes a bad one, every working-party is shot to pieces; if a man is killed or wounded his brains or his entrails always protrude from his body; no one ever seems to have a rest. Hundreds of games of football were played every day on the Western Front . . . but how often does one hear of a game in a 'War book'? Attacks succeed one another with lightning rapidity. The soldier is represented as a depressed and mournful spectre helplessly wandering about until death brought his miseries to an end.

For Falls, this kind of compression was not a literary privilege, because the point was not literary effect. The texts claimed to be representing the real war of its combatants, but they were only offering a piece of it as the whole.[94]

Falls knew that this approach was justified as anti-war propaganda, but he argued against it for several reasons. "In the first place," he wrote, "propaganda founded upon a distortion of the truth and an appeal to the emotions rather than to reason is apt to defeat its own object in the long run." This reasoning appears particularly flawed in the post-Nazi era, of course, but Falls cannot be held responsible for not knowing that. "Secondly," he continued, "many of these books have not had even momentarily the propagandist effect intended upon the minds of a good proportion of their readers . . . they have instead created or pandered to a lust for horror, brutality, and filth, which is in itself disquieting and dangerous." The next reason, however, showed how much of his concern was about perceptions of the present, rather than the past. Falls's third reason, he wrote, "will appeal only to those who still believe in the virtues of British patriotism, honour, and devotion to an ideal – the constant belittlement of motives, of intelligence, and of zeal is nauseous." This seemed more important to him, perhaps, than his final reason, though he

[94] Falls, *War Books*, pp. ix–xii.

wanted to present it otherwise: "to pretend that no good came out of the War is frankly an absurdity. The fruits of victory may taste to us as bitter as the fruits of defeat to our late enemies. But how would the fruits of defeat have tasted to us and our Allies?" Ignoring these important issues was especially unfair to the memory of those who had fought and died, he argued. "Let us all do what we can to make war impossible. Let us not forget what the War generation suffered," he wrote, "but do not let us pretend that either those who died or those who came through are best served in this fashion."[95] The disillusionist school of war literature was deeply problematic to men like Falls not because the war had not been horrible – they were more than willing to agree that it was. To dwell on that only, however, and to argue that coping with its horrors was beyond the capacities of British soldiers, was to malign the past (including the dead), to criticize the present, and even to jeopardize the future of the nation.

Jerrold, a veteran of Gallipoli and France and a military historian, offered many of the same arguments, but put them considerably more strongly. Falls had used a star system to rate highly a number of disillusionist books because of their literary merits, including those by Sassoon, Blunden, Graves, and even Remarque. Jerrold, who ostensibly was reviewing sixteen books but was really just using them as a platform, also made the distinction that "of the books to which I am going to refer, none is indifferent and many are extremely fine." That, he argued, was not the point. Instead, "it is my purpose to show that they present a picture of war which is fundamentally false even when it is superficially true, and which is statistically false even when it is incidentally true." Like Falls, he felt these problems made the books "a danger to the cause of peace," because "all causes which derive their inspiration from lies ultimately fail." He, too, denied that "the war was avoidable and futile," or that "it was recognised as futile by those who fought in it." Jerrold also spent considerable time disproving the frequency of events presented in the war books. Each incident might have been historically correct, but the books ignored the majority of other, equally historically correct periods, thus giving a narrow view of the life of the trench soldier. As he put it, it was "very striking in these books, how every ration party, every fatigue party and every wiring party is the subject of murderous fire, and how a slightly wounded man is unknown." He proceeded to support his argument statistically. Like other critics, Jerrold, too, buttressed his main point by denying the idea that nothing good had come of the war.[96]

[95] Falls, *War Books*, pp. ix–xii.   [96] Jerrold, *Lie*, pp. 9, 18, 20–21, 25.

For the British authors who understood the concept of honor (unlike their American and German counterparts), Jerrold was willing to concede that "the deception practiced is largely unconscious." Though "the statistical falsity" was "true to the belief of the writers," it was still false and therefore dangerous. The reason for Jerrold's vehement opposition was explicit: the past needed to be accurately portrayed in order to defend the present and protect the future. It was only, he suggested, a younger generation who could accept this new view of the war, a generation that had not experienced combat itself. And the effects, he argued, would be costly indeed. "Only if the generation now growing up in Europe and America can all, and all at once, be taught to realise that the war of 1914 was, in 1914, inevitable," he wrote, "will they learn not to ride their silly hobby horses so that another war will be equally inevitable."[97] The new depictions of the war as horrifically pointless were unacceptable less because of what they said about the past and even more for the risks they portended for the future.

Falls, and especially Jerrold, did not go unnoticed. Now the reviewers became the reviewed, as both texts were the subject of critical attention. Eric Partridge, who admired Blunden and Graves as well as Edmonds, wrote that Jerrold had provided "a very pungent antidote to much 'tosh' and 'slush.'" He concluded that The Lie About the War was a "notable brochure, refreshing in its sanity, decency, and penetration," which made it "just what is needed by the general public to enable it to distinguish the genuine from the spurious, the normal from the abnormal."[98] Others disagreed of course, and "M.P.," writing in The New Adelphi, spent some time taking apart what he considered to be Jerrold's more egregious arguments. Certainly some writers had exploited the war, but that should not be a major concern, as they "will be amply balanced" by stories of false heroism. Again, the past was being evaluated in terms of its impact on the future: "peace is not endangered by tales of shattered nerves or scenes of such exquisite tenderness as Remarque shows." Instead, "its chief danger comes from those whom the war taught nothing better than to think in divisions" rather than individuals.[99] Everyone on all sides of the controversy seemed to agree that the goal was world peace. The dispute over how to achieve and maintain that goal, though, exposed a gulf so profound in its breadth that the people on opposite sides seemed unable even to hear one another.

The Times Literary Supplement weighed in on both the war books controversy and the texts analyzing it with a review essay called "The

---

[97] Jerrold, Lie, pp. 39, 48.   [98] Partridge, "War Continues," p. 63.
[99] M.P., "Rehabilitating Mars," New Adelphi, 3, 3 (March–May 1930), pp. 217–220.

Garlands Wither," in June 1930. It narrated, as so many articles did, the evolution of war representations, culminating in the disillusionist school that seemed so predominant by 1929. "It was some time before a strong protest was made" against this type of war book, the anonymous author wrote, because the situation had created a bit of a dilemma for many veterans. Again, the concern about the future was presented as paramount. Not only was "it right that the younger generation should hear something of the horrors of war," but critics "were for the most part as anxious as the writers [of the books] that there should be no more war, and felt that any attempt to contradict or criticize what was obviously anti-war propaganda involved the assumption of some responsibility." To demonstrate the reasonableness of this opposition when it occurred, it was important that not only "half a militarist" like Charles Edmonds or "wholly one" like Ernst Jünger spoke against the disillusionist school, but also Edmund Blunden, "a hearty hater of war." To this movement aiming to correct what its proponents saw as extreme misperceptions, the reviewer joined his voice. Like others, he was anxious to be clear that his goal was not "to belittle the agonies and endurances of the troops in France." They were real, and they were awful. The emphasis on the cruder aspects of life, however, was misplaced and unnecessary. On seeing the repeatedly drunken officers in *Journey's End*, the reviewer had wondered where, in 1918, they had been lucky enough to find a sufficiently generous supply of whisky to make such inebriation possible. He also asked why the drunkenness was "more significant" in "Poperinghe ... than in Shaftesbury-avenue?" What good did the realism do: would "bad language ... strengthen the League of Nations? Are visits to brothels in Amiens or Béthune any more edifying than visits to brothels in London or Chicago?" These scenes were not about remembering the war, but "intended merely to shock, to excite, and to pander the latent brutality of their readers." Ironically, just as authors of the disillusionist school often blamed women at home for not understanding the true horrors of the war, so this reviewer wrote of the inaccuracies of "the very books about which many women were heard to rhapsodize."[100] The fault by definition could not lie with the soldiers who knew better, so women vicariously reading novels safe at home became reasonable targets.

The real problem, however, was one of representativeness. The reviewer agreed with Jerrold that the most serious "lie about the War" was "the closing-up of scenes not in themselves unfaithful." This made it seem that "every sector of the front is always in turmoil; every salvo seems to hit a ration party; friends and comrades hit are nearly always

---

[100] "Garlands," p. 486.

killed; there is hardly a hint of the unceasing and not unsuccessful efforts to provide comforts and recreation, in which British troops, especially in France, were certainly more fortunate than those of any other belligerent nation." Again, it was not just that these books were wrong, but that they were dangerous; it was not mere petty criticism of inaccuracies, but the articulation of an often all too vague fear about the future of the British nation and people. Though he agreed that "the serious, reasoned case against war is overwhelming," conflict could not be avoided merely by believing that it was too awful to happen again. "The nation which acts upon the delusion that war is impossible just because it is horrible," he wrote, "will be rudely undeceived by one in a more primitive moral state." War should be avoided because "as a means of policy it is outworn," like duels or clan warfare. To accomplish this required "cool heads and reasonable arguments," however. "Hysterical denunciations, belittlement of the honourable motives of the past, the pretence that the Great War was nothing but mud and blood, drink and lechery," would not help. These misconceptions of the fundamental state of the British citizen, he concluded, "will not take us far."[101] Again, concern over the future was a reason to argue about memories of the past.

Echoing many of his fellow reviewers, the author of "The Garlands Wither" praised efforts to debunk inaccurate details in the assumption that such errors invalidated the overall message of any given book. This was one of the many aspects of the review that provoked a lengthy letter of rebuttal from Robert Graves himself. Graves questioned the very meaning of "truth," positing that it was not an absolute, as so many reviewers seemed to be claiming. Instead, he argued that truth was relative. Graves identified four different types of war books – unit or campaign histories, personal memoirs of combatants, propaganda novels, and genre novels. A definition of "truthfulness" that was restricted to an attention to accurate details, he argued, applied only to the first of these categories. It was less relevant to memoirs, and not just because it was difficult to keep a diary in the trenches or because a soldier doing his job well would not have had much time to write about it. Brilliantly, Graves took his logic a step well beyond anyone else, claiming that memoirs were not "truthful" about the war *unless* they were inaccurate about the details. If one had really experienced the worst that trench warfare had to offer, it would be impossible to maintain accuracy in its representation. Such was the power and result of its horror. As for the third category, propaganda could only be judged by its effectiveness in achieving its goals of

[101] "Garlands," p. 486.

persuasion, so "truthfulness" was entirely irrelevant there. Graves then dismissed the rest of the criticism by claiming that the subject of "The Garlands Wither" had been primarily "genre novels," which were in fact not trying to tell any fundamental truths. In fact, they were "to be read no more and no less seriously than the detective novels listed in your Fiction Briefs." The tropes of the war criticized by those opposed to the disillusionist school were no different from their corresponding common characteristics in mysteries, so "it would be absurd to apply to them Mr. Jerrold's statistical test of frequency in actual experience." Genre authors were just following "what your admirable Fiction Briefs reviewer calls 'the rules of the game' [presenting] the highlights of war . . . from the debauched Waac to the crucified Canadian, and . . . the hero shall *not* in the end be awarded the Victoria Cross."[102] Because these characteristics had become conventional – the very criticism, of course, of some reviewers – Graves exempted them from serious consideration. In one pithy letter, he excused the vast majority of books concerning the war from examination for factual veracity.

Depicting the war retrospectively in literature was at least as much a debate about the present insecurities of Britain and especially the nation's future as it was concerned about the past, as book reviews from the late 1920s and early 1930se clearly demonstrated. The widespread acceptance of disillusionment as the soldier's story of the war was itself a postwar phenomenon, which was strongly and vociferously resisted at the time.[103] Yet the soldier's story was culturally triumphant, and became accepted as the "real" history of the war. Though some reviews later in the 1930s continued to call for an alternative to the soldier's story of disillusionment, they failed to spark further debate because they were, in effect, beating a dead horse.[104] The further the war receded in chronological terms, the more differences in its depiction were similarly blurred into this story. Issues that caused debate in 1929 blended more easily into each other, particularly after another war had come along to push the Great War further into the shadows. The story of the war that has entered popular culture was a product much more of the time in which it was created than of the time it ostensibly represented, as detailed comparison of texts by the same author from each of the two

---

[102] Robert Graves, "Correspondence: The Garlands Wither," *TLS*, June 26, 1930, p. 534.
[103] "Trauma provokes conservative as well as radical response": Light, *Forever England*, p. 200.
[104] See, for example, Alec Waugh, "New Literature – The Happy Warrior," *London Mercury*, 31, 181 (November 1934), p. 79; A. V. Cookman, "An Infant in Arms," *London Mercury*, 32, 188 (June 1935), p. 192.

periods makes clear. Graves and Sassoon were the key players, whether they meant to be or not, in the creation and perpetuation of the soldier's story. Other writers – including women like Vera Brittain and Irene Rathbone – were then left with little choice but to re-remember their own experience.

In 1922, the soldier-poet and future memoirist Robert Graves wrote a rather unpleasant letter to his old friend Siegfried Sassoon. Over the years, their correspondence was often bitter and angry, and intentionally hurtful. In the last years of the war itself, and for some time after the Armistice, Graves claimed to have emotionally distanced himself from the trench experience. "You identify me in your mind with a certain Robert Graves now dead," he wrote, "whose bones and detritus" were in his war poetry as well "the land of memory." He told Sassoon, "Don't." Instead, Graves wrote, "I am using his name, rank and initials and his old clothes but I am no more than his son and heir."[1] Graves was declaring, in no uncertain terms, that he had changed fundamentally since the war years – and also, perhaps, that Sassoon had not. Sassoon and Graves served together in the Royal Welch Fusiliers during the war and bonded over their mutual interest in poetry and literature. Once out of shared combat, however, they increasingly had difficulties with each other. Graves initially proved himself more capable at setting aside the war and moving on with his life, to the distress of Sassoon. Though both returned to the subject of the Great War and its impact, authoring books that have become canonical texts of the conflict, they did so in radically different ways, ultimately creating a serious rupture of the friendship.

Their books, however, with a few others, have become key to the soldier's story. Sassoon's first volume was widely praised and won the Hawthornden Prize in 1929, and the subsequent volumes were eagerly anticipated and welcomed.[2] Graves's memoir was a phenomenon from its publication, selling 20,000 copies in the first five days.[3] Graves's 1957 revised edition was also very positively reviewed in the literary and popular

---

[1] Graves to Sassoon, 31 May 1922: Robert Graves (Paul O'Prey, ed.), *In Broken Images: Selected Correspondence* (Mt. Kisco, NY: Moyer Bell, 1982), p. 134.
[2] See, for example, *The Times*, July 13, 1929, September 19, 1930, September 4, 1936; and reviews discussed in more detail below.
[3] See Richard Perceval Graves, *Robert Graves: The Years with Laura, 1926–1940* (New York: Viking, 1990), pp. 131–137.

press. Their status as the key figures in war literature only solidified over the decades, confirmed not just in the popular mind but by scholarly attention. Paul Fussell, in *The Great War and Modern Memory*, identified Graves, Sassoon, and Edmund Blunden as the central authors of war literature, and devoted significant sections of his pathbreaking study to each of the three men.[4] By doing so, of course, he further strengthened the view of their centrality to the canon of war accounts. Though Blunden's *Undertones of War* was perhaps the most unequivocally praised at the time of publication, the writings of Sassoon and Graves have maintained a more powerful popular presence. Sassoon and Graves have also both left behind considerable private prose from the war years themselves, including letters and a detailed diary. Because of the importance of this potential for direct comparison over time, I focus here only on Graves and Sassoon, and not Blunden. When close readings of personal writings from 1914–1918 are contrasted with retrospective texts, then the evolution of the soldier's story and its relation to contemporary moments rather than to the war itself are thrown into sharp relief.

Graves and Sassoon, of course, were not the only people writing about the war. Other authors, however, then had to deal with the new idea of war experience that these men helped establish. The soldier's story was "the truth about the war," by people – men – who had experienced it, seen it, suffered through it, and been changed by it. This was also the claim, however, of women like Vera Brittain and Irene Rathbone. The only legitimate "experience," according to the soldier's story, was that of the infantry soldier. Many other narratives, in turn, began to be recast. Veterans who were not in the infantry, other active non-combatants, and especially women reimagined themselves as survivors surrounded by devastating carnage (whether physical or emotional). They were writing their own soldier's stories.

For well-known women authors, this was often a process of reclaiming the validation for parallel service that they had been granted during the war years, and had been an important part of their personal identity. When the trench took over the cultural history of the war, however, there was no room in it to give credit to women. (Within the soldier's story, the only real role left for women, if they were acknowledged at all, was one of impediment, or at best ignorance.) Facing their own exclusion in memory, they too began to reconstruct their narratives in order to fit with the accepted model of war experience. They presented themselves as war workers who had served their nation, often at high personal cost, just as their brothers had in the army. Following my readings of Graves

---

[4] Paul Fussell, *The Great War and Modern Memory* (Oxford: Oxford University Press, 1975).

and Sassoon, therefore, I focus here on two female authors of the 1930s, Irene Rathbone and Vera Brittain, for whom both wartime and retrospective narratives are also available, in order to explicate this process of re-remembering. They constructed their war memories in keeping with contemporary portrayals of war service, just as their wartime accounts reflected the common social imagery of those years. Where these new texts succeeded, as well as where they did not, reveals the workings of a British society at a time that it increasingly feared would be "interwar" rather than "postwar."

Robert Graves: the evolution of all that

Robert Graves's cynical memoir *Good-bye to All That* is now often considered an anti-war tract (though in fact it is also quite pro-militarist and is in many ways a story of a love affair with the Royal Welch Fusiliers). In it, Graves described aspects of his war experience quite differently in 1929 than he had in his personal correspondence during the war years. For decades, both scholars and soldiers have pointed out the many factual errors in the book. As Paul Fussell wrote, "any man with some experience and a bent toward the literal can easily catch Graves out in his fictions and exaggerations"; he then proceeded to debunk some of the better ones himself.[5] Graves himself cynically acknowledged the influence of popular expectations on his construction of the text. Though he was trying to make a point about the war and its impact, he also needed money and wanted to write a book that would sell well. He maintained, however, that these flourishes did not undermine the fundamental veracity of the portrayal. Graves's creativity, in any case, went beyond amusing but impossible stories of gunners heating tea-water by firing off a few rounds (the water would have ended up laced with unappetizing machine oil) or tapping out songs in response to the German guns by removing rounds from the ammunition belts (which would have jammed the guns entirely rather than merely creating a pause in the rhythm). This, then, is neither a further assessment of his accuracy nor a study of his life, but a comparison of his writings from two distinct time periods. Over the years, Graves changed important details of his experience to fit his postwar disillusionment (and not just his prewar and wartime cynicism).

Graves spent time near the beginning of his memoir documenting some of the appalling – and inaccurate – allegations of anti-German

---

[5] Fussell, *Great War*, p. 206. For him, its literary rather than documentary tendencies were its strength, and "it is valuable just because it is not true in that way" (p. 207).

propaganda.[6] "Though I discounted perhaps twenty per cent of the atroc-
ity details as wartime exaggeration," he wrote, "that was not, of course,
sufficient." Hatred of "the Hun" was one of the stereotypical characteristics of the early phases of the war; later, experienced and exhausted
survivors came to be described as recognizing that soldiers on both sides
were human beings, none of them entirely sure why they were trying to
kill each other. *Good-bye to All That* maintained this humane evaluation
of the enemy from the beginning. Graves had family in Germany, and
in the early pages of the memoir he remembered the summers he passed
there as a child, along with "my cousin Wilhelm – later shot down in an
air battle by a school-fellow of mine." The irony was obvious: a playfel-
low killed by a school-fellow, with no real difference between the two. In
1929, Graves remembered his cousin lying in the loft "picking off mice
with an air-gun."[7] However, this taste for shooting seemed much more
uncomprehendingly malicious in an earlier, wartime account. "I see in the
Mail today," Graves wrote to his mentor Edward Marsh in August 1916,
"that a damnably nasty German cousin of mine has been killed flying."
He went on to recount a time when one of Graves's sisters had admired
a squirrel, and Wilhelm immediately shot it. The cousin was presented
as the model of Teutonic mindless violence: "he couldn't understand her
tears of rage. She'd admired the squirrel: he'd got it for her and was prepared to skin it then and there for her." Wilhelm was "a brute [who]
used to climb up the only greengage tree in the orchard . . . and throw us
down the stones." In 1916, Graves concluded, "how I hated him."[8] All
animosity, however, was absent from the postwar version. In a story of
waste on both sides, the emphasis had to be on the bonds of family rather
than the bitter rivalries of childhood.

The movement away from anti-German sentiment was far from the
only postwar revision Graves made for his memoir. As he was a poet,
it should come as no surprise that poetry and poets played a significant
role in his wartime writings as well as his memoir. In *Good-bye to All
That*, Graves did not mention the well-known idealistic pro-war poet
Rupert Brooke until his postwar section, when the local rector asked
him to read some war poetry at a memorial service. Graves defied what
he represented as social expectations. "Instead of Rupert Brooke on the

---

[6] On atrocities and their cultural and political impact, see Nicoletta F. Gullace, *"The Blood
of Our Sons": Men, Women, and the Renogotiation of British Citizenship During the Great
War* (New York: Palgrave Macmillan, 2002), especially ch. 2, "The Rape of Belgium and
Wartime Imagination."

[7] Robert Graves, *Good-bye to All That* (New York: Doubleday, 1929; 2nd edn. [revised],
1957), pp. 67, 5, 24.

[8] Graves to Edward Marsh, August 7, 1916: Graves, *Broken Images*, p. 60.

glorious dead," he wrote, "I read some of the more painful poems by Sassoon and Wilfred Owen about men dying from gas-poisoning, and about buttocks of corpses bulging from the mud."[9] Brooke died in 1915, in uniform but never having seen any combat. Retrospectively, Brooke symbolized those people who had not experienced the war and therefore could not understand it.

In his correspondence, however, Graves revealed himself to have been an admirer of Brooke's. In January 1915, he wrote to Marsh that he had "bought Rupert Brooke's *Poems* . . . I think he is really good."[10] Even after Graves gained direct combat experience in the Battle of Loos, he praised Brooke's poem "The Soldier." He then sent "Rupert's two books" to his friend and fellow poet Siegfried Sassoon.[11] It was not until 1917 that an edge began to creep into Graves' references to Brooke; he praised Sassoon's poetry as "original . . . [with] no ode either to Kitchener or Rupert Brooke."[12] Later that year, however, Graves was still referring to Brooke's work as "the better sort of poetry," along with Sassoon's and Robert Nichols's.[13] This ongoing attention to Brooke was entirely absent from Graves' more cynical memoir, which presented an earlier disillusionment with the war than his correspondence suggests.

Nichols, too, was rewritten. Repeatedly in correspondence during the war years, Graves referred to himself, Nichols, and Sassoon as the hope for the future of poetry. To Sassoon, Graves wrote of "we three inevitables, two Roberts and a Siegfried, rising side by side on the roll of fame."[14] He was pleased that Nichols, whom he described as "a very staunch friend," had the right approach to the war. "As usual," Graves wrote, "we're right when the other poets are wrong."[15] In *Good-bye to All That*, however, Nichols was dismissed contemptuously. According to the postwar Graves, he "served only three weeks in France, with the gunners, and got involved in no show," and he "started a legend of Siegfried, himself and me as the new Three Musketeers, though the three of us had never once been together in the same room."[16] Nichols's lack of active service defined him in Graves's 1929 eyes; he had not been in the trenches, so he could not

[9] Graves, *Good-bye*, p. 318.
[10] Graves to Marsh, January 22, 1915: Graves, *Broken Images*, p. 30.
[11] Graves to Marsh, February 24, 1916; Graves to Sassoon, [early May 1916]: Graves, *Broken Images*, pp. 39, 47.
[12] Graves to Robert Nichols, January 7, 1917: Graves, *Broken Images*, p. 62.
[13] Graves to Sassoon, July 31, 1917: Graves, *Broken Images*, p. 80.
[14] Graves to Sassoon, no date [November 1917]: Graves, *Broken Images*, p. 87.
[15] Graves to Robert Ross, June 30, 1917: Margery Ross (ed.), *Robert Ross, Friend of Friends: Letters to Robert Ross, Art Critic and Writer, Together with Extracts from His Published Articles* (London: Jonathan Cape, 1952), p. 309.
[16] Graves, *Good-bye*, pp. 295–296.

be a good poet. Whatever the merits of his poetry, Nichols's inexperience made him a casualty of the soldier's story.

Graves staked his own claim as a war poet early on. According to *Good-bye to All That*, Sassoon complained in 1915 that "the war should not be written about in such a realistic way" as Graves was doing. Sassoon "had not yet been in the trenches," and Graves predicted "that he would soon change his style."[17] Sassoon, of course, came to admire Graves's work. In 1916, having heard the erroneous report that Graves had died of wounds, Sassoon wrote in his diary that "Robert might have been a great poet."[18] In January 1917, he was still confident that Graves would be "a magical name for young poets in 1980, if only he survives this carnage."[19] Yet, by the autumn of 1917, it was Sassoon who criticized Graves for ignoring harsh realities and therefore not writing the good poetry that needed to be written. "It's all very well for you to talk about 'good form' and acting like a 'gentleman'" about the conduct of the war, Sassoon wrote to his friend, but "to me that's a very estimable form of suicidal stupidity and credulity." He continued, condemningly, "if you had real courage you wouldn't acquiesce as you do."[20] Graves responded that Sassoon's "poems are damned good, but perfectly horrific as they're meant to be." He continued, "Do cheer up... Don't send me any more corpse poems."[21]

Graves cited this exchange in *Good-bye to All That*, but reimagined its context and significance. In the memoir, it was about Sassoon's ill-fated and ineffective public protest against the war, when he refused to continue serving unless the government made its war aims clear. Sassoon, Graves wrote, "reprehended the attitude I had taken in July, when I reminded him that the Regiment would either think him a coward or regard his protest as a lapse from good form." Instead, "it was suicidal stupidity and credulity... to identify oneself in any way with good form; a man of real courage would not acquiesce as I did." The exchange became one about past behavior, rather than present insufficiencies. In this revisiting, Graves had merely been impatient with Sassoon's attempt to tilt at windmills. Graves shifted the correspondence from an indictment of his own willingness to focus on himself (rather than the war) into a criticism of "Siegfried's unconquerable idealism [that] changed direction with his environment."[22] He himself remained the thoughtfully engaged soldier.

[17] Graves, *Good-bye*, pp. 174–175.
[18] July 21, 1916: Siegfried Sassoon (Rupert Hart-Davis, ed.), *Diaries 1915–1918* (London: Faber and Faber, 1983), p. 98.
[19] January 10, 1917: Sassoon, *Diaries*, p. 117.
[20] Sassoon to Graves, October 19, 1917: quoted in Sassoon, *Diaries*, p. 192.
[21] Graves to Sassoon, [November 1917]: Graves, *Broken Images*, p. 87.
[22] Graves, *Good-bye*, p. 275.

Graves's environment in 1917 affected his writing, however unclear that was by 1929. He was, in fact, both physically and emotionally removed from Sassoon's corpses. In England, while recovering from wounds, Graves was working on a book of romance verse called *Country Sentiment*. It was a far cry from his early war poetry, and Sassoon considered it inappropriate and unimportant, which his friend did not appreciate. As Graves, recently married to Nancy Nicholson, wrote indignantly later:

I can't write otherwise than I am now except with hypocrisy for I am bloody happy and bloody young (with only very occasional lapses) and passionate anger is most ungrateful . . . Worrying about the war is no longer a sacred duty with me . . . Curse me to hell: I shall hate it: but I must be honest according to my lights however dim they have grown.[23]

Graves was not writing about the war, but he tried to use it to his own advantage nonetheless. Invoking their shared combat experience, Graves asked Sassoon to accept his current activities not because they were friends, but because he should "be kind to me . . . for the sake of Fricourt now again overrun by Welch troops, and the woods beyond."[24] Graves tried to play the trump card of shared combat experience, bolstered by regimental loyalty. This was not, however, how Sassoon viewed the effect of the war, and he could not grasp Graves's new perspective. Graves seemed indeed happy; he was married and his wife was illustrating his new poems, which were much admired by "the seventeen-year-old girls and other romantics for whom they are intended." He was not worrying about the war, and so he was not writing about it. He even invoked the good he could do the nation in his new cadet training position to counter Sassoon's accusations of abandoning the war and his comrades. In retrospect, however, *Country Sentiment* was described quite differently by Graves. By 1929, the war seemed even more unavoidable as a topic of consideration, and as his marriage had failed, Nicholson seemed less so. In *Good-bye to All That*, in an effort "to forget about the War," Graves explained that he "was writing . . . a book of romantic poems and ballads."[25] With that simple turn of phrase – "to forget about the war" – the project that was originally the least about the conflict became essentially connected to it in memory.

Though Sassoon and Graves remained in contact for years after the Armistice, the division between them seems to have begun by 1917. Though sympathetic to the ideal being expressed, Graves could not understand Sassoon's action in his famous war protest and was more

---

[23] Graves to Sassoon, August 26, 1918: Graves, *Broken Images*, p. 101.
[24] Graves to Sassoon, August 26, 1918: Graves, *Broken Images*, p. 102.
[25] Graves, *Good-bye*, p. 277.

concerned with the logistics of preventing a court martial and getting Sassoon into hospital than with any principle involved. The second two volumes of Sassoon's *Memoirs* series bear witness to the profound gulf that had been created between the two writers, and the autobiographical texts that followed the trilogy of novels avoided mentioning Graves at all. Damningly, when Sassoon adapted sections of his diary for his protagonist George Sherston's use in *Sherston's Progress*, an entry about Graves and the incomprehensibility of leave is attributed not to David Cromlech, the Graves counterpart, but to Sherston's Aunt Evelyn.[26] Graves's view had been transmogrified into that of a civilian, and a woman at that. He became someone who was fundamentally incapable of understanding the realities of living in the trenches, rather than someone who had himself experienced, and condemned, that life.

This was not how Graves portrayed himself, of course, as his accounts of the end of the war attest. In the disillusionist school, the Armistice was almost invariably portrayed as a time of sadness rather than joy. To be happy was to demonstrate that you had failed to grasp the waste of the years of conflict. Graves's description in *Good-bye to All That* was very much in keeping with the model of the lonely survivor. "I heard at the same time of the deaths of Frank Jones-Bateman . . . and Wilfred Owen," he wrote, "Armistice-night hysteria did not touch our camp much." Instead, "the news sent me out walking alone . . . cursing and sobbing and thinking of the dead."[27] In 1918, however, Graves told Robert Nichols of his excitement. "Isn't it extraordinary to feel that the War's won at last," he wrote; "I keep a small silk Union Jack at the stairhead to remind me of it so that I shan't grouse at the petty annoyances of peace." He continued by criticizing the local population in Wales for the quietness of their celebrations.[28]

Even before the end of the war, though, Graves was sure he had a story to tell. He originally believed he could best tell his story as a novel, and he began it when he was in Britain after being wounded in 1916. He wrote to Robert Ross that he was "settl[ing] down to write the finest war-book (awful word) yet written," and was confident that "it should write quite easily as I haven't got to grout about after incidents: to choose will be the only difficulty."[29] The project proved more difficult than he anticipated, however, and four weeks later he confessed, "I stopped about ten days ago

---

[26] See Siegfried Sassoon, *Sherston's Progress* (London: Faber and Faber, 1936), p. 127.

[27] Graves, *Good-bye*, pp. 277–278.

[28] Graves to Nichols, [November 1918]: Graves, *Broken Images*, p. 104. See also Samuel Hynes, *A War Imagined: The First World War and English Culture* (London: The Bodley Head, 1990), pp. 434–435.

[29] Graves to Robert Ross, September 16, 1916: Ross, *Robert Ross*, p. 290.

at the 6th chapter because I was getting a bit weary."[30] In *Good-bye to All That*, Graves explained that "having stupidly written" his first efforts "as a novel," he was forced "to re-translate it into history."[31] He would write the soldier's story, with the authority of first-hand experience behind its claims for significance. In 1929, it was described as "an accurate and unembarrassed account of his life...apparently limited only by what is directly libelous."[32] Despite a number of caveats and concessions to factual criticism over the decades, Graves still described the work in 1952 as "a straight autobiography."[33] Experience was essential to the soldier's story, so Graves's account had to be true even if it were not.

"Truth," however, could only be judged by former comrades-in-arms. One of the hallmarks of the soldier's story was the claim that these narratives were written for informed audiences, allegedly the only ones who could understand them (though Graves and others were clearly also hoping their books would be widely read). Sassoon criticized the factual mistakes in *Good-bye to All That* because though they were "not noticeable to 'the general public'...they are significant to those who shared your experiences." He explained, "I am testing your book as a private matter between you and me, which is perhaps more important than the momentary curiosity of 50,000 strangers." Sassoon felt, like many reviewers, that "if such chapters are any good as evidence about the war, they should be valid against the criticisms of your 'former comrades.'"[34] Graves, however, defended the errors as a function of his experience:

I would even paradoxically say that the memoirs of a man who went through some of the worst experiences of trench warfare are not truthful if they do not contain a high proportion of falsities. High-explosive barrages will make a temporary liar or visionary of anyone; the old trench-mind is at work in all overestimation of casualties, "unnecessary" dwelling on horrors, mixing of dates and confusion between trench rumours and scenes actually witnessed.[35]

His friend Sassoon had accused the book of all those things, having told Graves that "there are no *under*statements in your book." Sassoon then concluded, "nearly all war books fall into that trap (pitching the story too strong and forgetting the decent element)." By then, the negative aspects of the war were far more important to the rootless survivors. Ironically, Sassoon criticized *Good-bye to All That* because Graves utilized

---

[30] Graves to Ross, October 12, 1916: Ross, *Robert Ross*, p. 291.
[31] Graves, *Good-bye*, p. 91.   [32] Dust jacket notes, *Good-bye* (1929).
[33] Graves's footnote to his correspondence with Ross: Ross, *Robert Ross*, p. 291.
[34] Sassoon to Graves, February 7, 1930: Graves, *Broken Images*, p. 200.
[35] Graves, "Correspondence: The Garlands Wither": *Times Literary Supplement* (hereafter *TLS*), June 26, 1930, p. 354; also reprinted in Graves, *But It Still Goes On* (1930).

"the omniscience of twelve years afterwards."[36] This kind of retrospective "omniscience" would in turn become the self-declared cornerstone of Sassoon's own prose writings.

Sassoon's progress: writing, identity, and the war

Sassoon himself had no greater luck in pleasing all his peers with his war writings. When the first novel of his Sherston trilogy, *Memoirs of a Fox-Hunting Man*, was published, Graves criticized it both publicly in a review and privately in a letter to Sassoon for failing to capture the moral questions of the war, and for disguising important issues by fictionalizing them.[37] Sassoon responded that his book was not "a piece of facile autobiographical writing," and that the protagonist, George Sherston, was "only 1/5 of myself, but his narrative is carefully thought out and constructed."[38] As Sassoon had earlier explained, he "attempted to construct something delicate and restrained," but in contrast "you blurted out your hasty version as though you were writing for the *Daily Mail*."[39] Sassoon's self-imposed literary schizophrenia continued a constant subject of his prose analysis. His prewar self, he remembered in his later memoir, had three parts: the hunter, the London gentleman, "and the invisible being who shadowed the other two with his lordly ambition to produce poetry."[40] The would-be poet was essentially important to his identity, both before and throughout the war years. George Sherston was not, in fact, Siegfried Sassoon, and it is problematic that many scholars and anthologizers have written about the Sherston novels as if he were.[41] Though Sassoon's fictional trilogy is clearly more than semi-autobiographical, Sherston was not a writer, making him fundamentally different from Sassoon himself. As Sassoon continued with the series in the 1930s, however, he grew increasingly frustrated with his fictional counterpart; significant portions of the third volume, *Sherston's Progress*, are based closely (though with some crucial differences) on Sassoon's

---

[36] Sassoon to Graves, March 2, 1930: Graves, *Broken Images*, p. 209 (emphasis in original).
[37] Graves to Sassoon, February 20, 1930: Graves, *Broken Images*, p. 203.
[38] Sassoon to Graves, March 2, 1930: Graves, *Broken Images*, p. 208.
[39] Sassoon to Graves, February 7, 1930: Graves, *Broken Images*, p. 199.
[40] Siegfried Sassoon, *The Weald of Youth* (London: Faber and Faber, 1942), pp. 266–267.
[41] As an example, even in *Great War and Modern Memory*, a text fundamentally aware of the *Memoirs* as fiction (see especially pp. 102–104), Fussell refers to Sassoon's shopping expedition prior to returning to the trenches in 1916, and cites *Memoirs of an Infantry Officer*. Sassoon may have made such purchases, but we cannot be sure of that from a source that refers to the fictional George Sherston: p. 65, p. 340 (n. 64). Less scrupulous texts, and especially anthologies, merely treat Sherston as if he and Sassoon were one and the same.

own wartime diary. Having then completed the trilogy of novels, Sassoon set out to try again. Between 1939 and 1946 he published three volumes of more conventional memoirs. These books focused more closely on his literary identity at the expense of his military activities. Sassoon has become an icon of disillusionment because of his famous war protest and subsequent "rehabilitation," described intimately both in his own work and by Graves. Sassoon's presentation of his wartime experience, however, evolved considerably over the decades which he spent rewriting it. Comparing the two literary versions of his life with his own wartime journals and letters illustrates the progression of his war views.

The most obvious difference, of course, is the absence of poetry and writing from Sherston's life. Though he had yet to achieve any tangible success, the dream of being a recognized poet was a driving force for the wartime Sassoon, who repeatedly recorded in his diary his desire for writing. In December 1915, though exulting in the opportunity for active experience of the war, Sassoon wrote in France that he "wish[ed] the Kaiser would let me go back to my work at writing poems . . . the good work was bound to come along sooner or later."[42] The idea of "experience," and how it would affect his poetry, was a major factor in how he viewed the war. As he wrote from the trenches in March 1916, the "great thing is to get as many sensations as possible . . . I want to get a good name in the Battalion, for the sake of poetry and poets."[43] Without those experiences, he had produced only "a sheaf of minor verse, mostly derived from memory."[44] The war, he suggested, actually gave advantages to both the poet and the poetry. Sassoon would serve bravely, even recklessly, to "let people see that poets can fight as well as anyone else."[45] He hoped that abandoning caution and embracing danger and depth of feeling would create great poetry, and declared that "if I'm alive in July 1926 I'll be a decent poet at last."[46] Continuing combat experience did not change this overall view, and even after the interlude of his protest, he continued to maintain the link between the war and his best poetry.

Sassoon was preoccupied with the relationship between the war, life on active service, and his writing. In the final volume of his autobiography, *Siegfried's Journey* (1946), he referred to the "complex advantage of being a soldier-poet" that was "denied" to Sherston and had helped Sassoon himself through the difficulties of disillusionment. Why, then, did he make

[42] December 17, 1915: Sassoon, *Diaries*, p. 26.
[43] March 31, 1916: Sassoon, *Diaries*, p. 51.
[44] December 17, 1915, July 19, 1916: Sassoon, *Diaries*, pp. 26, 96–97.
[45] April 4, 1916: Sassoon, *Diaries*, p. 53.   [46] July 19, 1916: Sassoon, *Diaries*, p. 97.

Sherston merely "a simplified version of my outdoor self" rather than a poet?[47] Though popular culture now associates the First World War with its poets, that connection was not so clear in the 1920s. Sherston was not a poet because Sassoon was fictionalizing his own life in order to create a broader indictment of war. Sassoon wrote in *Memoirs of an Infantry Officer* that "those who expect a universalization of the Great War must look for it elsewhere."[48] This is disingenuous, however; Sassoon's message would be powerful only if he could present himself as typical of the young officers of his day. He was writing about a vision of England he hoped everyone would recognize in order to contrast it with the horrors of military conflict. To have injected his own literary efforts into the pastoral picture and its counterpart of bloodshed would have been atypical, so he left them out. In the final volume of the first trilogy, he explicitly recognized the artificiality of this construct. Sassoon wrote, in Sherston's voice, that "our inconsistencies are often what make us most interesting, and it is possible that, in my zeal to construct these memoirs carefully, I have eliminated too many of my own self-contradictions."[49]

Readers had good reason to be confused by the relationship between Sassoon and Sherston. Though *Memoirs of a Fox-Hunting Man* was originally published anonymously, the note on the dust jacket declared that "this is fiction, but with a difference – for the author ... has himself lived the life of his hero." When Blunden accepted the Hawthorden Prize on an absent Sassoon's behalf in 1929, *The Times* quoted him promising that "Mr. Sassoon's next volume would continue his autobiography."[50] This set a clear precedent. The dust jacket of the trade edition of *Memoirs of an Infantry Officer* (1930) explained that "the details of Sherston's active-service experiences are fact, not invention," and its review in *The Times* referred to the "delicate accuracy" displayed in the "discovering and disclosing the truth of his own motives, actions, and reactions."[51] Continuing in the same manner, the dust jacket for *Sherston's Progress* (1936) drew explicit parallels between the lives of Sherston and Sassoon.

Sassoon himself later significantly elided the two. In the explicitly non-fictional *Weald of Youth*, Sassoon regularly referred to the fictional *Memoirs* for details of his own life. He even went so far as to add a fictional element to his autobiography in order to claim the validity of the *Memoirs* novels. Though he was now writing what he referred to as "this 'real autobiography' of mine," he was leery of "trespassing on Sherston's territory."

[47] Siegfried Sassoon, *Siegfried's Journey* (New York: Viking, 1946), p. 103.
[48] Siegfried Sassoon, *Memoirs of an Infantry Officer* (London: Faber and Faber, 1930), p. 13.
[49] Sassoon, *Sherston's Progress*, p. 147.   [50] *The Times*, July 13, 1929, 11e.
[51] *The Times*, September 19, 1930.

To preserve the illusion of shared identity, he adopted the pretense that "Aunt Evelyn," the character who stood in for his mother in his fictions, was visiting his real mother at the family home of Weirleigh. "Having thus ushered out my dilemma (which was a collision between fictionalized reality and essayized autobiography)," he explained, "I can now proceed with equanimity."[52] Some critics agreed with this blurring of identities, and Edmund Blunden maintained in 1946 that "the touch of fiction was not more than a touch, and the 'Fox-Hunting Man' series remains in the class of memoirs."[53] This covers over, however, a multitude of choices Sassoon made in the creation of Sherston's history.

Sassoon, in fact, spent the rest of his life writing about the present in terms of the past. He described what he called "the art of reminiscence" as "to show myself as I am now in relation to what I was during the War."[54] Sassoon's texts, however, have entered popular culture as being about the war years themselves, and their fictional, constructed aspects are often dismissed. There is only a brief interval between the conclusion of the Sherston texts and the appearance of the first of the more traditional memoirs, *The Old Century and Seven More Years*. There, the middle-aged author contemplated how he as a child would have reacted to his literary "future resuscitation." He imagined the young Sassoon asking him, "What's resuscitation?," and only being able to answer that "it means 'to imbue one's past life with saturations of subsequent experience.'"[55] Again, the retrospective viewpoint is at the center of these texts; they are not stories of the war, but stories of *remembering* the war. Memory, rather than experience, is at their heart.

Obviously, the books are about his life, but Sassoon constructed careful narratives in order to make an argument about the changes he had lived through in England, rather than focusing on himself. In many ways Sassoon remained an unreformed Georgian; he had little patience with modernism, though his own books have become canonical to the literature of disillusionment. He believed throughout his life that poetry should be about beauty. His books, then, were at their best when he was writing from his depth of admiration for prewar life; he had a gift for capturing the pastoral in compelling ways. This is not to say, however, that he was presenting an unreflective account of the era. The modernists looked to the future; Sassoon lived continuously in the past, celebrating it over the

---

52 Sassoon, *Weald*, p. 73.
53 Edmund Blunden, "A Poet Reviews His Journey: Mr. Sassoon's Star," *TLS*, January 5, 1946, p. 6.
54 Sassoon, *Sherston's Progress*, p. 37.
55 Siegfried Sassoon, *The Old Century and Seven More Years* (New York: Viking, 1939), pp. 118–119.

present. He indicted the war for the grievous crime of killing the vision of the past that he cared about. He even argued that he had done this most successfully in the fictionalized prose of the *Memoirs*, rather than the contemporary wartime anger of his best-known poetry. In the last year of his life, he wrote that he was "still inclined to think that the war poems (the significant and successful ones) will end up as mere appendices to the matured humanity of the Memoirs."[56] Sassoon wrote in *Infantry Officer* that he was "no believer in wild denunciations of the War" but was "merely describing [his] own experiences of it." He thus dismissed his own past protest as "wild" but continued to denounce the war, in more gentle but perhaps no less devastating ways. His used the material of his own life to construct carefully a more effective cautionary tale than his legendary (but ultimately unsuccessful) war protest of 1917 had proved to be.

From the diary to Sherston to the reflective older man, Sassoon's portrayal of the war was a function of the author at each different historical period rather than of the war itself. The experiences, in fact, were continually being reconstructed. In 1916, for example, Sassoon was invalided home to England with a gastric infection. His journey from London on the hospital train seems to have remained a powerful memory, as it was marked in turn in his journal, a poem, *Memoirs of an Infantry Officer*, and *Siegfried's Journey*. From the windows of the train, Sassoon watched civilians paying their respects to the hospital-bound soldiers. In a section of his diary in which he described himself in the third person – a technique he occasionally employed – he described the "grateful stay-at-homes" who waved, and a middle-aged man on a bicycle who took "one hand off handlebars to wave feeble and jocular gratitude." As a result, "the soul of the officer glows with fiery passion as he thinks 'All this I've been fighting for; and now I'm safe home again I begin to think it was worth while.'" This tempered enthusiasm was also ironic, as he simultaneously "wondered how he could avoid being sent out again."[57]

Sassoon immediately employed that irony in a poem, though without its contrasting sense of latent patriotism. In hospital, he wrote "Stretcher-Case" about a similar train journey. Again, in his effort to create a more universal voice, he changed himself as the narrator. "Stretcher-Case" used the voice of a wounded enlisted soldier (wounds being more "typical" than illness, of course, and rankers more prevalent than officers). The soldier, upon recovering consciousness, "remembered that his

---

[56] Quoted in Paul Moeyes, *Siegfried Sassoon: Scorched Glory. A Critical Study* (New York: St. Martin's Press, 1997), p. 195.

[57] August 2, 1916: Sassoon, *Diaries*, p. 100.

name was Brown" – a far contrast from the distinguished surname of Sassoon. Rather than be inspired by the tributes of real human beings, however ambivalent he might have felt about them, this soldier is reassured by the commonplaces of "railway advertisements of 'Lung Tonic, Mustard, Liver Pills, and Beer.'" Sassoon described the creation of this poem much later in *Siegfried's Journey* as an opportunity to release his "overflowing" abundance of "stored-up impressions and emotional reactions to the extraordinary things I had observed and undergone." His stay in hospital meant "I should now be able to work off some of the poetry bottled up in me."[58]

This emotional outlet was not available, of course, to George Sherston, as he – unlike the Sassoon of either 1916 or 1946 – was not a poet. In *Infantry Officer*, the entire scene was rendered with a more pastoral tone, reflective of the lost England Sassoon so frequently invoked in the *Memoirs*. The "grateful stay-at-homes" of the diary – a double-edged description, surely – became, more mildly, "peaceful stay-at-homes." The "middle-aged" waver became "elderly," and therefore perhaps more evocative of the past. Similarly, his gratitude, previously "jocular," became "comprehensive," and "everything seemed happy and homely." Sherston, not unlike the younger Sassoon, was "delivered from the idea of death," but was not trying to avoid a return to combat.[59] The mental complexities described in the journal were significantly simplified; the ambiguities of motivation were removed along with the poetry, in order to make a point more simple and more general about how Britain had changed during the war (and not for the better, in Sassoon's eyes).

Like Graves, Sassoon's personal writings also illustrate changing attitudes toward the enemy. Early in 1916, he encountered an old schoolfellow when the First Royal Welch relieved the Twelfth Middlesex in the line. Sassoon noted laconically in his diary that "their billeting officer is C. H. S. Runge. Hadn't seen him since I was at private school with him. His two cousins, whom I used to know, are fighting for the other side."[60] Sassoon offered neither condemnation nor empathy toward the Germans in this brief entry, but he made the incident do much more work when he rewrote it for *Memoirs of a Fox-Hunting Man*, more than a decade later. Here, the reader was introduced to "Regel (which he now pronounced Regal)," having been forced to Anglicize the pronunciation of his name. (Both Siegfried Sassoon and Robert von Ranke Graves also discussed the occasional difficulties they encountered with Germanic names.) Having finished their work, the two went on and "talked for a while of old days."

---

[58] Sassoon, *Siegfried's Journey*, pp. 7–8.   [59] Sassoon, *Infantry Officer*, pp. 90–91.
[60] February 1, 1916: Sassoon, *Diaries*, p. 37.

Though Sherston had not at first recognized Regel, he thought to ask after "cousin Willie . . . for want of anything else to say." This proved an awkward inquiry, and Regel "replied (in a low voice, for there were two other officers in the room), 'He's on the other side – in the artillery.'" Only then did Sherston remember that "Willie (a very nice boy) had always gone home to Hanover for the holidays. And now he might be sending a five-nine shell over at us for all we, or he, knew."[61] Unlike the unemotional account of the diary, here Regel had to be embarrassed by his family connections, and did not want his fellow officers to know that his relations with Germany were so close and so recent. The incident is another example of the ironies of the war: Regel (and Sherston) and Willie, former school-fellows, now doing their best to kill each other, entirely unbeknownst to one another. This cynical appreciation was entirely absent from the succinct wartime version of the incident that Sassoon had recorded in his diary.

By the publication of *The Old Century*, the tone had shifted further. This first volume of Sassoon's "real autobiography" did not deal with the war years directly, but was filled with references to them. A fort he and his brothers built as children was "not unlike one of the above-ground dugouts I was in during the war," for example. Revisiting a summer holiday cottage led, circuitously, to the story of his brother's death in the Dardanelles. Similarly, when describing his formal education, Sassoon recounted that he had been at school with "those two nice German boys, first cousins, who afterwards fought against one another in a war that neither of them wanted."[62] Now he had moved beyond the irony of school-fellows and family members turned enemies unawares, and the statement is far more directly in opposition to the war itself. Runge, himself English, was turned into a German like his cousin. There was no sense in either Sassoon's diary or Sherston's encounter that Runge/Regel was opposed to the war; in fact, Regel was eager to demonstrate his patriotism. Sherston did not even recognize Regel at first, having "forgotten his existence" – and presumably therefore that of his cousin as well.[63] The sentiment of being forced into an undesirable conflict by powers beyond the control of those fighting in it, however, was a key part of the soldier's story as it developed. This was particularly so by the late 1930s, when Sassoon was painfully aware that another war with Germany loomed. He attributed this postwar attitude to his wartime colleagues, then, in the service of his literary arguments.

---

[61] Siegfried Sassoon, *Memoirs of a Fox-Hunting Man* (London: Faber and Faber, 1928), p. 291.
[62] Sassoon, *Old Century*, pp. 151, 116–117, 174.   [63] Sassoon, *Fox-Hunting Man*, p. 291.

Perhaps the clearest example of Sassoon's rewriting of the past in the service of the present can be found where it might seem least likely to appear: Part III of *Sherston's Progress*, which consists entirely of relatively close transcriptions of Sassoon's own wartime diary. Rupert Hart-Davis, Sassoon's literary executor and editor of the published diaries, stated that the whole Sherston trilogy was "autobiography disguised as fiction," and "Part III of *Sherston's Progress* consists entirely of quotations" from the diaries.[64] Dominic Hibberd, reviewing the paperback reissue of *Sherston's Progress* which coincided with the publication of the diaries in 1983, wrote that "Sassoon himself got bored" with Sherston, and therefore "took to copying directly from the 1918 diary."[65] The critic Paul Moeyes, while arguing that the diary section suggested that the author was increasingly tired of the trilogy and his less complex and sophisticated counterpart, still averred that the published diaries "confirm that there are only minor changes and omissions."[66] The changes may be small, but they are significant.

Some of the changes are minor and understandable. As a writer, Sassoon could not resist the chance to clarify his prose and clean up his syntax, which he did regularly throughout the "entries." Sassoon was also writing when a number of his military peers were alive and able to recognize barely masked portraits, which led to some changes.[67] Sassoon had also used "diary" entries in *Memoirs of a Fox-Hunting Man*, where he deleted a reference to Robert Graves as well as a number of phrases. He also adjusted the date format to fit more neatly with Sassoon's efforts to tell a more general story, not grounded in specific events but in shared experience.[68]

Sassoon also deleted all references to sex. Where men on leave described in the diary were "eating and drinking and being bored, and looking for lust," in Sherston's version they were merely "eating and drinking and being bored."[69] This elision is particularly careful with any suggestion of homoeroticism. Watching men on shipboard, Sassoon wrote that "they lie in indolent attitudes, and their minds are just as stoical as the 'average young officer's' I suppose." He recorded that "I like to see them leaning against each other with their arms round one another – it is pathetic

[64] Rupert Hart-Davis, "Introduction," in Sassoon, *Diaries*, p. 9.
[65] Dominic Hibberd, "A Pilgrim in Flanders," *TLS*, April 22, 1983, p. 395.
[66] Moeyes, *Sassoon*, p. 193.
[67] See, for example, May 19, 1918: Sassoon, *Diaries*, pp. 251–252; Sassoon, *Sherston's Progress*, p. 121.
[68] Sassoon, *Fox-Hunting Man*, pp. 275–276; the entries correspond to November 25–29, 1915. A 1918 entry was also included, and therefore deleted from its corresponding "diary" section of *Sherston's Progress*. See also Moeyes, *Sassoon*, p. 193.
[69] March 4, 1918: Sassoon, *Diaries*, p. 219; *Sherston's Progress*, p. 95.

and beautiful and human (but that is only a sexual emotion in me – to like them in those attitudes)."[70] For Sherston, it was just that "leaning against each other in indolent attitudes, the men seem much nearer the realities of life than the average officer."[71] Sassoon, unlike Sherston, was coming to emotional terms with his sexuality during the war years. For Sherston to have expressed sexual feelings, especially toward men, would have jolted him out of the universal public persona Sassoon was trying to portray. Additionally, though Sassoon had male lovers in the 1920s and early 1930s, by the time he was working on *Sherston's Progress* he had married Hester Gatty, and his son George was born in 1936. He may, therefore, have been less comfortable with his own sexual history.

There are also a significant number of changes that shift Sassoon's representation of the war. In February, 1918, both Sassoon and Sherston picked primroses; Sassoon commented "how touching!" while Sherston wondered more gloomily "when I shall see another."[72] In April 1918, both described anticipating "trudging away from Arcadia" behind a column of men and mules carrying heavy baggage; Sherston alone added the depressed postscript that he would have "not much more liberty than a mule itself."[73] The mules continued to be important, though. While Sassoon the next day recorded that "a mule brays among the murmur of men's voices," only Sherston felt that the animal's participation was a protest, adding that it was "probably saying what it thinks about the war."[74] Birds, too, were anthropomorphized to make Sassoon's retrospective arguments stronger. Both personas went to the zoo in Boulogne in May 1918, where each heard a lone blackbird singing among more brightly colored avian companions. Sassoon wrote that the bird "sat and sang his heart out, quite indifferent to the others," and that "it was pathetic to see and hear him." Sherston, in contrast, began by criticizing the zoo itself – "not much there, owing to war" – and then went on to describe the blackbird as being "rather the worse for wear." Here, the independent music did not inspire mere pathos; instead, more specifically, "he made me think of a prisoner of war."[75] Where Sassoon in 1918 described beauty amid carnage, he turned it in Sherston's eyes and pen into only depression and darkness.

---

[70] May 4, 1918: Sassoon, *Diaries*, p. 242.

[71] Sassoon, *Sherston's Progress*, p. 114. See also Moeyes, *Sassoon*, p. 271, n. 36.

[72] February 13, 1918: Sassoon, *Diaries*, p. 212; Sassoon, *Sherston's Progress*, p. 8.

[73] April 7, 1918: Sassoon, *Diaries*, p. 230; Sassoon, *Sherston's Progress*, p. 105.

[74] April 8, 1918: Sassoon, *Diaries*, p. 230; Sassoon, *Sherston's Progress*, p. 105. In my editions, the diary entry is dated 8 April 7:00 p.m., and the fictional version 7 April 8:00 p.m.

[75] May 8, 1918: Sassoon, *Diaries*, p. 246; Sassoon, *Sherston's Progress*, pp. 116–117.

Similarly, the diary entry for May 13 records that Sassoon saw the "country looking very beautiful," and it inspired him to quote Thomas Hardy that "the May month flaps its glad green leaves like wings."[76] In 1936, though, the tone was entirely different. In Sherston's entry, he agreed about the "country looking very beautiful," but he continued that "May is a deceptive time of year to arrive anywhere," as "it creates an illusion of youth and prosperity, as though the world were trying to be friendly, and happiness somewhere ahead of one."[77] Instead of invoking joy with one of his favorite authors, Sassoon rewrote the passage to suggest illusion and foreknowledge of loss, as well as the absence of any possibility of future happiness. Again, the complexities of original emotion – including beauty even among the horrors of war – were simplified in the service of Sassoon's primary argument against the disastrous combat and the changes it brought about. The contrast heightened the poignancy, and the soldier's story lay behind the rewriting.

It should not be surprising, perhaps, that Sassoon treated his diaries as material to work with rather than sacrosanct utterances, even when "quoting" from them. His published writings contained several denigrating references to the journals themselves. In *Infantry Officer*, Sassoon wrote (quoting his own diary) that after being wounded Sherston "was able to write" that "I am still feeling warlike and quite prepared to go back to the Battalion in a few weeks." However, "in spite of [his] self-defensive scribble," he was sent to London and "by no means sorry to be carried through the crowd of patriotic spectators."[78] Sassoon was not just offering his postwar perspective on his wartime activities; he was recasting his own contemporary ambivalences in terms of his matured thoughts. This reconstruction is even clearer in *Siegfried's Journey*, when he insisted that "the diary indeed discloses very little of my actual state of mind about the war." He explained retrospectively that this was because "the young man was liable to regard his words as likely to be read after he'd been killed in action. It did not occur to him that the posterity that perused them would be merely himself." In contrast, "I now wish that my former self had allowed for the possibility of my some day writing a book about him!" The mature Sassoon, who by that point had spent much of the past two decades rethinking and rewriting his war, entirely discounted any validity of emotion from the diaries themselves. He rejected the confusion and ambivalence that repeatedly appeared from entry to entry by denying that it revealed his "actual state of mind," because "elevated feelings" could only be, after the fact, something "resort[ed] to" in order

[76] May 13, 1918: Sassoon, *Diaries*, p. 248.   [77] Sassoon, *Sherston's Progress*, p. 117.
[78] Sassoon, *Infantry Officer*, p. 171.

to "keep... [his] courage up." Sassoon wrote, "I find, here and there, a scrap of simple unaffected utterance," which could be used in the crafting of autobiography.[79] What the wartime diaries suggest, however, is that Sassoon's emotional life was far from simple or unaffected, and to recast it as such says much more about the author's perspective on the war and Britain in 1946 than in 1916.

Sassoon knew, and stated explicitly, that he was using the past to comment on the present, rather than trying to offer a "true" picture of the war. He was also aware of the complexities of memory, perhaps particularly as related to the trauma of war. In *Infantry Officer*, he wrote that "time seems to have obliterated the laughter of the war. I cannot hear it in my head." In retrospect, he only heard the irony of that laughter, "when we all knew that we'd got to do an attack that night," and explained it by the simple device of "some rum inside us."[80] He was necessarily reconstructing his experience from the perspective of his present, having survived both war and war protest, and having been disillusioned at least as much by postwar society as by his military service itself. It was not possible to recapture what it felt like to live those moments, with that frame of reference. In any case, he was not trying to. Sassoon had Sherston recall "a half-dug communication trench whose existence I have only this moment remembered (which shows how difficult it is to recover the details of war experience)."[81] His poetry of the 1930s, too, demonstrated this increasing distance from the events that obsessed his mind. In 1934 he published, in *Vigils*, a poem called "War Experience." Here he offered the image of a bombardment on the Somme, where "almost unbelieved-in looms / The day-break sentry staring over Kiel Trench crater."[82] His own past was becoming increasingly unreal, unbelievable, even doubted, while remaining fundamental to his conceptions of the present.

At the end of his last volume of prose writings, Sassoon attempted to come to grips with the complex relation between the past and the present. "It needs no pointing out," he wrote, "that there is an essential disparity between being alive and memorizing it long afterwards." But the "memorizer" – that is, the writer of memoirs – "must also bear this in mind, that his passage through time was a confused experiment, and that external circumstances had yet to become static and solidly discernible." He cited "an eminent Victorian" who maintained that "we read

---

[79] Sassoon, *Siegfried's Journey*, pp. 61–62.   [80] Sassoon, *Infantry Officer*, p. 61.

[81] Sassoon, *Infantry Officer*, p. 68.

[82] Edmund Blunden therefore suggested that Sassoon was "revisiting far-off things with gentleness": Blunden, "Mr. Sassoon's Trilogy," *TLS*, September 5, 1936, p. 709. See also Moeyes, *Sassoon*, p. 129.

the past by the light of the present," and compared "the living present to a jig-saw puzzle loose in its box," because "not until afterwards can we fit the pieces together and make a coherent picture of them." In his writing he had "often been conscious of this process." He therefore attempted to assemble the puzzle for his younger self, to "reconstruct an outline which represents everything as though it had been arranged for him beforehand." This was a new perspective, though, as "throughout the journey... he was like someone driving a motor-car on a foggy night, only able to see a few yards ahead of him." Sassoon knew that in doing so he was presenting an illusion, but could "only suggest that somebody with more metaphysical ability than I can command should investigate this discrepancy between the art of autobiography and the rudimentariness of reality."

He wondered, too, whether "the immediacy of our existence amounts to little more than animality, and... our ordered understanding of it is only assembled through afterthought and retrospection," a clear description of his approach to the dilemma. He then disclaimed any responsibility for the results of the process, suggesting he was "overstraining my limited intelligence" so that he had to "extricate myself from these obstrusities."[83] As his own words made clear, Sassoon's aim was never to reconstruct his specific lived experience of the Great War, but to use his autobiographical details to create a more coherent portrait of society before, during, and especially after the years of conflict. His work is popularly known through misinterpretation. He aimed for a unified story of the universal, and has been credited instead with the specific powerful tale of an individual.

By 1957, when *Good-bye to All That* was reissued, Sassoon had come to approve of Graves's memoir, on the grounds that it would help "remind the new generation of what 1914–18 was for those who endured it."[84] Their differences in representation and detail, so important during the publishing revolution, were forgotten in the shadow of age and another world war; complexities and differences, clear in the wartime years, and still vitally important to these men in the late 1920s, were ultimately simplified into a unified soldier's story. It was a vision of the war centered on the trench and therefore exclusive of all other experiences, including those that had been valued during the war itself. As a result, other war workers, and especially women, were left wondering how their contributions fit into the new history of the war.

[83] Sassoon, *Siegfried's Journey*, pp. 336–337.
[84] Sassoon to Graves, December 7, 1957: Graves, *Broken Images*, p. 347.

Irene Rathbone: she who was young

In the summer of 1918, Irene Rathbone was the 26-year-old daughter of an upper-middle class and politically radical Liverpool family. She was an experienced war worker, having spent part of 1915 in a YMCA canteen in Boulogne and then served as a VAD nurse in a number of London hospitals. She was also a would-be actress, prone to dramatic assessments of everyday life; a self-described socialist who had nonetheless deeply internalized the class divisions of her day; and a terrible flirt. The diary she kept of her war work that summer, when she returned to France and YMCA work in support of the Third Army rest camp established at St. Valery, makes all this vividly clear.[85] By 1932, Irene Rathbone was forty years old. Her favored younger brother and her fiancé both survived the war only to die soon after (one of influenza leading to pneumonia, the other while serving in the Middle East). She never married. She was living independently, though she maintained close connections to her family and took her responsibilities as a daughter very seriously. That year, she published her semi-autobiographical novel of how the war had changed her generation, *We That Were Young*. As its title indicated, it was about coming of age and beyond for what had come to be called "the lost generation," whose members were left dead or disillusioned; the use of "that" rather than "who" suggested that their very human status was negated by the war. It was very much a story of the 1930s, a retrospective view of the impact of the war that was clearer fourteen years after the Armistice than it had been at the time. A comparison of the St. Valery diary and the section of novel based on it makes the contrast between the two perspectives apparent. The diary was written in the summer of 1918, the last one of the war. After four years of conflict and three years of war work, Irene Rathbone was not yet voicing the disillusionment and devastation – or the sense of fundamentally changed identity – that came to be associated with the publications of the late 1920s and 1930s (including her own). Irene Rathbone of 1932, though reading her own diary, could see 1918 only through postwar eyes.

Important differences between the two texts are clear from the outset of the St. Valery section of the novel. Joan Seddon, Irene Rathbone's fictional counterpart, had been serving as a VAD nurse in London military hospitals. She was having health problems, however, and "a series of septic fingers" led to doctor's orders that "she must have a complete rest

---

[85] Irene Rathbone, *Diary, Valery-sur-Somme (APOS 59 BEF). Summer 1918*, 3 vols., Imperial War Museum Department of Documents 90/30/1.

from nursing, and only take it up again – if at all – later in the year."[86] Conveniently, Joan's friend Betty, who had been working in YMCA canteens since 1915, wrote to invite her to come help with the new Third Army rest camp. Forced to leave nursing, at least for a while, she turned to work that was equally safe in its connotations of femininity. Her decision to abandon nursing in favor of canteening was presented as reluctant, out of her control, and only temporary, though it was also greeted with some relief. "So she put away her VAD clothes – feeling a little apologetic toward them – 'until next winter,'" Rathbone wrote, but "her heart rose inside of her."[87] Seddon was excited by her new opportunity, but it was only when she was freed from her hospital obligation that she could accept work that was sure to be both more pleasant and more social.

Irene Rathbone, unlike Seddon, had control over her war work. She was tired from nursing, and frustrated by the complicated position of VADs in military hospitals, but she was under no medical compunction to leave. Her cousin Maidie, Betty's role model for this period, wrote to ask Rathbone to join them in St. Valery. Rathbone responded with enthusiasm:

Here is a chance of good work for a summer... under exceptionally delightful conditions, hard work, but a wonderful change from hospital; work with friends, in a nice atmosphere with no discipline... I seize the chance with both hands – it would have been madness not to. I was getting played out as a VAD.[88]

Rathbone continued to make derogatory references to her nursing experiences. "Every now and then," she wrote, "it comes over me with special force what a delightful life this is," especially when "I think with a shudder that I might easily be still in hospital."[89] In fact, Rathbone stopped nursing some time before she left for France. Both decisions – to leave nursing and then go to France with the YMCA – were hers. Many young middle-class women, of course, worked part-time and locally while living at home. Though it might have been socially challenging if she had not been involved in any war work at all, she was not necessarily expected to contribute her life to the effort full-time, as a soldier was. In rewriting her story, though, Rathbone was working within the parameters of the soldier's story. Joan had to feel compelled to continue her fully committed

[86] Irene Rathbone, *We That Were Young* (New York: The Feminist Press, 1989 [1932]), p. 368.
[87] Rathbone, *We That Were Young*, p. 369.
[88] Rathbone, *Diary*, first entry (undated, June 1918).
[89] Rathbone, *Diary*, August 8, 1918.

service, or else her ultimate disillusionment would not have seemed as powerful.

To fit with the soldier's story, canteening work also had to be character-ized as difficult, even if it was not as exhausting as nursing. Otherwise, the postwar contrast between extensive exertion and its corresponding lack of reward would not have been powerful enough. Irene Rathbone noticed in 1918 (with more than a little distaste) the way her companions perspired when working in the hot tent. She wrote in her diary that "while serv-ing out fish and chips the perspiration *literally* rained off Kit's face and splashed upon the table!"[90] This seems to have been a bit much for the younger Rathbone's delicate sensibilities. In contrast, it was Joan Seddon herself who was awarded the sweat of real exertion retrospectively; and she "dump[ed] down plates on the counter, splash[ing] pools of per-spiration beside them."[91] Similarly, while Rathbone's diary was full of references to ample time off, Joan Seddon's schedule was far busier. As part of the transformation into the female version of the soldier's story, the work had to be both hard and constant, entirely divorced from customary peacetime leisure activities.

Rathbone consistently imbued Seddon with a greater awareness of the pathos and humanity of the war's tragedies than was apparent in the 1918 diaries. Both texts, for example, described a dinner hosted by some of the officers at a restaurant. As with most social events, this meal was detailed at considerable length in the diaries. Rathbone described the men present and her topics of discussion with each one. With Hobbs, it was "French marriages, Swinburne, Anatole France, and crepe de chine nighties; with de Roubaiye ... trenches, retreats, and the cavalry; with little Brownrigg, his wife and kid and home life." She was frustrated though, that the man she found most attractive was too far away from her, engaged in conversation with her cousin. This disappointment was augmented when she learned that he was married: "he would be of course – they are all so much nicer when they are." The officers escorted the women home, where Rathbone found another worker dining with a YMCA Christian (as the officials were called). Their conversation was "very boring," as he "talked 'Tommy' and 'religion' and the 'Oxford book of mystic verse'" – topics without the fascination of military maneuvers or marriages British and French. Rathbone therefore retired to her diary and bed.[92] Though this dinner took place on July 1, there was no mention of the second anniversary of the Battle of the Somme, the event that later would be

---

so closely associated with the slaughter of idealistic innocents and the resulting disillusionment of the survivors.[93]

In *We That Were Young*, however, Joan Seddon had quite a different evening. The dinner itself merited only a brief mention. The point of the account, in fact, was to set up a contrast with Seddon's return to the house, where she encountered Barbara, another of the canteen workers. Barbara (who had no direct counterpart in the diaries) had not come to the dinner. Since the deaths in action of both her brother and fiancé, she was "definitely 'off' festivities." Instead, she focused on the work and the war, because "the fact that the war's still going on makes me feel that [the dead]'re still in it – still fighting somewhere." In fact, she continued, "I don't suppose I *shall* realise – until peace." This was the profound conclusion Rathbone gave to Joan Seddon's social evening; "she wouldn't realise – thousands of women wouldn't realise – until peace."[94] In the postwar version, the dinner was not about playing matchmaking games and being bored by serious thoughts. Instead, it used the constructed character of the woman who had lost so much to the conflict to make a most sobering point about death, war, and the wasteland of sorrow that still awaited the lonely women who survived. Her point was about life *after* the war rather than about 1918. To make sure the reader clearly understood this, Rathbone revisited it at the end of the chapter. Then, Joan Seddon greeted the Armistice in loneliness from her family's house in England. She described herself as "armysick" (in contrast to "homesick"), echoing the conviction presented by many soldiers that no one at home understood them. Rather than celebrating the end of the years of death, Rathbone had Seddon looking ahead to the future for those who had lost their loves, and for whom the cease-fire was the end of a "powerful and blessed drug."[95] This is an essentially retrospective perception.

Seddon also exhibited a more modern interpretation of morality than had her younger model. Both narratives described two local prostitutes. The young Rathbone's attitude toward these women was markedly different from that exhibited retrospectively through Seddon. The diary recorded disgust and frustration. "There are horrible facts about the army as well as splendid ones," Rathbone wrote, "one knows this all the time

---

93 Rathbone explained that the war did not have much day-to-day impact on her life or perceptions, even working in France with soldiers just down from the front: "The war news is good. When particularly so I allude to it, or if particularly bad I should, otherwise in a rather silly personal record of daily life such as this, communiqués of the war are out of place": Rathbone, *Diary*, August 9, 1918. In *We That Were Young*, more accurate and specific military information was added: Rathbone, *We That Were Young*, p. 396, for example.

94 Rathbone, *We That Were Young*, pp. 380–381.

95 Rathbone, *We That Were Young*, p. 408.

of course, but now and then one is brought right up against something which turns one sick and angry." She added that "it seems incredible that nothing can be done," and wondered if the local YMCA authority "could use his power in any way to get them turned out [as] the harm they do must be immense."[96] In *We That Were Young*, however, this vehement anger was attributed to one of the Christians, and Joan, "though saddened and sick at heart, was unable to feel so ferociously about it all."[97] Seddon was not as naïve as Rathbone had been.

Rathbone was particularly concerned because "if it were only the hardened older men who resorted there one could bear it better, but they get the under-aged boys into their clutches." She regretted that

there is nothing to do, I suppose, as far as we are concerned, but continue to be ourselves. In this work the threads we hold them by are so intangible . . . They have not to be specially viciously bent to fall victims to all the beastly influences that crowd in the passage of armies. Weakness, idleness, boredom, is quite enough. They may have been heroes at the Front. How hard things are for them! How hard. What we are seeing now is the extinguishing and degrading of an entire generation. Oh war! war![98]

Rathbone, in 1918, reached the somewhat novel conclusion that it was not slaughter, betrayal, and disillusionment that created the "lost generation" so discussed in the postwar years. Instead, immorality was the culprit, despite the best efforts of the "YM Ladies."

This diary passage was rewritten in *We That Were Young*, but Rathbone used many of the same words and phrases to reach quite different conclusions:

It was all natural enough; and a soldier had no need to be especially vicious if, after coming back from months of hell to a period of idleness, he wanted "love." The pity was that no better sort was provided. Boys who should still have been at home – still at school – first learnt of it like this. Yet there were people (her Uncle Robert was one) who talked of the "uplifting influence of war," and of how it "made men of boys." It certainly did. The little Scotch orderly who helped at the hut had been sent to hospital diseased. That was a case she knew of, but there were probably dozens – hundreds – of others.

No, there was nothing to be done, Joan supposed. Nothing but to go on, in one's rather futile way, making that centre of respectability, the YM, as attractive as possible.[99]

There were no references to venereal disease in the discussion in the diary, and nothing that would suggest any understanding of a need for "love." The younger Rathbone saw the front as the location of heroism,

---

[96] Rathbone, *Diary*, July 7, 1918.   [97] Rathbone, *We That Were Young*, p. 385.

[98] Rathbone, *Diary*, July 7, 1918.   [99] Rathbone, *We That Were Young*, p. 385.

not "months of hell." Perhaps most tellingly, the blame for the costs of prostitution and its effects on the soldiers shifted. In 1918, it was the women themselves who had the men in "their clutches." In 1932, the real culprit was the older men back home, like Seddon's Uncle Robert, who still believed there were personally redeeming aspects of the war. This was very much in keeping with the soldier's story, where non-combatants safe in Britain betrayed the men fighting and dying at the front. Of course, that version of the war often blamed not just older men but also women. Rathbone, as one who saw herself as part of the war generation, naturally excluded herself from the ranks of the exploiters.

This effort to include women workers among those who served, parallel to (if not the equals of) the fighting men, was an important undercurrent to Rathbone's retrospective revisions. Some of the changes were subtle; Joan Seddon, for example, never made references that could undermine her own importance or the value of her contribution to the war effort. The young diarist did, though, writing that "all this clack about what the women of England are doing makes me sick."[100] She even wondered, "are we or are we not any good at all . . . [if] we *are* an influence for good, what a passive influence it is, and how little exertion it requires on our part."[101] Seddon's efforts would never have been so minimized. Rathbone even hoped to leave canteen work and become an actress in one of the traveling theater companies that entertained the troops. "THERE is my job, I feel it and know it!" she wrote, "it would be doing the thing I cared for most in the world, and at the same time good war work."[102] A powerful combination, indeed. (This dramatic preference was entirely absent from Joan Seddon's summer at St. Valery, however. Seddon, after all, hoped to return to the ideal of nursing, as soon as she was well enough. It was a flightier character, Pamela, who had ambitions for the stage.) There was room for Rathbone in 1918 to belittle her activities and still be sure of appreciation and respect but that assurance was lost retrospectively. Still, the move from nursing to canteening to (ideally) acting did not suggest a desire to maintain intimacy of contact with the soldiers themselves. Each step moved her further from work for their physical well-being, whatever her alleged hopes for their emotional satisfaction.

In 1932, Rathbone (through Joan Seddon) was staking a claim for legitimacy of experience, for membership in a war generation that included both men and women. Both the diary and the novel acknowledged difficult relations with the commander of the camp, who was less than pleased to have women in his facility. Rathbone often complained

---

[100] Rathbone, *Diary*, June 22, 1918.   [101] Rathbone, *Diary*, August 23, 1918.
[102] Rathbone, *Diary*, July 2, 1918.

in her diary that Col. Lawson was obstructive. As she wrote, she wished he "would only be friendly toward us, allow us to drop in frequently to the [officers'] mess, and generally treat us as a vital part of the camp" (modest requests, of course).[103] In retrospect, however, though he was no more helpful, Rathbone needed to make the colonel an aberration, one of a minority who failed to understand the importance of the women's contributions. According to the diary, the visiting adjutant general of the Third Army asked Kit Beale about relations with Lawson. As head of the female canteen workers, she was diplomatically silent.[104] In the fictional version, however, there was complicity between the visiting officer and the canteener. When asked, "with the suspicion of a twinkle," if the colonel were treating the women well, "Betty's dark eyelashes flickered, but she made no reply." This was because "none was needed. The [deputy adjutant general] perfectly understood, and, remarking that the weather was very fine, saluted and strode off."[105] The dialogue did not change in any significant way, but the characterization of the high-ranking visitor provided validation for the efforts of the women workers. It was the colonel, rather than the women, who was excluded from the real conversation. If the army staff appreciated their work, then women were indeed legitimate members of the war generation.

Memory, of course, is a tricky thing, as Rathbone discovered. One diary entry, for example, gushed about a picturesque French farm and an amusing picnic, concluding that the day was one "I shall never forget." When reviewing the diary for her fictional revision, Rathbone wrote "HAVE completely. I.R. 1930" in the margin.[106] The changes between the diary and the novel, however, were not just about forgetting; they were about re-remembering, revising the past to fit the present, both consciously and unconsciously. Joan Seddon was far more idealistic yet less naïve than the young Irene Rathbone, who spent much of the summer discussing her love life in her diary (including the absence of the man of her dreams).[107] Seddon was much busier and more tired than her prototype, who not only seemed to have quite a bit of leisure time, but was thriving on the canteen work surrounded by admiring and appreciative men. After spending another relaxing day reading among the clover and enjoying the warm weather, Rathbone wrote in her diary that "if these days could go on for ever how easy it would be to endure life. Dear fields! Dear Summer! Dear, dear camp."[108] This is a starkly different picture

---

[103] Rathbone, *Diary*, July 17, 1918.   [104] Rathbone, *Diary*, July 25, 1918.
[105] Rathbone, *We That Were Young*, p. 384.   [106] Rathbone, *Diary*, September 22, 1918.
[107] Rathbone, *Diary*, August 7, 1918, July 14, 1918, July 17, 1918.
[108] Rathbone, *Diary*, August 14, 1918.

of the summer of 1918 from that of exhaustion and disillusionment following years of attack and retreat retrospectively associated with the war generation. Rathbone even wrote, "I have been happier and younger this summer than for ages and ages."[109] She knew this experience was separate from the war itself, which impinged in relatively minor ways on her life; on a similar day, she wrote that "To imagine 'the line' is almost an impossibility."[110] She was not yet a disillusioned survivor; that was a significantly postwar perspective.

The summer of 1918 for Rathbone was a rejuvenating beginning rather than a stultifying continuation. Seddon, in contrast, was not permitted such pleasures, unless they were brief and instructive. Her cousin Jack (like Rathbone's cousin Jeff) came to take her for a drive one day, and they had a lovely outing. This visit, however, contrasted the constraining effects of the war with the former liberties of its victims: Jack (unlike Jeff) was soon to lose his arm in combat, putting an effective end to his driving days.[111] In their jaded postwar days, Joan went to clubs with Jack and learned to dance with him despite his inability to lead. Having a shared experience as a member of the war generation, she could understand his losses, so he was comfortable with her, as he could not be with other people.[112] The soldier's story did not include women; Rathbone was one of those trying to write them back in.

Vera Brittain's generation

Rathbone was arguing that men and women alike had been young together, served together, and paid the cultural price together; for them, generation was more important than gender. This was Vera Brittain's argument in *Testament of Youth* as well.[113] As she explained in 1968, she was inspired to write her memoir during the war books boom:

I began to ask myself: "Why should these young men have the war to themselves? Didn't women have their war as well? They weren't all, as these men make them

---

[109] Rathbone, *Diary*, August 14, 1918.   [110] Rathbone, *Diary*, August 12, 1918.
[111] Rathbone, *Diary*, September 11, 1918; Rathbone, *We That Were Young*, pp. 395–402.
[112] Rathbone, *We That Were Young*, pp. 441–442.
[113] Brittain is almost certainly the best-known woman war worker of the First World War (perhaps accompanied in the popular mind, at some distance, by Lady Diana Manners and Enid Bagnold). She followed the success of *Testament of Youth* with *Testament of Friendship* and *Testament of Experience* in addition to a number of novels. *Testament of Youth* was dramatized for the BBC in 1979 and was rebroadcast on PBS's popular *Masterpiece Theatre*. When A & E Home Video released the series on videotape, they called it "one of television's truly great dramas" and "one of the most inspiring stories of a generation born to tragedy and triumph." The definitive biography is Deborah Gorham, *Vera Brittain: A Feminist Life* (Oxford: Blackwell, 1996).

out to be, only suffering wives and mothers, or callous parasites, or mercenary prostitutes. Does no one remember the women who began their war service with such high ideals or how grimly they carried on when that flaming faith had crumbled into the gray ashes of disillusion?"

From "high ideals" to the "gray ashes of disillusion" – it was the soldier's story in a nutshell, only Brittain was claiming it for women. Inspired, she "studied the memoirs of Blunden, Sassoon, and Graves" – the three leaders of the cultural canon – and concluded that "my story is as interesting as theirs [and] I see things other than they have seen, and some of the things they perceived, I see differently." As she looked over her letters and diary, she described realizing "how typical they were, not so much in terms of women's experience, as that of an entire generation."[114] Ultimately, however, she justified her right to speak through the risks shared between women and soldiers. A single story could epitomize the experience of loss for both men and women not just because of their joint spiritual deaths, but because women "could, and did, die the deaths of men" in wartime, "which made them equals in death as in life."[115] Given the power of the soldier's story, Brittain felt compelled to invoke the risk of death for both sexes in supporting her argument. She failed to acknowledge the patently obvious, however: that risk was far from equally distributed. Her blatant omission undermined the power of her claims for shared, gender-blind experience.

The memoir shows a sharp a contrast to the diary and letters on which it is based.[116] In *Testament of Youth*, Brittain first presented the war as an irritation. The opening lines made this point clearly: "When the Great War broke out, it came to me not as a superlative tragedy, but as an interruption of the most exasperating kind to my personal plans." The first chapters went on to focus on her childhood and education up to 1914, but she maintained this assertion upon reaching the war years. Though she had passed the entrance exams for Oxford, her father initially refused

[114] Vera Brittain, "War Service in Perspective," in George A. Panichas (ed.), *Promise of Greatness: The War of 1914–1918* (New York: John Day, 1968), pp. 368–369.

[115] Brittain, "War Service," p. 376. This is typical of Brittain's position as a postwar "equalitarian" feminist, in contrast to the new feminism focusing on sexual difference; see especially Susan Kingsley Kent, *Making Peace: The Reconstruction of Gender in Interwar Britain* (Princeton: Princeton University Press, 1993).

[116] Gorham argues that "because *Testament of Youth* is as much a classic war story as an anti-war statement, its author falls victim to the tradition in which war stories simplify moral and emotional realities," especially in her relationships to the four young men who play a large part in her narrative. Though this is certainly an important point, my argument is about changing perceptions of the war, about the interaction of history and memory. See Gorham, *Brittain*, pp. 79–83.

to think of her leaving home now that war had begun. Brittain recalled:

By means of what then appeared to have been a very long struggle, I had made for myself a way of escape from my hated provincial prison – and now the hard-won road to freedom was to be closed for me by a Serbian bomb hurled from the other end of Europe at an Austrian archduke.

... the War at first seemed to me an infuriating personal interruption rather than a world-wide catastrophe.

Brittain wrote that she had "entirely failed to notice in the daily papers of June 29th an account of the assassination, on the previous morning, of a European potentate whose name was unknown to me, in a Balkan town of which I had never heard."[117] Her overwhelming use of irony made her distance from such events patently clear to her postwar readers.

Her diary, however, contained three weeks of wartime entries before Brittain learned of her acceptance to Oxford and her father's subsequent resistance. Three weeks is a lot of lived time, and the war to the 1914 Brittain was many things before it became at all a "personal interruption." In fact, she dwelled extensively on it as a "world-wide catastrophe." On July 25 she recorded Austria's ultimatum to Serbia, and followed up with an entry on the two countries' declarations of a state of war on July 29. She was aware of some of the potential wider ramifications, and wrote that "it is feared that the whole of Europe will be involved." She noted the mobilization of the German army, and the family worked to locate a sold-out newspaper to get the latest news.[118]

In *Testament of Youth*, Brittain denigrated this real awareness of the international crisis by juxtaposing it with the details of her everyday life. "My diary for August 3rd, 1914," she wrote, "contains a most incongruous mixture of war and tennis," and she went on to cite details of the match and her partner.[119] She did not mention her excitement of the time. "To-day has been far too exciting to enable me to feel at all like sleep," she bubbled in her diary, "in fact it is one of the most thrilling I have ever lived through, though without doubt there are many more to come." She continued dramatically, with a much greater sense of world import than personal effect, that "that which has been so long anticipated by some and scoffed at by others has come to pass at last – Armageddon in Europe!" The two hours after breakfast that she spent with the newspapers had a

[117] Vera Brittain, *Testament of Youth: An Autobiographical Study of the Years 1900–1925* (New York: Penguin, 1989 [1933]), pp. 17, 93, 85.

[118] July 25, 1914, July 29, 1914, August 1, 1914, August 2, 1914: Vera Brittain (Alan Bishop, ed.), *Chronicle of Youth: The War Diary 1913–1917* (New York: William Morrow, 1982), pp. 82–84.

[119] Brittain, *Testament*, p. 94.

greater impact on her diary entry than the tennis match did, but Brittain's retrospective selection of detail gave a very different idea of her wartime priorities for her memoir. In fact, she continued to document the progress of the war effort on an almost daily basis.[120]

Entries burst with details as she learned them: "the great fear now," she wrote the day before Britain's declaration of war, "is that our bungling Government will declare England's neutrality." Staying out of the war was unacceptable, because "if we at this critical juncture were to refuse to help our friend France, we should be guilty of the grossest treachery and sacrifice our credit forever."[121] This line was actually excerpted in her memoir, but in a context that discredited its emotion. "My diary for those few days," she wrote, "reflects *The Times* in its most pontifical mood." In a brazen failure to acknowledge her earlier self, Brittain continued: "I prefer to think that my real sentiments were more truly represented by an entry written nearly a month later," when she was dismayed by German casualties.[122] The older Brittain chose to highlight the single passage that best matched her later feelings.

She did not actually offer any significant criticism of the war until a letter she wrote to Roland Leighton (to whom she would later become engaged) in February 1915. The war was six months old at that point, and much of the professional British army had suffered significant casualties. Leighton, along with Brittain's brother Edward and other male friends, was in uniform, training to go to the front. Brittain herself was at Oxford, in whose churches "so many of the congregation are soldiers." She was always hearing that "the call of our country is the call of God," and wondered, "is it?" Spring was coming, and she wrote to Leighton that "at this time of the year it seems that everything ought to be creative, not destructive, and that we should encourage things to live and not die."[123] In *Testament*, Brittain cited this letter and used it as a contrast to the more pro-militarist stance of Leighton, who wrote expressing his horror of civilian culture in wartime.[124] These differences of opinion, however, were not as stark as she later made them seem; Brittain had previously written to Leighton that she did "not know how [Oxford undergraduates]

---

[120] August 3, 1914, August 4, 1914ff.: Brittain, *Chronicle*, pp. 83ff. References to the progress of the war effort continued regularly, but as *Chronicle* is an edited collection, I cannot make any assertions about their comprehensiveness.

[121] August 3, 1914: Brittain, *Chronicle*, p. 84.   [122] Brittain, *Testament*, p. 97.

[123] Brittain to Roland Leighton, February 28, 1915: Alan Bishop and Mark Bostridge (eds.), *Letters from a Lost Generation. First World War Letters of Vera Brittain and Four Friends: Roland Leighton, Edward Brittain, Victor Richardson, Geoffrey Thurlow* (Boston: Northeastern University Press, 1998), p. 56.

[124] Brittain, *Testament*, pp. 125–127; for Leighton's letter, see Leighton to Brittain, February 15, 1915: Bishop and Bostridge, *Lost Generation*, pp. 55–56.

can endure not to be in khaki."[125] She was a full participant in the culture that called for healthy unmarried young men to be in uniform, and she had not renounced this stance by February.

Her correspondence also showed moments of powerful opposition to the costs of the war.[126] These assertions, however, were an aberration from her more usual tone, though her enthusiasm certainly became muted by sadness as men she cared about deeply were killed. Leighton's death in December 1915 did not make her opposed to the war; instead, it became even more important for her to justify the cause for which he had given his life. "I do condemn War in theory most strongly, as I suppose everyone who is not a lunatic or a fanatic does," Brittain wrote to her brother Edward, "but there are some things worse than even War, and I believe even wholesale murder to be preferable to atrophy and weakness." She continued, decisively, that "when the War in question is a War *on* War, all the usual objections are changed into the opposite commendations."[127] In her retrospective *Testament*, a sense of tragedy surrounded Leighton's death because it seemed pointless, but it is entirely absent from Brittain's wartime writings. In fact, she regularly wrote that she wished she were a man and could fight. Brittain told Leighton two months after the outbreak of war that "whether it is noble or barbarous I am quite sure that had I been a boy I should have gone off to take part in it long ago; indeed I have wasted many moments regretting that I am a girl." The excitement outweighed the principles, but unfortunately "women get all the dreariness of war and none of its exhilaration."[128] This militarist stance was hard for the older Brittain to comprehend, and she dismissed this sentiment in *Testament of Youth* by explaining that "obviously I was suffering, like so many women in 1914, from an inferiority complex."[129] The frustrated and envious empathy, though, was far from transient in her wartime writings. In March 1915, for example, she confided to her diary that "I know well enough really why [Leighton] wants to go, why if I were a man *I* should want to go."[130]

[125] Brittain to Leighton, October 18, 1914: Bishop and Bostridge, *Lost Generation*, p. 33.

[126] See, for example, Brittain to Leighton, October 10, 1915: Bishop and Bostridge, *Lost Generation*, p. 176.

[127] Brittain to Edward Brittain, January 24, 1916: Bishop and Bostridge, *Lost Generation*, p. 222. See also Gorham, *Brittain*, pp. 81, 120–121.

[128] Brittain to Leighton, October 1, 1914: Bishop and Bostridge, *Lost Generation*, pp. 30–31.

[129] Brittain, *Testament*, p. 104.

[130] March 19, 1915: Brittain, *Chronicle*, p. 157. Similarly, she wrote to Leighton (with an important heterosexual romantic caveat) that "I would give anything to be a man for the duration of the war, and change back again of *course* when it was over": Brittain to Leighton, April 15, 1915: Bishop and Bostridge, *Lost Generation*, p. 81. After the Battle

From the outbreak of war, then, Brittain was eager to be as active as she could be. She immediately began, as she recorded in her diary, "the only work it seems possible as yet for women to do – the making of garments for the soldiers." She "started knitting sleeping-helmets," but "as I have forgotten how to knit, and was never very brilliant when I knew, I seemed to be an object of some amusement." Despite this reaction, she was sure that "even when one is not skilful it is better to proceed slowly than to do *nothing* to help."[131] This incident, too, survived in the memoir, but presented in an entirely different manner. Brittain wrote in 1933 that "I even took to knitting for the soldiers, though only for a very short time"; as "utterly incompetent at all forms of needlework, I found the simplest bed-socks and sleeping-helmets altogether beyond me." Her desire to "help" had entirely vanished, and the use of "even" thoroughly denigrated her effort. Moving on from her less-than-successful knitting efforts, Brittain proceeded to first aid and home nursing classes. "In order to have something to take me away from the stormy atmosphere at home," she recalled, "I went in for and passed both of these elementary examinations."[132] The situation at home was indeed tense. Brittain's brother Edward was battling their father over his desire to enter the military. In her diary, however, the classes were not an escape from that unpleasant situation, but instead were a means to a very definite end: the possibility of volunteer nursing. "This afternoon I went to the St. John's bandaging class," she wrote four days after the outbreak of war, "of course I have never been to one before, never having taken a real interest, but I managed to take in quite a lot and learnt how to do 3 different kinds of bandages." This felt like a real accomplishment, but she was frustrated that "with the greatest industry in the world . . . one cannot get a certificate and therefore cannot volunteer as a nurse for six weeks."[133] From the beginning, then, Brittain was thinking about the possibility of nursing. Though the circumstances at times were not congenial, she took the work seriously, and was quite concerned three weeks later over the "dreadful" certificate exams, especially as she "did not acquit [herself] magnificently."[134]

---

of Loos, "I cursed Providence because I was not a man and in it all": September 28, 1915: Brittain, *Chronicle*, pp. 281–282. Even after Leighton's death, Brittain wrote to her brother that his letters "made me wish desperately that I were a man and could train myself to play that 'Great Game with Death'": Brittain to Edward Brittain, February 19–20, 1916: Bishop and Bostridge, *Lost Generation*, p. 231.

[131] August 6, 1914: Brittain, *Chronicle*, p. 89 (emphasis in original).

[132] Brittain, *Testament*, pp. 100–101.   [133] August 8, 1914: Brittain, *Chronicle*, p. 90.

[134] August 26, 1914: Brittain, *Chronicle*, p. 96. See also Brittain to Leighton, August 23, 1914: Bishop and Bostridge, *Lost Generation*, p. 27.

Another important transformation between the diary and the memoir concerned Brittain's brother, Edward. Eighteen when the war broke out, Edward eventually was commissioned, served, was decorated, and died fighting in Italy in 1918. Vera Brittain also lost her fiancé and two close male friends in the war. In keeping with the soldier's story, of course, these young men had to have been, as Brittain retrospectively described Edward, "not only willing but anxious to risk their lives in order to save the face of a Foreign Secretary who had committed his country to an armed policy without consulting it beforehand." The war clearly had no point – it could not improve the world, only the reputation of a politician. The irony of young men sacrificing everything for such a petty cause was meant to be thunderingly obvious. Her generation's willingness to commit itself, she explained later, was a result of the public school system and its Officer Training Corps (OTC), which "had already served their purpose in the national exploitation of youth by its elders," and "which stood for militaristic heroism unimpaired by the damping exercise of reason." A product of this unsound system, Edward continued to petition for his father's permission to enter the army, as "his enforced subservience seemed to him synonymous with everlasting disgrace."[135] In her memoir, Brittain seemed already to have known that the soldier's story would call on the civilians at home to betray the active participants in the war effort.

Edward, in fact, did not "suddenly [get] very keen" about military service until the next day, when Vera herself "showed [him] an appeal in *The Times* and the *Chronicle* for young unmarried men between the ages of 18 and 30 to join the army."[136] *Her* impetus sparked *his* enthusiastic commitment. Vera Brittain was sure Edward was doing the right thing; as she wrote, "dreary as life is without his presence here, dreary as are the prospects of what may lie before him, yet I would not have his decision back, or keep him here." The public school ethos, in fact, was used to condemn Mr. Brittain rather than to explain his son. As she wrote in her diary, "E[dward] said that Daddy, not being a public school man or having had any training, could not possibly understand the impossibility of his remaining in inglorious safety while others, scarcely older than he, were offering their all." Brittain was clearly a willing participant in the pro-war enthusiasm of the day. "Not that other people's opinions matter to us," she wrote, "only they represent prestige and it is hard luck on Edward to be misjudged for what is not his fault." Her brother's motivations were

---

[135] Brittain, *Testament*, pp. 99–100.
[136] August 5, 1914: Brittain, *Chronicle*, p. 88.

unimpeachable, but "Daddy does not care about E.'s honour or courage so long as he is safe."[137]

When faced with her father's obstinacy about Edward's service along with her mother's inability (though allegedly agreeing with her children) to contradict her husband, Vera concluded that "it is left to Edward and I to live up to our name of 'Brittain.'" Patriots in name, they had also to be in action. Mr. Brittain was battered down by pressure from his son, his friends and colleagues, and his wife and daughter, who "tried to make him see it from the point of view of honour." He finally, despite what Vera called his "unconquerable aversion to Edward's doing anything for his country," conceded and allowed his only son to train for a commission.[138] Knowing her brother's ultimate fate, however, Vera Brittain could not retrospectively admit her own complicity in this effort. Her contemporary relief at her father's concession, though, was clear in the letter she wrote Roland Leighton:

I expect you will be glad that Edward is allowed to do something definite at last... You have no idea the domestic storms that have been necessary in order to achieve this object; I have come in for a good many because I have persistently urged from the beginning of the war that Edward ought at least to try for something. Not that I am in the slightest degree a militarist... But it seems to me that to refrain from fighting in a cause like this because you do not approve of warfare would be about as sensible as refusing to defend yourself against the attacks of a madman because you did not consider lunacy an enlightened or desirable condition.[139]

Her reservations at that time were about war in general, not the European war of 1914 in particular, and she had no doubts what her brother's role should be. This was, understandably, an uncomfortable memory.

Brittain continued to express her support of the war effort vicariously through her brother's participation. When he was leaving to begin training for a commission, Edward nearly missed his train. Vera recorded that "we have said 'He must depart' and he has departed, leaving home laughing, with a delighted sense that he is not to be one of those men who will be branded for life because they have not taken part in the greatest struggle of modern times."[140] The chills of foreboding that accompanied seeing her brother in uniform in *Testament of Youth* were also entirely absent from her wartime writings.[141] Vera was physically near Edward that autumn, as

---

[137] August 7, 1914, September 2, 1914: Brittain, *Chronicle*, pp. 89–90, 101. It is hard not to sympathize with Mr. Brittain.

[138] September 2, 1914, September 3, 1914, September 4, 1914: Brittain, *Chronicle*, pp. 101–103.

[139] Brittain to Leighton, September 6, 1914: Bishop and Bostridge, *Lost Generation*, p. 29.

[140] September 11, 1914: Brittain, *Chronicle*, pp. 106–107.

[141] Brittain, *Testament*, p. 96.

he was training in Oxford, where she was now a student at Somerville. At the time, she wrote to her mother that he was "looking so nice in his officer uniform."[142] Retrospectively, however, Brittain remembered that "he looked so handsome in his new second-lieutenant's uniform that the fear which I had felt when he returned from Aldershot on the eve of the War suddenly clutched me again." To make the impending disaster ironically clear, she "said good-bye to him...almost opposite the place where the Oxford War Memorial was to be erected ten years afterwards 'In memory of those who fought and those who fell.'"[143] In the memoir, he was unknowingly foreshadowing his own death, a dramatic irony that simply could not have been perceived at the time.

The younger Brittain was not without ambivalence, however, despite her apparent embrace of the patriotism that surrounded her. She was, as she later remembered, ecstatic about her opportunity to attend Oxford when she learned that she had passed the requisite exams. She admitted, too, that "I will not say anything but that I am glad [Edward was joining the army], but I cannot pretend not to be sorry." In particular, "Oxford will not be the same if he is not there." In response, she translated Oxford into her own war service. She was not attending for personal fulfillment, because

Not self-satisfaction, but self-sacrifice, is the order of the day. And I am determined to give up the now futile attempt to see what happiness I can get for myself out of Oxford, and instead to see what *use* I can be both in it and the world in general – by acting directly on behalf of war claims when I can do so, and when I cannot, by helping in the more indirect way of advising the perplexed and comforting the distressed.[144]

Important as both the education she desired and the escape from what she later termed "provincial young lady-hood" were to her, the young Brittain still felt the need to transform university life into patriotic service.

Eventually, however, she left the university for hospital work. Nursing held a special attraction for Brittain, and like many women of her socio-economic position, she came to consider it as the gendered parallel to military service. This became an especially powerful emotional argument for her, given her deepening attachment (primarily via correspondence) with Leighton. It was no coincidence that his departure for the Western front coincided with Brittain's dissatisfaction with Oxford as a substitute

---

[142] Brittain to Edith Brittain, November 18, 1914: Bishop and Bostridge, *Lost Generation*, p. 36.

[143] Brittain, *Testament*, p. 111. As he never matriculated, Edward Brittain's name is not on the memorial.

[144] August 27–28, 1914: Brittain, *Chronicle*, pp. 97–99 (emphasis in original).

for more active war service. Similarly, her choice was nursing, which permitted close interaction with other soldiers as proxies for the one soldier she was focused on. Her first real commitment to long-term nursing was articulated when she had gone longer than she expected without a letter from Leighton. She then declared that "if he dies I shall sign on as a Red Cross Nurse for a year."[145] In retrospect she explained that nursing "was not, perhaps, an obvious choice for a Somerville exhibitioner," displaying her continuing feeling of superiority toward the qualifications of trained nurses. However, she "was then in no mood for the routine Civil Service posts which represented the only type of 'intellectual' war-work offered to uncertificated young women."[146] From her educated and experienced perspective of 1933 such a disclaimer might have been necessary, but as the diary showed, nursing was the specific work her community considered appropriate for her. They – and she – saw amateur nursing as her version of military service. As she explained in a letter to Leighton, "I am longing to begin nursing [as] I am anxious to play my small part in what is only another division of the same strife that you are in now."[147] Nursing was the work that offered a bond for the wartime Brittain with the soldiers who were at the center of her emotional life. Earlier, when Edward Brittain left to return to his army unit, his sister had described the scene: "we all assembled there on the station, Edward and I, soldier and nurse, and Mother and Daddy."[148] His work and hers, his war identity and hers, were clearly paired.

When Brittain committed herself to nurse in military hospitals overseas, she wrote that "if I had refused to put down my name I should despise myself as much as I would a [Territorial] regiment that wouldn't volunteer for foreign service."[149] If men who had expected to serve in England were now called on to fight abroad, then Brittain also felt required to go. In retrospect, however, she shifted her emphasis. She volunteered for overseas service, she wrote, not because it was a patriotic duty but because "now that Roland was irretrievably gone and my decision [to defer studies at] Oxford had finally been made, there seemed to be no reason for withholding my name." The focus here was on why she might not have signed up, rather than why, in fact, she did. Rather than being about emotion, "it was the logical conclusion... of service in

---

[145] April 13, 1915: Brittain, *Chronicle*, pp. 173–174.
[146] Brittain, *Testament*, p. 146.
[147] Brittain to Leighton, May 26, 1915: Bishop and Bostridge, *Lost Generation*, p. 113.
[148] August 5, 1915: Brittain, *Chronicle*, p. 228.
[149] March 6, 1915: Brittain, *Chronicle*, p. 320. See also May 12, 1915, June 12, 1915, August 22, 1915, August 23, 1915: Brittain, *Chronicle*, pp. 195, 207, 252, 261–262. See also Leighton to Brittain, June 3, 1915; Brittain to Leighton, July 24, 1915, August 8, 1915: Bishop and Bostridge, *Lost Generation*, pp. 117, 175, 140–141.

England, though quite a number of VADs refused to sign because their parents wouldn't like it, or they were too inexperienced, or had had pneumonia when they were five years old."[150] Though she presented herself as being superior to those women whose commitments to war work were less complete than her own, in her retrospective story, her patriotism had to be muted.

In her reconstruction of the soldier's story, it was important for Brittain to document the disillusionment of the men she cared about. Experience of the war, especially for those who lived until its later years, had to result in an increasingly non-militarist perspective. Thus while Brittain detailed in her memoir Roland Leighton's machinations to get to the front in 1914–1915, she failed to mention those of his school-fellow, Victor Richardson. Richardson joined the army early on but was stricken with a near-fatal case of cerebral meningitis. He recovered, and was put on home service. Though the army was content to keep him in England, Richardson, especially after Leighton's death and Edward Brittain's service in France, was eager to go to the front. Vera Brittain mentioned none of this in her memoir, however, only noting that in 1916 she learned from her brother "the surprising news that Victor had gone unexpectedly to the front."[151] More than two years of trench warfare and the experiences of his comrades had not dampened Richardson's perceived obligation to serve. More than that, Richardson described a real satisfaction in his active military service. He even joked that "really I am beginning to agree with the Rifleman who when some dear old lady said 'What a terrible War it is,' replied 'Yes Mum, but better than no War.'"[152] He also fairly soon began to consider a permanent career in the army, and was eventually recommended by his commanding officer for a permanent commission.[153] Given the strained relations that often existed between volunteers and army regulars, this was no mean feat.

Vera Brittain did more than fail to document Victor Richardson's continuing personal engagement with the military and the war. To the contrary, she presented him as a critic of the war and its supporters, and matured beyond his years by the experience. She wrote of one serious letter in particular, which "accustomed though I was by 1917 to the sudden tragic maturities of trench life" still "moved me to intolerable pity."

---

[150] Brittain, *Testament*, p. 260.   [151] Brittain, *Testament*, p. 306.

[152] Richardson to Brittain, October 31, 1916: Bishop and Bostridge, *Lost Generation*, pp. 284–285. See also Thurlow to Edward Brittain, December 5, 1916; Thurlow to Vera Brittain, December 15, 1916: Bishop and Bostridge, *Lost Generation*, pp. 295–296, 300.

[153] Richardson to Brittain, November 18, 1916, March 4, 1917: Bishop and Bostridge, *Lost Generation*, pp. 292, 324.

Brittain described Richardson's letter, in which he discussed soldiers' motivations, as "a meditation" that was "then very characteristic of the more thoughtful young officer, who found himself committed to months of cold and fear and discomfort by the quick warmth of a moment's elusive impulse." Again, she retrospectively denigrated the depth of commitment that had led the young soldiers to volunteer, and their extensive efforts to be posted overseas. She described his conclusion: "although the invasion of Belgium, and the example set by friends, and perhaps even 'Heroism in the Abstract,' had a share in it all, the only true explanation that could be given by ninety percent of the British Expeditionary Force was" the soldiers' song which ran "We're here because We're here because We're here…"[154] Richardson, of course, had spent considerably longer than "a moment" in his efforts to get on active service, as had both Edward Brittain and Leighton. Similarly, while he did indeed ascribe the lyrical motivations to nine-tenths of the army as a whole, he described his own position quite differently. He wrote that it was "mainly I think, as far as I am concerned, to prevent the repetition in England of what happened in Belgium in August 1914. Still more perhaps because one's friends are here. Perhaps too, 'heroism in the abstract' has a share in it all."[155] The same factors were rearranged in priority. At this late stage of his war experience, facing potential death in the battle of Arras, he still wanted to affirm his commitment to the ideals of self-sacrifice, honor, comradeship, and patriotism he had also articulated earlier. Brittain, however, with her knowledge of Richardson's death, could not retrospectively acknowledge the continuing power of those motivations.

Though at times she presented her younger self as conflicted, Brittain was firm in her implementation of the final essential component of her soldier's story: her ultimate disillusionment, rejected by the society that had gone on without her. Her presentation, of course, was more than merely personal; a committed and active pacifist, she meant her memoir as a tract to persuade others, not merely as the record of an individual life. In *Testament of Youth*, Brittain's depiction of her postwar return to Oxford was one of loneliness, depression, exclusion, and frustration. She described her fellow students as either bored by or contemptuous of her war experiences, so that she wished she had herself died in the conflict.[156] However, as her biographer Deborah Gorham has effectively demonstrated, her letters showed a very different picture. "We never see the exhausted, humourless, intensely sad, lonely and world-weary persona," Gorham argued, "she is lively, she is acutely observant of and

---

[154] Brittain, *Testament*, pp. 335–336.
[155] Richardson to Brittain, March 24, 1917: Bishop and Bostridge, *Lost Generation*, p. 326.
[156] Brittain, *Testament*, pp. 467–493.

intrigued by her surroundings, she is enthusiastic about Oxford and she is very much involved with family and friends." She was, according to Gorham, "very much her prewar self."[157] Her disillusionment and cynicism must, therefore, have crystallized later – at some point in the decade after 1919, after the Armistice but before she began *Testament of Youth*. As with Rathbone, however, to maintain her status as a member of the war generation, the changes in her life had to result from her experiences of the war itself, and not from after the war. Her return to Oxford, then, was recast to suggest the emotionally devastated survivor, lost because the only world she knew had vanished while she was serving. She positioned herself with the special knowledge of one who had experienced and therefore knew, separate from those who could not understand because they were not there.

The translation of the soldier's story

In some ways, Rathbone and Brittain were successful in their attempts to stake claims for the validity of their own service. Fundamentally, however, their efforts failed. Books by women, of course, were not usually discussed or analyzed along side those that told the "real" story of the war: the story of combat, the story of men. *We That Were Young* was reviewed in the *Times Literary Supplement*, but not by Cyril Falls, Orlo Williams, or any of the regular reviewers of war books written by men. Instead, Ruth Baily praised it as "a very good War-book." She felt that it was not a good novel, because the characters were too well delineated, their dialogue was unnatural, and the plot at times too sentimental. It succeeded, however, "as a record, as the recovery and communication of a strange experience." Though Rathbone may have been disappointed with the criticism of her writing skill, she could be sure that the novel was read (at least by Baily) just as she intended it to be. Baily explained that the book centered on "the women of the 'leisured classes,' who were young in 1914 and became War-workers of one kind or another when their brothers went to the front." The parallel was explicit: the brothers were soldiers, and the sisters also served. The review sounded like so many of those that addressed books by men: it praised the "vividness" of the narrative, it rejoiced in the novelty of its perspective, and it invoked the authority of "the author's contemporaries." Baily felt that the novel met the key requirement of realism: "there is no vagueness, unreality, or sentiment in the descriptions of daily life in the canteen, the hospitals, or the munitions factory." As a result, "at the end of the book we feel that we have lived and worked in

[157] Gorham, *Brittain*, p. 139.

these places."[158] As with the trench narratives, the hallowed details gave the reader purchase on a specific claim to reality. Nonetheless, the novel did not make a dent in the monolith that the soldier's story had become. It sold poorly, and was popularly seen as irrelevant to the history of the experience of the war, because it was only about women.

A year and a half later, Vera Brittain's memoir made more of a stir. Better written, more emotionally engaging, it also had a stronger claim on authority because it was explicitly positioned as non-fiction. Reviews, with a few notable exceptions, were very positive. Iolo Williams called it "well worth doing – as a record of spiritual growth, as a memorial to sacrifices nobly made, and as a testimony to the horror and waste of war." In the recent "era of autobiographies by those still young in years," *Testament of Youth* "must have a high place."[159] The same might have been written about *Good-bye to All That* or the George Sherston *Memoirs* series. P. D. James, reviewing the reissue in 1978, called it "one of those books which help both form and define the mood of its time." She remembered "the fierce excitement and emotion which it aroused on publication in 1933, particularly in those of us born in the years immediately after the First World War, children of the survivors of the holocaust, who first read it in our youth."[160] Like *All Quiet on the Western Front*, perhaps the story resonated most powerfully with people trying to understand the experience they themselves had been too young to have. They wanted the emotion, the detail, the power, and they were fundamentally uncritical readers at a moment where the legitimate authority repeatedly invoked was specifically that of someone else's personal experience. *Testament of Youth* became by far the best-known account of a woman's experience in the war, and as a result Brittain was often the only female writer included in analyses of war books.[161] Her argument, though, that she represented

---

[158] Ruth Baily, "We That Were Young," *TLS*, February 25, 1932, p. 130.

[159] Iolo Williams, "Testament of Youth," *TLS*, August 31, 1933, p. 571. For negative reviews, see especially the *New Statesman*. Williams had served in a variety of military and non-military capacities during the war. His usual reviewing strengths, according to the *TLS*, however, were poetry, flowers and countryside, marine art, reptiles, and libraries (French and Welsh).

[160] P. D. James, "The Women Who Went to War," *TLS*, May 5, 1978, p. 492. James wrote that "Vera Brittain was intelligent, courageous, determined, high-minded and idealistic; one only wishes one could like her more."

[161] This was not merely a phenomenon of the 1930s, but has continued. In 1980, for example, when Simon Schama reviewed *The Generation of 1914* by Robert Wohl, he described the "chapter of British writers" as covering "what is by now a fairly familiar platoon of literary warriors and scapegraces: Brooke, Sassoon, Wilfred Owen, Robert Graves, Vera Brittain, Richard Aldington and T. E. Lawrence": Schama, "To and From the Slaughter," *TLS*, May 16, 1980, pp. 559–560. The absence of Blunden illustrates the declining attention paid to his memoir since the period of its publication.

the whole experience of the war, of its service, its loss, and its disillusionment, was not what led to the popularity of the book. Rather than being
perceived as typical of the generation as a whole, Brittain instead embodied the female mourner, who had lost all the men she loved.[162] The
deaths of Edward Brittain, Victor Richardson, Geoffrey Thurlow, and
especially Roland Leighton transformed Vera Brittain into the prototype
of the survivor. The review in *The Times* made this point explicitly. In a
"Shorter Notice," it described "the chief strength of the book" not as a
narrative of events (or the chronicle of a generation) but as "the record
of the author's own spiritual life through the vicissitudes and sorrows
that befell her." Where men's narratives were presented as clear-eyed
truth telling, Brittain's representation of experience was coded as feeling. Though the reviewer felt the book was at times irritating and even
irrelevant, "it is nevertheless a moving story of sorrow and of a conso-
lation achieved without oblivion of the past."[163] Instead of challenging
the gender distinctions of the soldier's story, ultimately Brittain fit neatly
and safely within their confines. She captured popular empathy not because of her own risks and service, but because she was left alone at the
end of it all. There was no room for women within the soldier's story as
established by Graves, Sassoon, and the rest of the disillusionist school.
Rathbone and Brittain (and the other women who identified with them)
were – in a phrase adapted from the title of a 1930 novel – the "stepdaughters of war." Despite their best efforts, they were no longer fully
included, after the Armistice, in the family of veterans. Like their brothers' narratives before them, however, their reimagined war experiences
would have a profound and complex impact on the later memories of
other, less renowned, veterans of war work and service.

---

[162] On woman as mourner, see Susan R. Grayzel, *Women's Identities at War: Gender,
Motherhood, and Politics in Britain and France During the First World War* (Chapel
Hill: University of North Carolina Press, 1999), and Jay Winter, *Sites of Memory,
Sites of Mourning: The Great War in European Cultural History* (Cambridge: Cambridge
University Press, 1995).
[163] *The Times*, September 1, 1933, 6f.

7   Still fighting: memory enters history

In 1976, a former VAD, C. E. Tisdall, decided to write down her memories of the Great War. No longer a young woman, she wanted to share her past. She hoped in particular that "some of today's younger generation, especially those of my own family, might be interested to learn something of those 'old unhappy far-off days, and battles long ago' from someone who had actually experienced them at first hand." Tisdall concluded the Preface to her typescript memoir by explaining that though her "own part in the work of the [London Ambulance] Column was intermittent and quite insignificant... the effect upon [her] was deep and permanent." In fact, she averred, "in a long and very varied life my time with the ambulances was probably the greatest experience of all."[1]

Tisdall's descriptions of her work exemplify the tensions within many war narratives written after the 1930s. The war had, retrospectively, become inextricably linked with disillusion and pointless horror and sacrifice. Bernard Martin, who volunteered as soon as he came of age, reacted positively to "a righteous war, a great and glorious adventure, patriotic and God on our side too." Martin then retrospectively dismissed that enthusiasm and depth of feeling, however, declaring that "I find it hard now to believe I could have been so stupid at the age of seventeen."[2] It is a powerful indictment; his former self was not just young, or naive, or innocent, but in fact stupid – not knowing something of the nature of warfare that the mature author argued he should have. From the perspective of life beyond the soldier's story, it had become difficult to see how the war could have been viewed in any other way. This is, of course, the evolving story of the war itself, but it did not prove universal. At the same time, positive descriptions of the war and its effects on its participants, broadly defined, proved resilient. This opposition is clear in Tisdall's text: though she introduced her memoir with a poetic reference

---

[1] Miss C. E. Tisdall, Imperial War Museum Department of Documents (hereafter IWM-DD) 92/22/1.

[2] Bernard Martin, *Poor Bloody Infantry: A Subaltern on the Western Front 1916–1917* (London: John Murray, 1987), pp. 3–5.

to "unhappy" times, the war was also "the greatest experience of all" – significant, epic, important – not at all an empty waste. Additionally, she positioned herself as a qualified judge because she had been there, "at first hand." Similarly, A. B. Beauman, a professional soldier who explicitly condemned command mistakes, "appalling conditions," and "many lives . . . uselessly wasted," still maintained that "I can honestly say that this was one of the happiest periods of my life."[3] Gender and especially socioeconomic position affected depictions – women and especially men who had talked about service during the war were most likely to remember disillusionment, for example. There was, however, an internal tension in many of these texts between the wartime ideas of work and service on the one hand, and the retrospective effort to present the war as the soldier's story on the other. These later war stories are themselves battles over how to remember the 1914–1918 experience.

Claims of personal satisfaction in the war, even for non-combatants, do not meld easily with the popular modernist view of the war as described so compellingly by the poets of the trench. Such accounts have failed to substantively change the accepted image of the war because they seemed too alien – too different simply to amend accepted views, too unbelievable to change them, and therefore more or less ignored. In 1929, for example, at the height of the war books controversy, Mrs. C. S. Peel quoted an anonymous VAD who described the period she spent working in the wards as "the happiest I ever spent."[4] Almost sixty years later, however, another study quoted the same passage, with the caveat that "the memories of a VAD who found life in a hospital 'the happiest time I ever spent' also jar."[5] Happiness is not consistent with the dominant soldier's story, yet it was far from a unique claim, and we should not be too quick to dismiss it as propaganda, either. It was typical of the war period, and remained a powerful undercurrent afterwards. As Alison Light has written, the "dialectic between old and new, between past and present, between holding on and letting go, between conserving and moving on, is a constant one."[6]

Peel, a popular social commentator, remarked in 1929 on the contentment expressed by many young women. Because they had worked hard

---

[3] A. B. Beauman, *Then a Soldier* (London: Macmillan, 1960), pp. 55, 48.

[4] Mrs. C. S. Peel, *How We Lived Then, 1914–1918: A Sketch of Social and Domestic Life in England During the War* (London: John Lane, 1929), pp. 132–133. See also Angela Woollacott, *On Her Their Lives Depend: Munitions Workers in the Great War* (Berkeley: University of California Press, 1994), pp. 208–209.

[5] Gail Braybon and Penny Summerfield, *Out of the Cage: Women's Experiences in Two World Wars* (London: Pandora, 1987), p. 64.

[6] Alison Light, *Forever England: Femininity, Literature, and Conservatism Between the Wars* (London: Routledge, 1991), p. 19.

in new and useful ways, they had experienced "a happiness which many of them had never known before." But she hastened to make clear that her praise for the women's success in unusual positions and under trying circumstances was not akin to the wartime language of parity that was so often used to encourage female labor participation. It was 1929, not 1917, and "never," she stated emphatically, "although arduous and occasionally dangerous work was demanded of them, did it compare in the smallest degree with that demanded of the fighting men."[7] In little more than a decade, women war workers had shifted from the separate-but-parallel peers of their brothers in arms to something so different that comparison between the two groups was no longer conceivable. This position was not unique either to Peel or to the interwar period, of course. The historian Arthur Marwick, from the vantage point of fifty more years, averred that "it involves no denigration of women's role in peace and in war to remark that this equation of women's sufferings at home with the sordid hellishness and desperate danger of the trenches borders on the outrageous."[8] War "experience" had become a gendered competition – an inverted one where the bigger losers won. The key delineating factor was defined as risk of death, to preclude any rational opposition to the hierarchy of the trench. Of course, the very need of these authors, half a century apart, to claim so authoritatively that it was impossible to compare men and women workers is itself a testament to the durability of the idea (first put forth during the war years themselves) that men and women had contributed equally to the victory. If it were truly impossible to consider the contributions of women and men together – if no one were continuing to maintain such a comparison – then it would not have been necessary to deny it, especially so categorically. Whatever amateur and professional scholars have argued since, a considerable number (though certainly not all) of participants and witnesses have maintained this parity.

In 1914–1918, women were seen as necessary to win the war. As a result, different populations were appealed to as equal contributors to the national effort. This idea of parity provided both validation and justification to many women who, even though they did not put their lives in any real danger, certainly profoundly changed their lifestyles. For many women, as well as many men, the war was a transformative experience that shaped their self-identities for the rest of their lives. This was why, facing the dominance of a history that claimed that the only legitimate war story was that of the loss, disillusion, and devastation now associated with the trenches, many women (like many men) retold their own

---

[7] Peel, *Lived Then*, p. 137.

[8] Arthur Marwick, *Women at War, 1914–1918* (London: Fontana/Imperial War Museum, 1977), p. 44.

accounts to maintain that idea of parity. This retelling, of course, served to further marginalize the position of the women. The trench story was grounded in death – in its risk and its pervasiveness. Men had suffered undeniably horrific casualties. Since women memoirists could not with any plausibility claim that relation with mortality, their efforts to posit an understanding of the war were taken as further evidence of how little, in fact, they comprehended.

Women were not the only wartime participants excluded from the soldier's story. Male non-combatants remained marginalized. Additionally, military men who had not served in the trenches – even though they spent considerable time on active service – found themselves needing to claim the legitimacy of their own histories, and could do so only in relation to the soldier's story. Staff officers and higher ranks had long been mocked for being out of touch with the conflict. Now, though, even combat soldiers like gunners and pilots did not fit neatly into the new account. Because the trench story was so powerful, other narratives were understood in relation to it, rather than on their own terms. R. G. Loosmore, editor of R. B. Talbot Kelly's memoir of service in the artillery, wrote that the gunner's positive version of the war was opposed to the better-known disillusionist texts. Loosmore warned that people "who believe it is dangerous, perhaps wicked, to publish anything that declares there was another side to the war will disapprove of Talbot Kelly's memoirs. The attitude they reveal," he continued, "is unfashionable, but not of course unique." Loosmore then cited other authors with similar points of view. His list included Liddell Hart, who wrote of the war that "I know that for my own part I am more glad of that experience than of anything else I have known," and G. H. Greenwell, who counted "the years 1914–1918 as amongst the happiest I have ever spent."[9] Loosmore needed to justify the validity of Talbot Kelly's perspective so that it would not be dismissed as an aberration.

Yet Talbot Kelly himself put the relationship between his story and the others quite differently. He first acknowledged the role of memory: "I am one of those people who, luckily, remember the good things in their life rather than the bad." This discussion of selective memory, though, was a prelude to his real point: it was not just that memories differed but that the nature of war service itself was variable. "Those others . . . were mostly infantrymen living a restricted trench life, week in and week out, with discomfort and danger," he wrote, "whereas I as a gunner was able to move about on the battlefield at large, seeing far more and, although

---

[9] R. G. Loosmore, "Editor's Introduction": R. B. Talbot Kelly, *A Subaltern's Odyssey: A Memoir of the Great War 1915–1917* (London: William Kimber, 1980), p. 17.

frequently in danger, finding something by the way to ease the burden of war."[10] Talbot Kelly positioned his memoir as complementary, rather than oppositional, to the trench stories, though he still felt obligated to engage them. Even his own editor, though, could not imagine him outside the received history.

Narratives of British war experience after the 1930s, in fact, bear evidence of two, often contradictory ways of representing the war. Much of the wartime language of work and service proved to be quite durable, offering different gender- and class-specific perspectives that could be quite positive. In tension with this view of experience, however, was the soldier's story of disillusion and devastation, loss and useless sacrifice. Populations that had been more likely to think about service during the war itself were also more likely to remember their lives within the confines of the soldier's story, but honor and sacrifice still remained powerful values to many diverse writers. People who had seen their war efforts as work continued to be likely to do so. Their stories, though, were often drowned out by those so eloquently told by writers with greater education, a tradition of personal writing, and the powerful command of the language which stemmed in part from years of reading and writing poetry. In some contexts, ideas of value and devastation worked against each other, while elsewhere they combined to create a contradictory yet coherent view of the war, years removed from the events themselves. The war over the war as remembered was still being fought.

Compensations of war: happiness, comradeship, and class

Retrospective descriptions of happiness in war work abound among men and women from different class positions, though they often battled with the conventions of the soldier's story. May Cannan, a VAD in Oxford, claimed that "it was wet, cold and dark as I went home and the newsboys called in the streets the war news that was always bad." Here, she demonstrates the power of the soldier's story of the war: though news might not often have been good, on most days there was none at all, and the armies remained entrenched. Due to propaganda efforts, even bad war news was frequently presented very positively (if erroneously) in the press. Yet Cannan remembered "news that was always bad," in keeping with a vision of war constantly active in its destruction. Despite this, however, she concluded that "I would not have missed it for the

---

[10] Talbot Kelly, *Subaltern's Odyssey*, pp. 19, 166.

world."[11] In contrast to her earlier tone, here Cannan sounds similar to young officers like P. D. Ravenscroft, who as an old man remembered his sadness at demobilization in April 1919. "Forgetting all the horrors of the war," he wrote, "I felt that this was the end of one of the happiest periods of my life."[12] The two approaches to describing war experience, that of devastation and that of value, were again working simultaneously.

Though Cannan came from a socially elite and well-educated background – her Oxford VAD detachment found inspiration by posting the poetry of Rupert Brooke on the walls over the dishwashing sink – this kind of juxtaposition of ways of thinking about the war is in fact remarkable for its cross-class nature. Ada Potter, daughter of a joiner and builder, enlisted in the WAAC and served as a telegraphist in the later years of the war. In her typescript memoir, she wrote that the war "had been a great experience." She acknowledged that "sometimes there had been strain," however "like all young people we had enjoyed what relaxation came our way." Her account, in fact, describes a number of social experiences, including a rhapsodic narrative of her first dance. Yet her memoir clearly also follows the representative model of the soldier's story: when she returned home on leave, "I felt as if I'd come from the moon ... There did not seem to be a war." Like a soldier, she felt that non-combatants in Britain "did not seem to want to know. Not that I would have spoken about it." This division between those participating actively in the war and those at home – which was only truly perceived by the combatant, and could not (and should not) be communicated – was one of the hallmarks of the soldier's story. Here, of course, it was adapted to a woman operating a telegraph far behind the lines in France. Though Potter's experience was different from that of an infantry soldier, she remembered it as equally incommunicable. "My attitude to war," Potter then concluded, "is that it is utterly vile."[13]

Descriptions of satisfaction found in many memoirs across class lines were often dependent on the nature of the work being done. Mrs. P. L. Stephens, who worked in munitions and as a motorcyclist attached to a Royal Air Force (RAF) aerodrome, wrote four pages of reminiscences as she neared her eightieth birthday. Her account focused almost exclusively on the work and the people doing it, with special attention paid to evolving relations between men and women. The war itself was not a factor in her account until the last sentences, when she and her colleagues

---

[11] Miss M. W. Cannan, IWM-DD P360.

[12] P. D. Ravenscroft (Antony Bird, ed.), *Unversed in Arms: A Subaltern on the Western Front. The First World War Diary of P. D. Ravenscroft MC* (Swindon, Crowood, 1990), p. 165.

[13] Miss A. Potter, Peter Liddle 1914–1918 Personal Experience Archive, University of Leeds (hereafter PL) Women.

celebrated the Armistice. Stephens's memories were often happy. When they were not, it was specifically because of the nature of the work she was involved in.[14] Similarly, the young officer Francis Law remembered refusing an extended leave he was entitled to after eighteen consecutive months' service at the front. Though he referred to the conflict retrospectively as "a ghastly war," he had not wanted to go home because he "was fit and happy where [he] was."[15] Work was also the reason behind the happiness Tina Gray felt. A VAD, she returned home from France after her thirteen-month contract was completed because she felt her family needed her in England. She was very reluctant, however, "for I loved the work and the having to make my own place, and the independence." The war was a catastrophe, she wrote, but it created valuable and enjoyable new opportunities for her. Though Gray was herself a volunteer, and described her friends as all "either nursing or working in canteens," similarly for nominal pay (if any), her memoirs resonate with ideals of work rather than the service more typically identifiable with women of her social position.[16] She was, indeed, exceptional among VADs. For Gray, the war proved to be a transformative experience by exposing her to medicine, not just as a means of patriotic participation but as a profession. Following the Armistice, Gray was one of only thirteen former VADs who used the Red Cross Society/Order of St. John's training scholarships to attend medical school.[17] She became a doctor.

More typically, Dorothy McCann, well educated and well enough placed socially to be among the first groups of VADs sent over to France, still invoked the language of service when she wrote her reminiscence in 1977, at the age of eighty-seven. "I feel I was very privileged to be given the opportunity of doing what I did," she recorded, and though the conditions were difficult, and not what she was accustomed to, "I wouldn't have swopped those years for the gayest in the world." McCann was well traveled, having attended school in Dresden, and she was actually

---

[14] Mrs. P. L. Stephens, IWM-DD P348.

[15] Francis Law, *A Man at Arms: Memoirs of Two World Wars* (London: Collins, 1983), pp. 100, 73.

[16] Dr. T. Gray, PL Women. On war as a liberating experience, see Sandra M. Gilbert and Susan Gubar, *No Man's Land: The Place of the Woman Writer in the Twentieth Century*, vol. II, *Sexchanges* (New Haven: Yale University Press, 1991), and Gilbert's article, "Soldier's Heart: Literary Men, Literary Women, and the Great War," in Margaret Randolph Higonnet, et al. (eds.), *Behind the Lines: Gender and the Two World Wars* (New Haven: Yale University Press, 1989).

[17] All VADs were eligible to apply; a total of 557 scholarships were awarded. The largest two groups trained in midwifery (134) and nursing (129); most were generally associated with health, education, and welfare: *British Red Cross Society / Order of St. John Joint War Committee Reports 1914–1919* (1921), p. 203: Red Cross British Society Archives, Barnett Hill, Guildford (hereafter BRCS).

in Austria at the outbreak of war in 1914. Yet she saw VAD nursing as a great opportunity, "the greatest adventure in our lives."[18] Rose Isabella (Betty) Leared, six years younger than McCann, came from a similar background and also finished her education on the continent. She joined the Women's Legion as a driver and then was transferred into the WAAC to go overseas. Her memoir, written more than twenty years earlier than McCann's, focused less on the seriousness of the nation's cause, and more on the joy of being young and in the thick of things. Certainly the conditions were challenging in France, Leared remembered, but "Did we care? Not a bit! We were young, we kept falling in and out of love, we had got our fingers into the War pie . . . And so we laughed our way through those years." Laughter, in fact, was her most powerful memory: "we laughed at one another, we laughed at our cars, we laughed at our passengers, and most important of all, we laughed at ourselves."[19] Former VAD Marge Stead was succinct when she looked back on her war work in England and France from the perspective of 1977: "All a wonderful experience."[20]

The specific form of happiness most frequently mentioned in retrospective accounts of the war, though, is one that is quite consistent with the soldier's story: that of a powerful and deep comradeship among those who lived through the war together. Loyalty and friendship were a consistent theme of the trench poets (though Graves, for one, seemed incapable of maintaining any of those friendships after the constraints of war were removed). Yet even these descriptions could show the tension between old and new portrayals of the war. A. B. Beauman, a professional soldier, wrote that in "the wonderful comradeship of a historic regular battalion" there was "ample compensation" for "the periods of intense fear and periods of great sadness after the battalion had suffered heavy casualties." His pride in his profession as a regular soldier, not just a wartime volunteer, was apparent in his attitude toward the work at hand. It mattered very much to him that he served in a regular battalion with a long record of military achievement, and that in the current war he was "doing a job really worthwhile."[21] As a result, though on a number of occasions he criticized command decisions and military tactics, his memoirs demonstrated his lifelong conviction that the war itself was justified and important.

Camaraderie was a recurrent theme in informal memoirs as well as their published counterparts. A soldier in the ranks, Joseph Murray, remembered that he was glad to return to the front line. He "longed for the friendship of real men, men that understood what war was all about, to be among men where trust was mutual and everything was shared, the good

---

[18] Mrs. D. McCann, IWM-DD P371.   [19] Mrs. R. I. Leared, IWM-DD 73/34/1.
[20] Mrs. Marge Stead, PL Women.   [21] Beauman, *Then a Soldier*, p. 48.

and the bad, the delights and the sorrows."[22] Similarly, another soldier wrote that "I had such friends then as I had never had before or since – friends with whom one lived in a complete bond of thoughts as well as goods."[23] Women, too, invoked this characteristic of the soldier's story. Olive Taylor, a working-class woman who left domestic service to take a job in a munitions factory and ultimately served in the WAAC, recalled feeling "free" when she was finally discharged. Her memory of the work itself was not positive, and she wrote that "I look back on my service as having done fourteen months' hard labour." However, she concluded, "the Espri [sic] de Corps and loyalty of the girls I shall always treasure."[24]

For Louise Downer, who came from a family of teachers and joined the WAAC "to help win the war," the bond she felt with her comrades was part of her satisfaction that women had proven their worth. The war had provided a special opportunity for work, under a rubric of patriotism: "we answered the nation's need for Women to do the jobs never been done before by the female sex." They rose to the challenge, and "we did match the men and woman for woman gave of our best under very adverse circumstances and with no training whatever." This idea of equal contributions by men and women still mattered to her fifty years later, when she told the gathered crowd at the "Jubilee Dinner of QMAAC 1917–1967" that "without our help in 1917 and onwards there would have been no shortening of the War and no Women's services as there are to-day." Downer wrote that the Jubilee dinner had been a special experience for her, when "I felt happy to be with my own 'kind' and to re-live again the Good Comradeship of the past." Two years later, at a WAAC reunion luncheon, she spoke of "a comradeship that we find nowhere else in the world," and averred that "by our service in so many ways we helped to shorten the war and prove that the women of the future could never again be ignored."[25] Her contribution to the crisis was the subject of satisfaction, not regret, and comradeship was key to her view.

Beryl Hutchinson remembered this same mixture of pride in service and delight in friendship. She was a member of the First Aid Nursing Yeomanry (FANY), and therefore of a socially elite background. Hutchinson claimed that "the most important aspect of all [was] the feeling of comradeship with every man and woman, Senior General to FANY

[22] Joseph Murray, *Call to Arms: From Gallipoli to the Western Front* (London: William Kimber, 1980), p. 142.

[23] Quoted in Peter Liddle, *Voices of War: Front Line and Home Front 1914–1918* (London: Leo Cooper, 1988), p. 222.

[24] Miss O. M. Taylor, IWM-DD 83/17/1.

[25] Mrs. L. Downer, IWM-DD 79/15/1. The WAAC was officially renamed Queen Mary's Army Auxiliary Corps (QMAAC).

Bugler to aged and wobbly Base Detail stretcher bearer, with whom one had shared the conditions, the life of dedication." Men and women alike were included in her representation, though she did not mention any active combatants. In fact, she remained defiant about the motivations of war workers in the face of the subsequent focus on disillusionment and worthless sacrifice. "We may have been naive, lived with illusion," she wrote, "but we all had the feeling that we really were keeping the world fit to live in, that our many sacrifices had been worthwhile." She explicitly invoked the concept of service, because "my generation had absorbed the idea of responsibility." As a result, "in that Spring of 1919 we felt the biggest task, the utmost sacrifice had been made and the world was a better place."[26] Their idealism was clearly still intact after the Armistice. Women's wartime narratives, in contrast, had not emphasized this comradeship of service, instead focusing more on the war and the soldiers. Shared fellowship was more clearly articulated in women's retrospective narratives after it had played a prominent role in the soldier's story. At the same time, these women continued to see their contributions as parallel to men's, though they were increasingly isolated in this perception. The women themselves, as they aged, did not forget. The different perspectives became joined in their memories: the trench parallels were used to claim legitimacy, the contribution to feel valuable, the friendship for a shared understanding.

The ideal of comradeship articulated in the soldier's story, however, does not stand up to cross-class pressures any better than similar claims did during the war. Then, the "classless" state of the trench, where all men fought together side by side regardless of their prewar social status or educational background, was identified with the national unity essential to victory. It was consolidated in the soldier's story, not from a shared patriotism, of course, but from a shared tragedy, a shared experience of terror, loss, and disillusionment. The bond among soldiers who had served in the trenches was described as the strongest possible kind. These men understood the war as no one else could, and that made them the most desirable companions – often, the only acceptable ones – for each other. The 1980 memoir of Joseph Murray, an enlisted volunteer, typified the traditional account of the common experience of the trench overcoming social divides. Murray wrote of the comfort and relief of returning to the front line (even though he described it as "Hell") because "in the forward area there is no real distinction, no classification – a weed is as exotic as an orchid." The commonplace had no less chance of survival than the special, and "there is a wonderful feeling of comradeship

[26] Beryl Hutchinson, IWM-DD 74/105/1.

among the lads in the line."[27] Retrospectively, however, it is clear that the trenches, common risk notwithstanding, were riven by the same class distinctions and tensions that permeated the rest of British society. The uniform, far from masking social stratification, was in fact a symbol of it, as enlisted men had their clothing and supplies provided by the military, but officers bought their own, tailor-made. Even then, the devil was in the details. A "temporary gentleman" – an officer drawn from the lower middle classes, who would not have been considered for a commission in the pre-war peacetime army – might give away his social background by using the wrong tailor, leading to a cut not quite right, or a khaki that was too buff or even, heaven forbid, practically yellow. Many veterans remembered these distinctions, even if they were glossed over by some well-known former officers.

Francis Law praised the "true comradeship that embraced everyone" as the only possible "good which emerged from the horrors and hazards of trench life." Because soldiers were dependent on each other in the face of great peril, he explained that "we shared a common humanity and recognized this profoundly though it was never put into words." As a result, "a generous feeling of understanding, appreciation and respect developed naturally." At the same time, he exposed in his memoir many of the ways that class remained a powerful force, even on active service. His very praise of the men emphasized that they were a separate population. "No one could serve with men like these without admiring them," he wrote. In battle, and through more daily travails, "it was the uncomplaining, sustained courage, good humour, and fortitude of our guardsmen that remained." He knew this because of his frequent interaction with the men, and "their leaders, particularly we junior ones in hourly contact with such splendid men, had every reason to be proud, respectful and humbled by their example." Law's strong praise, however, used language that emphasized the separation between the two groups. So did his efforts to improve their conditions. During troop movements, Law wrote, "being less heavily laden than our men, many of us tried to help those in distress by carrying their packs or rifles." His advice on leading men in the ranks also made the men seem alien: "strong personal, sympathetic leadership is desirable everywhere, but it is essential in the handling of Scottish and Irish soldiers, who must be led, not driven."[28] It would be hard indeed to argue that this was a portrait of equality in the trenches.

George Coppard remembered those same heavy packs from the perspective of one required to march in them, seemingly endlessly. His account described the different conditions for officers and enlisted men.

[27] Murray, *Call to Arms*, p. 75.   [28] Law, *Man at Arms*, pp. 61–62, 78, 54, 50.

Additionally, it was a comment on the social situation that made such disparity possible then, and on how class perceptions had since changed:

Junior officers had things a little easier for they marched in "light order," or with a dummy pack with little or nothing in it and a cane under their arms. Any belongings of a weighty nature were packed in their valises by their batman and put on transport. As if to remind us of the inferiority of our station, the colonel and company COs, looking soldierly and unfatigued, rode well-groomed horses. Looking at it today it seems a display of class privilege, but fifty years ago the Tommy accepted it as the natural order of things, for the changes enjoyed by the masses now were not even thought of.

It may have seemed "natural" to accept such disparity, but that did not mean that differences in condition were not resented by the enlisted men. Coppard remembered marching away from the front, when the eighty-pound packs seemed a bit lighter because they were going in the right direction, and the senior officers rode, "as befitted their station." When the captain dismounted, he would find small faults with men in the ranks, which caused the sergeants "to get all pepped up and start yelling commands." Coppard recorded that "there was no visible reaction against this, but every Tommy muttered 'Bastards!' under his breath, I'll wager."[29] The classlessness perceived by the elites was, at best, superficial. A little scratching quickly penetrated the veneer.

Military scholars have recognized the perpetuation of these strong class divisions so notably absent from the popularly known soldier's story. Ian Beckett argued that social interaction between officers and men "was far from being recognised as a universality of experience by the rank and file." As a result "there are thus distinct dangers in accepting the postwar disillusionment of a Robert Graves or a Siegfried Sassoon and their longing for the unity of the front line as in any way representative."[30] Similarly, Keith Simpson asserted that "there was still a considerable social divide between the ranks."[31] However, cultural scholars of the war have continued to maintain this special cross-class comradeship. Modris Eksteins, for example, argued that "in the trenches social barriers broke down as intellectuals became dependent on working-class men and aristocrats on crop farmers" – as fine a propagandistic note as any sounded during the war years.[32] A newfound affection on the part of the officers for their men

---

[29] George Coppard, *With a Machine Gun to Cambrai* (London: Imperial War Museum, 1980), pp. 16–17, 50–51.

[30] Ian Beckett, "The Nation in Arms, 1914–1918," in Beckett and Keith Simpson (eds.), *A Nation in Arms: A Social Study of the British Army in the First World War* (Manchester: Manchester University Press, 1985), p. 22.

[31] Keith Simpson, "The Officers," in Beckett and Simpson, *Nation in Arms*, p. 68.

[32] Modris Eksteins, *Rites of Spring: The Great War and the Birth of the Modern Age* (New York: Doubleday, 1989), p. 230.

was certainly a recurring theme in soldiers' narratives. However, as with Law, it was often worded in ways that emphasized the depth of the social gulf between the two groups. Perhaps most tellingly, this novel fondness was remarkably one-sided; enlisted accounts, though at times mentioning loyalty, did not generally refer to any enlightened comradeship across traditional class lines.

Among women, the story is remarkably similar. During the war itself, there were many claims of aristocrats working beside parlormaids, university students along with shopgirls. As with trench stories, however, this was more about showing a diverse nation united in a common effort than any kind of undistorted reflection of real work situations. Like the men, however, stories of classlessness did not fade away, but were told almost exclusively from the perspective of the "educated." Peggy Hamilton, for example, a middle-class woman who chose to work in a munitions factory, was described by a friend as "completely immune from the conception of 'class.'" Like the officers of the soldier's story, she not only "accepted people for what they were," but "her anger and indignation were reserved for officialdom and bungling in high places." Hamilton herself wrote of her coworkers that she enjoyed "being just an ordinary worker pushing my way through the gates with hundreds of others." She mocked the titled ladies who seemed to think that their occasional presence in the factory canteen was itself a treat for the regular employees. When an elite woman began to criticize munitions workers for earning too much and buying their legendary (and infamous) fur coats, Hamilton recorded that she sprang to her colleagues' defense. She recalled warmly asserting that "no one I knew owned a fur coat" – her experience and acquaintance denied the stereotype of the profligate munitions worker spending excessive amounts of money on her body. The other woman, undaunted, continued that the wages were still higher than what the workers were formerly accustomed to, "and they don't know how to spend it." Hamilton's spirited defense continued, insisting that just as the financial decisions of the wealthy were not the business of those less fortunate, whether they knew "how to spend their money" or not, so "it's nothing to do with the rich how their poor spend their money either."[33] Though she presented her own strong support for her fellow workers, her position made clear how very aware indeed she was of her different class status.

[33] Peggy Hamilton, *Three Years or the Duration: The Memoirs of a Munition Worker 1914–1918* (London: Peter Owen, 1978), pp. 9–10, 37, 33–34, 48. In fact, the famous fur coats always seemed to belong to someone else. Ethel Wilby, a former domestic servant and barmaid, began munitions work "at the time when they were slowing down on making them, coming to the end of the war, and you weren't making the money like they did in the first place, when they were supposed to have bought fur coats and goodness knows what with the money they earned": Mrs. E. Wilby, IWM-DD 92/49/1.

C. E. Tisdall, the VAD with the London Ambulance Column, fit her 1976 memories neatly into the traditional story of classlessness. "In spite of the more conventional conditions prevailing at that time we had not a scrap of class consciousness between us," she wrote, "we knew each other only by our surnames, but I suspected that there were some minor titles on the team." Despite her suspicions, she described "no distinction between an aristocrat and a little clerk, or any intermediate type." This may have been so officially, but it was clear from Tisdall's descriptions that an awareness of these differences clearly remained, and was the subject of ongoing speculation. Within the work environment, however, she remembered that she did not know that two VADs were "mistress and maid" until accompanying them to their flat for cocoa, when one began to serve the other.[34] Tisdall expected such distinctions to be noticeable, and ultimately, they were.

It is possible that this masking of social origins might have occurred in a relatively small ambulance column in London, but it was certainly not the case in the large women's services. As with men in the army, women were placed as "officers" or in the "ranks" based almost exclusively on their class position. They then lived and worked in very different conditions from each other. Rachel Haire-Foster, who was proud of her "Social Service Certificate from the London School of Economics," had been a social worker. She wrote that she wanted to join the General Service VADs (GSVAD) in the ranks, as she had worked "always, I felt, from the outside." She explained that "I thought I would be of more value to society later on if I could experience life for a time as an 'under-dog.'" She said she was disappointed to learn that the Red Cross would not consider her for the ranks, however; instead they made her commandant of a new General Service detachment being posted to Salonika.[35] Katharine Furse recalled with frustration that these social distinctions were made from the planning stages of the new GSVAD. "My colleagues," Furse wrote, felt "that nursing was such superior work that the VAD. Nursing Members should not be mixed up with the others performing more menial occupations." The military parallel was explicit, and "the Nursing Member ranked as an officer, but the cook and the clerk would be replacing RAMC orderlies in the ranks and it was thought that this would make great difficulties."[36] With an interesting mix of pronouns, first inclusive and then self-separating, Haire-Foster wrote that "as most

[34] Miss C. E. Tisdall, IWM-DD 92/22/1.   [35] Mrs. R. Haire-Foster, IWM-DD P347.
[36] Katharine Furse, *Hearts and Pomegranates: The Story of Forty-Five Years 1875–1920* (London: Peter Davies, 1940), p. 342. These differences were clearly perceived. Winifred Hodgkiss, at Ipswich High School preparing to go up to Girton, recalled that "some girls left to take up nursing as VADs," but "I do not remember any going into the Women's

of us were from the working classes they simply could not understand Army discipline." These ideas made efficient work challenging, she suggested, as "they were quite unable to understand why, if they were prepared to forfeit a day's pay, they shouldn't lose a day's work." (This criticism, of course, is evocative of those leveled at women munitions workers during the war.) Though the women were "very lively and affectionate," Haire-Foster felt that her supervisory job would have been easier if the women had been "more or less educated" – a euphemism for middle-class.[37]

Olive Taylor, like George Coppard, remembered these kinds of distinctions from within the ranks. Even during hot nights in the summer of 1918, enlisted WAACs had to keep the windows of their huts closed, "perhaps in case a soldier might creep in." Taylor and her colleagues, however, "were very annoyed to find a large cooltent [sic] had been erected for the officers." The WAACS "thought this most unfair," she wrote, and they determined not to accept the difference meekly. After making sure the structure was unoccupied, "we met at the tent and at a given signal got the ropes off the pegs and let the whole thing down and fled." Though "a big inquiry" was conducted, the women were not caught or punished, as "one trait stood out amongst us girls and that was loyalty to each other." This loyalty did not extend to their officers, who were clearly seen as entirely different.

Taylor and her friends also resented the discipline and what they certainly perceived as condescension in the control exercised over their personal lives. It became a game among the women to try to avoid the compulsory lectures frequently given by the officers on behavior, or the claim "that an awful disease could be caught through a kiss." When she was forced to attend, Taylor once instigated, to the joy of her companions, the circulation of a (mildly) disrespectful note: "She has nothing on under her coat-dress." Yet this very incident of rebellion also showed how powerful the constraints remained; though the note was "quietly enjoyed" by the congregated WAACs, "of course no one dare giggle."[38] Social distinctions were obvious on both sides, but class protest remained almost entirely contained. Comradeship was a powerful part of Taylor's recollection, but it did not surmount the barriers of class perceptions. The components of both wartime inclusiveness and the shared horror of the soldier's story failed to overcome the perspective of the socially excluded. Middle-class authors may have insisted on remembering equality,

Services": *Ipswich High School GPDST, 1878–1978* (privately published, no date), p. 19: Girls' Public Day School Trust Central Archives (hereafter GPDST).
[37] Mrs. R. Haire-Foster, IWM-DD P347.   [38] Miss O. M. Taylor, IWM-DD 83/17/1.

but their working-class counterparts continued to recall fundamental distinctions.

Work, service, and memory

Ideas of work and service that were so fundamental to descriptions of wartime experience also proved highly durable in memory, despite the dominance of the soldier's story. People who saw their war contributions as work held onto that conception especially tenaciously. Professionals, who were least influenced by idealism during the war, were also least likely to describe retrospective disillusionment. Conversely, a lasting focus on voluntarism and service could simultaneously be adapted to the soldier's story. Memoirs embraced disillusion while still maintaining the validity of service and its importance to the ongoing success of British society.

Many old soldiers have continued to think of their time in uniform as work. Because they were separate from the soldier's story, somehow they were not part of the debate over it. Though pride in work skillfully performed had no place in the traditional soldier's story, it was clearly not an uncommon alternate narrative. In 1933, Frank Richard's memoir, *Old Soldiers Never Die*, was praised in *The Times* for the perspective it offered on "the old soldier's sense of responsibility and concentration on the job in hand."[39] Talbot Kelly's memoir, its editor claimed, showed "something comparatively rare in war memoirs: the satisfaction of the professional in the efficient exercise of his own skills."[40] Similarly, Joseph Murray, an enlisted volunteer, felt real pride in the tasks he and his colleagues in the ranks had learned to accomplish, on and off the field. As they approached a French village, he remembered in 1980, "we don't need any prompting, we automatically become parade soldiers ... demonstrating ... [we] could march as well as any others." This was not just a matter of show, as "[we] had proved that we were second to none where fighting was concerned ... We were top of the class and proud of it."[41] Though a volunteer, his pride in his work was clear.

Conflicts over ways to remember the war exposed the workings of class in postwar culture. Virginia Woolf, of course, was never a supporter of the war. Her opinions, however, fell more gently on the popular ear after the triumph of the soldier's story. Woolf, in *Three Guineas*, criticized the women who – from what she described as a misplaced sense of patriotic service – had enabled the war (and the killing) to continue. An

---

[39] *The Times*, September 1, 1933, 6f. This short review immediately followed the discussion of Vera Brittain's *Testament of Youth*.
[40] Loosmore, "Introduction," p. 24.   [41] Murray, *Call to Arms*, pp. 150–152.

unemployed weaver, Agnes Smith, responded to Woolf in a letter. "You say glibly that the working woman could refuse to nurse and to make munitions – and so stop the war," Smith wrote; "a working woman who refuses to work will starve – and there is nothing like stark hunger for blasting ideals."[42] Woolf's assumptions were grounded in a vision of the war that insisted that women who worked did so because of the "need" of the nation, responding to a call to service. Smith lambasted Woolf for failing to understand the role of class position – of economic need – in making decisions about work. Smith's discussion, in 1938, of how "hunger blast[ed] ideals" is particularly telling: the ideal referred to here was pacifism, not patriotism. The view of the war had changed indeed.

Ideas of service, though, had not faded away even by the 1970s. Margaret Adams spent time as a VAD and with the Land Army before becoming a driver at the Vickers's Arms Factory. Adams, a student at Cheltenham when the war broke out, made a clear distinction in her memories between the kind of work she performed as part of the national effort and her later professional activities. Upon leaving school, she recalled in 1977, "before training in a career for myself, I was able to 'serve' in various ways."[43] Adams was, however, unable to use the term without the somewhat ironic inclusion of quotation marks, setting it off from standard language. C. E. Tisdall, the London Ambulance Column driver, recalled another young woman "whose parents would not allow her to work in the ambulances, so she spent all day putting clean covers on pillows." Though the fellow volunteer admitted she would have preferred the more exciting ambulance work, Tisdall averred in 1976 that "her service was as much necessary, dedicated and self-sacrificing as that of anyone else – albeit terribly boring. All honour to her!"[44] Clearly, these were still values that merited praise from Tisdall's perspective. It was the motivation of service, rather than the details of the work, that mattered.

National service could even at times become more powerful retrospectively. Jenny Swann's account of her time in the ranks of the WAAC focused primarily on the work. She also concluded, however, that "this country owe a debt to all the thousands of women who answered the call to do the men's jobs while they went to fight." Swann claimed their value through a key element of the soldier's story: the risk – and loss – of life. "Many of our girls died overseas," she continued, "I was lucky to come home."[45] Statistically, of course, this was not true; the vast majority of

---

[42] Agnes Smith to Virginia Woolf, November 7, 1938, quoted in Woollacott, *Lives Depend*, p. 165.

[43] Mrs. M. H. Adams, IWM-DD P348.   [44] Miss C. E. Tisdall, IWM-DD 92/22/1.

[45] Miss J. Swann, IWM-DD Misc. 61, Item 947.

WAACs came safely home. Swann may have been lucky, but not sur-prisingly so. The few who did not come home, however – and especially those killed in the bombing that accompanied the German advance of spring 1918 – were held up by those who wanted to make a claim for the service of women within the structures established by the postwar trench story. As female deaths from enemy action were a rare commodity, they were especially valuable symbolically for the appropriation of a historical model that was firmly based on the casualties of war.

The concept of service stayed especially strong among women in-volved with the Voluntary Aid Detachments. Katharine Furse, the origi-nal VAD commandant (who also served as the first head of the WRNS), remained deeply committed to the ideals of service that she had espoused in wartime. The stories of disillusionment that became so popular in the late 1920s and 1930s did not even tinge Furse's memories of war work and her confidence in the superiority of voluntarism over professionalism remained unshaken. "I became," she wrote in 1940, "a great believer in voluntary or unpaid workers." She insisted that this "very precious system" of voluntarism was not about class or the need to earn a liv-ing, but about a level of devotion and people's personal commitment "to contribute vocational service to those who are less fortunate than themselves." (This altruism, of course, rings a bit hollow from someone of her socioeconomic status.) Furse continued by defining "making a willing sacrifice for the benefit of others" as "one of the finest privileges of humanity." This positive idea of service was explicitly contrasted to "the attitude of professional workers toward the amateur." In fact, when VADs "failed in their duty," she argued that "their failure could often be traced to the way in which they were treated by those under whom they worked."[46] She still maintained that the professionals were undermining the service of the volunteers. For Furse, certainly, the war in the wards did not end with the Armistice.

Work, service, and the battle for the wards

The differences between wartime descriptions and memories were not always marked. Retrospective accounts continued to maintain a vision of tension and misunderstanding between VADs and trained nurses, though it was somewhat qualified by an awareness of the distance of time. Social distinctions between women who worked and women who did not were not diminished in the postwar period – if anything, they were perhaps sharpened retrospectively. This ongoing cultural separation meant that

---

[46] Furse, *Hearts and Pomegranates*, pp. 329–330.

both groups continued to rely on self-justifications. Kit Dodsworth, a volunteer in France, wrote unsympathetically of the arrival overseas of a group of trained nurses from the Cambridge Hospital. The new arrivals were "very smart and grand and very critical of our rather rough-and-ready fittings and habits." One nurse was sent to Dodsworth's ward. The new nurse was allegedly horrified by the difference in conditions from a British facility. Instead of the "wonderful linen cupboards" of the Cambridge Hospital, they were forced to use upended packing cases. Dodsworth, presenting herself as the voice of experience, testily reminded the nurse that "we were now on Active Service."[47] Dodsworth's account was full of similar incidents. She remembered the controversy over titles; it was only the arrival of the Cambridge nurses that resulted in the VADs being denied the unearned title of "Sister." An enlisted patient recorded in Dodsworth's autograph book: "Laugh and the Nurse laughs with you; Sister enters and you laugh alone." This, she commented, was "very typical of ward life after the arrival of the new sisters." At that time, "life was indeed miserable."

These aspects of her account were very similar to VAD wartime accounts of their relations with trained nurses. Retrospectively, however, the older Dodsworth also tempered the more extreme portions of her memoir. "I do not think that it was really half as bad as I imagined," she wrote, "it was only I was overwrought and just full of nerves." New, inexperienced VADs arrived "and were quite obviously unable to take on any responsible work," she later realized. "At that time though, when we were all very much on edge with overtiredness, it seemed all very irritating" that the VADs were denied real nursing work.[48] Her perspective shifted considerably by the time of her memoir. No longer a young woman and the war long over, she was far less invested in the battle between service and professionalization than she had once been. Dodsworth's specific memories of conflict with trained nurses remained as acidic as many wartime accounts. Her explanatory narratives, however, were now subtly tempered by a more tolerant realization of the differing perspectives of the two groups of women.

Mrs. E. Briggs Constable, another VAD, also retrospectively qualified her memories of relations with the nurses. Constable admitted that "I made rude remarks about a few [nurses] in the privacy of my diary," though even then, she asserted, "sometimes changed my mind when I came to work closely with them, or to know them better personally." Though she tried retrospectively to diminish the significance of these conflicts, her acknowledgment that she had to discuss "relations with

---

[47] Mrs. Vaughan Phillips, PL Women.   [48] Mrs. Vaughan Phillips, PL Women.

the trained staff" in her memoir shows how fundamental that interaction was to most accounts of women's hospital work. "There was certainly discipline," Constable wrote, "but that's what they were there for, or rather, that's what we expected to get, as part of our training, and it was accepted as such."[49] Here, perhaps, Constable was exposing her own perspective as the daughter of a doctor; most volunteers did not describe themselves as part of a training relationship. They were there, the argument went, to take care of soldiers, not to be forced to learn the niceties of nursing as it was practiced. Constable, in contrast, was raised to respect hospital routines. She therefore wrote that she did not expect that they should change in any substantive way for "volunteers" who were "in this thing of our own free will." Of the infamous discipline, she argued that "surely only someone with a persecution complex could have called it 'bullying.'" Once in France, she continued, relations improved further. Looking back, she suggested that "we VADs grew up a little bit, and perhaps the sisters grew down a little bit," leading to "generally a very pleasant working partnership."[50] This retrospective view showed a moderating of tension much less common in wartime accounts of the wards, perhaps better demonstrating the passage of time after the war than during it. Similarly, Tina Gray, the former VAD who became a doctor, wrote of the "mixed reception" she and her colleagues received from the trained nurses when they arrived at a hospital. Some of the professionals "seemed to consider or pretend to consider us a nuisance," while "others gave us the most un-nursing jobs to do, like cleaning the radiators when the heat was on." Yet, like Constable, Gray showed a distinctive admiration of the professionals. One Matron "was a wonderful surgical nurse and her aseptic technique I never saw bettered."[51] This kind of appreciation was necessarily retrospective, given Gray's future career as a surgeon.

The special relationship so frequently described between the VADs and the patients, quite different from the way the soldiers and the trained nurses were presented as interacting, was widely acknowledged. Personal interaction with the patients was frowned upon in nursing training; Kit Dodsworth was therefore awarded the "horrid punishment" of working in the Sisters' Mess rather than in her "beloved wards," because she laughed too much with them. Even after she returned to medical care she wrote that she "still continued to get 'strafed' for laughing."[52] May Cannan, the VAD in Oxford, remembered that patients "would always do their best to 'cover up'" if there were troubles with the trained staff;

[49] Mrs. E. Briggs Constable, PL Women.   [50] Mrs. E. Briggs Constable, PL Women.
[51] Dr. T. Gray, PL Women.   [52] Mrs. Vaughan Phillips, PL Women.

the soldiers "invariably took our part."[53] From the other perspective, Sister Henrietta Hall remembered an incident with some of her patients, who because of gassing or illness had no wounds apparent to the casual observer. The men once went into town unnecessarily bandaged in order to garner female sympathy and attention. As, according to Hall, "it was obvious that it was a professional job" and the soldiers had also gotten access to restricted crutches, she knew they must have had help in carrying out their plan. "Obviously it wouldn't have been my Staff nurse," Hall remembered; clearly no real trained nurse would have colluded with patients like that. Instead, she assumed the responsibility lay with the five VADs she supervised, "because they were very sympathetic to the boys." The VADs all denied involvement, but Hall did not believe them. "It seems very funny, looking back," she concluded, "but at the time I had to be very strict."[54] Again, the lines of conflict, once razor sharp, became softer with both the passing years and the firm establishment of professional nursing standards. Hall could afford to be amused by the VADs' lack of discipline, when it no longer threatened to undermine the credibility of her ward; she could even complement their skills by calling the bandages a "professional job."

Other members of the nursing community, however, experienced no such tempering in their accounts of VADs. In 1967, fifty years after the war, Gerald Bowman's history of the Royal College of Nursing was as one-sided in favor of the trained staff as anything written by Katharine Furse had been in her support of the volunteers. His account of the war years was filled with snide references to VADs, "who allowed it to be known that they did not consider themselves to be on a level with 'ordinary nurses.'" He explained that "they were, of course, right, but not quite in the way they imagined." While Bowman grudgingly wrote that "in justice to the VADs, a large proportion of them did useful work throughout the war," he also made clear the root of the real problem. Productive or not, VADs "were thoroughly and very understandably unpopular with the nursing profession, and when the war ended many of the qualified nurses had reason to suspect that the VADs would be competing with them unfairly in the professional employment market."[55] He presented no particular evidence for this claim.

This also worked better as an explanation for tensions after the war, rather than a way to understand the conflicts that arose during the war

[53] Miss M. W. Cannan, IWM-DD P360.
[54] Quoted in Lyn Macdonald, *The Roses of No Man's Land* (London: Michael Joseph, 1980), p. 155.
[55] Gerald Bowman, *The Lamp and the Book: The Story of the RCN 1916–1966* (London: Queen Anne Press, 1967), pp. 64–67.

itself, when nurses were likely to be thinking more of their present professional status than of their future employment searches. Some VADs
did wish to continue hospital work after the Armistice, and a number
were awarded scholarships by the Red Cross and the Order of St. John
to cover the costs of training as a nurse. The vast majority, though, left
the work altogether; their interest had been in the war rather than the
wards. According to Bowman, however (again without offering any supporting statistics), VADs "applied in large numbers for registration at
the [Royal] College," but then discovered that "only a three year certificate of training from an approved hospital could gain them membership." Bowman suggested that this rejection caused an increase in the
status of the registration process among the nurses themselves. News
of the unsuccessful overtures "brought full confidence in the College
among all the qualified and practising nurses and nurses in training for
whom it had been founded."[56] In Bowman's account, they now knew
they could rely on uniform enforcement of the standards for training and
registration.

The story of conflict in the wards has primarily been told from the
perspective of the VADs, and therefore without much sympathy for the
position of the nursing profession. During the war, Enid Bagnold was
the subject of a flurry of attention when her *Diary Without Dates* was
published. In it, she condemned what she described as senseless routines along with what she perceived as a lack of empathy on the part of
the nurses. She was summarily dismissed from her hospital position when
the book appeared. Mary Borden's critically acclaimed short stories, published in 1929 as *The Forbidden Zone*, repeatedly positioned nurses as
being motivated by their profession rather than any fundamental – and
necessary – understanding of human beings. One "excellent nurse," Pim,
was not concerned with her patient (who clearly fascinated Borden) as
a man; rather, she "was interested in his wounds and in saving his life."
According to Borden, "she had come to the front to nurse the French because she had been told that they needed nurses more in the French army
than in England; but she was not interested in French men, nor in any
man." This was because "she knew no men. She knew only her patients."
In Borden's elegant prose, Pim's fight to save the young Frenchman's life
became insufficient effort because she could not really understand him.
For Borden, training was not enough; empathy was required. In another
story, Borden begged another nurse to allow a soldier – scheduled to be
executed – to die in the hospital as he wished. Here, compassion was
posited as being in opposition to the "highly trained" nurse's "traditions,

[56] Bowman, *Lamp*, pp. 64–67.

her professional conscience, [and] the honour of her calling."[57] (The nurse did, though, ultimately agree.)

Most famously, however, the nurses were done in by Vera Brittain's best-selling *Testament of Youth* in 1933. Though Brittain praised a few of the nurses she worked with, and most notably became friends with one while serving at a hospital in France, her condemnation of the profession as a whole was profound and unambiguous. Her portraits were not subtle. In fact, nurses she liked were usually described as being attractive, while the majority whom she criticized were inevitably physically unappealing. Since her account remains the best-known narrative of British women's experience in the war, this characterization had significant impact, and other writers, in turn, have felt the need to address it. May Cannan, for example, wrote "I think [Brittain] was unfortunate" in her descriptions of tribulations at the hands of trained staff. However, "I was told the same thing by many of my friends who nursed, and we did have experience of it ourselves."[58] Simultaneously, Cannan identified Brittain's account as both unusual and typical, a difference perhaps of number than of kind.

This focus on the perspective of the VAD has translated into the secondary literature as well. Histories like Arthur Marwick's *Women at War 1914–1918* presented the complaints of the VADs but not the countering objections of the nurses. When he described the War Office's decision to maintain overall control of VADs in military hospitals, Marwick explained that Katharine Furse, VAD commandant, "rightly felt [that] justifiable grievances of many VADs serving in France were simply not being considered."[59] More popular accounts like Lyn Macdonald's *The Roses of No Man's Land* and David Mitchell's *Monstrous Regiment* have focused on the healing aspects of the work being performed by women in the wards, a perspective which precluded clarification of the conflict between the different populations. Finally, literary studies like Claire Tylee's *The Great War and Women's Consciousness* and Sharon Ouditt's *Fighting Forces, Writing Women*, among others, have focused on the narratives of VADs because these women were the ones who were educated in a literary tradition that valued personal writing, and have therefore left the texts that made them more vocal defenders of their own war experiences – at the expense, perhaps, of those women who worked beside them. (This self-selection, of course, parallels that of the junior officers who played such a dominating role in the definition of the soldier's story.) In her focus on VADs, in fact, Ouditt even referred to them as "military nurse[s]," a title correctly restricted to the trained members of the regular and reserve

[57] Mary Borden, *The Forbidden Zone* (London: William Heinemann, 1929), pp. 71, 105.
[58] Miss M. W. Cannan, IWM-DD P360.   [59] Marwick, *Women*, pp. 83–85, 91.

military nursing services.[60] The most significant retrospective shift in narratives of conflict in the wards, then, was not the revisions and tempering of many personal accounts – though that assuredly occurred. Instead, it was the effective silencing of one-half of the debate.

Work and service: sex and the war

VADs, because of their privileged social backgrounds and the feminine nature of their work, lived away from home in close proximity to (often unclothed) men without having their "morality" impugned. Working-class women, of course, faced much greater social condemnation. Forcing the enlisted WAACs to keep their windows shut in order to prevent illicit fraternization with soldiers when their officers were given much more personal freedom, as Olive Taylor recalled, was typical of differing class expectations. While issues of "morality" never seemed to be far from authorities' minds, they were certainly applied differently to the disparate populations of women war workers, in accord with expectations based on socioeconomic background. For some, rules were considered sufficient; for others, more physical restraints (like closed windows and bed checks) were applied. Charlotte Dalton remembered "a *severe* lecture" from Katharine Furse before leaving with her VAD contingent for France. That was considered adequate prevention for these women. Dalton alleged that trained nurses were the real social offenders, "even to crawling in under wire fences *and* meeting young men in the forest." Then serious problems occurred, she claimed, after the arrival of the WAACs. Nurses may have met with men illicitly, but the WAACs allegedly did more, and "maternity wards had to be made available."[61] Her cosmology of sexual promiscuity closely correlated with perceived class position.

Public concerns about sexual behavior were applied up and down the socioeconomic scale, but they were acted on differently. Katharine Furse insisted that she "knew enough about men and women and their relationships to be tolerant of perfectly natural behaviour." However, she was sure that in order for the new VAD service to be successful in the popular eye, "they should establish a reputation for almost exaggerated seriousness," as that "was safer than too great leniency at first."[62] Kit Dodsworth remembered the strictness with which these policies were implemented, and the lack of enthusiasm with which they were received. On board the hospital ship *Aragon* in the harbor at Malta on Christmas Day,

---

[60] Sharon Ouditt, *Fighting Forces, Writing Women: Identity and Ideology in the First World War* (London: Routledge, 1994), p. 9.
[61] Mrs. G. Mackay Brown, IWM-DD PP/MCR/168.
[62] Furse, *Hearts and Pomegranates*, p. 321.

Dodsworth and her fellow VADs were frustrated by their matron's stern refusal to allow them to dance with the officers. Even the best efforts of the ship's captain and the colonel commanding the troops resulted, after much persuasion, only in the tearful matron closing her eyes to dancing occurring on deck.[63] Men could afford to be more lenient about bending rules because their status in wartime was beyond criticism. For the matron, though, the limited extent of her real authority had been painfully demonstrated.

The real public concern, of course, was not with the morality of the predominantly socially elite nursing VADs, but with the newly independent working-class women in the factories and the ranks of the auxiliary military organizations. Wartime accounts, then, focused on stories of unwed pregnancy in the ranks, like those Dalton recalled hearing. Retrospective accounts, however, generally struck a different tone. Sexual mores and sexual practices had changed and become considerably more open. At the same time, women as a visible and critical presence in the labor force were no longer a novelty. Dalton still blamed WAACs as part of her effort to vindicate the behavior of VADs in comparison, and some soldiers like Joseph Murray continued to express shock at the actions of officer-patients and their nurses at Paris-Plage.[64] Most women, however, were able to be much more matter-of-fact about their own activities and those of their coworkers. Ada Potter, a WAAC near Boulogne, remembered friendships that became romances and then engagements, "but in civilian life nothing came of it," suggesting the feeling of separation from any regular existence that came with active service.[65] An "engagement" perhaps legitimated a different level of sexual interaction, but it too, like so many things, was just "for the duration." Olive Taylor, stationed at the WAAC post at Aldershot, recalled the challenge of racing to break new rules as soon as they were posted. She and her friends, she wrote, also evaluated the moral codes of different groups of soldiers. The Irish Guards included "some very nice boys," but the women learned not to trust the Coldstream Guards, who were more forceful and sexually demanding. "What did it matter to them," she wrote, "if a girl lost her character and ended up in the workhouse with a baby?" The women colluded to avoid being caught by inspecting officers, and saved their special animosity for the women police officers. These were practically seen as traitors, as "what kind of women could volunteer for such a position we could not envisage." Taylor prided herself on her ability to fool the authorities, recalling

---

[63] Mrs. Vaughan Phillips, PL Women.   [64] Murray, *Call to Arms*, p. 72.
[65] Miss A. Potter, PL Women.

that despite many broken rules, her discharge papers read "Work in the Corps, very good, personal character, excellent." (She may not have been quite as successful as she remembered, as her actual discharge papers, included in her file at the Imperial War Museum, describe her as "very good" on both counts.)[66] Of course, the fact that "personal character" was a category on the discharge documents is itself a telling detail about the kind and amount of supervision considered appropriate for women in the ranks.

Betty Leared remembered the specific physical and emotional preparation for service in France the WAACs underwent. The women were "inoculated, vaccinated, drilled and lectured" – specifically, to "be friendly with the men, girls, but don't let them get silly." Leared also believed that the WAACs in London had been given some lectures on venereal disease, which she had not attended. (As a driver attached to the WAAC from the Women's Legion when she went overseas, Leared was not grouped consistently with the women of the ranks.) In her memoir, Leared was open with stories about drunkenness among the drivers as well as both flirtations and more serious liaisons with soldiers. She described a rivalry with a neighboring group of VADs, where each seemed to compete to be able to tell more immoral stories about each other, "hoping thereby to restore our [own] damaged prestige." She defended women who became pregnant, and their partners as well, preferring to blame, in wartime, "the girl's parents, and in a much lesser degree, the Corps to which the girl belonged." The women needed, she argued, more compassionate attention at home and, emphatically, better sex education. In wartime, she suggested, her countrywomen who stayed in England had only extreme opinions of those who worked abroad. "Either we were heroic martyrs carrying on our work under continual shell fire or bombardment from the air," she wrote, "or we were the lowest type of womanhood, which had made its way to France solely in pursuit of men and pleasure." Retrospectively, Leared hoped there would be room to see that "in reality few of us came under either category." Instead, "we were just ordinary people who had drifted into foreign service more by accident than by good management."[67] Patriotism, as a salutary motivation, was entirely absent from this retrospective analysis of war workers. Leared simply wanted to remove the lenses of class expectations and examine the women workers on their own terms. She argued that it was time to rewrite the history of British society at war.

[66] Miss O. M. Taylor, IWM-DD 83/17/1.   [67] Mrs. R. I. Leared, IWM-DD 73/34/1.

Re-remembering the war as lived

In 1921, the Joint War Committee Report prepared by the British Red Cross Society and the Order of St. John stated that "while sixteen British Military Medals were awarded for special acts of bravery, it is pleasant to be able to add that no Voluntary Aid Detachment Member serving in France under the control of the Joint War Committee lost her life through enemy action."[68] For the authorities responsible for placing women in potentially dangerous situations near the combat zones, this was a victory. The report could not say that VADs had not died overseas, as some succumbed to illness, presumably at rates higher than those faced by their counterparts who were home in Britain living in more hygienic surroundings and not in daily contact with diseased bodily fluids. When a VAD, like any other non-combatant woman serving in France, did die, she was accorded a funeral with full military honors. The British military custom (unlike the American) is to bury fallen soldiers at their last battlefields rather than to try to bring the bodies home to their families. This cultural tradition was applied to women serving overseas as well, even though the physical obstacles of returning remains from France to England were far from insurmountable. Photographs show parades of troops lined up to honor coffins draped with the national flag before proceeding to burial in military cemeteries.

These ceremonies were not restricted to the often socially privileged VADs – or, even, necessarily, to those serving overseas. Olive Castle remembered when a fellow WAAC, a clerk in Aldershot, died of tuberculosis (in itself, clearly not a war-related fatality). The clerk's only relative was a fiancé serving in the trenches in France, who, in an ironic twist of usual wartime gender roles, was called to her deathbed. "When she was buried," Castle recounted, "she was given Full Military Honors, – guncarriage team of black horses, coffin with Union Jack, full military band, and some hundreds of us, taken from the whole area, to parade and line the streets." Castle described how the woman "was buried in the Military Cemetery, among famous names and was given the salvo over her open grave, just like the high-ranking instead of a humble WAAC clerk."[69] The symbolic message was unmistakable: the WAAC had died in service to her nation, whatever the specific circumstances of her demise. The event clearly made a powerful impression on Castle, who, sixty years later, remembered even the details of the fiancé's handkerchief covering his face as he walked. Both these historical moments – the wartime funeral and

[68] *War Committee Reports*, p. 340: BRCS.
[69] Mrs. O. Castle, IWM-DD Misc. 61, Item 948.

the elderly memory – mark how powerful ideas about women's mortality in wartime could be.

Death, here, was a metaphor as well as a physical reality. Though of course the Joint Committee was eager to demonstrate how well cared-for their VADs in fact were, many postwar sources put forward the idea that equality of risk – even if fewer faced it – symbolized equality of service. The Jubilee Book of the Girls' Public Day School Trust, celebrating its fiftieth anniversary in 1923, wrote about the schools' Old Girls, "some of whom," during the war, "fell for their country as gallantly as any brother in arms." The account also mentioned "so many . . . whom to-day wear the riband of the Order of the British Empire, for deeds of valour under fire, or for duller deeds of heroic endurance in Base hospitals or in nursing homes." One footnote served for both these claims, yet it documented only the variety of military distinctions awarded, from "DBE, 1" to "Foreign Decorations, 8." It offered no supporting statistics for fatalities among the alumnae who had served – apparently, judging from the description, only as nurses rather than in any other areas of war work open to women.[70]

These claims, while positing a parallel degree of ultimate risk, could not pretend to equality in number. Some women died, but clearly nowhere near as many as men. In putting forth these assertions (both during and immediately following the war) about the risks to life and limb faced by women war workers, the argument was one about the ultimate *willingness* to sacrifice in the name of the nation, rather than about the price actually paid. It was their eagerness to "do their bit," which made these women the cultural partners of men in the war effort. The very language, "to do *your* bit," even implied that the "bit" might not be the same for everyone – and, given norms of class and gender, indeed it was not. A decade or so later, however, the dominance of the soldier's story swept away that broad mantle of approval. Risk of death, along with the emotional devastation that was described as the inevitable result of trench service, were the defining characteristics of war experience as it was newly (and narrowly) defined. As a result, women and other non-combatants who still valued the differentiated parity of war contribution that they had been granted in the war itself began to re-remember their experiences in ways that kept, as closely as possible, to the model of the soldier's story. Claims for emotional devastation might have been successful, but those that focused on mortality fell flat because they were patently not, in fact, comparable. "Different but equal" could

[70] Laurie Magnus, *The Jubilee Book of the Girls' Public Day School Trust 1873–1923* (Cambridge: Cambridge University Press, 1923), p. 188.

not translate, retrospectively, into (almost) the same, and therefore also acceptable.

This trench-centered vision of the conflict, thoroughly ensconced by the 1930s, remained relatively uncontested until the 1980s. In fact, it received one of its greatest boosts, just as it might have been fading. New memoirs began to be published in increasingly greater number as their authors found the available time that came with retirement and grown families in combination with the retrospective contemplation that often accompanies increasing age. These diverse "veterans" were looking back over the formative events of their lives, and the spurt of memoirs was accompanied by a revival of the battlefield tourism that had initially sprung up in the 1920s. The publication of Paul Fussell's *The Great War and Modern Memory* in 1975, however, further established Robert Graves, Siegfried Sassoon, Wilfred Owen, and Edmund Blunden as the canonical war authors by declaring them so. These choices, of course, continued to restrict the view of the war to the depths of the trenches. Memories of war, for Fussell, only encompassed the recollections of combat soldiers serving in the front lines; the home front had no place at all, either in making its own claims or in understanding those made by soldiers. In the 1970s and 1980s, however, more and more voices with a variety of perspectives began to articulate their memories of war. Some of these accounts were in published and polished form, but more were informal narratives, often intended for grandchildren, and then sent, perhaps as an afterthought, to the Imperial War Museum (which itself solicited both written and oral recollections) or the Liddle Collection at the University of Leeds. Some accounts were donated by family members, after their authors' deaths. This wealth of new, diverse sources, in combination with increasing interest among professional historians, literary critics, and the reading public in women and working people, began to change ideas and expand knowledge about specific populations that previously had not been the subjects of extended analysis.

Many of these reminiscences of war work began with memories of joining up. Some authors said they were motivated by patriotic conviction, others because the work seemed exciting, and still others from a sense of obligation. Retrospectively, the more service-oriented an author had been during the war itself, the more likely he or she was to justify volunteering in terms of the disillusionment posited by the soldier's story. Some writers thus felt the need to look back pityingly at their younger, more naïve selves. Others, though, continued to maintain the validity of their original motivations. Many, like WAAC telegraphist Ada Potter, were very aware of the different cultural perspective of their readers. As she wrote, with some self-deprecation, "it must be difficult [to understand] now how patriotic we youngsters were then." Potter, upon hearing from colleagues that the Post Office was looking for women to replace male telegraphists in France, "immediately begged them to be sure to put my name down I was sure there would be dozens applying." She had been working hard, with long shifts, but wrote that "somehow giving one's all in France seemed so much more worthwhile."[71]

Volunteer soldiers, too, continued to defend their original motivations. W. T. Colyer, at work when the war began, remembered: "I wished to goodness I were in the army. I felt restless, excited, eager to do something for the cause of England. And then the impulse came, sending blood tingling all over my body: why not join the army now?"[72] Similarly, a civil servant, W. R. Owen, explained to his modern readers that joining up "was not a sentimental whim"; he and his friends "were genuinely moved."[73] He felt obliged to assert his own sincerity to younger generations. George Coppard, who served in the ranks, remembered that "News placards screamed out at every street corner and military bands blared out their martial music in the main streets of Croydon." For an impressionable young man like Coppard, he wrote, "this was too much for me to resist, and as if drawn by a magnet I knew I had to enlist right away."[74] Though only sixteen years old, the sentiment as he remembered it was a powerful motivation that resonated across classes. Working men who filled the army's ranks responded, after all, in much greater real numbers than their future officers.

Women also remembered being moved by official recruitment efforts. Louise Downer saw "a Large Poster asking for Women to join the Army and help win the War." She remembered vividly that "the Picture had a Woman in Uniform and said 'Your Country needs *YOU*.' That settled it for me. I thought that is what I'll do – I'll go help win the War."[75] Eighteen-year-old Dorothy Dunbar, "urged by a feeling of restlessness and the conviction that she should be 'doing her bit,'" learned to drive and ultimately joined the WRAF.[76] Ruth Manning, a VAD, remembered being equally enthusiastic. When she was selected to work at a military hospital, "I felt so proud and pleased to be considered suitable to volunteer."[77] Serving on behalf of the war effort was not just an obligation, but a privilege, even in retrospect. Indeed, for some, the war was an

---

[71] Miss A. Potter, PL Women.
[72] W. T. Colyer, IWM-DD 76/51/1 quoted in Peter Simkins, *Kitchener's Army: The Raising of the New Armies, 1914–1916* (Manchester: Manchester University Press, 1988), p. 168.
[73] W. R. Owen, letter dated July 16, 1963, quoted in Simkins, *Kitchener's Army*, p. 168.
[74] Coppard, *Cambrai*, p. 1.
[75] Mrs. L. Downer, IWM-DD 79/15/1.   [76] Miss D. M. Dunbar, IWM-DD 88/2/1.
[77] Miss R. B. Manning, IWM-DD 80/21/1.

opportunity. For a professional soldier like A. B. Beauman, "mobilisation started in a spirit of exhilarating excitement . . . After all we were regular soldiers and our business was war."[78]

Attitudes toward enlistment, in fact, could be quite contradictory, both as lived and as remembered. Olive Taylor, who left domestic service for a munitions factory and then the WAAC, carefully pointed out in her manuscript memoir that her brother had rebelled against the pressures exerted by the gentry in their village. He "said he would go when he was ready – not when other people told him." He was not objecting to enlistment, she explained, merely trying to keep his actions within his own control. Her father, in fact, enlisted as well: "he was over the age limit, but he felt he ought to." Taylor herself said she ended a relationship with a beau "because he wouldn't enlist as a soldier." Though she did not refer to the ideals of patriotism or service when describing the war contributions of herself and her family, there was an obvious depiction of obligation and she did include a moral conclusion. Years later, she and her husband met the beau who would not join the military, by then "old and lame and lonely." Though most of the details of her story were intended to illustrate an argument about changing sexual mores, she also drew a comparison between the married couple (who had served) and the elderly bachelor (who had not) that was telling about her ongoing attitude toward war work. The beau was not praised for having resisted involvement in the useless war; instead, he was condemned to a pitiful last phase of his life.[79] His choice, in her eyes, was still presented as the wrong one.

Memories of the end of the war prove to be as revealing as those of the beginning of involvement were. The Armistice of November 1918 played an important part in the soldier's story. Though personal accounts always mentioned mass celebrations and festivities, in the story of disillusionment, it was always someone else – someone less sensitive and aware – who was feeling joy.[80] As Francis Law, a volunteer who became a regular soldier, remembered, "whatever may have gone on in London and in Paris that day, there was little rejoicing on our part." His thoughts were "far removed from rejoicing, remembering only too vividly the lost ones whose sacrifices now seemed in vain, and whose absence in the years ahead would be sorely missed in ruined homes and in the country at large." He

---

[78] Beauman, *Then a Soldier*, p. 27.   [79] Miss O. M. Taylor, IWM-DD 83/17/1.

[80] As Samuel Hynes argued, "every diarist recorded it," but those entries only marked how "out there in the rain other people, dreadful people, were celebrating in dreadful ways." Instead, for Hynes, a somber Thomas Hardy poem "seems to me to get the mood of 11/11/18 – at least as *thoughtful* Englishmen felt it – exactly right": *War Imagined*, pp. 254, 256 (my emphasis).

concluded, in the tradition of the lost generation, that "the bravest and the best were always sacrificed from the outset." Law in memory, however, was clearly thinking about a future Britain that Law, in 1918, could not yet know about. "We were to pay most bitterly for this terrible waste for decades," he continued, and we "are still paying and will do so for generations."[81] His memory of the past was really an argument about the future. Similarly, Diana Manners, secure in the knowledge that the man she loved was already safe in London, recalled that "after so much bitter loss it was unnatural to be jubilant. The dead were in our minds to the exclusion of the survivors." As a result, "the Armistice so prayed-for seemed a day of mourning." Though she confessed to having dinner at the Ritz Hotel with her mother and some friends, she "could not bear the carnival and slipped secretly away."[82] It was always other people who celebrated, people less sensitive, and less aware of the costs of the war, both personal and national. For some writers, though, the picture could be muddier, combining the two perspectives. C. E. Tisdall remembered that "I think most of us experienced a conflict of emotions . . . overwhelming relief, intense thankfulness . . . joy . . . but for the many thousands who would not return, or whose bodies were shattered, renewed grief."[83]

From reading the well-known elite texts alone, one would wonder who, in fact, did any celebrating at all. By examining lesser-known personal writings, however, it seems that a lot of people were jubilant at the end of the war. People who had imagined their war contribution as service were more likely to remember the Armistice as a solemn time, while those who saw what they were doing as a form of work were ready and eager to celebrate the end of more than four years of death and conflict. Celebrations were, in any case, clearly widespread. Mrs. P. L. Stephens, a motorcyclist attached to the RAF at the Armistice, described it as "a joyous and never-to-be-forgotten occasion." Rules about social interaction were relaxed, and a number of men and women from the aerodrome went into Nottingham to celebrate. Stephens described this wistfully as one of the best times of her youth: "how good it was to be *young* at that time, rather than now, at almost 80!!"[84] Amy Watkins devoted about a quarter of her one-page reminiscence of her war work to the Armistice. A Land Girl, she remembered that November 11, 1918, "was a cold foggy morning . . . in a very muddy field." When she and her fellow laborers heard the sirens from factories in nearby Hereford announcing the end of the war, "for a moment we just stood and stared then did a wild dance

---

[81] Law, *Man at Arms*, pp. 96–97.
[82] Diana Cooper, *The Rainbow Comes and Goes* (Boston: Houghton Mifflin, 1958), p. 219.
[83] Miss C. E. Tisdall, IWM-DD 92/22/1.
[84] Mrs. P. L. Stephens, IWM-DD P348 (emphasis in original).

in the mud." Watkins made no mention of an end to killing, or of any form of solemnity. Instead, she concluded shortly, "So by Xmas 1918 I was back home."[85] Normal life was restored.

Mrs. M. Parker, a Red Cross ambulance driver attached to the Women's Legion in Aldershot, wrote that she was glad to be on leave in London at the time of the Armistice. In her account, it was an opportunity for everyone to celebrate together, mindless of national differences. "I was most happy to join in all the rejoicing," she remembered, "troops of all nationalities were jostling each other and Waterloo station when I eventually got there was one seething mass of Troops of Canadians, New Zealanders, and others."[86] Tina Gray, the VAD who later trained as a doctor, described the joy of the soldiers in her care. Even the seriously hurt soldiers thought of celebration rather than mourning, she remembered. "The impression remains of smiling faces and raised laughing voices and general excitement," Gray wrote. She was particularly struck by "one young soldier who had lost both feet and who was fitted with temporary – really stumps – tap dancing in them up and down the ward and into the corridor. He was full of gaiety and determined they wouldn't be a handicap."[87] This was not an unusual reaction in hospitals, even though the costs of war were always vivid there. Mrs. E. Briggs Constable, another VAD, was nursing in France. They waited "for the guns on Bon Secours hill, which we had heard so often during the air raids, to crash out once more to signal the Armistice." At first there was a "curious hush...after the last bang died away," because "the end of a war is as stunning as the beginning." After that silence, she wrote, joyous celebration ensued: "one of the orderlies, a quiet little man, gave a wild whoop, and did a cake-walk down the full length of the ward, and pandemonium broke out."[88] Despite being surrounded by physical reminders of the risk and dangers of warfare, their initial sentiments were described as those of joy and relief, not sadness at the price already paid, or sacrifices made in vain. In fact, one ambulance driver, Vivienne Prentice, used the idea of pointlessness only to refer to the defeated enemy. British soldiers, she remembered, "went wild with excitement [and] I had people sitting on the bonnet of my car, also on the roof, banging tins and shouting." It was not until she was driving by a camp for prisoners of war that ideas of waste entered her recollections: "I felt very sorry for the men behind the wire netting," she wrote, "they must have felt that all they had been through was in vain." For the victors, even from the perspective of 1985, her memories of the Armistice did not include any acknowledgment of

---

[85] Miss A. Watkins, IWM-DD 87/5/1.   [86] Mrs. M. Parker, PL Women.
[87] Dr. T. Gray, PL Women.   [88] Mrs. E. Briggs Constable, PL Women.

waste; it was just the vanquished who had suffered without purpose. She concluded her manuscript memoir, however, with the declaration that "war is so terrible, that we must do everything possible to prevent it."[89]

Similarly, Ethel Wilby, a munitions worker, remembered that "people linked arms with strangers, danced to barrel organs [and] I started to dance on the mat with joy." She joined the celebratory crowds, and "my friend Grace and I went to the Victoria Palace that night, where most of the artistes had had too much to drink, which made them all the funnier." She immediately tempered her memories of such unalloyed joy, however, with solemn reflections from the perspective of one who had by then lived through two world wars. "I should have thought with all the wars we've had it would be understood that wars don't benefit anybody," she wrote, "everybody's worse off really – except those who make munitions." She meant this conclusion as a contrast, however; it was a comment on how, in November 1918, "people were hoping they were going to get better things out of winning the war, so as to be better [off] than they were beforehand."[90] That promise, though, was unfulfilled and people learned to blame the war for their difficulties. Winifred Hodgkiss, who spent the war years first at Ipswich High School and then at Girton, considered herself special because she remembered having such considerations of the future even on Armistice Day itself. "Some of the students got into St. Mary's Church in Cambridge," she recalled in 1978, "and rang a wild peal on the bells. But too many of our friends . . . would not come back. As an historian I knew that the world had greatly changed."[91] Most people, however, in their joy at the end of the war, were not yet looking forward.

It was, of course, the solemn version of the Armistice that entered popular practice.[92] November 11 each year was commemorated not with celebration but with mourning and sadness. The privately published history of Sutton High School recounted how "Armistice Day with its Silence became solemn – the clock ticking between the tall windows, and Mademoiselle Berst quietly weeping [because] she had lost a father and three brothers 'morts pour la France.'"[93] Charles [Edmonds] Carrington, who wrote two memoirs about his army service,

---

[89] Mrs. V. Prentice, PL Women.   [90] Mrs. E. Wilby, IWM-DD 92/49/1.
[91] *Ipswich High School GPDST, 1878–1978*, p. 20: GPDST.
[92] For more on Armistice commemoration, see Adrian Gregory, *The Silence of Memory: Armistice Day, 1919–1946* (Oxford: Berg, 1994). See also Hugh Cecil and Peter Liddle (eds.), *At the Eleventh Hour: Reflections, Hopes, and Anxieties at the Closing of the Great War* (Barnsley: Leo Cooper, 1998); and Mark Connelly, *The Great War, Memory and Ritual: Commemoration in the City and East London, 1916–1939* (Woodbridge, UK: The Royal Historical Society/Boydell Press, 2002).
[93] *A School Remembers: Sutton High School GPDST, 1884–1964* (private published, no date), p. 62: GPDST.

explained how he experienced the evolution of the commemorations of November 11:

The first Armistice Day had been a carnival; the second Armistice Day, after its solemn pause at the Two Minutes' Silence... was a day of festivity again. For some years I was one of a group of friends who met, every Armistice Day, at the Café Royal for no end of a party, until we began to find ourselves out of key with the new age. Imperceptibly, the Feast-Day became a Fast-Day and one could hardly go brawling on the Sabbath. The do-gooders captured the Armistice, and the British Legion seemed to make its principle outing a day of mourning. To march to the Cenotaph was too much like attending one's own funeral, and I know many old soldiers who found it increasingly discomforting, year by year. We preferred our reunions in private with no pacifist propaganda.[94]

No one seemed happy with the commemorations; at the same time as Carrington's retreat, the British Legion was complaining that Armistice Day had been taken over by flapper hedonism – a holiday like any other in the late 1920s.

Carrington's first volume of memoirs, *A Subaltern's War* (1930), was hailed by conservative critics (and a vocal number of veterans) as a corrective to the developing soldier's story. He described the book as being based on sources that were "anterior to the pacifist reaction of the nineteen-thirties and... untainted by the influence of the later writers who invented the powerful image of 'disenchantment' or 'disillusion.'" His work, he continued, went "back to an earlier stage in the history of ideas."[95] That cultural battle was lost, however, and he found himself increasingly out of step with the popular memory of the war. Carrington and his colleagues were forced indoors, away from the public domination of the soldier's story. Their own perspectives – like many of those that did not fit neatly with the established account of disillusionment – were silenced, overlooked, or condemned. As veterans and former war workers aged, however, new stories began to be remembered that negotiated a delicate balance between disillusionment and enthusiasm, waste and nobility of purpose. Soon there will be no more new memories of the First World War, but the history of its experience continues to be rewritten.

[94] Charles Carrington, *Soldier from the Wars Returning* (London: Hutchinson, 1965), p. 258.
[95] Carrington, *Soldier*, p. 12.

Conclusion
Climbing out of the trenches

The remembered soldier's story, with its exclusive focus on combat trench experience by men, would not have been easily recognized as the story of the war during the 1914–1918 period itself. Then, of course, active non-combatants, especially if they were women, were "soldiers" of a sort, helping to "fight." Olive Dent called the members of the Voluntary Aid Detachments "a New Army of nurses" like "the New Army of men."[1] Ethel Alec-Tweedie referred to women munitions workers in a shell factory as "a veritable little soldier-women's army."[2] The Women's Army Auxiliary Corps, Women's Royal Naval Service, and Women's Royal Air Force were explicitly military in their names, and the two smaller services were subsumed equally with the men's services in the king's official gratitude on behalf of the nation.[3] Women in the Land Army, whose military name was much less representative of their duties, were told in their official handbook that they were "serving [their] Country just like the Soldiers and Sailors."[4] Even young Peggy Brown asserted in 1915 that "a nurse . . . is as good as a soldier."[5] Repeatedly, women's war efforts were given symbolic parity with those of men in uniform through the use of a language of militaristic organization. During the years of the war, contributions on behalf of the nation by both men and women were thus classed publicly as parallel in effort and necessity.

Yet this represented equivalence was highly gendered: only young men in the military were awarded the accolade of giving the most they could to the country in its hour of need, because they were offering their lives.

---

[1] Olive Dent, *A VAD in France* (London: Grant Richards, 1917), pp. 14–15.

[2] Ethel Alec-Tweedie, *Women and Soldiers* (London: John Lane, [1918]), p. 30.

[3] See, for example, M. H. Fletcher, *The WRNS: A History of the Women's Royal Naval Service* (London: B. T. Batsford, 1989), p. 23; "The King's Message to the Royal Air Force," certificate, Miss J. G. Lambert, Peter Liddle 1914–1918 Personal Experience Archive, University of Leeds (hereafter PL) Women.

[4] *Women's Land Army Handbook*, p. 5. See, for example, Miss D. Ferrar, Imperial War Museum Department of Documents (hereafter IWM-DD) 92/30/1.

[5] Dorothy Brown to Helen Beale, undated [early November 1915]: Beale Family Papers, Cobnor Cottage, Chidham, Chichester (hereafter BP).

In contrast, women in a variety of jobs, none of them being regularly life-threatening and many of them also being performed by men, were represented as doing their best, but always with the caveat that they were indeed women. This propaganda also cut across class boundaries, with praise for the working women in the Land Army sounding almost the same note of patriotic parity as that applied to the young "ladies" involved with the Voluntary Aid Detachments. In fact, an alleged wartime diminution of class barriers was often depicted, focusing on men and women of widely varying social positions serving side by side, whether in the trenches or on the munitions assembly line. To make this point more clearly, wartime publications meant for a broad audience often particularly (and unrepresentatively) emphasized work that seemed especially unusual for the socioeconomic position of the worker: the university student scrubbing hospital floors, or the daughter of an earl making bombs. In the construction of these individual experiences, the battle over how to talk about war work was simultaneously a contest over the roles of gender and class in early twentieth-century British society.

Personal texts, not intended for publication, make it vividly clear that ideas about class played a fundamental and defining role in ideas about war work for both men and women. For men, the focus remained on service in the military. Able-bodied young men were expected to serve actively, though this expectation was even stronger in the middle classes. By the late nineteenth century and continuing on into the twentieth century, boys of this socioeconomic group were usually educated at public schools, which shared a similar approach to both education and the ideal of national service. Though of course there was variation, they all focused on a classical education in the context of a strong emphasis on team sports. Through the public school system, these boys had been thoroughly and repeatedly exposed to ideals of honor and sacrifice, of contribution to team effort, and of the glory of the empire. Field Marshall Earl Roberts spoke at many of these schools annually, calling on the future young men to be ready to defend the empire, an attitude symbolized in Baden-Powell's choice of "Be Prepared" as the motto for his Boy Scouts.[6]

This education, of course, was part of an ongoing redefinition of masculinity. It valorized the ideas of sacrifice leading to glory, and honor that could often only be achieved through noble death, combined with an emphasis on individual physical and mental contributions for the greater benefit of the team. It also focused on good sportsmanship and playing by

[6] The Scouts were even told by the king in 1909 that "the habits of discipline which they are now acquiring as boys will enable them to do their duty as men should any danger threaten the Empire": quoted in W. J. Reader, *At Duty's Call: A Study in Obsolete Patriotism* (Manchester: Manchester University Press, 1988), p. 38.

the rules, as "gentlemen." Men of the working classes were also strongly encouraged to enter the army, a national effort made even more important because Britain was the only one of the European powers that did not employ conscription in the early years of the conflict. Reform in schooling in the late nineteenth century also had a significant impact on their ideas about personal responsibilities as citizens. Victorian educational reform resulted in the vast majority of children attending school until the age of fourteen, and literacy rates were close to universal by the outbreak of war. This education, aimed at the "followers" rather than the "leaders" of the nation, still emphasized the importance of the empire, and the role of the people in maintaining its glory. After all, it was on the shoulders of such men that the empire was carried.[7] Many working-class men, in turn, talked about a sense of obligation to join the army when war broke out. There were also, however, several strong mitigating factors. Enlistment rates show some correlation to fluctuations in civilian wage rates, particularly after the first months of the war. Also, enlisted men were clearly taking time to establish reasonable financial security for their families before leaving for the army. This was an issue of critical concern for them as it frequently was not for their future commanding officers who came from more economically endowed families.

Though working-class men enlisted in vast numbers – after all, the army required many more men in the ranks than officers – they also had alternatives to military service that might be individually acceptable. Among working-class men more reluctance to volunteer was articulated, if not actually felt (middle-class men may have felt similar compunctions but have refrained from voicing them as they differed so from the prevailing expectations of courage and service). In working-class or lower-middle class families, however, it was less unusual, and certainly less shocking, for a man in the army to write to his younger brother working in munitions that he should continue in the factory rather than enlisting. Harry Rice wrote this way to his brother Charles, stating that "I don't see how a fellow can keep away from helping altogether or in some way [but] you are of most use where you are so don't go breaking your neck to get off into some more active sphere."[8]

---

[7] For more on these concepts of masculinity, see J. A. Mangan and James Walvin (eds.), *Manliness and Morality: Middle-Class Masculinity in Britain and America, 1800–1940* (New York: St. Martin's Press, 1987); and George Mosse, *The Image of Man: The Creation of Modern Masculinity* (New York: Oxford University Press, 1996).

[8] Though Harry Rice became an officer, he was not of the traditional "officer classes." Instead, he was one of the men who benefited from the decreased expenses of a commission in wartime: H. P. Rice to Charles Rice, January 28, 1916: C. J. Rice, IWM-DD PP/MCR/116.

This kind of expression of individual approval, however, did not extend to popular opinion. Young men who did not enter the army – even those working in protected war-related industries – were quite generally condemned, and that condemnation was often expressed through denigration of the labor movement and industrial action. Ian Hay criticized striking munitions workers and miners in both *The First Hundred Thousand* and its sequel, *Carrying On*, in which they were grouped with conscientious objectors, politicians, and male ballet dancers as "pet aversions."[9] Anger and criticism also came from the ranks, as when Pvt. Horace Bruckshaw, serving in Gallipoli, recorded in his diary that the striking Welsh miners he was reading about in the *London Telegram* "ought all to be hung."[10] Middle-class families such as the Beales expressed similar outrage, including Harold Brown's declaration that the miners should be bombed, because it "might perhaps remind them that England is at war."[11]

If issues of class complicated ideas about men and war work, women presented an even more intricate picture. While official propaganda and recruiting efforts may even have placed greater emphasis on the contributions of women in munitions production, on the land, or in auxiliary military organizations than of those volunteering in hospitals, there were clear overall social distinctions. Some work, especially though not exclusively from a middle-class perspective, was seen as more appropriate for certain populations, and often correspondingly perceived to be more important to the war effort. For a woman, most commonly, being a volunteer nurse was supposed to be like being a soldier. Both were described as the ultimate gendered expression of patriotism, honor, and sacrifice in wartime.

While the connection between the public school ethos and enthusiasm for war in men has been extensively discussed, less attention has been paid to the role of education in women's attitudes. It is often forgotten or overlooked that in the late nineteenth and early twentieth centuries, girls' educational experiences in and out of school were more similar to their brothers' than they had ever been before. Middle-class daughters were now likely to be educated outside the home, whether at day or boarding schools, and they attended institutions that were consciously modeled

[9] Ian Hay, *The First Hundred Thousand: Being the Unofficial Chronicle of a Unit of "K(1)"* (Edinburgh and London: William Blackwood and Sons, 1916, 5th edn.), pp. 237, 310; Hay, *Carrying On – After the First Hundred Thousand* (Edinburgh and London: William Blackwood and Sons, 1917), pp. 181–183.

[10] September 3, 1915: Horace Bruckshaw (Martin Middlebrook, ed.), *The Diaries of Private Horace Bruckshaw, 1915–1916* (London: Scolar Press, 1979), p. 76.

[11] Harold Brown to Helen Beale, September 12, 1915: BP. See also Margaret S. Beale to Helen Beale, March 29, 1916; Helen Beale to Margaret A. Beale, July 26, [1918]; Dorothy Brown to Helen Beale, February 4, [1919]: BP.

on those where their brothers studied. These schools were appearing around the country, whether they had national reputations like Roedean or were more locally known like the institutions of the Girls' Public Day School Trust. Like their brothers, too, working-class girls also received more schooling than they had previously, thanks to national educational reform. It was also no longer legal to train them explicitly to enter domestic service. They were seen as the mothers of the empire, and therefore were exposed along with the men in their families to the nationalistic and imperial languages of triumph, glory, and patriotism. Like their brothers, they, in turn, responded to the declared need of the nation. Women of all classes did not necessarily privilege gender above other identities when they thought about themselves, particularly in a time of national crisis. As Imogen, the heroine of Rose Macaulay's *Told By an Idiot*, explained, "people of her age simply weren't non-combatants; that was how she felt about it . . . it seemed a disgrace to her, who had never before so completely realised that she was not, in point of fact, a young man."[12] Previously, Imogen, like many of her peers, had identified herself by class more strongly than by sex; "war," however, as Denise Riley has pointed out, "throws gender in sharp relief."[13] Women responded in great numbers across the social spectrum, though they all had to deal with the challenges of popular expectations about gender-appropriate behavior.

Whether they saw their efforts more as service or as work, the vast majority of workers seem to have felt good about their opportunity to contribute. Hard as it is at times for our modern ears to hear or our modern minds to comprehend, the patriotic language voiced by many of the men and women at the outbreak of the First World War was not mere rhetoric. Instead, it reflected powerful and deeply held convictions. Many middle-class women, when faced with the dilemma created by their sex and their need to do something active in the war effort, therefore resolved to find the war work which meant to them what soldiering meant to their men. For many of them, the obvious thing was volunteer nursing, and they received significant support from families, friends, and official sources in this parity of service.

Other kinds of war work, though, met with more ambivalent responses. Military organizations for women (unlike the armed forces for men) not only failed to provide similar approval to that granted to the VADs, but also were usually the subject of considerable debate and condemnation.

---

[12] Rose Macaulay, *Told By an Idiot* (New York: Boni & Liveright, 1924), p. 316.
[13] Denise Riley, "Some Peculiarities of Social Policy Concerning Women in Wartime and Postwar Britain," in Margaret Randolph Higonnet, et al. (eds.), *Behind the Lines: Gender and the Two World Wars* (New Haven: Yale University Press, 1987), p. 269.

When Helen Beale decided to leave volunteer nursing service to be an "officer" in the newly formed WRNS in early 1918, she experienced this real difference for herself. In contrast to the warm support for their efforts that she and so many other VADs had received, Beale now encountered significant and bitter opposition to her move. This criticism even included being accused of seeking "exciting work" and being "unpatriotic" by her Red Cross county director.[14] Organizing the WRNS in Dover, Beale met with substantial resistance from both the civilian and naval communities, as well as the continuing attitude that a woman could be interested in wearing a military-style uniform only for non-productive and self-serving reasons.

Military uniforms, as worn by women, were particularly condemned. Nursing uniforms, in contrast, were generally considered not just acceptable but desirable. As Ethel Alec-Tweedie explained, "in war days duchesses and society girls wear uniforms and love them"; patterns for them were sold at Selfridge's at the outbreak of the conflict.[15] Correspondingly, the language of parallel service to the country was often utilized during the war for volunteer nurses. At the same time, it was much more rarely applied outside official propaganda, recruiting sources, and some popular newspaper accounts and publications to women in other war work (including especially women in auxiliary and paramilitary organizations). To grant this kind of validity to military women would have been to undermine the social and gendered order of British society. If men were fighting to defend civilization, as often represented by the women at home, then women simply could not be soldiers without fundamentally disturbing that vision. In wartime, women were the defended, not the defenders; therefore "military women" was an oxymoron. This was perhaps especially true in the First World War, when so much of the language of justification of the conflict was heavily gender weighted. Belgium had been "raped," both literally and figuratively according to the propaganda. The honorable and masculine British soldier therefore went to defeat the horrible – and uncivilized – Hun, to protect the "womenfolk" (who represented society) from further such violations.

These criticisms found even stronger voice when applied to working-class women. The women's official military services paid a reasonable salary to "educated" women, partly because so many of the women they considered preferable were already committed to other forms of war work and needed to be wooed into the new services. Crucially, however, they

---

[14] Copy of letter from M. Pelham to Clare Blount, undated, enclosed with letter from Clare Blount to Helen Beale, January 8, 1918: BP.

[15] Alec-Tweedie, *Women and Soldiers*, p. 52.

also paid wages that were much higher than those in domestic service to the women in the "ranks," for work that was usually much less strenuous. This remuneration, however, undermined public ideas about correct motivation in wartime; working-class women who were rendered financially independent as a result of wartime work were threatening to the social and gendered order. In time of war, concerns about their increasing power could be expressed as criticism of their alleged insufficient patriotic motivation, at the same time as, in other contexts, the work was being praised as patriotic effort. Working-class women were portrayed as being inherently unable to respond with appropriate attitudes of sacrifice because their class position had not taught them such values. When the novelist Tennyson Jesse was sent to France by the Ministry of Information, she reported of the majority of women serving in the ranks of the WAAC that they lacked the "many reverences" that the "upper classes are brought up with." Instead, "the classes which, for want of a better word, I must call lower are for the most part brought up to think themselves as good as anyone else, and their rights as the chief thing in life." Indeed, the women were educated "without proper standards of impersonal enthusiasm and imaginative daring."[16] Ethel Alec-Tweedie agreed, complaining that "we have heard a great deal of late years about our Rights, but little enough about our Duty." She argued that "the upper and middle classes learn something of duty at school, but in lower middle and lower class education the word 'Duty' seems to be unknown."[17] Working-class women were thus trapped: they were criticized for not being sufficiently patriotic, but as the reason for that lack was alleged to be inherent in who they were, it in turn opened them up to additional condemnation.

David Mitchell echoed this point of view decades later, in his popular history of the First World War. When he discussed the WAAC, he explained that it "was not easy... to instill a sense of military pride and etiquette." As a result, "jewelry-bedecked Tommettes [sic] were apt to stroll arm in arm with Tommies, for all the world like parlormaids on their half day off."[18] A WAAC might well have been a parlormaid formerly, of course. In any case, this relatively discreet description of her social life – one which would have been appropriate for a woman in domestic service – was perceived somehow as problematic when the woman was wearing an official military uniform. Working-class women in uniform

---

[16] Quoted in David Mitchell, *Monstrous Regiment: The Story of the Women of the First World War* (New York: Macmillan, 1965), pp. 224–225.

[17] Alec-Tweedie, *Women and Soldiers*, p. 87.

[18] Mitchell, *Monstrous Regiment*, p. 224. Mitchell identifies "les soldates" and "les Tommettes" as the French nicknames for the WAAC members, and then proceeds to use "Tommettes" as if it were English; I have never encountered its use anywhere else.

were considered by many people to be dangerous to the social order. As a result, their morality was constantly under question, both in the press and in popular debate. This opinion was widespread, but of course not universal. Helen Beale wrote home with more tolerance of the social activities of the WRNS serving under her.[19] Ethel Alec-Tweedie, though she worried about class-based motivations, still supported the women. She argued that uniforms in general (which before the war women had hated to wear) now gave them an honor equal to that of soldiers. She even went so far as to state that men – and specifically men in the military – preferred a woman in uniform.[20] There were also repeated official efforts to redeem this reputation, but they were not remarkably successful. Members of the WAAC, WRNS, and WRAF could not be the female equal of soldiers, because their very existence as "khaki girls" undermined the image of the society that the soldiers were represented as fighting to preserve.

These criticisms were similar in both content and motivation to those made against working-class women entering traditionally male-dominated environments, particularly in the factories and agriculture. Women working in industry, especially in munitions factories, faced popular charges of failing to bring to the work sufficient patriotic motivation. They were also accused of sexual and social misconduct. Their wages were too high and they spent their money recklessly, the argument went. In particular, munitions workers were accused of being profligate with respect to their bodies, buying frivolous clothes, fancy underwear, and fur coats. This emphasis on physical attributes brought together the social and sexual criticism being leveled at the women workers. Control of their own bodies – and, to a greater degree than previously, their own living and working environments – made these women seem dangerous to the memory of the prewar social order.

The "masculine" work being done by these women was justified during the war because it was temporary: it was only "for the duration." In keeping with that approach to controlling the social threat the workers represented, a pervasive movement to return women to the household followed the war (in Britain as well as other countries).[21] Postwar efforts were, in fact, quite successful in removing women from their newfound jobs in industry. National priorities shifted, and "Tommy's sister" was

[19] Helen Beale to Dorothy Brown, March 14, 1918: BP.
[20] Alec-Tweedie, *Women and Soldiers*, pp. 52, 66.
[21] See Alison Light, *Forever England: Femininity, Literature, and Conservatism Between the Wars* (London: Routledge, 1991); Susan Kingsley Kent, *Making Peace: The Reconstruction of Gender in Interwar Britain* (Princeton: Princeton University Press, 1993); Deirdre Beddoe, *Back to Home and Duty: Women Between the Wars, 1918–1939* (London: Pandora, 1989). For France, see Mary Louise Roberts, *Civilization Without Sexes: Reconstructing Gender in Postwar France, 1917–1927* (Chicago: University of Chicago Press, 1994).

forced to leave the factories – allegedly, though not always in reality, for Tommy himself. Working women were no longer heroines. They could no longer be described in equal terms with men; their needs and preferences were in fact being sublimated to those of the men. The previous language of parity publicly employed during the war, one that had at times even inaccurately emphasized a shared risk of death, was denied in the postwar years.

For women of the leisured classes, it was less a case of leaving the specific jobs their men were to come home to than of returning to the world those men had allegedly fought to preserve. Women who did not have to work now should not work at all, or at least not outside the traditionally acceptable areas of family and social work (and not for remuneration). In some situations women could continue to be called "heroines," but only if it were clearly understood that they were inferior to the real "heroes." In this story of the war, women had "done their bit" when their country needed them, and (despite their natural tendencies) had risen to the emergency. Once the crisis was past, however, they were to return to their old patterns with relief. Whatever they might have been doing before the war, it was now all the more critical that they conform to the reinterpretation of traditional expectations. This was the only way to justify the sacrifices made by the soldiers, those who returned and especially those who did not.

In some ways, women resisted these efforts. Though forced out of many industrial jobs, working-class women overwhelmingly did not return to domestic service, and, when they did, they exercised much stronger control over its conditions. Many better-off women found within the new outcry about "surplus women" – a concept which certainly predated the war, but whose casualties revived it with a vengeance – a justification for living independently of husbands and families. Many women, of course, returned to prewar patterns contentedly, just as many had never left them in the first place. But the 1920s in Britain were a period when the "history" of the war was still developing. Individuals dealt with grief and loss. The nation invoked languages of sacrifice and glory as it unveiled the Cenotaph, along with war memorials in almost every town in the country.[22] This public focus on mourning rather than on the war as transformative experience, though, left room for many women to retain

---

[22] The vast majority of these omnipresent war memorials are devoted exclusively to men who died as a result of combat. One notable exception is the Scottish War Memorial, which was built at Edinburgh Castle. It includes an alcove dedicated both to those who served and those who died serving in the women's branches, including auxiliary military organizations, nursing services, the British Red Cross, the Order of St. John of Jerusalem, and the First Aid Nursing Yeomanry.

their self-conceptions as equal members of the war generation, at least temporarily.

A literary retrenchment

With the flood of war texts a decade after the Armistice, the trench became cemented not just as the primary way of understanding of the war but as the only legitimate one. The focus of the soldier's story was on waste and exploitation, on unnecessary sacrifice and daily gruesome bloodshed and decomposition, on men being mowed down in waves by machine guns (should they leave the safety of the trench). Valid voices, then, could only belong to those men who had shared this "experience." The case was put persuasively. The first phase of publication was dominated by former soldiers who were also established writers, men with a decade or more of publishing expertise, often poets who well knew the power contained in words. These men "understood" the "experience" of war generally and not just personally, and their representational abilities at times far exceeded their own familiarity with the major battles of the war. Their status as veterans made their authority appear unimpeachable, especially to the generation that came of age just after the war ended. Their version of the war would become its history.

There was significant opposition to this stance at the time. Charles Carrington initially wrote under the pen name Charles Edmonds about his experience as a junior officer in the war. He hoped that the "rather romantic tone" taken by the protagonist of his narrative "may strike a responsive chord in the ears of some old soldiers who are tired of the uniform disillusion of most authors of war books."[23] He was not trying to negate the importance of the trench; rather he devoted an appendix to the subject because he felt that "to be able to picture a soldier's life in France it is necessary to understand some of the principles of trench fighting which took so large a part in the Great War."[24] However, Carrington argued that the disillusionment that had become inseparable from the trench in war publications was inappropriate. "It is time," he wrote, "that the world remembered that among the fifteen million [combatants] there were other types as well as the conventional 'Prussian militarists,' and the equally conventional 'disillusioned' pessimists."[25] His concerns were shared by numerous figures from both inside and outside the military, and the press identified a "war books controversy." Women's narratives, too,

---

[23] Charles Edmonds [Charles Carrington], *A Subaltern's War* (New York: Minton, Balch and Company, 1930), p. 8.
[24] Edmonds, *Subaltern's War*, pp. 213–221.   [25] Edmonds, *Subaltern's War*, pp. 8–9.

criticized the soldier's story, as when the anonymous author of *WAAC: The Woman's Story of the War* declared in 1930 that she had "avoided trying to harrow readers' feelings with gruesome descriptions of battlefield and war-hospital horrors, for that has been done already – in [her] opinion overdone."[26] Resistance, however, gradually became overwhelmed by the representational power of the image of the trench. Being extreme, this view polarized the history of the war: all accounts were read as either supporting or opposing this view of trench life, with little room left for narratives of anything else. Facing this, narratives began to be rewritten to echo the carnage, loss, and personal destruction of the soldier's story. The history of the war, once broad, was narrowed to the perspective of the trench. Forced to compete rather than coexist with the horrors of infantry accounts, other stories were delegitimized and silenced.

The Great War and its impact have been under almost constant popular and scholarly reevaluation since 1914. More than twenty-five years ago, Paul Fussell published his seminal study on the literature of World War I, *The Great War and Modern Memory*. In it, he argued that modern modes of expression resulted from the horrors of the war, which could not be contained within the existing approaches. Samuel Hynes extended this argument in *A War Imagined: The First World War and English Culture*, positing a true modernist divide between 1914–1918 and the postwar years. More recently, Jay Winter has documented the ongoing prevalence of traditional expressions of culture in the postwar years. In the conclusion of *Sites of Memory, Sites of Mourning*, Winter pushed the modernist moment up to 1945: trench warfare did not render the previous languages of idealism meaningless, but Hiroshima and the Holocaust did. Perhaps the question might be examined, however, from a different perspective.[27] The transition can then be analyzed generationally rather than chronologically. There was no identifiable turning point – at the Somme, at the Armistice, or elsewhere – when traditional ways of imagining the war and one's role in it were no longer comprehensible. For many of the British men and women who were active participants in the First World War, the languages of honor, patriotism, and self-sacrifice for a greater good never lost their currency (as their later written memories attest). Though

---

[26] *WAAC: The Woman's Story of the War* (London: T. Werner Laurie, 1930), p. 5.

[27] For more on the debate over modernism and the First World War, see Trudi Tate, *Modernism, History, and the Great War* (Manchester: Manchester University Press, 1998); Angela K. Smith, *The Secret Battlefield: Women, Modernism, and the First World War* (Manchester: Manchester University Press, 2000); Douglas Mackaman and Michael Mays (eds.), *The First World War and the Cultures of Modernity* (Jackson: University Press of Mississippi, 2000); Allyson Booth, *Postcards from the Trenches: Negotiating the Space Between Modernism and the First World War* (New York: Oxford University Press, 1996).

some famous authors eloquently articulated a powerful story of disillusionment, this became the dominant historical view of the war because it was embraced by those who came after, not because it entirely changed the perceptions of many people who had fought and worked in the war itself.

In 1929, Augustine Birrell wrote that "no war in modern times has produced so abundant, so realistic and so well-composed a literature as the late War." He explained that "there were real men of letters in the trenches, French, German and English; and books have been written about it which, though cheaper to-day, are even more illuminative than the more costly productions of politicians."[28] It was, however, a very specific type of light that was shed by these texts. The story of disillusionment was a product of the late 1920s and early 1930s. Though some voices were silenced, particularly as Britain prepared to face another war in Europe, this did not mean that the critics had changed their minds. Many active people still held on to the motivations that had made them choose to become involved in the war in the first place. They also knew that these ideals were unfashionable, and were sometimes defensive or defiant about their own perspectives on the war. The story of disillusionment is certainly present in these memoirs – it would have been more than surprising if it had not been – but there was clear and powerful resistance to it. This tenacity led to a renegotiation of memories, with disillusionment and pride uneasily cohabiting (but the latter often still paramount). Though the British embraced irony and modern modes of expression at some point – perhaps sufficiently gradually that it is hard to pinpoint just when, leaving room for scholars to disagree – they did so generationally rather than chronologically. Many active participants in the Great War remained unrepentantly premodernist in their representations of their experience, even toward the end of the twentieth century.

Epilogue: telling war stories

The diary of Arthur Graeme West, a young officer killed in the First World War, made a long journey through the different stages of war stories analyzed here. In some very important ways, West's life resembled Siegfried Sassoon's. Both came from middle-class families, attended preparatory school and university, and joined the army in 1914. To be sure, West completed his degree at Oxford (though certainly not with distinction) while Sassoon came down from Cambridge long before his examinations. Both began their military service in the ranks but were later commissioned

---

[28] Augustine Birrell, "War," *Life & Letters*, 3, 8 (January 1929), p. 15.

as officers. Both found poetic voice in the war and its criticism, though that was not the only subject for either. Both, also, became committed to protest against the war, influenced at least in part by Bertrand Russell. Both have left prose works of their war experiences, meant to expose the harder realities of trench conflict. (Sassoon's, of course, is much better known.) There are two significant differences, however, between them. Though West wrote a letter of protest against the war, he, unlike Sassoon, did not mail it. And West, unlike Sassoon, was killed on the Western front, leaving any reinterpretation of his war experiences to others.

A selection of West's journal entries, along with some of his poetry, was published posthumously as *Diary of a Dead Officer*. The text was edited by Cyril Joad, a socialist and pacifist, who had been a school fellow of West's both at preparatory school and at Balliol.[29] They remained friends until West's death, and it was during a leave spent at Joad's family house that West became committed to his protest. Though West did not act on that decision during his life, Joad used the diary as a posthumous proxy for it. Joad took pains in his 1918 Introduction to claim that "the value of the Diary lies in its absolute frankness, its stark realism, its obvious truth and sincerity," and explained that "as far as possible it is given just as he wrote it." It is actually significantly edited, abridged, and selected, in order to make the indictment against the war and its costs even stronger. The importance of Joad's manipulation is not minimized because it was in the service of a cause that West was very likely to have agreed with. West, through editorial intervention, became in many ways the prototype of the disillusioned young volunteer, who joined the army for the right reasons, was deeply disturbed and fundamentally changed by what he experienced in France, expressed that disenchantment powerfully in verse, and then paid the ultimate price (for no reason). "Even his death was irrelevant," Joad wrote pointedly. West "died, it seems, in no blaze of glory," but instead was "struck by a chance sniper's bullet as he was leaving his trench."[30] He embodied the soldier's story.

Joad's editorial purpose – one close to West's heart – was pacifist. "If its detailed realism serves to correct in some measure the highly coloured picture of the soldier's life and thoughts to which the popular Press has accustomed us," he concluded, "it will not have been written in vain."[31] West, as the double meaning of the title Joad selected makes clear, was

---

[29] Joad published against the wishes of West's father, and therefore most probably in violation of copyright. (West died intestate, so his papers reverted automatically to his family.)

[30] C. J. [Cyril Joad], "Introduction," in Arthur Graeme West, *Diary of a Dead Officer* (London: Imperial War Museum, 1991 [1918]), p. xiv of facsimile text.

[31] C. J., "Introduction," p. xiv of facsimile text.

killed by the military system as much if not more than he was by the Germans: it was the diary kept by a *dead* officer, dead in spirit and philosophy before his bodily functions were forcibly stopped. In his 1991 Introduction to the facsimile reprint, Dominic Hibberd therefore referred to the text as one of "the finest examples of the myth-making process that was to reshape literary memories of the war for future generations." Hibberd documented the changes made by Joad, arguing that the resulting text "tends to underestimate West's happiness and spiritual courage," and makes him "sound more miserable than he really was in England." The edited West was denied emotions which were not in keeping with the image of the young disillusioned poet, including the love he shared with Dorothy MacKenzie and the hope for the future that it gave them both. The book had been published in cooperation by Allen & Unwin, "one of the few firms willing to take on pacifist material," and *The Herald*, a socialist newspaper. For Joad and Russell, Hibberd argued, "the *Diary* seemed urgently needed as a revelation and warning, a tract for the times." It found few readers when published, however, and "it was too blunt and artless, and perhaps too subversive, to appeal to the renewed fashion for 'war books' in the late twenties." Pacifism, however, is now beyond the scope of fashion, and so "the *Diary* can be read again ... [and] the book still carries the message that the two friends wanted the world to hear."[32]

Both introductions fit neatly into the history of war stories from each time period. West embodied the soldier's story, particularly as edited by Joad with the support of Russell and Ottoline Morrell. Hibberd identified the manipulations necessary to emphasize the story, but maintained the diary's ultimate pacifist message, still in keeping with what became the popular view of the war – hence its reprinting by the Imperial War Museum. These historically specific readings skip over an interim stage in the cultural meaning of the war, however, which the diary also fits into. West's volume, in fact, was not entirely overlooked during the 1929–1930 boom in war books. Hibberd quotes, in a footnote, Cyril Falls's discussion of the text in his *War Books*, but argues that Falls dismisses West's claims "as merely the result of personal and physical defects."[33] It is true that Falls attributed West's early rejection as an officer to his poor eyesight. It was not merely a "personal defect" that he invoked, though, when he wrote that West "had none of the protective armoury of callousness or use, which was so valuable to most of us," and therefore his life as a soldier on the Western front "must have been miserable." This fits, instead,

---

[32] Dominic Hibberd, "Introduction," in West, *Dead Officer*, pp. viii, xii–xvi.
[33] Hibberd, "Introduction," n. 14, p. xxii.

into the greater body of Falls's criticisms of the disillusioned approach to war books in general, and his concerns about intellectuals in particular as worthy observers. West, he was arguing, failed to defend himself against the war in the ways that other men had found possible to do, but he was far from unique in this. The one phrase of Falls's review that Hibberd did not quote, in fact, was the assertion that "there were probably many who felt like him." West was also presented, as were many of the books of which Falls (and colleagues sympathetic to his viewpoint) approved, as having "loathed it all," but "less from hatred of war itself than from dislike of what he called 'the herd' and the herd spirit."[34] Falls and his fellow critics who disapproved of the soldier's story strengthened their argument by admitting that the war was horrible at the same time as they disagreed with the significance other writers and critics ascribed to that horror.

Similarly, Eric Partridge shared with Falls both an appreciation for West's diary and a deep concern about the story of the war that seemed to be taking over the popular imagination. He also remembered West's diary when analyzing the war books controversy in 1930, and called it "profoundly moving." Partridge praised the book using the same terms Falls had, invoking a sense of realism without the uselessness later attributed to it. "West," he wrote, "suffered keenly but did not flinch."[35] In 1930, it was possible to read many texts that would later be entirely associated with the disillusioned view of the war as, in fact, positive alternatives to that interpretation. It was only as the controversy simplified and the disenchantment solidified that the lines of debate were shifted and polarized, in ways that modern readers take for granted but which would have surprised many 1930 reviewers. The evolution of the war story has been complex, and is still ongoing, and ideas about experience and memory always reflect their own times. There was no unified vision of a war being fought by the British, in 1914–1918 or later, and the stories people told reveal more enemies to society than just the German forces during the war. The British have been fighting many wars, on many fronts, all of them entrenched.

[34] Cyril Falls, *War Books: A Critical Guide* (London: Peter Davies, 1930), pp. 237–238.
[35] Eric Partridge, "The War Comes Into Its Own," *Window*, 1, 1 (January 1930), p. 90.

Select bibliography

ARCHIVAL SOURCES

Beale Family Papers (privately held), Cobnor Cottage, Chidham, Chichester (BP)
British Red Cross Society Archives, Barnett Hill, Guildford (BRCS)
Girls' Public Day School Trust Archive, London (GPDST)
Imperial War Museum, Department of Documents, London (IWM-DD)
The Peter Liddle 1914–1918 Personal Experience Collection, University of Leeds (PL)

PUBLISHED PRIMARY SOURCES

TEXTS WRITTEN DURING THE FIRST WORLD WAR

Alec-Tweedie, Ethel. *Women and Soldiers*. London: John Lane, [1918].
Asquith, Lady Cynthia. *Diaries 1915–1918*. London: Hutchinson, 1968.
Bagnold, Enid. *A Diary Without Dates*. London: Virago, 1978 (1918).
Billington, Mary Frances. *The Red Cross in War: Women's Part in the Relief of Suffering*. London: Hodder and Stoughton, 1914.
  The Roll-Call of Serving Women: A Record of Woman's Work for Combatants and Sufferers in the Great War. London: The Religious Tract Society, 1915.
Bishop, Alan, and Mark Bostridge (eds.). *Letters from a Lost Generation. First World War Letters of Vera Brittain and Four Friends: Roland Leighton, Edward Brittain, Victor Richardson, Geoffrey Thurlow*. Boston: Northeastern Press, 1998.
Booth, Mary. *With the BEF in France*. London: The Salvation Army, 1916.
Bowser, Thekla. *The Story of British VAD Work in the Great War*. London: A. Melrose, 1917 (2nd edn.).
Brittain, Vera (Alan Bishop, ed.). *Chronicle of Youth: The War Diary, 1913–1917*. New York: William Morrow, 1982.
Bruckshaw, Horace (Martin Middlebrook, ed.). *The Diaries of Private Horace Bruckshaw, 1915–1916*. London: Scolar Press, 1979.
"Carry On": British Women's Work in War Time. [London: Harrison, Jehring & Co., 1917].
Churchill, Jennie Randolph (ed.). *Women's War Work*. London: C. Arthur Pearson, 1916.
Cosens, Monica. *Lloyd George's Munition Girls*. London: Hutchinson [1916].
Dearmer, Mabel. *Letters from a Field Hospital*. London: Macmillan, 1916.

Delafield, E. M. *The War Workers.* New York: Alfred A. Knopf, 1918.

Dent, Olive. *A VAD in France.* London: Grant Richards, 1917.

Farmborough, Frances. *Nurse at the Russian Front: A Diary 1914–1918.* London: Constable, 1974.

Finzi, Kate John. *Eighteen Months in the War Zone: A Record of a Woman's Work on the Western Front.* London: Cassell and Co., 1916.

Haigh, R. H., and P. W. Turner (eds.). *The Long Carry: The Journal of Stretcher Bearer Frank Dunham, 1916–1918.* Oxford: Pergamon Press, 1970.

Haig Brown, R. M. *Ad Lucem: Some Addresses.* London: Oxford University Press (Humphrey Milford), 1931.

Hankey, Donald. *A Student in Arms.* London: Andrew Melrose, 1916, 1917.

Hay, Ian. *The First Hundred Thousand: Being the Unofficial Chronicle of a Unit of "K(1)."* Edinburgh and London: William Blackwood and Sons, 1916 (5th edn.).

Carrying On – After The First Hundred Thousand. Edinburgh and London: William Blackwood and Sons, 1917.

Leake, R. E. *Letters of a VAD.* London: Andrew Melrose, Ltd., [1918?].

Macauley, Rose. *Non-Combatants and Others.* London: Hodder and Stoughton, 1916.

Mack, Louise. *A Woman's Experience in the Great War.* London: T. F. Unwin, [1915].

Macnaughton, Sarah. *A Woman's Diary of the War.* London: Thomas Nelson and Sons, [1915].

McDougall, Grace. *A Nurse at the War: Nursing Adventures in Belgium and France.* New York: Robert M. McBride, 1917.

McLaren, Barbara. *Women of the War.* London: Hodder and Stoughton, 1917.

Morten, J. C. (Sheila Morten, ed.). *I Remain, Your Son Jack: Letters from the First World War.* Wilmslow, Cheshire: Sigma Press, 1993.

Navarro, Antonio de. *The Scottish Women's Hospital at the French Abbey of Royaumont.* London: George Allen & Unwin, 1917.

Ravenscroft, P. D. (Antony Bird, ed.). *Unversed in Arms: A Subaltern on the Western Front. The First World War Diary of P. D. Ravenscroft MC.* Swindon: Crowood, 1990.

Ross, Ishobel (Jess Dixon, ed.). *Little Grey Partridge: First World War Diary of Ishobel Ross Who Served with the Scottish Women's Hospitals Unit in Serbia.* Aberdeen: Aberdeen University Press, 1988.

Ross, Margery (ed.). *Robert Ross, Friend of Friends: Letters to Robert Ross, Art Critic and Writer, Together with Extracts from His Published Articles.* London: Jonathan Cape, 1952.

Sassoon, Siegfried (Rupert Hart-Davis, ed.). *Diaries 1915–1918.* London: Faber and Faber, 1983.

Stone, Gilbert (ed.). *Women War Workers: Accounts Contributed by Representative Workers of the Work Done by Women in the More Important Branches of War Employment.* New York: Thomas Y. Crowell, [1917].

Thurstan, Violetta. *Field Hospital and Flying Column: Being the Journal of an English Nursing Sister in Belgium & Russia.* London: G. P. Putnam's Sons, 1915.

Usborne, Mrs. H. *Women's Work in War Time: A Handbook of Employments.* London: T. W. Laurie, [1917].

Vaughan, Edwin Campion. *Some Desperate Glory: The World War I Diary of a British Officer, 1917.* New York: Simon & Schuster, 1981.
Vernède, R. E. *Letters to His Wife.* London: W. Collins Sons, 1917.
A War Nurse's Diary: Sketches from a Belgian Field Hospital. New York: Macmillan, 1918.
West, Arthur Graeme. *Diary of a Dead Officer: Being the Posthumous Papers of Arthur Graeme West.* London: Imperial War Museum Department of Printed Books, 1991 (diary orig. pub. London: Allen & Unwin, 1919).
"Wideawake, Captain." *Jovial Jottings from the Trenches.* London: George G. Harrap & Co., 1915.
Yates, L. Keyser. *The Woman's Part: A Record of Munitions Work.* London: Hodder and Stoughton, 1918.

TEXTS WRITTEN AFTER THE FIRST WORLD WAR

Bagnold, Enid. *Autobiography.* London: William Heinemann, 1969.
Beauchamp, Pat [P. B. Waddell]. *Fanny Goes to War.* London: John Murray, 1919.
Beauman, A. B. *Then a Soldier.* London: Macmillan, 1960.
Blunden, Edmund. *Undertones of War.* London: Penguin, 1982 (1928).
Borden, Mary. *The Forbidden Zone.* London: William Heinemann, 1929.
Brittain, Vera. "War Service in Perspective," in George A. Panichas (ed.), *Promise of Greatness: The War of 1914–1918.* New York: John Day, 1968.
    Testament of Youth: An Autobiographical Study of the Years 1900–1925. New York: Penguin, 1989 (1933).
Carrington, Charles. *Soldier from the Wars Returning.* London: Hutchinson, 1965.
Chapman, Guy. *A Passionate Prodigality: Fragments of Autobiography.* New York: Holt, Rinehart and Winston, 1966 (1933).
Cooper, Diana. *The Rainbow Comes and Goes.* Boston: Houghton Mifflin, 1958.
Coppard, George. *With a Machine Gun to Cambrai.* London: Imperial War Museum, 1980.
Douglas-Pennant, Violet. *Under the Search-Light: A Record of a Great Scandal.* London: George Allen and Unwin, 1922.
Dunn, J. C. *The War the Infantry Knew 1914–1919: A Chronicle of Service in France and Belgium.* London: Cardinal, 1989 (1938).
Edmonds, Charles [Charles Carrington]. *A Subaltern's War.* New York: Minton, Balch, and Company, 1930.
Falls, Cyril. *War Books: A Critical Guide.* London: Peter Davies, 1930.
Furse, Katharine. *Hearts and Pomegranates: The Story of Forty-Five Years 1875–1920.* London: Peter Davies, 1940.
Graves, Robert. *Good-bye to All That.* New York: Doubleday, 1929; 2nd edn. (revised), 1957.
Groom, W. H. A. *Poor Bloody Infantry: A Memoir of the First World War.* London: William Kimber, 1976.
Hamilton, Peggy. *Three Years or the Duration: The Memoirs of a Munition Worker 1914–1918.* London: Peter Owen, 1978.
Jerrold, Douglas. *The Lie About the War.* London: Faber and Faber, 1930.
    Georgian Adventure. New York: Charles Scribner's Sons, 1938.

Law, Francis. *A Man at Arms: Memoirs of Two World Wars.* London: Collins, 1983.

Lewis, Windham. *Blasting and Bombadiering.* London: Eyre and Spottiswoode, 1937.

Macaulay, Rose. *Told By an Idiot.* New York: Boni & Liveright, 1924.

MacManus, Emily E. P. *Matron of Guy's.* London: Andrew Melrose, 1956.

Martin, Bernard. *Poor Bloody Infantry: A Subaltern on the Western Front 1916–1917.* London: John Murray, 1987.

Murray, Flora. *Women as Army Surgeons: Being the History of the Women's Hospital Corps in Paris, Wimereux, and Endell Street, September 1914–October 1919.* London: Hodder & Stoughton, [1920].

Murray, Joseph. *Call to Arms: From Gallipoli to the Western Front.* London: William Kimber, 1980.

Pankhurst, E. Sylvia. *Homefront: A Mirror to Life in England During the First World War.* London: The Cresset Library, 1987 (1932).

Peel, Mrs. C. S. *How We Lived Then, 1914–1918: A Sketch of Social and Domestic Life in England During the War.* London: John Lane, 1929.

Rathbone, Irene. *We That Were Young.* New York: The Feminist Press, 1989 (1932).

Remarque, Erich Maria. *All Quiet on the Western Front.* New York: Fawcett, 1982 (English trans., 1929; orig. pub. *Im Westen Nichts Neues*, 1928).

Richards, Frank. *Old Soldiers Never Die.* London: Faber, 1933.

Ruck, Berta. *The Land Girl's Love Story.* New York: Dodd, Mead and Company, 1919.

Sassoon, Siegfried. *Memoirs of a Fox-Hunting Man.* London: Faber and Faber, 1928.

Memoirs of an Infantry Officer. London: Faber and Faber, 1930.

Sherston's Progress. London: Faber and Faber, 1936.

The Old Century and Seven More Years. New York: Viking, 1939.

The Weald of Youth. London: Faber and Faber, 1942.

Siegfried's Journey. New York: Viking, 1946.

Smith, Helen Zenna [Evadne Price]. *Not So Quiet... Stepdaughters of War.* London: Virago, 1988 (1930).

Talbot Kelly, R. B. *A Subaltern's Odyssey: A Memoir of the Great War 1915–1917.* London: William Kimber, 1980.

Tilsley, W. V. *Other Ranks.* London: Cobden-Sanderson, 1931.

WAAC: The Woman's Story of the War. London: T. Werner Laurie, 1930.

Wenzel, Marian, and John Cornish, compilers. *Auntie Mabel's War: An Account of Her Part in the Hostilities of 1914–1918.* London: Allen Lane, 1980.

ANTHOLOGIES OF TEXTS COVERING BOTH PERIODS

Cooper, Artemis (ed.). *A Durable Fire: The Letters of Duff and Diana Cooper, 1913–1950.* London: Hamish Hamilton, 1983.

Graves, Robert (Paul O'Prey, ed.). *In Broken Images: Selected Correspondence.* Mount Kisco, NY: Moyer Bell, 1982.

Fuller, Simon (ed.). *The Poetry of War 1914–1989.* London: BBC/Longman, 1990.

Jones, Nora, and Liz Ward (eds.). *The Forgotten Army: Women's Poetry of the First World War*. Beverley: Highgate Publications, 1991.

Reilly, Catherine (ed.). *Scars Upon My Heart: Women's Poetry and Verse of the First World War*. London: Virago, 1981.

SECONDARY SOURCES

Adam, Ruth. *A Woman's Place 1910–1975*. London: Chatto and Windus, 1975.

Anderson, Benedict. *Imagined Communities: Reflections on the Origins and Spread of Nationalism*. London: Verso, 1991.

Baly, Monica E. *Florence Nightingale and the Nursing Legacy*. London: Croom Helm, 1986.

Barlow, Adrian. *The Great War in British Literature*. Cambridge: Cambridge University Press, 2000.

Barnes, Maj. R. Money. *The British Army of 1914: Its History, Uniforms & Contemporary Continental Armies*. London: Seeley Service & Co., 1968.

Barnett, Correlli. *Britain and Her Army 1509–1970: A Military, Political and Social Survey*. New York: William Morrow, 1970.

Beauman, Nicola. *A Very Great Profession: The Woman's Novel 1914–1939*. London: Virago, 1983.

Becker, Jean-Jacques. *The Great War and the French People*. Leamington Spa, UK: Berg, 1985.

Beckett, Ian F. W. "The Nation in Arms, 1914–1918," in Beckett and Simpson, *Nation in Arms*, pp. 1–35.

Beckett, Ian F. W., and Keith Simpson (eds.). *A Nation in Arms: A Social Study of the British Army in the First World War*. Manchester: Manchester University Press, 1985.

Beddoe, Deirdre. *Back to Home and Duty: Women Between the Wars, 1918–1939*. London: Pandora, 1989.

Bet-El, Ilana Ruth. "Experience into Identity: The Writings of British Conscript Soldiers, 1916–1918." Unpublished Ph.D. thesis, University College London, 1991.

"Men and Soldiers: British Conscripts, Concepts of Masculinity, and the Great War," in Melman, *Borderlines* pp. 73–94.

Conscripts: Lost Legions of the Great War. Stroud: Sutton, 1999.

Booth, Allyson. *Postcards from the Trenches: Negotiating the Space Between Modernism and the First World War*. New York: Oxford University Press, 1996.

Bourke, Joanna. *Dismembering the Male: Men's Bodies, Britain, and the Great War*. Chicago: University of Chicago Press, 1996.

Bowman, Gerald. *The Lamp and the Book: The Story of the RCN 1916–1966*. London: Queen Anne Press, 1967.

Bracco, Rosa Maria. *Merchants of Hope: British Middlebrow Writers and the First World War, 1919–1939*. Oxford: Berg, 1993.

Braybon, Gail. *Women Workers in the First World War*. London: Croom Helm, 1981.

Braybon, Gail, and Penny Summerfield. *Out of the Cage: Women's Experiences in Two World Wars*. London: Pandora, 1987.

Brereton, F. S. *The Great War and the RAMC.* London: Constable, 1919.

Buitenhuis, Peter. *The Great War of Words: British, American, and Canadian Propaganda and Fiction, 1914–1933.* Vancouver: University of British Columbia Press, 1987.

Bullough, Vern, Bonnie Bullough, and Marietta Stanton (eds.). *Florence Nightingale and Her Era: A Collection of New Scholarship.* New York: Garland, 1990.

Bushaway, Bob. "Name Upon Name: The Great War and Remembrance," in Roy Porter (ed.), *Myths of the English*, pp. 136–167. Cambridge: Polity Press, 1992.

Calahan, Peter. *Belgian Refugee Relief in England During the Great War.* New York: Garland, 1982.

Cecil, Hugh. "The Literary Legacy of the War: the Post-war British War Novel – a Select Bibliography," in Peter H. Liddle (ed.), *Home Fires and Foreign Fields: British Social and Military Experience in the First World War*, pp. 205–230. London: Brassey's, 1985.

The Flower of Battle: How Britain Wrote the Great War. South Royalton, VT: Steerforth Press, 1996.

Coetzee, Frans, and Marilyn Shevin-Coetzee. *Authority, Identity and the Social History of the Great War.* Providence: Berghahn, 1995.

Cohen, Deborah. *The War Come Home: Disabled Veterans in Britain and Germany, 1914–1939.* Berkeley: University of California Press, 2001.

Condell, Diana, and Jean Liddiard. *Working for Victory? Images of Women in the First World War, 1914–1918.* London: Routledge & Kegan Paul, 1987.

Connelly, Mark. *The Great War, Memory and Ritual: Commemoration in the City and East London, 1916–1939.* Woodbridge, UK: The Royal Historical Society and Boydell Press, 2002.

Cooke, Miriam, and Angela Woollacott (eds.). *Gendering War Talk.* Princeton: Princeton University Press, 1993.

Cowper, J. M. *A Short History of Queen Mary's Army Auxiliary Corps.* Women's Royal Army Corps Association, [1967].

Culleton, Claire. "Gender-Charged Munitions: The Language of World War I Munitions Reports." *Women's Studies International Forum*, 11, 2 (1988): 109–116.

Working-Class Culture, Women, and Britain, 1914–1921. New York: St. Martin's, 1999.

Damousi, Joy. *The Labour of Loss: Mourning, Memory, and Wartime Bereavement in Australia.* Cambridge: Cambridge University Press, 1999.

De Groot, Gerard J. *Blighty: British Society in the Era of the First World War.* New York: Longman, 1996.

Digby, Anne. *Making a Medical Living: Doctors and Patients in the English Market for Medicine, 1720–1911.* Cambridge: Cambridge University Press, 1994.

Downs, Laura Lee. *Manufacturing Inequality: Gender Division in the French and British Metalworking Industries, 1914–1939.* Ithaca: Cornell University Press, 1995.

Dunlop, John K. *The Development of the British Army 1899–1914.* London: Methuen, 1938.

Dyhouse, Carol. *Girls Growing Up in Late Victorian and Edwardian England.* London: Routledge, 1981.

Ecksteins, Modris. *Rites of Spring: The Great War and the Birth of the Modern Age.* New York: Doubleday, 1990 (1989).

Evans, Martin, and Ken Lunn. *War and Memory in the Twentieth Century.* Oxford: Berg, 1997.

Farwell, Byron. *Mr. Kipling's Army: All the Queen's Men.* New York: Norton, 1981.

Fentress, James, and Chris Wickham. *Social Memory.* Oxford: Blackwell, 1992.

Fletcher, M. H. *The WRNS: A History of the Women's Royal Naval Service.* London: B. T. Batsford, 1989.

Foucault, Michel. *The History of Sexuality: An Introduction, Volume I.* New York: Random House, 1978.

Fussell, Paul. *The Great War and Modern Memory.* Oxford: Oxford University Press, 1975.

Gallagher, Jean. *The World Wars Through the Female Gaze.* Carbondale, IL: Southern Illinois University Press, 1998.

Giddings, Robert. *The War Poets: The Lives and Writings of the 1914–1918 War Poets.* London: Bloomsbury, 1988.

Gilbert, Sandra M., and Susan Gubar. *No Man's Land: The Place of the Woman Writer in the Twentieth Century,* vol. II, *Sexchanges.* New Haven: Yale University Press, 1991.

Gillis, John (ed.). *Commemorations: The Politics of National Identity.* Princeton: Princeton University Press, 1994.

Girouard, Mark. *The Return to Camelot: Chivalry and the English Gentleman.* New Haven and London: Yale University Press, 1981.

Goldman, Dorothy (ed.). *Women and World War I: The Written Response.* London: Macmillan, 1993.

Goldstein, Jan. "Foucault Among the Sociologists: The Disciplines and the History of the Professions." *History and Theory,* 23 (May 1984): 170–192.

Gorham, Deborah. *Vera Brittain: A Feminist Life.* Oxford: Blackwell, 1996.

Gould, Jenny. "Women's Military Services in First World War Britain," in Higonnet, et al., *Behind the Lines,* pp. 114–125.

Grayzel, Susan R. *Women's Identities at War: Gender, Motherhood, and Politics in Britain and France During the First World War.* Chapel Hill: University of North Carolina Press, 1999.

Gregory, Adrian. *The Silence of Memory: Armistice Day, 1919–1946.* Oxford: Berg, 1994.

Griffiths, Gareth. *Women's Factory Work in World War I.* Phoenix Mill, UK: Alan Sutton, 1991.

Gullace, Nicoletta F. "White Feathers and Wounded Men: Female Patriotism and the Memory of the Great War," *Journal of British Studies,* 36, 2 (April 1997), 178–206.

"The Blood of Our Sons": Men, Women, and the Renegotiation of British Citizenship During the Great War. New York: Palgrave Macmillan, 2002.

Hanley, Lynne. *Writing War: Fiction, Gender, and Memory.* Amherst: University of Massachusetts Press, 1991.

Higonnet, Margaret Randolph, Jane Jenson, Sonya Michel, and Margaret Collins Weitz (eds.). *Behind the Lines: Gender and the Two World Wars*. New Haven: Yale University Press, 1989.

Hughes, Clive. "The New Armies," in Beckett and Simpson, *Nation in Arms*, pp. 99–125.

Hynes, Samuel. *The Edwardian Turn of Mind*. London: Pimlico, 1968.

A War Imagined: The First World War and English Culture. London: The Bodley Head, 1990.

Joyce, Patrick. "The Historical Meanings of Work: An Introduction," in Joyce (ed.), *The Historical Meanings of Work*, pp. 1–30. Cambridge: Cambridge University Press, 1987.

Kent, Susan Kingsley. *Making Peace: The Reconstruction of Gender in Interwar Britain*. Princeton: Princeton University Press, 1993.

Khan, Nosheen. *Women's Poetry of the First World War*. New York: Harvester Press, 1988.

King, Alex. *Memorials of the Great War in Britain: The Symbolism and Politics of Remembrance*. Oxford: Berg, 1998.

Laffin, John. *On The Western Front: Soldiers' Stories from France and Flanders 1914–1918*. Gloucester: Alan Sutton, 1985.

Lamm, Doron. "Emily Goes to War: Explaining the Recruitment to the Women's Army Auxiliary Corps in World War I," in Melman, *Borderlines*, pp. 377–395.

Laqueur, Thomas. "Memory and Naming in the Great War," in Gillis, *Commemorations*, pp. 150–167.

Lawrence, Margot. *Shadow of Swords: A Biography of Elsie Inglis*. London: Michael Joseph, 1971.

Le Goff, Jacques. (Steven Rendall and Elizabeth Claman, trans.) *History and Memory*. New York: Columbia University Press, 1992.

Leed, Eric J. *No Man's Land: Combat and Identity in World War I*. Cambridge: Cambridge University Press, 1979.

LeMahieu, D. L. *A Culture for Democracy: Mass Communication and the Cultivated Mind in Britain Between the Wars*. Oxford: Clarendon, 1988.

Leneman, Leah. "Medical Women in the First World War: Ranking Nowhere." *British Medical Journal*, 307, 6919 (December 18–25, 1993): 1592–1594.

Elsie Inglis: Founder of Battlefield Hospitals Run Entirely by Women. Edinburgh: Edinburgh National Museums of Scotland, 1998.

Lewis, Jane. *Women and Social Action in Victorian and Edwardian England*. Aldershot: Edward Elgar, 1991.

Liddle, Peter H. (ed.). *Home Fires and Foreign Fields: British Social and Military Experience in the First World War*. London: Brassey's, 1985.

Voices of War: Front Line and Home Front 1914–1918. London: Leo Cooper, 1988.

Liddle, Peter H., John Bourne, and Ian Whitehead (eds.). *The Great War, 1914–1945*. London: Harper Collins, 2000.

Light, Alison. *Forever England: Femininity, Literature, and Conservatism Between the Wars*. London: Routledge, 1991.

Lloyd, David W. *Battlefield Tourism: Pilgrimage and the Commemoration of the Great War in Britain, Australia and Canada, 1919–1939*. Oxford: Berg, 1998.

Macdonald, Lyn. *The Roses of No Man's Land*. London: Michael Joseph, 1980.

Mackaman, Douglas, and Michael Mays (eds.). *The First World War and the Cultures of Modernity*. Jackson: University Press of Mississippi, 2000.

MacLeod, Roy (ed.). *Government and Expertise: Specialists, Administrators, and Professionals, 1860–1919*. Cambridge: Cambridge University Press, 1988.

Maggs, Christopher J. *The Origins of General Nursing*. London: Croom Helm, 1983.

Mangan, J. A., and James Walvin (eds.). *Manliness and Morality: Middle-Class Masculinity in Britain and America, 1800–1940*. New York: St. Martin's Press, 1987.

Marwick, Arthur. *The Deluge: British Society and the First World War*. New York: Norton, 1965.

Women at War, 1914–1918. London: Fontana Paperbacks in association with Imperial War Museum, 1977.

McLaren, Eva Shaw. *A History of the Scottish Women's Hospitals*. London: Hodder and Stoughton, 1919.

Melman, Billie (ed.). *Borderlines: Genders and Identities in War and Peace, 1870–1930*. New York: Routledge, 1998.

Meyers, Judith. "'Comrade-Twin': Brothers and Doubles in the World War I Prose of May Sinclair, Katherine Anne Porter, Vera Brittain, Rebecca West, and Virginia Woolf." Unpublished Ph.D. dissertation, University of Washington, 1985.

Middlebrook, Martin. *Your Country Needs You! From Six to Sixty-Five Divisions*. Barnsley: Leo Cooper, 2000.

Middleton, Peter, and Tim Woods. *Literatures of Memory: History, Time and Space in Postwar Writing*. Manchester: Manchester University Press, 2000.

Mitchell, David. *Monstrous Regiment: The Story of the Women of the First World War*. New York: Macmillan, 1965.

Moberly Bell, E. *Storming the Citadel: The Rise of the Woman Doctor*. London: Constable, 1953.

Moeyes, Paul. *Siegfried Sassoon: Scorched Glory. A Critical Study*. New York: St. Martin's Press, 1997.

Moore, Judith. *A Zeal for Responsibility: The Struggle for Professional Nursing in Victorian England, 1868–1883*. Athens: University of Georgia Press, 1988.

Mosse, George. *Fallen Soldiers: Reshaping the Memory of the World Wars*. Oxford: Oxford University Press, 1990.

The Image of Man: The Creation of Modern Masculinity. New York: Oxford University Press, 1996.

Nora, Pierre. *Les Lieux de Memoire*. Paris: Gallimard, 1984.

O'Neill, H. C., and Edith A. Barnett. *Our Nurses, and The Work They Have to Do*. London: Ward, Lock, and Co., 1888.

Onions, John. *English Fiction and Drama of the Great War*. New York: St. Martin's Press, 1990.

Ouditt, Sharon. *Fighting Forces, Writing Women: Identity and Ideology in the First World War*. London: Routledge, 1994.

Panichas, George A. (ed.). *Promise of Greatness: The War of 1914–1918*. New York: John Day, 1968.

Parker, Peter. *The Old Lie: The Great War and the Public School Ethos.* London: Constable, 1987.

Parry, Noel, and José Parry. *The Rise of the Medical Profession: A Study of Collective Social Mobility.* London: Croom Helm, 1976.

Pavey, Agnes E. *The Story of the Growth of Nursing as an Art, a Vocation, and a Profession.* London: Faber and Faber, 1938.

Pedersen, Susan. "Gender, Welfare, and Citizenship in Britain During the Great War." *American Historical Review*, 95, 4 (October 1990): 983–1006.

   Family, Dependence, and the Origins of the Welfare State: Britain and France, 1914–1945. Cambridge: Cambridge University Press, 1993.

Perkin, Harold. *The Rise of Professional Society: England Since 1880.* London: Routledge, 1989.

Potter, Jane. "'Britain's Splendid Daughters.' Women on Active Service: Diaries and Novels of the Great War." Unpublished M.A. thesis, University of York, 1989.

Price, Mary, and Nonita Glenday. *Reluctant Revolutionaries: A Century of Headmistresses 1874–1974.* London: Pitman Publishing, 1974.

Quinn, Patrick J. *The Great War and the Missing Muse: The Early Writings of Robert Graves and Siegfried Sassoon.* Selinsgrove: Susquehanna University Press, 1994.

Raitt, Suzanne, and Trudi Tate. *Women's Fiction and the Great War.* New York: Oxford University Press, 1997.

Reader, W. J. *Professional Men: The Rise of the Professional Classes in Nineteenth-Century England.* London: Weidenfeld and Nicolson, 1966.

   At Duty's Call: A Study in Obsolete Patriotism. Manchester: Manchester University Press, 1988.

Riley, Denise. "Some Peculiarities of Social Policy Concerning Women in Wartime and Postwar Britain," in Higonnet, et al., *Behind the Lines*, pp. 260–271.

Robert, Krisztina. "Gender, Class, and Patriotism: Women's Paramilitary Units in First World War Britain." *International History Review*, 19, 1 (February 1997): 52–65.

Rose, Jonathan. *The Edwardian Temperament, 1895–1919.* Athens, OH: Ohio University Press, 1986.

Samuel, Raphael (ed.). *Patriotism: The Making and Unmaking of British National Identity.* London: Routledge, 1989.

Sanger, Ernest. *Letters from Two World Wars: A Social History of English Attitudes to War 1914–1945.* Phoenix Mill, UK: Alan Sutton, 1993.

Scott, Joan W. "Rewriting History," in Higonnet, et al., *Behind the Lines*, pp. 19–30.

   "The Evidence of Experience," *Critical Inquiry*, 17 (Summer 1991): 773–797.

   "Experience," in Judith Butler and Joan W. Scott (eds.), *Feminists Theorize the Political*, pp. 22–40. New York: Routledge, 1992.

   Gender and the Politics of History. New York: Columbia University Press, 1988.

Sebba, Anne. *Enid Bagnold: The Authorized Biography.* London: Weidenfeld and Nicolson, 1986.

Seymour, Miranda. *Robert Graves: Life on the Edge.* New York: Henry Holt, 1995.

Seymour-Smith, Martin. *Robert Graves: His Life and Work.* New York: Holt, Rinehart and Winston, 1983.

Sheffield, G. D. *Leadership in the Trenches: Officer–Man Relations, Morale and Discipline in the British Army in the Era of the First World War.* New York: St. Martin's Press, 2000.

Sherman, Daniel J. *The Construction of Memory in Interwar France.* Chicago: University of Chicago Press, 1999.

Simkins, Peter. "Soldiers and Civilians: Billeting in Britain and France," in Beckett and Simpson, *Nation in Arms,* pp. 165–192.

Kitchener's Army: The Raising of the New Armies, 1914–1916. Manchester: Manchester University Press, 1988.

Simpson, Keith. "The British Soldier on the Western Front," in Liddle, *Home Fires and Foreign Fields,* pp. 135–158.

"The Officers," in Beckett and Simpson, *Nation in Arms,* pp. 63–97.

Smith, Angela K. *The Secret Battlefield: Women, Modernism, and the First World War.* Manchester: Manchester University Press, 2000.

Spiers, Edward M. *The Army and Society 1815–1914.* London: Longman, 1980.

"The Regular Army in 1914," in Beckett and Simpson, *Nation in Arms,* pp. 37–61.

Squier, Susan M. "Rose Macaulay (1881–1958)," in Bonnie Kime Scott (ed.), *The Gender of Modernism: A Critical Anthology,* pp. 252–260. Bloomington: Indiana University Press, 1990.

Stephen, Martin. *The Price of Pity: Poetry, History, and Myth in the Great War.* London: Leo Cooper, 1996.

Sternlicht, Sanford. *Siegfried Sassoon.* New York: Twayne, 1993.

Summers, Anne. "Pride and Prejudice: Ladies and Nurses in the Crimean War." *History Workshop Journal,* 16 (1983): 33–56.

Angels and Citizens: British Women as Military Nurses 1854–1914. London: Routledge, 1988.

"Public Functions, Private Premises: Female Professional Identity and the Domestic-Service Paradigm in Britain, c. 1850–1930," in Melman, *Borderlines,* pp. 353–376.

Tait, H. P. *Dr. Elsie Maud Inglis, 1864–1917: A Great Lady Doctor.* Leith: Bridgland Press, [1965].

Tate, Trudi. *Modernism, History, and the Great War.* Manchester: Manchester University Press, 1998.

Thom, Deborah. "Women and Work in Wartime Britain," in Wall and Winter, *Upheaval of War,* pp. 297–326.

Nice Girls and Rude Girls: Women Workers in World War I. London: I. B. Tauris, 1998.

Tylee, Claire. *The Great War and Women's Consciousness: Images of Militarism and Womanhood in Women's Writings, 1914–1964.* London: Macmillan, 1990.

(ed.). *Women, the First World War and the Dramatic Imagination: International Essays (1914–1999).* Lewiston, NY: East Mellen Press, 2000.

Vance, Jonathan F. *Death So Noble: Memory, Meaning, and the First World War.* Vancouver: University of British Columbia Press, 1997.

Vicinus, Martha. *Independent Women: Work and Community for Single Women 1850–1920*. Chicago: University of Chicago Press, 1985.

Wall, Richard. "English and German Families and the First World War, 1914–1918," in Wall and Winter (eds.), *Upheaval of War*, pp. 43–106.

Wall, Richard, and Jay Winter (eds.). *The Upheaval of War: Family, Work and Welfare in Europe, 1914–1918*. Cambridge: Cambridge University Press, 1988.

Walsh, Mary Roth. *"Doctors Wanted: No Women Need Apply": Sexual Barriers in the Medical Profession, 1835–1975*. New Haven: Yale University Press, 1977.

Watson, Janet. "Khaki Girls, VADs, and Tommy's Sisters: Gender and Class in First World War Britain." *International History Review*, 19, 1 (February 1997): 32–51.

"The Paradox of Working Heroines: Conflict over the Changing Social Order in Wartime Britain, 1914–1918," in Mackaman and Mays, *First World War and the Cultures of Modernity*, pp. 81–103.

"Wars in the Wards: The Social Construction of Medical Work in First World War Britain," *Journal of British Studies*, 41, 4 (October 2002): 484–510.

Wenzel, Marian, and John Cornish (eds.). *Auntie Mabel's War: An Account of Her Part in the Hostilities of 1914–1918*. London: Allen Lane, 1980.

Whitehead, Ian R. *Doctors in the Great War*. London: Leo Cooper, 1999.

Williams, John. *The Other Battleground: The Home Fronts, Britain, France and Germany 1914–1918*. Chicago: John Regnery, 1972.

Wilson, Jean Moorcroft. *Siegfried Sassoon, The Making of a War Poet: A Biography 1886–1918*. New York: Routledge, 1999.

Wilson, Trevor. *The Myriad Faces of War: Britain and the Great War, 1914–1918*. Cambridge: Polity Press, 1986.

Winter, Denis. *Death's Men: Soldiers of the Great War*. London: Penguin, 1979 (1978).

Winter, J. M. *The Great War and the British People*. Cambridge, MA: Harvard University Press, 1986.

Sites of Memory, Sites of Mourning: The Great War in European Cultural History. Cambridge: Cambridge University Press, 1995.

Winter, Jay, Geoffrey Parker, and Mary R. Harbeck (eds.). *The Great War and the Twentieth Century*. New Haven: Yale University Press, 2000.

Winter, Jay, and Emmanuel Sivan (eds.). *War and Remembrance in the Twentieth Century*. Cambridge: Cambridge University Press, 1999.

Wohl, Robert. *The Generation of 1914*. Cambridge, MA: Harvard University Press, 1979.

Woollacott, Angela. "Sisters and Brothers in Arms: Family, Class, and Gendering in World War I Britain," in Cooke and Woollacott, *Gendering War Talk*, pp. 128–147.

"Khaki Fever and Its Control: Gender, Class, Age and Sexual Morality on the British Homefront in World War I." *Journal of Contemporary History*, 29 (April 1994): 325–347.

"Maternalism, Professionalism and Industrial Welfare Supervisors in World War I Britain." *Women's History Review*, 3 (March 1994): 29–56.

Woollacott, Angela. *On Her Their Lives Depend: Munitions Workers in the Great War*. Berkeley: University of California Press, 1994.

"From Moral to Professional Authority: Secularism, Social Work and Middle-Class Women's Self-Construction in World War I Britain." *Journal of Women's History*, 10, 2 (Summer 1998): 85–111.

"Dressed to Kill: Clothes, Cultural Meaning and First World War Munitions Workers," in Moira Donald and Linda Hurcombe (eds.), *Representations of Gender from Prehistory to the Present*, pp. 198–217. New York: St. Martin's Press, 2000.

Zimmern, Alice. *The Renaissance of Girls' Education in England: A Record of Fifty Years' Progress*. London: A. D. Innes & Company, 1898.

Index

325

Studies in the Social and Cultural History of Modern Warfare

Titles in the series:

10 *The Spirit of 1914: Militarism, Myth and Mobilization in Germany*
    Jeffrey Verhey
    ISBN 0 521 77137 4

11 *German Anglophobia and the Great War, 1914–1918*
    Matthew Stibbe
    ISBN 0 521 78296 1

12 *Life Between Memory and Hope: The Survivors of the Holocaust in
    Occupied Germany*
    Zeev W. Mankowitz
    ISBN 0 521 81105 8

13 *Commemorating the Irish Civil War: History and Memory, 1923–2000*
    Anne Dolan
    ISBN 0 521 81904 0

14 *Jews and Gender in Liberation France*
    Karen H. Adler
    ISBN 0 521 79048 4

15 *America and the Armenian Genocide of 1915*
    Edited by Jay Winter
    ISBN 0521 82958 5

16 *Fighting Different Wars: Experience, Memory, and the First World War
    in Britain*
    Janet S. K. Watson
    ISBN 0 521 83153 9